Capacity Building for IT in Education in Developing Countries

IFIP – The International Federation for Information Processing

IFIP was founded in 1960 under the auspices of UNESCO, following the First World Computer Congress held in Paris the previous year. An umbrella organization for societies working in information processing, IFIP's aim is two-fold: to support information processing within its member countries and to encourage technology transfer to developing nations. As its mission statement clearly states,

> IFIP's mission is to be the leading, truly international, apolitical organization which encourages and assists in the development, exploitation and application of information technology for the benefit of all people.

IFIP is a non-profitmaking organization, run almost solely by 2500 volunteers. It operates through a number of technical committees, which organize events and publications. IFIP's events range from an international congress to local seminars, but the most important are:

- the IFIP World Computer Congress, held every second year;
- open conferences;
- working conferences.

The flagship event is the IFIP World Computer Congress, at which both invited and contributed papers are presented. Contributed papers are rigorously refereed and the rejection rate is high.

As with the Congress, participation in the open conferences is open to all and papers may be invited or submitted. Again, submitted papers are stringently refereed.

The working conferences are structured differently. They are usually run by a working group and attendance is small and by invitation only. Their purpose is to create an atmosphere conducive to innovation and development. Refereeing is less rigorous and papers are subjected to extensive group discussion.

Publications arising from IFIP events vary. The papers presented at the IFIP World Computer Congress and at open conferences are published as conference proceedings, while the results of the working conferences are often published as collections of selected and edited papers.

Any national society whose primary activity is in information may apply to become a full member of IFIP, although full membership is restricted to one society per country. Full members are entitled to vote at the annual General Assembly, National societies preferring a less committed involvement may apply for associate or corresponding membership. Associate members enjoy the same benefits as full members, but without voting rights. Corresponding members are not represented in IFIP bodies. Affiliated membership is open to non-national societies, and individual and honorary membership schemes are also offered.

Capacity Building for IT in Education in Developing Countries

IFIP TC3 WG3.1, 3.4 & 3.5 Working Conference on Capacity Building for IT in Education in Developing Countries
19-25 August 1997, Harare, Zimbabwe

Edited by

Gail Marshall
Gail Marshall & Associates
St. Louis
USA

and

Mikko Ruohonen
Turku School of Economics & Business Administration
Turku
Finland

First edition 1998

Originally published by Chapman & Hall in 1998
MyCopy version of the original edition 1998

DOI 10.1007/978-0-387-35195-7

A catalogue record for this book is available from the British Library

Printed on permanent acid-free text paper, manufactured in accordance with ANSI/NISO Z39.48-1992 (Permanence of Paper).
www.springer.com/mycopy

CONTENTS

Preface

Deryn Watson

CapBIT 97, Capacity Building for Information Technologies in Education in Developing Countries, from which this publication derives, was an invited IFIP working conference sponsored by Working Groups in secondary (WG 3.1), elementary (WG 3.5), and vocational and professional (WG 3.4) education under the auspices of IFIP Technical Committee for Education (TC3). The conference was held in Harare, Zimbabwe 25th - 29th August 1997.

CapBIT '97 was the first time that the IFIP Technical Committee for Education had held a conference in a developing country. When the Computer Society of Zimbabwe offered to host the event, we determined that the location and conference topic reflect the importance of issues facing countries at all stages of development - especially Information Technologies (IT) development. Information Technologies have become, within a short time, one of the basic building blocks of modern industrial society. Understanding IT, and mastering basic skills and concepts of IT, are now regarded as part of the core education of all people around the world, alongside reading and writing. IT now permeates the business environment and underpins the success of modern corporations as well as providing government with cost-effective civil service systems. At the same time, the tools and technologies of IT are of value in the process of learning, and in the organisation and management of learning institutions.

In developing countries there are capacity-building deficiencies, including human resource development problems and physical infrastructure problems, which hinder progress in the use of IT. The successful implementation of IT at national levels depends on national policy, government support, and the cooperation and coordination of all key players. In particular, realistic plans would appear to depend upon knowledge of needs, practices, experiences, peer support, and the accessibility of resources - both human and technical.

It seemed that a working conference involving IT practitioners and planners from developing and more developed countries would provide a collaborative environment where past experiences could be shared, current constraints explained and plans could be developed in the light of models from a variety of experiences. So delegates from all levels of the educational arena were invited - including IT practitioners in education; key people involved in policy making in governments and agencies; primary, secondary and post-secondary teachers and lecturers; representatives of professional IT societies and organisations; teacher educators; members of the research community; and IT business professionals and suppliers.

Seven topics were chosen to form the backbone of the conference agenda, through invited papers and discussion groups. They were:

- IT as tools for teaching and learning at all levels;
- the role of professional and educational bodies;
- IT as a teaching subject;

Capacity Building for IT in Education in Developing Countries
G. Marshall & M. Ruohonen (Eds.)

- Experiences from a variety of national policies, initiatives and strategies;
- IT as tools for educational administration and support;
- Building resource accessibility in developing countries - physical resources, skills and knowledge;
- Action plans for proposed projects at local and national levels.

This book reflects the uniqueness of the CapBIT conference in a number of ways. The core of the book is the collection of invited papers that were delivered at the conference - papers which were invited to reflect the range of topics and experiences in the field. The papers provided insights into the individual and collective problems facing IT use in education. But to that core are added two further features. Firstly, synopses of four workshops, devoted to specific capacity building applications and concerns of the delegates, demonstrate the range of possibilities available. Secondly there are reports from the discussion groups held during the conference. Each CapBIT delegate met daily with colleagues to review key points of the invited papers and explore the implications in the light of their individual experiences.

There were discussion groups on each of the following topics:

- policies, strategies and initiatives for ICT in education;
- building resource accessibility in developing countries;
- IT in institutional administration and management;
- IT in education delivery and learning;
- the role of teachers in planning for change;
- IT in curriculum and courseware development.

From their discussions, each group reported in the form of recommendations for others in the IT community, whether from more developed or less developed countries. These recommendations are a tangible outcome from the five working days in Harare. Their inclusion in this book will enable others to reflect on, borrow from, implement, evaluate and transform according to local conditions, regional resources and national policies.

The CapBIT delegates returned to their own countries impressed by the beauty of Zimbabwe and the hospitality of her people, delighted by meeting new friends and greeting again longtime colleagues, and dedicated to the idea of continuing the long but rewarding task of developing IT plans, practices and policies within their own countries as well as contributing to the successful worldwide use of IT as a major tool for education.

Thus the event and this publication are unique in a number of ways. These are reflected in the content of the welcoming remarks which are reproduced here. The actuality of bringing an international working conference to Zimbabwe and the excitement that was generated locally is clear. The aim of the Programme Committee was that this book should not just reflect the work during Harare but also act as a benchmark publication from which we all hope that further positive action shall occur. Indeed the Programme Committee is most grateful to the Commonwealth Secretariat, which supported the publication of this book.

Welcome remarks

Vice Principal Owen Mavengere, Harare Polytechnic

It gives me great pleasure to see many academics and scholars who have come from different countries to attend this very important Capacity Building conference. We regard this conference as important for three reasons:

1. It has placed the Harare Polytechnic on the international map in terms of educational Information Technology.
2. It has afforded an opportunity to the lecturers of Harare Polytechnic to freely rub shoulders with other academics and technologists from other colleges of higher learning, thereby exchanging notes in terms of training.
3. It has provided Harare Polytechnic with free information in terms of the latest technological developments in other countries.

A glance around this hall shows that we have people from 33 different countries. This clearly indicates that delegates from these countries know that the conference is of great importance to their training institutions. It is hoped that the delegates who are here will link up with each other and maintain permanent educational ties for a long time to come.

Allow me to give a brief history of Harare Polytechnic. The Salisbury Technical School was opened in 1926 by Mr. Richard Deary. Salisbury changed to Harare at independence in 1980. With the passage of time, many courses were introduced. Today the College has eleven divisions. The college has a staggering enrolment of 7000 students. A large proportion of these are in the Division of Business Education, which has well over 3000 students pursuing various courses.

Let me express my utmost appreciation to the Computer Society from Zimbabwe and Dr. Watson for having honoured Harare Polytechnic by requesting us to host this conference. Allow me to thank all the staff members of the College who have worked tirelessly preparing for the event.

On behalf of the staff and students, welcome to our Polytechnic and I hope you all enjoy our hospitality.

Arthur Sithole, Chair of Organising Committee

I feel honoured to welcome all you delegates to our conference. The Computer Society of Zimbabwe (CSZ) is the leading computer body that informs and advises policy makers and IT users in Zimbabwe, that represents the interests of its members, and encourages professionalism and ethics in the application of IT. CSZ is deeply honoured to be hosting this event in association with IFIP.

This event crowns a two year planning process at a local level through the Organising Committee as well as the Programme Committee at an international level. The CSZ invested a lot of money, time and effort since it considers the issues about to be discussed as crucial for the socioeconomic development of our nations.

We have therefore invited you all here as key stakeholders in the field to share ideas on how to achieve the objectives of empowering developing countries with IT in order that they take charge of their own development in the field of education and training in an efficient and effective manner.

The issue in general is not that there are no developments regarding IT in education in developing or 'emerging' nations. Papers to be presented during the course of the working conference will testify to this. The key questions we need to deal with regarding developing countries are:

- Why has it been so difficult to plan and invest in IT in education for efficiency and effectiveness?
- Where IT investment in education was realised, why is the resource under-utilised?
- What is being done or has been done elsewhere to deal with these negative valued situations?
- What can be done to transform this sad state of affairs?
- What roles can the IFIP community, governments, private sector and others play to convert these states into positive desired solutions?

I put it to all of us that very few of our schools, particularly government owned and those in rural areas, have access to IT in developing countries. Secondly the majority of those that have the technology are using outdated equipment or have equipment gathering dust because they cannot afford to maintain and upgrade. I am confident that realistically achievable outputs or action plans will emerge form this working conference.

Allow me, on behalf of the Computer Society of Zimbabwe, to acknowledge with thanks the efforts by members of the international programme committee as well as the local organising committee for making the dream of the event come true; and in particular to thank Geoff Fairall, the Chief Executive and Liezel Crawford, the Secretariat.

My thanks would not be complete without mentioning Barclays Bank of Zimbabwe, Central Africa Building Society, Commonwealth Secretariat, COMSA, Delta Systems, Harare Polytechnic, IBM, IFIP, Local Authorities Pension Fund, Old Mutual, Speciss Computers, Trust Academy, ZBC-TV, and others for their sponsorship and support of this working conference.

Brian Samways, Chair of IFIP Technical Committee for Education

Although IFIP have come to Zimbabwe for its General Assembly meeting in 1991, this is a 'first time' for the Technical Committee for Education and its Working Groups. In fact it is also the 'first time' for three of our Working Groups to hold a joint working conference - WG 3.1 on secondary education, WG 3.4 on professional and vocational education, and WG 3.5 on elementary education.

I believe that our organisers, Deryn Watson, Arthur Sithole and Geoff Fairall, have created the ideal situation for capacity building. The conference programme offers many opportunities for the sharing of ideas and the discussion of ways forward. I would ask that you all make 'links' which can continue the work of the conference after the delegates leave Harare. As in the past, I hope that the good work of the conference and the contacts made will be sustained for a long time into the future. Finally I thank Zimbabwe for allowing IFIP to hold the conference in their country.

Deryn Watson, Chair of CapBIT Programme Committee

Welcome to CapBIT 97. I am delighted that so many of you, 120 from 33 different nations, have travelled to take part in this working conference. I applaud the considerable efforts you have had to make, especially financial, to get here.

The purpose of this event is to provide a working environment for all delegates to contribute to the discussion of the important topic - IT for education in developing countries. The programme has been designed around paper sessions, discussion groups, and workshops. After five days of discussion, informed by the content of the papers, and the experience and knowledge which each delegate brings to the discussions groups, we will collect our ideas into an information market place, designed to inform each other and provide a basis for the development of ongoing strategic and activity plans for further action. These discussions will culminate in a panel at which the perspective of a number of donor agencies will be presented with the intention of ensuring that future actions, both national and international, may bear fruit. Thus we hope to have a deeper understanding of the range of issues and various prescriptions for forward action than we do now.

This conference design is a unique aspect of IFIP education working conferences - the actual participation of all delegates within focused discussion groups in order to make it an active rather than passive event. A further unique feature is that these discussions will be reported alongside the papers in the conference book. This will provide a benchmark by ensuring that this event lasts beyond the actual week, and the ideas and discussions you as delegates generate are disseminated widely.

It is our hope that this conference will stimulate and inform governments and agencies active in this area. It is also our intention that the working relationships formed during this week shall form the basis of new networks across regions and nations, from which further debate and collaboration will ensue.

We have planned to make it as happy and sociable event as possible. So although it will be hard work, we hope it will also be fun and that the camaraderie thus engendered will ensure that the networks we plan have a real chance to succeed. I have outlined how we have planned for the conference but its success is totally dependent upon you, its delegates. Welcome.

Introduction

Gail Marshall and Mikko Ruohonen

In every culture telling stories about how events occur and why they occur is an important activity that distributes information and ensures a collective understanding. Similarly, gathering together to discuss issues and demonstrate skills is an age-old form of self and community development. So it was with the Harare conference. During the week of the conference, capacity building occurred daily as delegates shared their experiences with IT and worked together to forge a community of professionals dedicated to creating a hospitable and practical climate for IT in their own countries, and to continue sharing insights and expertise long after the conference ended.

Development is often thought of as a straightforward linear process - one starts from Ground Zero and quickly accumulates experience and expertise. In fact, development, whether of human beings or organizations, is a fitful process. Forward motion is unpredictable, and often accompanied by obstacles, wrong turns and regressions. The conference highlighted the fact that all countries are 'developing' with respect to IT use. New technologies, appearing almost daily, cause shifts in policies and practices, and call for reallocations of a wide range of resources. All countries are 'undeveloped' in the resources needed for IT adoption, implementation and institutionalisation since insufficient resources - time, money, expertise - are currently being allocated. This is as true in Paris as in Papua New Guinea.

The delegates recognized that while per capita income may be a dividing line separating 'developed' from 'developing' countries, the search for solutions to a host of common problems unites IT users around the globe. For example, IT adds a new level of complexity - acquiring equipment, training users and reconceptualising past practices - that places extraordinary demands on the IT community and, at the same time, creates dislocation in day-to-day life, whether in the village or the megalopolis.

The conference, with its attention to education from the preschool level to the workplace, impressed on the delegates the need to consider IT as an integral part of the educational process. Young children, it was said, need IT-based experiences to acquire literacy in the language of their country; mature workers, it was said, need IT-based experiences to equip them for the ever-changing workplace in Sydney Australia or Harare, Zimbabwe.

While each of us is a unique human being, we operate in a complex social context with established mores. Increasingly pressure, either from within or without, to incorporate skills and strategies necessary for survival and success is creating a demand for a wider use of IT in educational settings. As IT-using educators we know that teachers, school administrators and government officials must learn to use IT as part of educational practice. But the old ways - government

Capacity Building for IT in Education in Developing Countries
G. Marshall & M. Ruohonen (Eds.)

policies and management principles, for example - constrain our ability to use IT to the fullest. Similarly, the complexity of IT integration - altering curriculum, reshaping teaching practices and developing software - acts as a brake on the straightforward, widespread use of IT around the globe.

Nevertheless, telling stories about large scale national projects and smaller but equally powerful initiatives as well as sharing experiences and making recommendations as occurred at the Harare conference serves not only the delegates to the CapBIT conference but also readers of the conference proceedings so they may cope more successfully with the complexity associated with IT adoption and institutionalisation, and thus assure the continuation of capacity building worldwide.

National perspectives

Peter Bollerslev, elected to the presidency of IFIP shortly after the Harare conference took place, discusses the Nordic countries' approach to capacity building for Information Technology. His analysis of the many and varied activities initiated by the members of the Nordic Committee on Educational Software and Technology highlights the importance of collaboration among countries. Bollerslev also shows us the role that shared culture and pedagogical traditions play in facilitating planning and practice. Strategies successfully employed in the Nordic region might provide a blueprint for other countries in a region as they proceed through IT adoption-implementation-institutionalization phases.

Sunday Ojo and Ben Awuah's case study of Botswana's plans and practices provides an interesting counterpoint to Bollerslev's story. Working with more limited resources than the Nordic countries, they, like their Nordic colleagues, realize the importance of curriculum building, teacher education and evaluation. Realistic in their appraisal of constraints facing them, they also look to a future in which IT plays a major role in the day-to-day lives of their countrymen.

Geoffrey Kiangi, from Namibia, while also emphasising the constraints facing many developing countries' attempts to integrate IT into education, says that social, vocational, pedagogical and catalytic factors compel policy makers in developing countries to plan for the widespread adoption of IT. So Kiangi, echoing themes articulated by Bollerslev, Ojo and Awuah, says emphasis must be placed on education, not technology. That message will resonate through the stories told in this volume.

The importance of teachers' collaboration on curriculum development and their active role in software development, described by Bollerslev as an important component of teachers' education about IT, receives confirmation in Hogenbirk's story. His description of an ambitious and successful project in The Netherlands shows that by enlisting teachers in the design of IT-based lessons, the revision of the curriculum to reflect the role of IT becomes a powerful tool for teacher education - not only for teachers who participated directly in the curriculum development process but also for their colleagues who watched the process and learned by working alongside their IT-innovating colleagues. Hogenbirk's discussion of the 'Schools with SPIRIT' project reminds us of the crucial role involved teachers play in the successful adoption of innovations.

Capacity building is and will be a continuous process. Sindre Røsvik tell us how Norway, which has been using IT in the classroom for many years, has embarked on a major school reform initiative in which IT plays a central role. Like The Netherlands's initiative, Norway's is comprehensive, but Røsvik questions whether financial resources and government plans for allocating responsibility are sufficient to ensure success of the reforms. The tension between what is planned and the resources allocated for the plans will be a theme that will be replayed again and again as commentators describe attempts at IT-based capacity building.

The importance of planning and the essential role that government plays in the process of initiating and institutionalizing IT in schools is reiterated by Alex Fung in his description of Hong Kong's present and future use of IT. While describing Hong Kong's plans for the installation of large scale information management systems, Fung also says that resource provisioning for educational management should not supersede strategic planning directed at developing peoples' capacity to use IT across a wide range of educational situations. The importance of a holistic view of IT in education, the key role that teacher education plays in the successful use of IT, the crucial role that government plays, and the positive impact of collaboration among all stakeholders are cited by Fung as essential elements in present and future capacity building.

Hari Gopal Shrestha's story of his work in Nepal on behalf of IT implementation and integration reminds us that collaboration and planning do not happen spontaneously. Instead they require patience, vigilance and persistence; they require the diligent efforts of one or more leaders who see what IT can do, mobilize forces to accomplish the vision, and then continue to share and shape the vision as new possibilities are presented by the emergence of new technologies. In each case - curriculum development, teacher education and resource provisioning, Shrestha had to take the initiative in order to promote the widespread adoption of IT in Nepal. Although he mentions support from colleagues in other countries, a critical ingredient in developing and maintaining one's own capacities, it is clear that Shrestha's 'on the ground' efforts were essential elements in the growth of IT use in education in Nepal. Many other participants in the Harare conference have experienced the isolation faced by Shrestha and combating isolation remains a major problem in IT-based capacity building. The end result, building the skills of a generation or more of students and teachers, is worth the price, according to Shrestha.

Building skills in the national context

Skills development is at the forefront of Arthur Sithole's discussion of Zimbabwe's plans for IT use. Stressing the need for his country to develop an IT-competent workforce, Sithole cites the need for strategic planning, the need to stimulate IT-focused training opportunities, and the need to continually monitor the processes and products of that training.

Uche Modum's description of Nigeria's efforts to work with IT emphasises the importance of a country's economic, social and political infrastructures as both constraints on capacity building and as necessary ingredients in the implementation of plans for broad-based IT use. Wealth of natural resources, says Modum, does not ensure the successful implementation of IT if political, social and economic conditions are unfavourable at one or more points in time. Her analysis of Nigeria's past and present situation, where IT use has grown dramatically in spite of the economic downturn is inspiring; her view that Nigeria continues to face economic difficulties that will compromise future IT-based growth is a story familiar to many in the IT community.

Deane Arganbright's discussion of capacity building in Papua New Guinea shows the role that steady work and careful planning can play in developing a core of IT-enabled students. Working in a remote area of the world and challenged by limited financial resources as well as climatic constraints, Arganbright and his colleagues have developed a curriculum - based on applications programs - to train the workforce for today's and tomorrow's challenges. Emphasising problem solving as much as basic computer literacy, Arganbright's program is easily replicable and may serve as a model for other countries seeking to build IT-based competencies.

Targetted projects

Portable computers provide a strategy for implementing IT in situations where desktop computers may be impractical for one reason or another. Anne McDougall analyzes the implications of portable computers used as essential elements of an Australian school's IT strategy. When students use portable computers in each class throughout a school day, says McDougall, IT knowledge and skills improve, and so does cooperation among students. Better problem solving and increased student responsibility for learning can be seen where the portable computer is used as fluidly as the pencil. McDougall points out that the constraints associated with portable computer use - the need for battery charging, the cost of procurement and the staffs' anxiety about managing and using the computers - must be recognized but proposes that portable computers might be a viable way for many countries to enhance their IT-based capacity building.

Often IT adoption and implementation has been a helter-skelter process - a few computers installed and teachers trained haphazardly. Sam Gumbo describes a Zimbabwe-based project designed to bring coherence to schools' IT use. As part of the process of introducing IT to a group of schools in Zimbabwe, appropriate implementation strategies will be analyzed, and teacher training will be coordinated and evaluated as a new phase of capacity building begins in Zimbabwe.

New strategies for empowering school administrators to take a major role in planning for and using IT is the focus of Bil Newman's discussion of an Internet-based project for school principals in Australia. By teaching school principals located in the remote Australian outback how to access the Internet and use it as a means of school-to-school communication, the Australian Principals Association Professional Development Council has changed principals' attitudes towards IT and enhanced their ability to play a leadership role in IT-based decision making in their schools. The model has powerful implications for others working to develop capacities for IT use.

Zhang Ji-Ping and Jef Moonen present another facet of telecommunications as a tool for capacity building. By collaborating both face-to-face and over long distances via telecommunications, East China Normal University and the University of Twente, The Netherlands, have provided distance courses which will eventually be used by 60 Chinese universities. The project, sponsored by AT&T, illustrates the tremendous potential of IT to put needed resources in place around the globe.

Not only for the here-and-now but for the future, telecommunications can be a powerful tool for linking people with one another. IT can also be a major ingredient in the development of positive attitudes towards lifelong learning. Anton Knierzinger's discussion of Upper Austria's 'Education Highway' project sets forth criteria for Internet use - learning will be more project-oriented, more problem-oriented and more activity-based. Specifying four essentials - time, motivation, sources of advice and evaluation/research - Knierzinger sets the stage for other countries to design and deliver similar projects as part of their capacity-building programs.

Classroom-based initiatives

Just as the 'Upper Austria' project recognizes how students can benefit from Internet use, Rachel Cohen sets out the strategies for using IT to prevent illiteracy among young children. Based on her carefully developed program of written and oral language development activities in French IT-equipped settings, Cohen provides a conceptual framework for young children's use of technology. She accompanies that framework with guidance on managing instruction for young children in IT-equipped classrooms. Her belief that early intervention is crucial for the full flowering of each child's potential is an important message for those seeking to use IT to create a major educational impact.

Márta Turcsányi-Szabó sees Logo as a powerful tool for increasing students' literacy with informatics. Knowing about the computer and knowing by using the computer, in her view, are complementary, and of equal importance. She describes how pre-service teachers can be shown how Logo can be used to convey important ideas, thus ensuring that teachers-to-be will use IT in educationally meaningful ways as soon as they begin their teaching careers. The curriculum developed at Loránd Eötvös University in Hungary may be adopted by others who wish to move from a computer literacy to a computer empowerment level of capacity building.

Research for IT-based education

Research on the essential elements of curriculum is the central issue in Mikko Ruohonen and Olayele Adelakun's paper. Taking the current level of curriculum development for IT in Nigerian universities as a starting point, the Finland-based researchers say that Information Systems education is vitally needed in developing countries in order to develop the necessary human resource capacities needed for current and future IT adoption and utilisation. Their recommendation for a model Information Systems curriculum is a valuable resource for any country, whatever its stage of capacity building.

Deryn Watson of the UK cautions us not to think that providing resources will translate into successful implementation. Citing numerous studies which describe the limited impact of IT on education, Watson says that teachers' slow adoption of and adaptation to IT is rooted in complexity - differing perceptions of IT, problems associated with any type of change in schools and problems associated with professional concerns of teachers. Watson advises those charged with capacity building for teachers to work with teachers while designing and delivering staff development instead of ignoring their concerns, a caution that applies to developed as well as developing countries.

Watson's work highlights the importance of good research and evaluation studies as a means of guiding us towards future capacity building. Gail Marshall, USA, presents a summary of the kinds of resources - human resources, cultural traditions, models of evaluations, tests and measures, observation instruments and surveys - which have been used in pre-IT settings and which will help decision makers collect data as they analyze attempts at institutionalizing IT.

Resource acquisition, allocation and utilisation

The important role human resources - especially educational and professional bodies - can play in capacity building is carefully described by Peter Juliff. He presents specific suggestions about the programs and policies that those bodies have enacted in Australia, and the models can serve as guidelines for involving a broad range of professionals - from schools, universities, corporations and government agencies - in capacity building efforts.

Dudley Dolan, based in Ireland, addresses another instance of the way governmental bodies and other IT-expert professionals can work toward skill building for IT use. To ensure a uniform standard of competence for all IT users, the European computer driving licence has been established as a mechanism for assessing skill and for certifying performance with technology. Designed to change as IT competencies need to change, the European computer driving licence can serve as a standard for workplace capacity building in developed and developing countries.

Skill is also the focal point of James Isaacs's discussion of the importance of information literacy. Situated at a major Indian training centre, Isaacs draws a clear distinction between skills required for a world governed by the generation and use of materials, and a world governed by the generation and use of information. Education, he says, must change radically to equip citizens to meet the challenges of an information-driven world. Developing countries, where educational decision making is still fluid, have a special advantage and can succeed in 'leapfrogging' ahead of developed countries, where educational policies and practices have long-standing rituals and constraints, says Isaacs, who describes his work in helping IT users gather and analyze information worldwide.

Successful planning and procurement for Information Technology, says Ian Mitchell, results from a careful analysis of the local situation, and a straightforward specification of what is needed and why. Based on field experience acquired as a consultant from New Zealand to projects around the world, Mitchell provides ingredients for success - respect cultural sensitivities, work within the constraints of local conditions, keep projects small and consider all the ramifications of technology demands versus resources. His advice serves as a primer for consultants and for those seeking aid from funding agencies.

Adrie Visscher's work on Information Technology at the University of Twente, The Netherlands presents a primer of another sort. Visscher has skillfully analyzed the many demands placed on school administrators and staff. Visscher has developed a design strategy for maximizing data use and minimizing the redundancy associated with operations on school data. He stresses the importance of government's involvement in the adoption and institutionalization of such management systems.

Data at another level - statistics on a wide range of indices including per capita kilowatt hour consumption, the number of radios, TVs and computers per 1 000 inhabitants for developed and developing countries - are presented by Marsha Williams, USA, to show the disparity in resource dispersal between the 'have' and 'have not' countries. Collaboration and communication, conducted with respect on all sides, is essential, says Williams, in order to support equitable resource use and the universal quest for knowledge.

A curriculum for the future

Strategies for promoting knowledge acquisition are important features of the 'Creating Learning Networks for African Teachers' project, sponsored by UNESCO's Learning Without Frontiers initiative. David Berg and Jeannette Vogelaar's report on the project emphasises the ways current educational policies and practices must change in order to foster the lifelong learning - a requirement for survival in the Information Age. Berg and Vogelaar stress the complexity associated with IT-based change but suggest that many current constraints associated with schools' IT use may be overcome by encouraging communication and collaboration among teachers. Their descriptions of the pilot projects sponsored by UNESCO show the role that large-scale organizations such as UNESCO can play in capacity building.

Tom van Weert's presentation of the UNESCO/IFIP secondary school curriculum brings us full circle. Through his work at the School of Informatics, University of Nijmegen, The Netherlands and his leadership in IFIP, van Weert has contributed to the capacity building of colleagues around the world.

The UNESCO/IFIP curriculum is an important instance of the capacity building spirit. Bollerslev spoke of collaboration and the UNESCO/IFIP curriculum is tangible proof of the power that comes from a group of professionals pooling their talents. Ojo and Awuah discussed efforts at curriculum building and the UNESCO/IFIP curriculum provides a fundamental platform around which countries can organize instruction in IT topics.

Throughout the discussions of capacity building - whether from India or Norway or Namibia - we have seen both similarities in approaches to IT-based problem solving, and differences in conditions and solutions. By working on the similarities arrived at through diverse experiences, say van Weert, we will have a starting point for effective IT policy making. Again and again discussions have focused on fundamental issues and van Weert says attention must be paid to the fundamentals above all. Highlighting the need for qualified IT professionals, he reinforces the message of Kiangi, Modum and Dolan. As with Isaacs, Juliff and Watson, who see competence with IT as the sine qua non for personal and professional growth, van Weert presents a curriculum that is a road map for today's and tomorrow's teachers.

The UNESCO/IFIP curriculum is developmental - a perspective endorsed by Cohen and Turcsányi-Szabó. It acknowledges that students at different ages need different types of experiences. But as students learn more about technology at earlier ages, the depth and breadth of their IT-based educational experiences must increase. The UNESCO/IFIP curriculum provides that flexibility.

In emphasising the dynamic nature of IT and reporting a curriculum with matching dynamic possibilities van Weert offers us a paradigm for all countries, whether developed or developing. Stable concepts must be the building blocks of capacity building; IT must be thoroughly integrated across a wide range of subjects; and collaboration is an essential strategy for planning and practice in our increasingly information-laden world.

Workshop presentations

Another aspect of capacity building is the demonstration of actual practice and the conference was fortunate to have several skilled practitioners present workshops where they modeled the kinds of day-to-day practices using IT that they had developed through their experience with IT.

Although many conference participants stressed the need to integrate IT across the curriculum, it was agreed that IT as a specialized subject still had a place in the education of all. Peter Hubwieser, Germany, presented a workshop, based on his work with Steffen Friedrich. The workshop emphasised three major aspects of informatics teaching: why should we teach informatics; what should we teach in informatics courses; and how should we teach informatics.

The workshop also stressed the idea that informatics as a subject should also enable students to use, control, and judge IT and its consequences. The workshop said that representations of information - real life situations that must be modeled - should be a focal point of instruction and presented ways to change, exchange and communicate data.

In her workshop on the use of hypermedia and the Internet, Karen Norwood, USA, stated the advantages of using hypermedia over traditional media - the appeal to different learning styles, the provision for students' creativity and the preparation of students for the 21st century, among other benefits. She then showed participants how use of the hypermedia and Internet can help students navigate through various domains of knowledge. The advantage of hypermedia and the Internet as tools for teaching mathematical topics that would be too difficult without technology's capacity for representation was also demonstrated in the workshop.

The work of a group of mathematicians working at the Instituto Matemetica Applicata, Genoa, Italy formed the basis of Guiliana Dettori's workshop on mathematical problem solving in IT settings. After defining IT and stressing the benefits of integrating IT into a subject such as mathematics, the workshop defined problem solving, elaborated the benefits of using IT in problem solving settings and demonstrated how IT can be used to foster mathematical problem solving. The workshop also presented several topics related to IT use for discussion and asked participants to compare national situations in order to share strategies for success.

Paul Nicholson, Australia, after critiquing the traditional Western models of research in IT, described action research and then led the workshop participants through a series of activities in scenario-based research. The plan of the workshop included asking participants to brainstorm where they are in the course of IT use and development, what can change in their own practice, and how they can plan for change. Provision was made for the participants to work alone, to share their situations with others, and to benefit from the advice and experiences of others.

Discussion Group recommendations

The Discussion Groups worked on a series of issues related to curriculum development, policy making and resource utilisation. Each Discussion Group had a formal meeting each day where the issues, constraints and prospects were discussed, and informal discussions also took place at lunch each day and in the coffee hours that forged bonds of collegiality among the delegates. The work of the Discussion Groups shows how devising strategies can be a powerful collaborative activity for capacity building.

Discussion Group 1 divided in to three sections. The curriculum and courseware development section reviewed the current situation in IT use in elementary education, and agreed on the importance of children's early access to IT. Specific examples of good IT practice with young children were offered - using computers to facilitate writing; CD-ROM use to facilitate listening; and problem solving software use to develop thinking, creativity and communication.

The importance of appropriate local conditions for IT use, access to electricity, equipment and human resources trained for IT use in early learning settings, were described. The need to establish goals for IT use was also seen as a critical factor in the successful use of school-based IT use.

Recommendations included integrating IT into all subjects; standardizing equipment to facilitate training; choosing software carefully; and collaborating with other countries to exchange ideas and resources.

Another section of the group discussed secondary education and used a framework provided by Paul Nicholson - curriculum, hardware, courseware and collegiality - to focus its discussion. In the field of curriculum differences in approaches - integrating technology across the curriculum versus teaching computer literacy as a separate subject - were noted. It was also noted that courseware and software development in Zimbabwe is usually locally-based with little funding available for those development activities.

The group then explored what in the situation can change. Recommendations for the future included a suggestion that greater efforts at courseware/software production be made locally. It was also suggested that hardware configurations need to be reanalysed to provide a uniform platform base in schools.

The third section of Group 1 based their discussions on the role of teachers in planning for change and highlighted the importance of teacher education in IT as a vehicle for change. Critical factors which can be changed in order to provide a suitable environment for IT adoption include: developing consortia for curriculum planning and infrastructure projects; and changing the culture of teaching from the delivery of imposed curricula to the development of reflective, flexible practices.

Discussing how change can be implemented, the group suggested that relevant national IT policies be identified and clarified; teachers be trained to implement the UNESCO/IFIP curriculum; minimum IT competencies for graduating teachers be mandated; and dissemination processes such as conferences, journals and newsletters be widely adopted and used.

Discussion Group 2 examined policies, strategies and initiatives for ICT in education, and identified four perspectives - social, pedagogical, vocational and catalytic - for defining IT-based educational objectives. That framework led to the specification of objectives - using IT as a tool for personal functioning or for catalysing and improving the quality of the learning process, for example.

The group said that in order to achieve those objectives policies are needed for IT access, for teacher training and for provisioning an infrastructure. Once policies are in place, strategies must be implemented to ensure success and those plans must be linked to national development programs. It was advised that research centers for assembling and manufacturing IT tools should be established, and networking all schools to public offices, other schools and to the Internet should be accomplished.

Discussion Group 3 examined guidelines and directions for ICT policy in education, and formulated a set of guidelines for policy making. Objectives outlined by the group include encouraging business and employment growth, and enhancing service delivery. In setting guidelines for IT implementation the group stressed the importance of continuing government support for IT, focusing on IT in the broadest educational sense and not limiting IT to training a few computer literacy skills. The importance of support, especially providing on-going professional development opportunities, was seen as essential for capacity building.

Discussion Group 4 worked on strategies for IT education and delivery. Focal points for strategising included: the difficulties involved in planning and investing in IT to ensure maximum efficiency and effectiveness; remedies to overcome perceived difficulties; and roles to be played by the IFIP community and others in creating successful IT use. The group's collective experience was that there are mixed levels of computer literacy among staff, varying degrees of success in integrating IT into the curriculum, and varying levels of official control of syllabi.

The group said IT must be integrated in all aspects of the curriculum but provision must also be made for specialised study of IT. Skill development of teachers was cited as critically important in achieving IT goals. Learning as an active, not passive, process was emphasised and pilot projects, showing teachers what IT can do, were judged to make an important difference in IT diffusion.

IFIP can act as a facilitator, said the group, through the sharing of expertise, the enabling of dialogue, the promotion of standards and the encouragement of government agencies in formulating innovative policies.

Discussion Group 5 examined the role of IT in managing educational administration. The case of Zimbabwe, where a need for better control of data was cited as a need, was a focal point of the discussion while the experiences of Hong Kong and The Netherlands were provided as illustrations of IT-based educational management in other countries. As a result, a series of issues related to Zimbabwe were highlighted. Among the issues discussed was the need for the development of a comprehensive information management system policy. The need to communicate that policy to stakeholders and the need for well thought-out plans for design and implementation were also seen as important steps for Zimbabwe to take in managing data.

From those recommendations an action plan, calling for the participation of professional bodies, and the development of seminars designed to introduce and train people to use the systems, was devised.

Discussion Group 6 addressed the issue of building resource accessibility in developing countries. The group agreed that the first step must be clarifying the problem. Hardware and software needs should then be identified as well as human and infrastructure resources available for IT use. Accessibility and portability were identified as critical and inhibiting factors.

The group said every child in a developing country must have fun in 'hands on' IT experience and to achieve this goal the short-term objectives were identified, but the group also said comprehensive national policies must be developed. The group stressed the importance of providing computers for teachers. They also discussed ways donors might be sought, and emphasised the importance of government commitment to IT procurement and use.

Conclusion

All those attending the CapBIT conference knew that capacity building for IT in education in developing countries does not stop when the last speaker has spoken and the last delegate has left for home. Instead, all delegates shared the sobering realization that capacity building had just taken another step forward. But all participants of the conference were wiser in the knowledge of what their brothers and sisters around the globe had accomplished before arriving at the conference, richer in the knowledge of the plans, resources and possibilities available for IT-users, and more understanding of the potential for expanding IT use in their own countries and around the world.

PART I

National Perspectives

1

Nordic cooperation on Communication and Information Technologies and didactics in education

Peter Bollerslev
Director
Center for Applied Informatics in Teacher Education
Peder Hvitfeldts Straede 4,3
DK-1173 Copenhagen K, Denmark
Tele + 45 33 91 40 96; Fax + 45 33 91 46 96
E-mail: peter.bollerslev@sembsc.dk

Abstract
Implementing and applying each new development in Information Technology (IT) in education is a task requiring considerable resources. At the same time it is obvious that investment in IT is crucial for the development of any nation. The Nordic countries are very small. However, they share cultural backgrounds and educational traditions. Together they constitute a strong block capable of creating and building up expertise in the field of IT. The Nordic Committee on Educational Software and Technology, and, subsequently, IDUN have coordinated the Nordic collaboration during each phase of IT in education.

Keywords
Capacity building, competencies, developed countries, software, teacher education

1 INTRODUCTION

The five Nordic countries - Denmark, Finland, Iceland, Norway and Sweden - are situated farthest north in Europe. The Nordic Council of Ministers, a

Capacity Building for IT in Education in Developing Countries
G. Marshall & M. Ruohonen (Eds.)

committee responsible for collaboration between the governments in the Nordic countries, was established in 1971. Greenland, the Faroe Islands and the Aland Islands also participate, and the Nordic Council of Ministers makes decisions which are binding for all the countries when the decision has been taken unanimously.

In 1986 the Nordic Council of Ministers for Culture and Education entrusted the Nordic Committee on Educational Software and Technology with planning and organization of a broadly based Nordic collaboration on new Information Technologies (IT) in schools scheduled to start in 1987. The initial mandate was to develop competence in the use of IT in schools and develop high quality educational software.

In 1988 the committee's terms of reference were expanded to encompass all aspects of new technologies in education - information and documentation, development work and questions of standardization, product development, teacher education, and increased international collaboration. The mandate given by the Nordic Council of Ministers in 1988 emphasized that such activities should apply to the entire education system from primary and lower secondary schools, grammar schools, and vocational education and training to teacher education and adult education. The mandate of the Nordic Committee on Educational Software and Technology expired on 31 December 1994.

From January 1995 the IDUN project has continued the collaboration established by the Nordic Committee. This discussion explains how the Nordic Committee on Educational Software and Technology has carried out its work, describes the results achieved and how the work has influenced the collaboration between countries. The discussion will also describe how the collaboration has influenced the development of IT planning and implementation in each of the countries. Finally the activities the IDUN project has scheduled and already implemented are described.

2 STARTING POINT AND WORKING METHODS

Nordic collaboration on IT hardware and software issues for education has undoubtedly had the advantage of drawing on a shared fundamental view of education since the similar educational traditions provide a solid foundation for collaboration on the development of competence.

The Committee's objective was to exploit the potential of IT both as a means of renewing teaching individual subjects, and as a tool to amplify and complement teaching, especially with the help of sound educational software programs.

Nordic collaboration in the new and demanding field allowed the countries to effectively exploit the resources made available for the use of each new technology in education, for example by sharing the development costs of new software products or by coordinating research in a new area instead of carrying out the same work in parallel in all the Nordic countries. Another objective of the Committee's work was to build up a shared Nordic experience through reasonable contributions from the individual countries.

Coordination of the whole range of activities was carried out by the secretariat of the Nordic Committee. The working methods used to implement the various projects varied depending on the size and nature of the project in question. A project was often the result of a joint effort with the aim of achieving a result or product which could be of use in the entire Nordic area. In other cases projects were implemented by sharing tasks among the countries. The final product was later made available to all the countries. A third working method was based upon the exploitation of a special, national competence.

The case of jointly-implemented projects applies principally to the information and documentation area, agreements and standardization, teacher education, and international collaboration. A real division of labour occurred when it came to major competence-based projects and to the product development area.

It should be noted that a basic aim in such a collaboration is that national, public agreements which were previously applicable to an individual country should, wherever possible, cover the Nordic area. Agreements of this kind for the Nordic area mean, amongst other things, that services and products can be licensed in the Nordic area on the same conditions as in the country which was originally part of the agreement.

It is also important to note that the rapid expansion of the exchange of information and experience in all the areas accorded priority had a number of positive consequences when viewed from a national perspective. The intensified exchange of information, both centrally and at the regional level, led to common trends in the framework and developments within the IT area in the Nordic countries, both from a technical viewpoint and an educational one.

The increased exchange of information has even contributed to the avoidance of errors at national level in areas undergoing rapid development as countries have been able to take advantage of research and insights gained in other Nordic countries. For example, the advanced studies in Expert Systems, which were carried out in Norway in cooperation with MIT in USA, has given valuable input to the Nordic research in the area generally. In this connection it is important to emphasize that the budget of the Nordic Committee only covered the marginal costs for the implementation of most project activities. The lion's share of the costs was borne nationally. However, thanks to joint project planning, a division of labour among the member countries and the exchange of software products has led to savings at national level.

Activities and Achievements

When the project started in 1987 the ministers gave priority to the work with information about and documentation of the results of projects on the introduction of IT into education, issues of standardization of hardware as well as software to be used in education, research and development in IT in education, competence in teachers using IT and development of educational software, agreements and contracts for the common Nordic use of software developed in one of the countries, teacher education, and international cooperation with specific reference to IT in education.

The following categories will be used in the description of the results of the Nordic cooperation: information and documentation; research and development, and competence initiatives; product development, standards and agreements; teacher education; and international collaboration.

Information and documentation

The exchange of information and experience in their various forms has been one of the main initiatives throughout the entire collaborative process. Central authorities in each of the member countries send all relevant material - acts and regulations, agreements, reports, informative publications, educational materials and educational software relating to IT - on a regular basis to the Secretariat. Incoming materials are usually distributed at monthly intervals to the appropriate national bodies in the Nordic area. In many cases, the exchange of material has enabled the countries to use each other's suggestions and reports at the national level thus saving both money and duplication of effort.

A second activity under the aegis of the Committee has been study visits to member countries. Central authorities, institutions, schools and individual teachers have received contacts and suggestions concerning proposed study visits in various Nordic countries from the Secretariat.

The study visits took place at all levels from ministry to schools. Political and administrative experiences as well as classroom experiences were exchanged. The results are reported having been very helpful and sometimes having avoided repetition in other countries of failures already experienced in one country. Of course, projects with positive results have been copied from one Nordic country to another.

For a number of years, the exchange of information and experience has been followed up by an annual meeting of decision makers in the field of educational software and technology. Discussions at their three-day meetings have covered Nordic collaboration, development trends and guidelines for future work. As collaboration took root, annual meetings were replaced with national advisory panels who recommend on proposals for project activities through the Committee members.

The Committee's twice-yearly Nordic journal *Nytt om data i skolan* (*News on Computers in Schools*) is an important component of information-sharing activities. The journal was necessary because most member countries lacked a journal which regularly provided information on developments in IT in the various educational sectors. Rather than start five national journals in this field, a Nordic journal providing relevant Nordic and national content was felt to be a cost-effective alternative.

The Committee has also promoted Nordic catalogues of educational software for the entire educational field. Such catalogues did not exist at national level nor was there a standard for software description. For this reason the Committee commissioned the drafting of a joint Nordic standard for the description of software covering both the product and its hardware requirements in detail. The standard was then used to prepare Nordic catalogues, which were produced in collaboration with national institutions specializing in IT. As a result, the structure of the catalogues is identical in each Nordic country and is easy for teachers to use. Each country's catalogues cover both publicly and commercially-developed educational software, either written in or translated into, the language of that country.

The Committee has also produced many publications over the years in order to disseminate ideas and experiences about educational opportunities afforded by the use of IT in education. The publications vary in content and objectives. In some cases they are summaries and lists, for example covering research and development projects in the Nordic area. Some of them are general analyses or scenarios in various sectors, for example educational software requirements in schools, new technologies in adult education or the use of expert systems in education. They may also be reports from workshops and seminars, or course material. Publication is either by the secretariat, often in collaboration with appropriate national institutions, or via a private publisher who takes on the task of publishing the materials on a commercial basis.

Major reports are printed in sufficient numbers and are sent to member countries for distribution under national supervision. Reports with a more limited readership are distributed in the form of master copies, one per country. The individual countries can thereafter decide on the printing run and the distribution pattern themselves.

A by-product of collaboration, which had not been anticipated in the action plan but which has become an important part of information exchange among the member countries, was that the more the work of the Committee became known, the more the Committee's secretariat functions metamorphosed into a Nordic resource centre for the use of IT in education. In addition to coordinating formalized collaboration, the Committee's secretariat now acts as a resource centre which can promote informal cooperation in the Nordic region.

Research and Development and Competence Initiatives

One of the main initiatives of the Committee was to increase Nordic competence and expertise in the field of IT in education. The Committee had very little experience on which to base its work. While countries such as France, the United Kingdom, USA and Canada launched major initiatives in IT in the early 1980s, the Nordic countries were taken by surprise by the rapidly expanding development of IT in education. Concerted planning was initiated in the Nordic countries at about the same time as guidelines for Nordic collaboration were being written. The shared problems of the member countries did, however, constitute a good foundation for Nordic collaboration. While there were doubts as to the thrust of the programme there was agreement that IT had come to stay and it would be necessary to keep abreast of the educational and technical aspects of international achievements in the field. The Committee used an international conference, organized by the Swedish Ministry of Education and Cultural Affairs, as its point of departure. Some of the most prominent experts in the field of IT in education from France, England, Scotland and USA were invited to the conference, which took place in Sollentuna, Sweden in 1986.

The Committee then commenced work on developing Nordic competence and expertise with the Nordic teachers who had participated in the conference in order to place the Nordic region at the forefront of international developments in IT. A key objective was that IT not be seen exclusively as an aid but also as a means of facilitating the renewal of education in a wide range of school subjects.

To increase Nordic competence with software design, multimedia, interactive video, computer-aided tools, expert systems, system dynamics, databases, telecommunications, collaboration on icons, music, curriculum development and emerging technologies the Committee engaged in many different activities. Previously member countries had built up their expertise by sending representatives to conferences or on study trips. There is no doubt that this is still a viable approach. But a rational and cost-effective solution proved to be the use of Nordic experts with the required international expertise who provided information about international developments and trends, and also contributed their expertise to their peers from all the Nordic countries. This expertise could afterwards be disseminated more widely through national workshops.

The dissemination effect has been very high - especially when it comes to courses in software design. From the start, the Committee's views on the development of educational software for many subject areas and school levels was that the initiative and much of the design work should come from teachers themselves. For this reason the Committee organized a number of general and tailor-made design courses for teachers. The software design courses were a mix of general design courses, design courses for special education and subject-related design courses. More than 60 joint workshops, seminars and other competence building sessions were held within the Nordic community. Over 800 teachers from the Nordic region have participated in the design courses.

The Committee developed a specific tutor training model for the courses. The venue for courses alternated among the member countries so half of the tutors and programmers on a course were from the host country. The remainder consisted of experienced tutors and programmers from the remaining Nordic countries. The new national tutors were intensively trained with the aid of skilled experienced Nordic tutors for the week of the course's duration. Tutor training continued during the design course itself by getting a new and an experienced tutor to work as a pair for a fortnight, the duration of the course. Over the years more than 100 Nordic tutors and programmers have been trained through this process, and the training of experienced national teams has facilitated the transfer of Nordic design courses for teachers to national contexts.

Courses in software design held at the national level based on the Nordic courses and the training of national tutors and programmers soon emerged to intensify the building up of expertise and software development. Experienced speakers and tutors were soon being exchanged far and wide across borders.

Nordic work on program design has developed a new kind of software development culture in the Nordic countries and has been adopted by a number of private publishers. The philosophy of open educational software such as the 'marketplace' model (Crossley and Green, 1985) has been the starting point for most of the software programs produced at Nordic level.

When staffing workshops, seminars and other staff development sessions, the Committee wanted to study new areas subject to increasing development at the international level at the earliest stage possible to assess their significance for education. The Committee was interested not only in the pedagogical aspects of international developments but also in developing Nordic expertise for the common good and for private enterprise - a justification for carrying out advanced workshops in the various sectors of computer technology as Nordic pilot projects, after which achievements and results could be disseminated at the national level.

From a financial point of view it is evident that workshops are cheaper to arrange as joint Nordic initiatives than to do so on a country-by-country basis. The costs of international expertise needed in a Nordic development programme are already so high that a joint initiative benefits all countries involved. Coordinating development in a specific field is a good example of rationalistic profits for all Nordic countries. The cost effectiveness cannot be accurately accounted for but there is no doubt that software development paid for once and coupled with costs of translation, is far cheaper than developing costs multiplied by five Nordic countries. When you add to that what you may gain from cooperation over the borders with no need to convert software and even the fact that the same tools may be used for development of educational software, the advantages of the model chosen become even more apparent. There are undoubtedly cases where national workshops in priority areas are required and in such cases the Committee has given the other member countries the opportunity to take part with a limited number of participants per country through a separate agreement.

Product Development, Standards and Agreements

The area of product development, which understandably has been the most expensive of the Committee's activities, has had a major influence on the division of tasks among the member countries. In this area it is imperative that countries make full use of each other's capacity and, with the aid of agreements, ensure that educational products are inexpensive to use across borders. Agreements on joint standards have also supported national adaptations of each other's productions. The commissioning and production of Nordic software for education was one of the main priorities of the Council of Ministers. A model for exchange of software emerged, as a result of which more than 100 programs of good quality are available to the educational sector in the Nordic area.

The basic concept is simple. Since 1987, representatives of the member countries meet on an annual basis at workshops designed to evaluate the previous year's production of publicly and privately produced educational software. On average some 50-60 programs are shown each time. After the presentation the member countries rate the programs they are most interested in, and on the basis of this expression of interest, enter into a Nordic agreement covering programs to be used in all member countries. Normally the contract covers 4 programs from each country, which means that each country receives 16 programs from the other countries for this investment.

The Committee also arranges an adaptation workshop on an annual basis some months after the Nordic software contract has been signed. Software authors or persons with the necessary knowledge are brought together with programmers from each of the countries to work on translations and adaptations. The result is that a majority of programs covered by the agreement can be translated to all five Nordic languages in 4 days. An additional and significant advantage is achieved in connection with the workshops. In the course of work on adaptation one can see where the problems lay and, on a joint basis, agree upon common standards and models for future software development.

The Nordic model for software development has been most advantageous for the countries involved and has been adopted at European level by the European Union in Brussels. The EPES-project (European Pool of Educational Software) was begun in the summer of 1992 under the aegis of ORFEUS, Denmark. A workshop was arranged in Aarhus, Denmark in which 12 European countries participated. A European agreement covering two programs per country was signed and a yearly translation workshop has been arranged.

Teacher Education

Teacher education has also been an area accorded high priority by the Committee in order to increase expertise in areas such as multimedia, expert systems and system dynamics. Many of the initiatives have been described above but the Committee has also held many courses for teachers and teacher educators in a range of subjects with the objective of showing how IT can be used in the classroom.

The Committee's work on the development of special Nordic software was based on the hope that individual teachers would become interested and then generate ideas for software programs in many subjects and levels. This was why the Committee began its activities with special design courses for teachers.

In the general design courses as many as 120 teachers from primary and secondary schools, vocational education and training, adult education, teacher education and tertiary education took part in each course. Training took place over a two-week period in the summer through combined lectures in plenum and group work under the leadership of tutors and programmers who were themselves being provided with ongoing training at Nordic level. Teachers worked intensively with their ideas in groups of two to four. Towards the end of the course, the first draft designs could be tested with the aid of programmers. The major objective of the courses was to obtain a useable draft design which could form the basis of a finished piece of software. The objective was achieved in that out of the approximately 30 groups of each course eight to ten of the groups reached a draft which lent itself to being implemented as a finished product. A second objective, of which the participants were hardly aware, was to promote discussions of IT's potential for education. With 100 or more teachers from different countries, and with a variety of backgrounds, subjects and levels, spontaneous and intense discussions occurred around the clock. A new awareness of the advantages of IT emerged among the teachers who took part in the courses.

Courses in software design held at national level based on the Nordic courses and the training of national tutors and programmers soon emerged to intensify the building up of expertise and software development. Experienced speakers and tutors were soon being exchanged from far and wide across borders. When all member countries had launched their own teaching programmes the Committee discontinued general design courses in favour of subject-related courses.

Teacher educators are among the weakest links in the effort to integrate IT into Nordic education. In every country teacher educators are key determinants of the success or failure of IT's impact on the school of the future. But teacher educators have a more limited knowledge of the educational potential of IT than classroom teachers. So the Nordic Committee arranged pilot courses in IT which brought together national policy-makers and administrators to put together an action plan for teacher education. The target group was teacher educators for primary and lower secondary schools, upper secondary schools, and vocational education and training. The best method was practically-oriented workshops on the presentation and use of educational software in the teaching of all relevant subject areas.

Bringing together teacher educators from different institutions on a subject-by-subject basis provides not only national networks forming the foundation for future work but also Nordic contacts for the exchange of ideas and experience.

International Collaboration

At first the Committee's work aimed at the consolidation of Nordic collaboration. At the same time the Committee believed that the task of following international developments in computer technologies was a clear and important one. To be continually informed of educational and technical developments covering both software and hardware is of importance to the Nordic countries. The Committee continually intensified its relations with other countries and international organizations and has presented its work and results at a number of international conferences (Bollerslev, 1995).

Evaluation

In 1993 the Committee engaged the services of an international expert, Mike Aston, from the Advisory Unit, Computers in Education in the United Kingdom, who was given the task of assessing both activities and achievements in an international context. Aston's evaluation was clearly positive. Amongst other things he noted that 'The collaboration between the 5 Nordic countries is unique in this field. Neither the European Community nor the Gulf Cooperation Council, comprising 6 nations, have achieved anything like the degree of human networking and sharing of research, development and product generated by the Nordic Committee on Educational Software and Technology. This is in itself an asset which could be exploited' (Aston, 1993).

In its conclusions the report notes that 'The cooperation achieved by the programme in the fields of technology, the development of software and know-how in education has been remarkable, given the economic and human resources made available' (Aston, 1993).

3 CONTINUING THE COLLABORATION: THE IDUN PROJECT

The mandate of the Nordic Committee expired in 1994 but the work was continued in the IDUN project (IDUN was the goddess of renewal in Valhalla who was responsible, amongst other things, for the apples the gods ate so as not to age) with the same project director and the same secretariat.

The Council of Ministers gave priority to six main areas in the action plan for IDUN: Information Technology and educational policy; implementation; the development and exchange of educational materials including educational software; distance education; shared access to data networks and databases; and intellectual property rights and agreements in connection with software, databases and data networks.

IDUN's role is the follow-up and transferal of the activities previously conducted by the Nordic Committee but the rapidly growing areas of distance education and networking have also become focal points. The plan of operations for IDUN also notes that special emphasis should be put on the implementation of teacher education and says surveys of research and development should adopt a European perspective. A look at the completed and scheduled activities for 1996/97 shows that we still have a very intense Nordic collaboration in the field of IT in education. Recent activities for IDUN include a wide variety of planning meetings, workshops and continuing work with software development.

Three Nordic planning groups, each comprised of one person from each Nordic country, have planned and conducted conferences on IT and pedagogy, pedagogical/didactic issues in distance education, and IT and the library. A Nordic group has drawn up a plan for national courses for teacher educators on the use of IT and pedagogy. The courses are to be tested at a number of teacher education colleges in each country and eventually they will become compulsory in the training of teacher educators in the Nordic area.

Other IDUN activities include a Nordic group that has planned a course programme aimed at teacher educators on the subject of the computer as a tool in teaching. The course is to be carried out on the Internet and is operational with participants from all Nordic countries from March 1997. Other planning groups are working in the areas of special education to generate strategies for Nordic software development and exchange among the Nordic countries. Similarly, planning for a multimedia design course aimed at both commercial publishers and public companies is occurring, and a planning group has prepared a course for editors from publishing companies on the subject of IT, educational materials and subject related didactics.

The 1997 program evaluation and exchange workshop has taken place, and 20 new programs will be ready for distribution in the Nordic countries in the summer of 1997 and, as a result of a seminar, 15 titles from the Nordic software agreement have been translated into Greenlandic, the Faroe and the Lapp languages. Finally reports on adult education and information technology, Nordic research and development and intellectual property rights have been issued.

4 CONCLUSION

The Committee's results - both through the Nordic Council's work and then through the IDUN project - can be considered an exceptional success as interviews of key persons from ministries, educational authorities and other agencies in the Nordic countries, and a few other countries show. For example, one participant said, 'Software has been developed on the basis of Nordic ideas. Cooperation has led to an understanding of what it is really all about. And paradoxically it has given us resources at national level as well' (Bollerslev, 1991). Another participant said, 'Taking part has been a challenge. It [the collaboration] has created an inter-Nordic forum and it has influenced national development. Many problems which would have been difficult to tackle on your own, have been solved successfully' (Bollerslev, 1991).

5 REFERENCES

Aston, M. (1993) Nordic Council Committee on Educational Software and Technology. Evaluation 1993. Copenhagen, Denmark.

Bollerslev, P. (1991) Evaluation of The Nordic Committee on Educational Software and Technology. Copenhagen, Denmark.

Crossley, K. (1985) *A Practical Guide for Teachers: Designing Computer Lessonware*. Lessonware Services Incorporated, Ontario, Canada.

6 BIOGRAPHY

Peter Bollerslev has taught mathematics and informatics at colleges of education for many years. He was Her Majesty's Inspector in Teacher Education for more than 20 years. He is now director of the Center for Applied Informatics in Teacher Education. Peter Bollerslev has authored and co-authored more than 250 textbooks for schools and colleges, and has been involved in IFIP since mid 1970s. He has served as chairman of WG 3.1 for six years and for another six years was chairman of TC3. At present he is the Danish representative to the IFIP General Assembly. In his spare time he is a keen golfer and bridge player.

2

Building resource capacity for IT education and training in schools - the case of Botswana

Sunday Ojo and Ben Awuah
Department of Computer Science
University of Botswana
Private Bag 0022
Gaborone, Botswana
Fax + 267 3552784
E-mail: ojoso@noka.ub.bw

Abstract
Botswana provides an interesting case study of some issues and challenges in building the human resource capacity necessary for a programme of IT education and training in schools. Present and future education and training options for building capacity are discussed. A framework for building appropriate human resource capacity is also proposed in form of recommendations. The issues and challenges raised in Botswana's program of IT education and training in schools are not unique to Botswana, and, consequently, the proposed framework can be generalized, with appropriate adaptations, to different contexts in developing countries.

Keywords
Capacity building, curriculum development, developing countries, skills, teaching materials

1 INTRODUCTION

Information Technology (IT) is essential to developing countries if they wish to modernize their infrastructures, survive economically, compete internationally and communicate electronically for trade and other purposes (Hawkridge, 1990). The

Capacity Building for IT in Education in Developing Countries
G. Marshall & M. Ruohonen (Eds.)

modern successful industrial economy worldwide is IT-driven. Thus each society must be IT-aware, and the present and future workforce must be prepared to make the best use of IT.

Botswana has recognized the need to increase the technological skills of its people to better compete in world markets. The Botswana education policy aims to prepare Botswana for the transition from a traditional agriculture-based economy to an IT-based industrial economy. To imbibe the IT culture early enough, most societies are introducing computer education in schools. In Botswana, the introduction of IT education and training (IT E&T) in schools is aimed at ensuring a basic level of competence for most, and in the long run, for all young people countrywide. The intention of the programme is not to produce computer experts out of the students but to give them the basic computer knowledge and skills to make them computer literate, and enable them pursue computer studies without being intimidated by the computer. After the acquisition of the skills it is expected that the students will be able to use IT across the subjects of the curriculum (Curriculum Development Division, 1996).

The availability of human resources to the successful implementation of a programme such as this cannot be over-emphasized. Therefore, the main focus of this paper is on human resource capacity building for IT E&T at the secondary school level of education in Botswana. The key objective is to examine the various options available for human resource capacity building strategies.

2 IT EDUCATION AND TRAINING IN BOTSWANA'S SCHOOLS

2.1 Structure of Botswana's education system

The Botswana education system can be stratified into: preprimary, primary, secondary, and post-secondary levels of education. The preprimary level is wholly a private affair and so no reliable statistics are available. There are 629 public and 71 private primary schools. The secondary level is divided into two-year (or three-year) junior secondary and three-year senior secondary schools. At present, there are 209 junior secondary and about 27 senior secondary schools. At the post-secondary level, there are four primary teacher training colleges and two colleges of education (for training junior secondary teachers). There are also six vocational training centres and one university - to which are affiliated the two colleges of education and a college of agriculture.

2.2 Supply of computers to schools

According to Nganunu (1993), computers started finding their way into Botswana's secondary schools around 1982. School computers were usually donated by local businesses, Parent-Teacher Associations and nongovernmental organizations. Interested teachers and students were mainly exposed to computers through computer clubs in schools. Computers in the junior secondary schools (JSSs) were used mainly for administrative rather than educational purposes. The Ministry of Education came up with the idea of providing every senior secondary student with basic computer literacy in 1988 (Nganunu, 1993). The government started playing a proactive role in around 1991 and set up an inter-ministerial Government Computer Steering Committee (GCSC), with a national sub-committee on Computer Education and Training. The sub-committee was set up to advise the GCSC on pre-service and in-service education and training needs for the required human resources.

By 1992, the government had supplied five Macintosh computers each to all the senior secondary schools to enable them introduce computer awareness courses to teachers and students. One of the secondary schools which had started an 'O' level computer studies programme since 1986 was given an additional eight computers. One of the two colleges of education was also supplied with five PCs. The initiative was not based on any clearly-defined policy on computer education in schools. Recently, seven out of the 209 junior secondary schools were provided with laboratories equipped with 10 Macintoshes and 10 IBM PCs. The seven schools are currently being used for a trial run of a computer awareness programme for the junior secondary schools.

2.3 National policy on IT E&T in schools

In the Botswana Government White Paper (Botswana Government, 1994) on the Report of the National Commission on Education (NCE, 1993) the need to acquire computer literacy in secondary schools for both teachers and students was recognized. The White Paper made the following policy statements:

- that computers should be provided at the proposed resource centres for primary schools;
- that each student of a junior secondary school should take a basic computer awareness course;
- that all senior secondary school teachers should acquire computer literacy and the schools should be allocated enough computers to enable all students to develop computer skills.

Those policy statements have provided the basis for the various steps taken on behalf of IT E&T in schools in recent times.

2.4 Syllabus development

Senior secondary school computer awareness course development.
A task force was set up by the Ministry of Education to develop the necessary computer awareness programme for senior secondary schools. The task force carried out an initial survey as a basis for its recommendations.

The task force came up with a framework for developing the programme, which involved the use of teachers from selected schools. In the end it was decided that a consultant will be employed to develop a national syllabus for IT E&T in the senior secondary schools. To date the plan has not materialized. Senior secondary schools offering computer studies as an 'O' level subject make use of the Cambridge 'O' level syllabus.

Junior secondary school computer awareness course development.

In early 1996 a task force was set up by the Curriculum Division of the Department of Curriculum Development and Evaluation, Ministry of Education to come up with a computer awareness syllabus for the three-year junior secondary schools. The process of syllabus development was started with a consultancy which looked into the logistics for the development and implementation of the programme.

The three-year junior secondary school syllabus was launched in April 1997. The modules in the syllabus include: computer skills, keyboarding skills, productivity tools, word processing, spreadsheets, databases and graphics. The aim is to introduce computing to students through infusion into the subject areas. A trial run of the implementation of the syllabus is currently going on in seven selected junior secondary schools. According to the officer in charge, things are going well in some of the schools and not so well in others.

Presently there is no similar syllabus for the senior secondary schools. The plan is to have a national computer studies syllabus for senior secondary schools in the near future.

Human resource development efforts

The Teacher Training Development Unit (TTDU) of the Ministry of Education was charged with the responsibility of putting in place a programme to train the In-service Education Officers with computer awareness skills to enable them develop a syllabus and carry out teaching sessions in the secondary schools for teachers. The activities are aimed at laying a foundation for the teachers to acquire the skills and enable them to teach computer awareness as a subject to students.

Vendors were initially engaged in training teachers on the management of the IT resources and the use of productivity software packages.

In 1994, based on the advice of the Commonwealth Secretariat in London, a consultant was employed to come up with a programme for 'Training the Trainers'. The consultants' proposal (Tekateka & Miyanda, 1994) was based on visits to selected schools. A key finding was that besides individual efforts of interested staff, there was no comprehensive strategy to build the human resource capability for IT E&T in schools. It was recommended that the Ministry of Education should initiate a programme of training 60 teachers in Gaborone, the capital city, starting in January 1995. It was also recommended that the programme should focus on providing a foundation for the understanding of IT as well as the effective use of computers in schools and industry. Each class of 10 students was to last for six weeks. The trainees should have acquired enough knowledge to use computers and be able to teach others basic computer awareness at the end of the course. A number of other observations were made in the report including:

- selection of teachers for training should not be limited to only mathematics and science teachers as this would give an incorrect impression on the status of computers in general;
- teaching a computer awareness course in itself is not a job that many teachers would want to do for the full working week so computer awareness teachers should still teach part-time in their own departments;
- teachers do not need a qualification to teach a computer awareness course. In this sense, the computer awareness course is a subject which is different from

all others. Teachers who are familiar with some basic knowledge of computers turn out to be competent computer awareness teachers; expertise is not required;

- there should be three to four teachers skilled in computers per school, with one of them appointed as the computer coordinator.

The Teacher Training Department (TTD) organized a number of training workshops for teachers in selected schools. At the beginning of 1997, under the auspices of the pre-service unit, one of the colleges of education started a computer education programme aimed at training teachers for the junior secondary schools' computer awareness programme.

A programme has commenced for the training of teachers in the seven selected schools through the in-service programme. All teachers, regardless of their teaching subjects, are being involved. It is planned that the scheme will be extended to other schools based on the outcome of the pilot programme in the selected schools.

The Botswana government's full commitment to the programme of introducing computers in schools is not doubted. Also, right from the outset it was obvious that the government realized the significance of building the human resource capacity necessary for a successful implementation of the programme but we believe that there is a need to adopt a more comprehensive strategic approach to building IT capacity.

3 HUMAN RESOURCE CAPACITY BUILDING - AVAILABLE OPTIONS

The options for human resource capacity building can be categorized into in-service and pre-service. The in-service option is aimed at enhancing the capacity of serving teachers to be able to teach and effectively utilize IT in their schools. The pre-service option deals with IT E&T for trainee teachers to build in them the capacity to teach and utilize IT in the schools where they may be teaching after leaving college.

3.1 Options for the in-service programme

Short courses in private computer training schools

The short courses are essentially prepackaged training programmes for PC-based applications. The teachers had difficulty transferring their PC-based training to using the Macintosh systems in their schools. This suggests some fundamental deficiency in the nature of the training. The decision to supply both Macintoshes and PCs to schools from now on may not be unconnected with this experience.

Vendor training programmes

Vendor-delivered programmes are designed and implemented by IT system vendors/suppliers, and are limited to equipping trainees with the knowledge and skills required to use the specific hardware and software systems being sold by the vendors. Such training is commonly narrow and skill-oriented, and does not adequately prepare the trainees for the broad challenge of IT deployment in the education sector in general.

Training workshops

The Teacher Training Department organizes workshops which are conducted by officials of the Ministry of Education or the INSET (in-service training) staff based at the University of Botswana's Department of Mathematics and Science Education. The workshops are more or less devoted to computer appreciation topics and are developed in-house with the assistance of consultants. It is questionable whether the workshops take an holistic view of the total knowledge and skill requirements for teaching, using and managing IT in schools..

Options for the pre-service programme

Options for training are also available at the teacher training colleges and at the university. The college of education option for the introduction of computer education into the curriculum of the colleges of education for training teachers for the junior secondary schools was started in early 1997 (Molepolole College of Education, 1997). It is a cross-curricular approach where all IT delivery is by subject teachers and students receive no specific IT teaching per se. The challenge is that IT education and training for the student teachers requires more than just impacting the basic knowledge of computing. It requires delivery of the appropriate methodology to use the knowledge within the context of other teaching subjects. Merging the subject matter contents with pedagogical approaches in a complementary manner is important Naturally, the course would require the availability of experienced teachers. Also, the focusing of the course mainly on computers in education seems a good strategy to ensure graduates are not lost to more lucrative jobs outside the education sector - *e.g.* to industry as is experienced in other countries (Ojo, 1994).

Options within the University of Botswana

As a matter of policy, the country's National Development Plan 7 expects all students passing through the university to be computer aware before they can graduate. Consequently, virtually all programmes have computer awareness modules or IT-related courses infused into the subjects.

Recently, the Department of Mathematics and Science Education (DMSE) came up with a proposal aimed at producing teachers for Computer Education during the National Development Plan 8 (NDP8) (DMSE, 1996). The proposal was made to start a B. Ed degree as well as postgraduate Diploma in Education (PGDE) programmes in computer science. The programmes are intended to provide teachers of computer studies for the senior secondary schools. The Ministry of Education and related agencies have relied on expatriates or deployed mathematics and science teachers with basic knowledge of computing to teach the subject. This has been the practice despite the shortfall of mathematics and science teachers at the senior secondary school level. Another important observation made in the proposal is that mathematics and science teachers who graduated from the university will not have studied enough computing courses during their training. Closely related to the limited exposure to computer studies of the teachers is the question of pedagogical issues of teaching a subject which they will not have covered in the teacher education programmes. The cadre of mathematics and science teachers might not be sufficiently well-prepared to handle computer studies because of its uniqueness. Therefore the major focus of the programme is to produce computer studies teachers for the nation's senior secondary schools. In addition, it is hoped that the graduates of the programmes will serve in junior secondary schools to coordinate the basic computer awareness course and offer technical and academic advice. It is thought that providing teachers in this way would ensure the sustainability of the computer awareness course at the junior secondary school level.

The Department of Mathematics and Science Education has recently requested the inclusion of computer science courses in the B. Ed. (Science) programme. In this way the B. Ed. (Computer Science) programme would be comprised of a combination of courses which are selected independently by the two departments from education and computer science courses.

One problem with the combined major programme is that there are usually no clearly-defined objectives for the kind of human resource development that the programme is aimed at producing. Disciplines such as biochemistry emerged from the combination of chemistry and biology with emergent properties of its own. The combination of education and computer science should ensure producing the right kind of teachers for IT E&T programmes in schools.

4 KEY ISSUES IN BUILDING THE HUMAN RESOURCE CAPACITY

4.1 Teacher trainers

At present there is an acute shortage of human resources to train the needed teachers. People with combination of IT knowledge and skills plus the relevant pedagogical skills are rare.

4.2 Rural-urban infrastructural disparity

Botswana is one of the developing countries which can boast of adequate electricity and telecommunications infrastructures - the availability of which is sine qua non for successful IT. However, as it is the case with most developing countries, the rural infrastructures are not comparable to those of the urban areas. How do we ensure that the schools in the rural areas are not unnecessarily disadvantaged? Do we need special training so teachers deployed to the rural schools know how to maintain and effectively utilize IT resources in the face of inadequate infrastructure?

4.3 Teaching materials

As mentioned in the preceding section, no teaching materials have been developed as of now and so the schools already involved in the programme mainly depend on operating system manuals. The implication of this is that teaching may have a purely technical focus, which is rather narrow. The development of appropriate teaching materials is a crucial operational issue.

4.4 Expatriate dependency

As with other developing countries, Botswana is still at a developmental stage. There is a high dependency on expatriates, especially in the areas of science and technology. A recent study (Christopher, 1993) showed that 80% of trainers in private IT training institutions in the country are expatriates. The situation is worse in the only university, where the percentage is even higher for expatriates involved in IT E&T. On the one hand, there is the urgency to meet the immediate developmental needs of the populace and the irresistible temptation to keep making use of imported expertise to achieve these targets/objectives. On the other hand is the need to develop the internal human resource capacity crucial to ensuring the sustainability of development. How would these apparently conflicting objectives be resolved to guarantee the sustainability of any programme of human resource capacity building for IT E&T in schools? This is another crucial issue.

4.5 Balancing investments in IT E&T with other pressing demands

IT E&T in schools is just one of several areas for which the country needs to develop human resources capacity. Balancing resource allocation among the competing areas of need is a critical issue. Making the issue even more critical is the fact that education is virtually free in the country and investments in education do not yield immediate observable dividends.

4.6 Indigenous capacity building

Getting students interested in science and technology disciplines remains a major problem. There is a limit to what can be achieved in building the required indigenous capacity without adequate local supply of potential trainees. Though the government has started encouraging interests through the awarding of scholarships, there is still a long way to go to attain adequate supply of locals in this area. Also, there has to be a more conscious effort to promote and encourage the development of local talents, a crucial factor in guaranteeing indigenous capacity development.

4.7 Curricular innovation

Faced with the need to adapt science teaching to the local needs of their respective countries, science educators have, for some years past, embarked on curricula innovation projects. IT E&T programme innovation requires an adaptation to local needs. Local needs analysis is a commonly neglected aspect of IT E&T programme development in Africa. This means that trainers who are experienced in this kind of task may be lacking. The implication is that there have to be appropriate mechanisms to monitor such changes as well as adequate flexibility built into IT E&T programmes in order to accommodate the changes. Generally, the task requires an innovative and adaptive approach, all of which makes IT E&T programme innovation a critical issue with an enormous pedagogical challenge.

4.8 Maintaining the human resources capacity

With particular reference to the B. Ed. (Computer Science) programme, we must ask how we ensure maintaining competitiveness of the programme against more attractive job markets. As a matter of strategy, we should aim at evolving a programme which provides competencies to:

- teach the secondary school computer studies syllabus;
- analyse, design, implement, evaluate and manage appropriate computers-in-education programmes;
- determine computing resource requirements and manage computer laboratory facilities in schools;
- utilize computers in education administration.

5 RECOMMENDATIONS

Botswana stands a good chance of evolving IT E&T programmes that appropriately address the various problems found in other African countries. Now we need to build more solidly on the various positive steps that have been taken so far through a more deliberate approach of developing trainers for IT E&T programmes in schools.

5.1 General capacity building

To achieve general capacity building we recommend the following a series of initiatives:

- Introduce general science and technology awareness programmes in both primary and secondary school levels aimed at creating a general science and technology culture in the students.
- Carry out a national needs analysis to provide a focus for all IT E&T programmes in schools. The analysis should be well-aligned with overall national socioeconomic goals.
- Develop a national curricula standard, innovatively designed and based on the result of the needs analysis.
- Provide a clear and definite scheme for evaluating/accrediting IT E&T programmes.
- Formulate IT E&T policies and strategic plans well-aligned to the overall national plan for human resources capacity development.
- Make a periodic review and update of all of the above to ensure that technological and contextual dynamics of IT are adequately catered for at every point in time.

5.2 Institutional resource capacity building

The human resource capacity required for IT E&T programmes in schools should be acquired through the existing teacher training infrastructures in colleges of education and the teacher training departments of the university with the following recommended actions:

- Computer studies should be introduced as a teaching subject for both the Bachelors and sub-degree teacher training programmes.
- In view of the scarcity of mathematics and science teachers, other categories of students, including social science and humanities education students, should be involved as trainee teachers in the programme to involve more teachers in IT instruction.
- To ensure availability of the graduates for the purpose for which they have been trained, there should be a clearly-stated government policy as well as appropriate incentive mechanisms aimed at avoiding losing students to greener pastures in other sectors.

5.3 Curriculum development

The subject matter content of the curricula for training trainers should take a sociotechnical perspective so that trainers can sensitize their trainees in schools to some of the contextual issues of IT in the country. Therefore it is recommended that:

- The development of the programmes should receive input from a broad spectrum of the various role players - educationists for methodological content, IT specialists for subject matter and material content, representatives of employers and government for sociophilosophical and policy content as well as specialists in relevant subject areas for contextual issues.
- The curricula for teachers should include building capacity for graduates who are adequately equipped to effectively function in various positions of responsibility for IT E&T in schools. Skills should include defining and planning schools' IT systems as well as designing, implementing and managing the development and operations of those systems. This requires adoption of a flexible paradigmatic framework and diversified curricula orientation to accommodate the diverse backgrounds of the prospective students to be trained for the IT E&T programme.

In any programme of training the required teachers must establish cooperation among relevant academic departments. The nature of such cooperation is cross-disciplinary and should involve the computer science department and relevant departments in engineering, social sciences, humanities and education. The cooperation should cover areas of teaching, research, seminar and curriculum development. The educationists are needed for handling the various pedagogical issues involved in teaching and curriculum development while others will be required for the contextual issues. This kind of cooperation is needed for evolving the socioscientific-humanistic paradigmatic integration that is required for the new point of view in IT E&T programmes. It would also enable the sharing of human and material resources for teaching and research such that the inadequacies of one department are covered by the strengths of another.

Periodic remedial training programmes for trainers in IT E&T programmes should occur to update their knowledge and give them the right orientation for producing appropriate human resources.

Appropriate programme evaluation and review bodies should be established to ensure continual relevance of the human resources being developed.

The establishment of an appropriate forum where IT trainers, researchers and other stakeholders can meet to share ideas, facilities, and engage in joint research and development project activities should be facilitated. Such a forum can be in the form of a well-equipped national IT Research, Development, Education and Training Centre. Such a centre should also serve as a base to generate ideas on the direction which IT E&T programmes should be going at each point in time.

6 CONCLUSION

The Botswana IT E&T programme should aim for innovations that can produce the right calibre of IT human resources. The programme should be carefully designed so that it is appropriately adapted to the sociocultural and organizational contexts of the country. This requires inward-looking rather than the usual dependence on imported expertise. It is hoped that the recommendations made for Botswana would prove helpful, not only to Botswana, but also to other developing countries sharing similar context of socioeconomic development.

7 REFERENCES

Botswana Government White Paper on the Revised National Policy on Education, No 2 (1994) Gaborone, Botswana.

Christopher, A. (1993) Report of a Survey on Existing and Planned Computer Training in Botswana. Gaborone, Botswana.

Curriculum Development Division of the Ministry of Education. (1996) Three-Year Junior Secondary Syllabus - Computer Awareness. Ministry of Education, Gaborone, Botswana.

Department of Mathematics & Science Education (1996) University of Botswana, NDP 8 Proposal, Ministry of Education, Gaborone, Botswana.

Hawkridge, D. (1990) Creative gales and computers in third world schools in *Computers and Education* (eds. O. Boyd-Barrett and E. Scanlon),

National Commission on Education Report (1993), Gaborone, Botswana.

Nganunu, M. (1993) Ministry of Education Policy on Computer Training, Department of Technical Education, Ministry of Education, Gaborone, Botswana.

Ojo, S.O. (1994) IT Education and Training in Africa - A Framework for Botswana. A paper presented at the Commonwealth Association of Science, Technology and Mathematics Educators (CASTME) International Conference, Gaborone, Botswana.

Tekateka, W. and Miyanda, S. (1993) Proposal to the Botswana Government for the 'Training the Trainers' Computer Programme, Access Information Systems Training Dept., Zambia.

8 BIOGRAPHY

S.O. Ojo holds a Ph.D. in Computer Science from the University of Glasgow. He is the University of Botswana's representative to the National Sub-committee on Computer Education and Training. Dr.Ojo was the President of the Botswana Information Technology Society (BITS) from 1993 to 1996.

E.B. Awuah holds a Ph.D. in Computer Science from the University of Reading, UK and is the Head of the Department of Computer Science, University of Botswana.

3

Computer education and human capacity building for Information Technology in Namibia

Geoffrey E. Kiangi
University of Namibia
Private Bag 13301, Windhoek, Namibia
Tele + 264 61 206 3620; Fax + 264 61 206 3030
E-mail: gkiangi@unam.na

Abstract

Namibia, like many other countries, acknowledges Information Technology's potential in accelerating educational reform. A recently developed computer education policy attempts to ensure that remote schools benefit from the technology by narrowing the gap between the advantaged and disadvantaged schools. Analysis of the policy and the efforts of NITA, the Computer Association of Namibia, to assist in training school teachers are reviewed. The contributions of tertiary institutions, including the University of Namibia, in developing human resources in Information Technology are also examined in order that other developing countries can draw meaningful lessons from Namibia's experience.

Keywords

National policies, computer science, Internet, curriculum development

1 INTRODUCTION

Education is a key ingredient in the economy and well-being of any country. Through education, the human resource potential of countries is enhanced and considerable sums of money are spent on human resource development.

Education has continuously undergone reformations. Even in Africa, where formal education is not more than half a century old, many reforms and reviews have been carried out to keep pace with academic and technological developments, and to ensure relevance and equity - although observers have also voiced concern

Capacity Building for IT in Education in Developing Countries
G. Marshall & M. Ruohonen (Eds.)

about the low level of computer use in the schools of developing countries. They have also warned about the wide gap between developed and developing countries (Kiangi, 1995).

Hawkridge (1991) states four reasons why African schools need computers:

- social - schools are required to prepare students for life. Since computers have pervaded industries, the workplace and the home, students should be expected to be able to handle computers;
- vocational - school children should have a basic knowledge of computers, knowledge that may prepare them for a career in computer science. They also need a foundation that will prepare them to apply computers in the areas in which they will eventually specialize, even if those areas are different from computer science;
- pedagogical - computers are tools through which other subjects can be learned. For example, it is possible to teach a language course by using computerized voices, images and text;
- catalytic - computers can also be used to assist students to learn how to handle information and solve problems without necessarily memorizing facts.

Computers can be a vehicle to encourage collaborative learning while, at the same time, computers catalyze efficiency in the management and administration of schools.

The four reasons given by Hawkridge were the main focal points around which the education policy for Namibia was developed. While they do form good arguments for introducing computer education, there are problems of implementation which will be reviewed later.

2 EDUCATION IN NAMIBIA

The Namibian educational system has undergone considerable changes since independence in 1990. The years since independence can be considered as a phase of education reform and transition, where major organizational, administrative and curricular changes occurred (Ministry of Basic Education and Culture, 1995). Immediately after independence universal education was instituted. A number of studies and discussion were conducted between 1990 and 1992 which shaped future directions. In 1993, *Towards Education for All* (Ministry of Education and Culture, 1993) translated earlier efforts into concrete implementable government policies. The major goals of the reform effort were outlined as access, equity, quality and democracy. While the goals are not unique to Namibia, the strategic planning that was adopted, and which is now giving dividends, is worth noting.

To manage the reform process, a National Institute for Education Development (NIED) was established within the Ministry of Basic Education and Culture. The major functions of the institute include: curriculum research and development; curriculum implementation, including professional development and in-service teacher training; coordination of pre-service teacher training; and the development and production of instructional materials (Kiangi, 1994).

In February 1995, following the initial phase of reform and transition, NIED conducted a global assessment of the new system to evaluate the effects of initiatives adopted in the reform process. Several positive achievements were noted. The number of candidates who sat for grade 12 in 1995 increased six-fold within a period of only 5 years. Many learners are now able to choose their field of study within close proximity to their homes. All senior secondary schools are applying a single unified system in admission, class size and teaching loads so the first two goals of access and equity are beginning to be realized.

There are also problems with the reform process. In some schools teacher inefficiency was noted as a serious problem and it was also noted that it is difficult to have common core subjects in all schools. Computer courses and the popular HIGSCE courses can only be offered by few privileged schools. Availability of textbooks was observed to be a big problem. The few textbooks in use are from Britain and have little relevance to the local situation.

Lack of qualified teachers is also a problem. Namibia has only half the needed teachers for secondary schools in terms of qualifications (University of Namibia, 1995). Proper physical facilities are lacking in many schools. About 21% of all classrooms in Namibian schools are constructed using sticks, mud and thatch. Promotion rates for some grades range from 43% to 92%. This means that if the rates remain the same, for every 100 learners starting grade 1 only 3 reach grade 12 (Ministry of Basic Education and Culture, 1995b). This is a very poor throughput and if all these problems are not addressed they can overshadow the benefits of the reform process.

3 COMPUTERS IN NAMIBIAN SCHOOLS

3.1 Courses

Three courses are offered at different grades: computer literacy (grades 5-7), computer practice (grades 8-10) and computer study (grades 11-12) (Ministry of Basic Education and Culture, 1995; 1996; Kiangi and Hamutenya, 1994).

Computer literacy covers word processing and drawing using programs such as *Paintbrush* and Logo. Computer practise courses cover programming and advanced elements of computer literacy. Computer study courses cover the social and economic implications of IT as well as system design concepts. Coverage in the courses provides basic knowledge only and does not make one employable as a computer expert.

3.2 Enrolments

Only a few schools are able to offer computer subjects. According to 1995 statistics only 67 (.05%) students took Computer literacy; only 2083 (2.6%) students took Computer practice; and only 251 (1%) students took Computer study (Ministry of Basic Education and Culture, 1995b). Many of the students enroled in computer courses are only from privileged private schools, resulting in very low enrolments given above.

3.3 Performance

Examination results for 1995 are very interesting. The Junior Certificate examination results showed 472 candidates sat for the exam and 12% were awarded grade A pass - the highest percentage of grade A passes for the 32 subjects that were examined.

IGCSE results showed that 131 students sat for computer studies and 19 % were awarded grade A - one of the three well-passed out of the 43 subjects.

The statistics indicate that computer subjects can be performed well but students lack access to computing resources. Many are denied computer education not because they do not have the ability but because schools lack computer resources or trained teachers. In some schools computers have been donated but collect dust because there are no computer-literate teachers. The 1992 figures indicate that there were only 10 qualified computer teachers for grade 12 (Kiangi and Hamutenya, 1994).

3.4 Computer Education policy

For a long time the reform process was carried without much regard to the provision of computer facilities to schools. To a large extent schools were left to decide how to resource themselves. As a consequence, only a few schools acquired computer resources and trained teachers. In early 1995 a debate started on the need to provide a directive for computer education. Kiangi (1995) emphasized that there was a compelling need to develop a computer education policy, stressing the fact that while there are sentiments that computer education is a luxury, especially in a country where schools are still struggling to erect buildings for classes, it is imperative that a policy be set so that the meager resources available for computer education are put to the best use. He cautioned that failing to provide computer subjects - leaving such decisions to individual schools will widen the gap between the privileged schools and the underprivileged. That will greatly undermine government efforts in achieving equity in education.

Since then, the UNESCO office in Namibia provided funds to develop a computer education policy under NIED's direction. A draft policy was prepared by a number of academics, experts and NIED staff. A workshop was convened, calling in a number of teachers to discuss the draft, which was finalized in 1996.

The Computer Education policy is divided into three parts:

- introduction - states the need for a computer education policy and describes how computers impact the society today;
- policy - integrates the computer education policy with existing government objectives and priorities, and identifies the rationales for providing computer education courses;
- implementation - identifies short term, medium term and long term objectives, develops strategies needed to achieve the objectives, and identifies target groups and institutions bearing responsibility for ensuring the success of policy objectives (Ministry of Basic Education and Culture, 1996)

Very little has been done since the policy was completed. A financial strategy, outlining how the disadvantaged schools can be helped, should have been included. To a large extent, a computer education policy is also a fiscal policy. Since the education policy was based on the four reasons advanced by Hawkridge (1991) - social, vocational, pedagogical and catalytic - it is important to note a few things. Many analysts have examined in detail the pedagogical and catalytic reasons relating to learning. It is interesting that while more literature exist on these two than on the other reasons, it is these reasons that are ignored when African schools decide to introduce computer education. Namibia, therefore, starts on the right footing. With regards to the pedagogical reason, Sewell (1990) argues that computers should be used within the framework of cognition, learning and information processing. He analyses in detail the use of computers as cognitive tools and concludes that computers can be used for cognitive growth. Computers enable expression of skills already existing in a much easier way and they encourage the development of new cognitive skills.

Brown (1985) observes that computers provide an empowering environment where learners can accomplish things they otherwise could not accomplish. Bruner (1966) discusses the social context of computer education in that as students work together on a computer in small groups and group discussions are activated, discussions which could not be achieved in conventional teaching. Such cooperation among learners results in 'group reciprocity' in which learning is enhanced by learners themselves.

Bruner seems to be in agreement with many others who identify as key contributions of computers to education: active involvement with the learning environment; reduction of mental drudgery; better manipulation of information; and enhancement of abstract thought. Analysts generally agree that if educational philosophies, cognitive psychology and computer science are brought more closely together, greater benefits in computer education will be achieved. Teachers, decision makers and researchers should be made aware of the extra benefits not covered in many computer policy statements.

3.5 Internet

The introduction of the Internet into Namibian schools has created great interest, although many schools do not know how to effectively use the tool. The dangers of providing Internet access are also great and Internet issues need a separate section in the policy. In fact, since Information Technology is a dynamic field, a mechanism for continuously monitoring IT developments and ensuring harmonious progress should be incorporated in the policy document.

4 COMPUTERS IN TERTIARY EDUCATION

The University of Namibia (UNAM) and the Polytechnic of Namibia are the largest tertiary institutions which offer computing as a specialty. Other tertiary institutions offer computing as a subject; none offer courses beyond computer literacy. Professional computer companies offer short courses on specialized computer application areas.

The University of Namibia in 1995 enrolled 3501 students, more than half of whom were first year students. Only 169 were science students, 20 of whom majored in computer science. The University does not offer a degree in computer science but offers a Bachelors of Science degree where computer science can be a major together with other science subjects. Students from other faculties can also major in computer science, but with difficulty. Only two to six candidates have graduated annually with B.Sc. degree in computer science, although the numbers are gradually increasing. Beginning 1996, all science students must undertake a computer literacy course.

The Polytechnic of Namibia had an enrollment of 3272 students in 1995. Nearly half of the students take Information Systems, which is equivalent to computer literacy. The Polytechnic also offers a Business Computing Diploma requiring a one-year National Computing Certificate (NCC) offered by National Computing Centre in UK as well as an additional two years of computer and business studies. Only a few candidates graduate each year with a Diploma in Business Computing and the NCC part of the course was phased out in 1997.

Winschiers (1996) attempted to analyze IT knowledge acquisition of students at the University and Polytechnic. She noted that cultural backgrounds inhibit acquisition of computer knowledge and result in poor conceptions of computer science by students. This observation challenges the way computer education is provided both at tertiary and secondary school levels, and has led the Department of Computing at the University of Namibia to embark upon a research project intended to develop on-line computer training methods taking into account individual students' education backgrounds.

Use of computers in distance education also receives considerable attention. At the end of 1996 the University of Namibia attempted to examine how computers can be used to provide distance education. The University is working with the United Nations Office of Outer Space in Vienna, together with 12 other African countries, in the COPINE project to develop a computerized satellite system which will be used for distance education and many other applications such as tele-medicine. The planning for this system is fairly well advanced.

5 KEY ELEMENTS FOR FUTURE DIRECTIONS

5.1 The computer education policy

The computer education policy has been finalized. The policy should be implemented. If a school does not have computers, it can organize visits to a nearby, better-endowed school in order to provide a basic understanding of computers. Once enthusiasm has been created within a school, it is to acquire computers from a number of donor sources, including the local community. There are additional benefits to the implementation of the policy. One study notes that cognitive abilities among African students are low (World Bank, 1988). Since computers are excellent cognitive tools, they can be used to enhance cognitive growth.

5.2 Government Internet connection

The government, through the Directorate of Public Service Information Technology Management in the Prime Minister's office, has embarked upon a comprehensive program of providing all government ministries access to the Internet. The system will provide capabilities to support dedicated and dial-up Internet users, and will allow migration to larger systems as Internet uses expand within the government. The system consists of a series of backbone routers providing a 256 kbps connection to Global One. A total of 25 servers located in various ministries and regional government centres will be provided.

In addition, the Directorate of Public Service Information Technology Management is initiating government-wide online computer training courses. The courses range from simple computer literacy courses to comprehensive specialized courses in different areas of computer applications. This leapfrogging in computer use at the government level is likely to have far-reaching implications. The education system will be under greater pressure to keep pace.

The university computerized satellite system to be launched in association with COPINE will be a powerful tool in providing education in a cost-effective manner. The Ministry of Education may wish to use this for in-service training since computer courses can be offered to school teachers via this system with significant effect.

5.3 Contribution of NITA

The Namibian Information Technology Association (NITA) has always had a keen interest in computer education. In the past, the Association has helped train school teachers on Information Technology. Currently, NITA is looking for ways to assist in training school teachers, hoping to boost computer interest in schools.

5.4 Introduction of Internet

The introduction of Internet to Namibia has provided an upsurge of interest in IT. Several Internet service providers have mushroomed, Internet cafes have been established and school children flock to them with great excitement. A number of well-endowed schools have obtained Internet connectivity and the upsurge of interest is likely to have profound effect on computer education.

5.5 Introduction of ISDN technology

Telecom Namibia is upgrading most telephone lines to a digital system. The ISDN architecture of all digital telephone lines should make it easy to interlink computers requiring 64 to 128 kbps throughputs over long distances. This will accelerate the building of a computer network infrastructure where schools can connect effortlessly, and be able to receive and transmit voice, data and images. Again, such an infrastructure will put pressure on schools to train for and utilize Information Technology.

5.6 The IT industry

While the level of application of Information Technology in the industry and organizations in Namibia is fairly high (Kiangi and Hamutenya, 1994; Winschiers, 1996), IT management in Namibia still has a long way to go. As with any other technology, Namibia is mainly a consumer rather than a developer of Information Technology. There is a critical shortage of IT experts and even the simplest Information Technology applications are developed outside the country. There is little effort either within the government or in industry to localize IT application development. The situation has adversely affected computer education in Namibia. Elsewhere, Ellis (1974) has commented, '...thinking about computers in education does not mean thinking about computers, it means thinking about education'. Government policies should encourage industry to use local manpower in developing IT applications and thereby catalyze IT human resource development.

6 CONCLUSION

The experience of Namibia in training learners and experts in Information Technology presents a mixed picture. Excellent efforts such as the development of a computerized satellite system for use in training and the completion of a computer education policy are set against the lack of appreciation on the part of executive authorities of the potential benefits Information Technology can provide to education.

The computerized satellite system that the University of Namibia is developing provides opportunities for a wide range of developments in education such as the in-service training of teachers. Online computer training shows some promise as a viable computer training method with such a system in place.

Namibia has an environment conducive to developing the required Information Technology human resources given the good telecommunication infrastructure, a strong IT user market and close proximity to South Africa, where expertise can be tapped. Given the small population and the large land area, IT applications are particularly attractive to Namibia. Tele-education and tele-medicine seem to be the only way by which goals of education and health for all can be achieved. In recognition of this, IT human resource development should be regarded as essential. Other countries can learn about the good efforts Namibia has attempted in IT human resource development but take note of areas that need strengthening as outlined above.

7 REFERENCES

Brown, D. (1985) Process versus product: A perspective on tools for communal and informal electronic learning, in Chen, M. and Paisley, W. (eds.), *Children and Microcomputers: Research on the Newest Medium*, Sage, Beverly Hills, CA.

Bruner, J. (1966) *Towards a Theory of Instruction*, Norton, New York.

Ellis, A.B. (1974) *The Use and Misuse of Computers in Education.* McGraw Hill, New York.

Hawkridge, D. (1991) Computers in Third World schools: African advances. *Educational and Training Technology International*, **28**(1), 55-70.
Kiangi, G. E. (1994) Science, Technology and Mathematics Education in Namibia, CASTME Technical Report. NIED, Ministry of Education and Culture, Windhoek, Namibia.
Kiangi, G.E. (1995) Computer Education and the need for a policy. *Journal for Education in Namibia*, **1**(2), 36-41.
Kiangi, G.E. and Hamutenya, N. (1994) Status of Informatics and Information Technology in Namibia. RINAF South Workshop on Information Technology Networking and Education, Bulawayo, Zimbabwe.
Ministry of Basic Education and Culture. (1996) Policy for Information Technology in Education in Namibia. NIED, Windhoek, Namibia.
Ministry of Basic Education and Culture. (1995) Annual Report. Windhoek, Namibia.
Ministry of Basic Education and Culture. (1995) Education Statistics. Education Management Information Systems (EMIS), Windhoek, Namibia.
Ministry of Education and Culture. (1993) *Towards Education for All: A Development Brief for Education, Culture and Training*. Gamsberg Macmillan, Windhoek, Namibia.
Sewell, D.F. (1990) *New Tools for New Minds*. Harvester Wheatsheaf, London.
University of Namibia. (1995) Proceedings of the (H)IGCSE colloquium on Teacher Education. Windhoek, Namibia.
Winschiers, H. (1996) Information Technology Diffusion in Namibia. Sim posio de Informatica Informatica e desenvolvimento, Maputo, Mozambique.
World Bank (1988) Education in Sub-Sahara Africa: Policies for Adjustment, Revitalization, and Expansion, A World Bank policy study. World Bank, Washington, D. C..

8 BIOGRAPHY

Geoffrey Kiangi holds a B.Sc. in Civil Engineering from the University of Dar es Salaam, Tanzania (1982), an M.Sc. Construction Engineering from Leeds University, UK, (1984) and a Ph.D. in Engineering Management and Computer Applications, Leeds University (1988). He has worked as a consulting engineer, site engineer and university lecturer at the University of Dar es Salaam, Tanzania and the University of Nairobi, Kenya. He is currently Head of Department of Computing at the University of Namibia. His research interests include software engineering, computer networks, technology management and optimization techniques in engineering. He has written books, several journal and conference papers as well as literature for children in these areas.

4

Schools with SPIRIT - capacity building in The Netherlands

Pieter Hogenbirk
Sectormanager PRINT
PRINT\VO
P. O. Box 15922, 3800 BN Amersfoort, The Netherlands
Tele + 31 33 4534283; Fax + 31 33 4534380
E-mail: P.Hogenbirk@Print.cps.nl

Abstract

For the last 12 years the Dutch government has supported the supply of computers, the development of educational software and the introduction of computers in the schools. Prior to 1993 several attempts were made to train teachers to use IT. In 1993 the PIT project used the strategy of networking teachers to use software in their own disciplines and encouraged them to develop their own materials. Teachers were also encouraged to share and learn from each other's experiences. Involving more than 50% of all lower secondary schools, over 2,000 teachers and over 30 curriculum specialists the strategy has relied on the commitment of the schools involved - Schools with SPIRIT - and on a multiplier effect in schools. According to an extensive external evaluation the PIT strategy appeared to be a very effective alternative to 'traditional' in-service training.

Keywords

Informatics, secondary education, networks, national policy, integration

1 INTRODUCTION

For 12 years (1985-1997) The Netherlands worked with national projects introducing Information Technology (IT) into secondary education. We will distinguish between the first seven years and the following five years. From 1987 until 1992 an infrastructure of hardware, software and humanware

Capacity Building for IT in Education in Developing Countries
G. Marshall & M. Ruohonen (Eds.)

resources was installed. After this period the average teacher was expected to use the computer in the curriculum but efforts were disappointing at best and the government decided to put emphasis on helping teachers use the computer as part of their everyday teaching.

For the past five years an ambitious program, the PIT project (PIT is an acronym for 'Project on Information Technology' but a 'School with PIT' in Dutch also means a 'School with Spirit') has been carried out to implement IT in lower secondary education.

2 THE FIRST PHASE OF THE NATIONAL POLICY 1986 - 1989

From 1986 - 1989 the New Information Technology for Secondary Education (NIVO), a national project for secondary education, was initiated. All secondary schools received 11 IBM-compatible computer configurations, 8084 XTs, a package of software tools - mainly application software - and obligatory training for at least three teachers per school in information literacy. Many teacher training courses, offered on a voluntary basis, were also developed and carried out. At the same time the development of educational software began under the motto 'Let thousand flowers bloom' and work began on the development of curricula in which IT is treated as an objective.

NIVO resulted in the de facto standardization of computer hardware in schools (Collis and De Vries, 1993) and gave an impetus to courseware development (Collis and Moonen, 1995). The project also started the process of changing existing curricula (Hall, Loucke and Rutherford, 1977). Almost 95 % of the schools actually did organize courses in information literacy. Above all, the project provided conditions to orient schools and teachers to the possibilities of IT and so IT became part of the agenda for most of the schools (Hogenbirk and Diepeveen, 1993).

3 THE SECOND PHASE OF THE NATIONAL POLICY 1989 - 1993

From 1989 until 1993 PRINT, the PRoject on the Implementation of New Technologies, was designed to continue the introduction of computers into education. PRINT is a temporary project organization, with the assignment to manage and coordinate all the national initiatives for Information Technology and education. The management team consists of 9 people, all from different institutes.

A new curriculum on aspects of informatics in physics, social science, economics, mathematics and Dutch (mothertongue) was completed. Courseware to be used year-by-year through the existing curriculum of school subjects was developed. A major research project on three pilot schools was conducted to obtain information about successful introduction strategies, resulting in trials of many activities introducing computers into classrooms.

The activities were designed for all schools in regional projects with support of the National Educational Advisory Centers. They were also designed for

The activities were designed for all schools in regional projects with support of the National Educational Advisory Centers. They were also designed for school managers by presenting strategies for planning the introduction of computers in their schools. Teachers in several disciplines received in-service training on the subjects of informatics and Information Technology.

Activities were also targeted at individual teachers who attended a single afternoon session devoted to learning one or more computer-assisted learning (CAL) packages, At the sessions they also learned to implement courseware to be used on a long-term basis throughout the curriculum.

The entire educational community received assistance in IT implementation through articles, written publications, posters, conferences and a help desk. At the same time sufficient courseware to cover large areas of the existing curricula was developed (Collis and De Vries, 1993) and objectives for IT implementation in school subjects were proposed (Collis and Moonen, 1995). The activities generated a great deal of experience in the use of computers (Hall, Loucke and Rutherford, 1977; Hogenbirk and Diepeveen, 1993) but expectations had been too high. The 'ship of education' is very large and hard to get moving. By 1993 the incidental use of IT as a tool in the daily practice of education was limited to a few teachers in a few subjects in a minority of schools (Pelgrum, Janssen Reinen and Plomp, 1993).

4 THE THIRD PHASE OF THE NATIONAL POLICY 1993 - 1997

In 1993 the Dutch government asked PRINT to initiate a project designed to help teachers in lower secondary classrooms use IT. The project was to last from 1993 to 1996. The scope was subsequently broadened to involve Communication Technology (ICT). The plan, designed for all students from 12 to 15, was introduced in 1993 and called for the project to become part of the new curriculum, called 'Basic Education'.

PRINT launched the Project on Information Technology (PIT) (Veen, Hogenbirk and Jansen, 1994). PRINT initiated three rounds of project participation (March 1993, March 1994 and September 1995) and invited every secondary school to compete for projects in three out of eight school subjects: Dutch (mothertongue), German, French, English, mathematics, physics and chemistry, biology and technical skills. In each discipline there was a choice of one out of four or five themes. PRINT chose the most promising schools and tried to honour their preferences for the subjects and themes as much as possible.

Table 1 shows a sample of the themes that teachers might work on with colleagues from other schools.

Table 1 Brief description of themes in the PIT project.

Subject	Theme	Goal
Dutch and	Theme 1: Learning problems	Using IT to remedy learning spelling problems.
	Theme 2: Differentiation in time and contents in the classroom Practice	Using IT to stimulate differentiation in time and contents among pupils in classroom practice.
English pupils	Theme 2: Study skills	Teaching and developing to concentrate by means of IT.
French	Theme 1: Computer-assisted instruction	Using software that offers considerable potential to realize the core objectives in French.
German	Theme 1: Remediation	A number of programs are to be demonstrated, tested in the classroom and evaluated, in each case emphasizing the remediation possibilities of the package.
Mathematics	Theme 1: Algebra and Statistics	A wide range of software may be applied when learning to process statistical data or to interpret and represent algebraical relations.
development, geometry classes curriculum as 'Mathematics 16'	Theme 2: Geometry	The evaluation, adaptation and implementation of software for in the new referred to from the age of 12 to will occur.

PRINT, 1994

The PIT schools were given incentives to participate, including free counseling and help with the implementation of technology. In rounds one and two they also received 24 000 guilders (about $12 000) per year to spend on hardware and software. The funds also paid for extra hours for the teachers involved in the project. In round 3 the money supplied by the government was limited to the organization of the project and the actual support of the teacher networks. Schools participating in round three had to fund all the other expenses themselves.

Interest in the PIT project was overwhelming. For the first and second rounds more than 500 schools applied and 125 schools were selected for the first round starting in 1993; in 1994 71 schools were selected for the second round; in round three 230 schools applied (and that was amazing given that the schools had to finance a large portion of the activities themselves) and all were allowed to participate.

Schools were selected for the project on the basis of their letters stating the school's motives for joining the project. Commitment of the school administration, equipment available and the level of teachers' involvement were also criteria used to select schools.

5 THE ORGANIZATION OF THE PIT PROJECT

Over the three rounds 77 teacher networks - theme groups - were formed, each consisting of one or two teachers from one or more subjects from approximately 15 schools. Each teacher network tackled one of the themes defined for its discipline. The networks met face to face six times in a school year.

The participating teachers were instructed and coached by theme group leaders from three national Educational Advisory Centers. Teachers exchanged information and professional insights, and worked on their personal and professional development. They also developed, commented on and evaluated new materials. Each PIT school was encouraged to participate in at least three networks in three different subjects in order to get a critical mass of IT users in every school. Each participating school had to appoint a PIT coordinator to manage the project at the school by giving support, and assisting in the making and implementation of school policy on IT.

School administrators signed a contract specifying the duties of PIT and the schools. The PIT coordinators and a member of the administration of each PIT school attended special sessions about project approach, implementation support and policy making during the course of the project.

6 EVALUATION OF THE PROJECTS

In order to monitor the project but also to evaluate the process of change in the schools and among their teachers, a evaluation plan was devised. With the wide range of activities going on in the PIT Project, three different sources of information were used: (1) the PIT coordinators, (2) the PIT teachers and (3) the theme group leaders. The evaluation for the first two rounds was carried out by the Faculty of Educational Science and Technology, Department of

Instrumentation Technology (ISM) of the University of Twente in The Netherlands (Collis and Moonen, 1995). The framework of the Concerns-Based Model (CBAM) (Hall, Loucke, and Rutherford, 1977) was chosen as a framework for assessing two major aspects of the project: the degree to which the PIT teachers moved to higher levels of IT use in instruction during their participation in the PIT project and the degree to which a multiplier effect occurred in the PIT schools - *i.e.*, did other teachers not directly participating in the PIT Project also move to higher levels of IT use according to the CBAM Model.

The CBAM Model as modified for teachers' reactions to computer-related innovations (Collis and De Vries, 1993) is shown in Table 2.

Table 2 CBAM Model Adapted for IT Use

Level of the CBAM model	Action toward the innovation
1. minimal awareness level	1. casual interest in getting information about the innovation
2. some knowledge	2. interest in browsing and exploring
3. some use of one or two types	3. tries some things in practice
4. regular use	4. makes some uses of IT routine in his/her instructional setting
5. regular use and leadership role	5. makes regular use of IT in instructional practice and also works in various ways to stimulate his/her colleagues to also make use of IT

(Hall, Loucke and Rutherrord, 1977)

The increased use of IT by the PIT teachers in their classrooms was a major outcome of the project. Data showed a significant increase in teachers' self-reported CBAM levels - from 2.57 at the start of the project in September 1993 to 3.73 at the conclusion of the project in May, 1995 (Hogenbirk, 1996).

PIT-coordinators were asked to indicate their assessment of the satisfaction of the PIT teachers with the project. The majority of the teachers were 'mostly satisfied' with the project and only a small constant percent of teacher was 'mostly negative'. In a setting where so many teachers of different backgrounds, different starting points of IT experience and different expectations on the personal were a factor outcome of the project the results are reassuring. A slight decrease in satisfaction in round 3 is assumed to be related to the fact that the evaluation took place in the middle of that project year and the third round consisted of only six meetings of the theme groups so there was less time for the teachers to get as involved as the participants of rounds 1 and 2.

Two sets of indicators were used to evaluate the multiplier effect of the project in the participating schools. The PIT teachers reported a significant change in the level of IT use by their non-PIT colleagues - from CBAM level 1.96 at the beginning of the project to 2.74 by May 1995. A majority of the PIT coordinators (70 %) stated that an increase in IT use by non-PIT teachers had occurred and another 18 % stated that the increase was growing (Collis and Moonen, 1995).

7 CONCLUSION

Encouraging groups of teachers to meet regularly and work together to explore a theme in their subject appears to be a powerful strategy for changing attitudes towards new types of educational behaviour- specifically toward IT. Important elements in the plan to change teachers' perceptions and activities for IT use include creating a critical mass of experts - teachers and others - in the schools, ensuring that sufficient software and hardware is available in the classrooms, and gathering teachers on the base of common interests and similar levels of IT expertise. Experience has also shown us that IT innovators must put an emphasis on the professional development of the teachers - especially on their exchanges of experiences - and projects must facilitate teachers directly as well as through the commitment and efforts of the school administration.

In our experience teachers' increased use of IT for classroom work will occur when there is a balanced mix of easy-to-use materials and less easy-to-achieve but important improvement of teaching methods through training and information exchanges among teachers. The members of the teacher networks must have the opportunity to call on help and support during the project as well as after the conclusion of the project, and project staff must make sure that physical face-to-face meetings occur to build a cooperative supportive group, continuing to support the cooperation - if possible - through the Internet. Of course the whole setup of the PIT project demands great human, infrastructural and financial resources. For other countries and situations select elements of the project suited to the local situation and conditions may prove to integrate learning to use IT with the teaching/learning process.

8 REFERENCES

Collis, B., & De Vries, P. (1993) *The Emerging Trans-European Network for Education and Training: Guidelines for Decision Makers*. Commission of the European Community, Task Force Human Resources, Education, Training and Youth, Brussels.

Collis, B. & Moonen, B. (1995) *The PIT Project: Final Evaluation Report*. Faculty of Educational Science and Technology, University of Twente, Enschede, The Netherlands.

Hall, G., Loucke, H., and Rutherford, W. (1977) Measuring stages of concern about an innovation. University of Texas Research and Development Center for Teacher Education, Austin, TX.

Hogenbirk, P. (1996) The PIT-project: A teacher networking approach for broad-scale use of ICT, in *Information Technology: Supporting Change through Teacher Education* (eds. Don Passey and Brian Samways), Chapman & Hall, London.

Hogenbirk, P. and Diepeveen, T. (1993) Towards an information society: The policy of changing education in the Netherlands, in *Informatics and Changes in Learning* (eds. D.C. Johnson and B. Samways), Elsevier Publishers, Amsterdam.

Pelgrum, W.J., Janssen Reinen, I.A.M. and Plomp, Tj. (1993) *Schools, Teachers, Students and Computers: A Cross-National Perspective*. IEA, The Hague.

Veen, W., Hogenbirk, P. and Jansen, F. (1994). The Implementation of Communication and Information Technologies in Teacher Education in the Netherlands, in *Workshop Teacher Education and Communication and Information Technologies: Issues and Experiences for Countries in Transition.* University of Twente, Enschede, The Netherlands.

PRINT. (1994) *PIT, Projects on Information Technology*, English version, available at the PRINT office, P. O. Box 1592, 3800 BN Amersfoort, The Netherlands.

9 BIOGRAPHY

Pieter Hogenbirk has been a teacher in secondary education. In 1987 he became project manager for the NIVO project and from 1989 he served as project manager of the PRINT project, coordinating the development and implementation of curricula, assessment, courseware and teacher training. He was the first chairman of the Dutch Society of Informatics Teachers. From 1993 he has been head of the PRINT management, with supervision of more than 100 ICT projects. Among these the PIT project was the largest. In 1996 he also became chairman of a consortium for developing a study planning and registration tool, and the Dutch government has assigned him to inaugurate the Dutch National Educational Network.

5

Information Technology in Norwegian education - consistency of strategic initiatives for implementing IT in primary education

Sindre Røsvik
Educational Director, Giske Kommune
Øvre Nordstrand, N- 6050 Valderøy, Norway
Tele + 47 70 18 20 05; Fax + 47 70 18 12 86
E-mail: sindre@mimer.no

Abstract

In August 1997 Norway started implementing a major school reform - Reform '97, a multiple reform on childhood, family, culture and education. Reform '97 is part of an overall educational reform from kindergarten to university, remaking the structure and content of education in primary and lower secondary school. Information Technology and its implications are focused as important elements of the educational reforms, mainly on content but to some degree on structure as well. Goals and means of IT in Norwegian educational policy include national plans for IT, new curriculum guidelines, methodological guides on subjects and competence-building plans. Consistency between national IT plans, the curriculum L97 and plans introduced to implement the reform are a major part of the national initiative. The effect of these plans, especially on IT, can be questioned because of the financial arrangements and diverse plans for assigning responsibility.

Keywords

Curriculum development, competencies, national policies, elementary education, secondary education, higher education

Capacity Building for IT in Education in Developing Countries
G. Marshall & M. Ruohonen (Eds.)

1 INTRODUCTION

After a period of intensive national experiments and projects from the mid 1980s onward Norway experienced some years of vacuum in the national efforts to support and promote use of Information and Communication Technologies (ICT). Some main national projects had failed and the political climate did not favour putting money into new initiatives.

During the 1990s education has been given substantial publicity and priority. From 1994 onward there has been an educational reform for upper secondary education, and, from August 1997, Reform '97 has focused on primary and lower secondary schools. Such comprehensive reforms are changing both the structure and content of the Norwegian education system. New curriculum guidelines (L97) are the most substantial elements of Reform '97. Competence-building programmes are being run to ensure the implementation of the curriculum.

Mass media and meetings have been used to introduce Reform '97 to students, parents and local authorities. It is emphasised that this is a major and comprehensive reform, changing not only structure and curriculum, but also ways of learning and working in schools, ways of evaluating students' work, grading, exams and other aspects of education. New learning materials have been introduced to all students in all subjects.

In this discussion our focus will be on national ICT initiatives and how they are dealt with in the national curriculum. The intention is to see if the different plans form a consistent strategy on ICT in primary education.

2 MAIN ELEMENTS OF NATIONAL PLANS ON ICT IN EDUCATION

During recent years ICT in education has been a part of a general public interest in technology. Elaboration of policy papers and debates have kept the level of attention high, with many questions being raised about implementation of the ICT policies given the lack of financing.

In 1995 the Norwegian plan,coordinated by The Ministry of Transport, set an agenda of challenges to deal with ICT. The report includes a chapter about the global local school, the importance of learning to use ICT and the use of ICT in learning. The report stresses the role of education in a modern society, the importance of mastering ICT and educational possibilities offered by ICT.

Following the general strategy document, the Ministry of Education elaborated plans for ICT in Norwegian Education through *A Plan for 1996 -1999* (Royal Ministry of Education, Research and Church Affairs, 1996).

A key formulation of the new directives is that teachers and students are to be personal users of ICT capable of using ICT in those parts of their learning to which ICT can add value. It is also expected that the students and teachers have the necessary grounding for making use of ICT at work and in their leisure time.

A main element of the plan is to clarify responsibilities of different levels, from the national to the classroom level. The national level covers the development of curriculum, a methodological guide and authorisation of learning material. Development of competence programmes is also a national responsibility and the plan includes initiatives to enable universities and teacher colleges to run programmes. School owners are to organise the implementation of the curriculum, competence building programmes, financing and other aspects of ICT use. Teachers and students are recognised as those who will finally implement the curriculum. To succeed they need support of different kinds.

The plan advocates main approaches for ICT use in schools: 'using to learn'; 'learning to use'; teacher training; and technical infrastructure and organisation. A plan of action is formulated through 31 different initiatives, or measures, mostly on using to learn (15 initiatives), while the rest of the measures are focused on learning to use, teacher training, technical conditions and organisation.

2.1 'Using to learn'

Information Technology in Norwegian education emphasises the integration of technology, without giving undue weight to technology. Instead the plan stresses ICT as a learning aid to support the learning process. ICT is to be used as a source of information and communication, to develop teaching and training methods, and to make different kinds of information collections. Relevant Norwegian information - texts, speeches, pictures, and other types of data - should be available to schools. Research and development projects must be run to offer new insights into the learning process. The importance of a lifelong perspective on learning and the greater opportunities offered by ICT as well as the establishment of new learning environments are underlined by the plan.

Such a plan challenges Norwegian mediators, publishers, libraries, broadcasters, software companies and other software manufacturers to develop and process information, and make it available to the educational sector.

2.2 'Learning to use'

Learning to use means getting familiar with and mastering ICT. From the first years of schooling it means playing with the computer, getting used to the keyboard and other devices. From the middle and upper level of primary school it means learning to use standard software.

According to the plan, learning to use ICT should be integrated into each subject to prepare for general use in studies and occupations. Courses should be introduced at the different levels to suit students' different needs, and to ensure opportunities for coherent and structured ICT training to adults.

2.3 Teacher training

Teacher training initiatives cover future education and refresher courses in ICT for teachers, the place of ICT in teacher training, the boosting of the competence of teachers training teachers, and research and development relating to the use of ICT .

A bottleneck in the implementation of the measures is a lack of competence in the implementing institutions. This has been an acknowledged problem but possible solutions are to buy or employ the needed competence along with upgrading the teacher training staff.

2.4 Technical infrastructure

The main initiatives under this measure are to consider establishment of a comprehensive electronic network for Norway's entire educational sector. Easing access to national and international data networks has been given priority. Software agreements will secure efficient and reasonable prices.

2.5 Organisation

Organisation deals with implementation of the plan as well as new ways of organising teaching and training as a consequence of introducing the use of ICT. Administrative possibilities opened by use of ICT are also dealt with.

Accompanying the plan are yearly action plans, dependent on budgets designed to realise the plan. The Ministry of Education has also conveyed questionnaires to follow the implementation of the plan in the schools, to check ICT investments and to provide other forms of monitoring.

3 MAIN ELEMENTS OF CURRICULUM 1997 (L97)

Main elements of the reforms are to develop a more holistic school system by strengthening the structures of education and by focusing on the content of education. The reforms also stress the importance of education in a modern society, both to the benefit of each individual and to society as a whole. Content and quality are emphasised in the reforms to raise motivation and to generate attention to users' ability to require new knowledge.

Objectives of the government can be summarised as:

- equal access to education and training for all independent of gender, ethnic origin, geographical, social background or disability;
- a belief that education should motivate all to acquire knowledge as a lifelong perspective;
- a belief that the content of Norwegian education must be of high quality in order to respond to the needs and requirements of the international community, and promote innovation.

Education and training are to be considered as part of a lifelong process, a continuing process on the part of individuals and organisations. Growing globalisation is also reflected in the reforms and the educational policy documents.

The new curriculum (L97) consists of three main parts. The first general part is common to primary, secondary and adult education. The second part describes principles and guidelines for primary and lower secondary education. The final part presents syllabi of subjects.

3.1 General part of L97

The general part of the plan provides a holistic vision of education by drawing on seven perspectives:

- the spiritual human being - basic values, cultural heritage and identity;

- the creative human being - creative abilities and creativity;
- the working human being - versatile and practical ability;
- the literally-educated human being - basic knowledge and general education;
- the social human being - cooperation and independence;
- the environmentally aware human being - nature, environment and technology.

Summing up all perspectives and values, education shall stimulate the development of the human as a whole to produce the integrated human.

3.2 Principles and guidelines for primary education

This section of the plan presents values and principles of the comprehensive school, balancing and focusing on community and individual adjustments, upbringing and learning environment, home and school, school and local community, cooperation within school, and local developmental work. It also explains the construction of the syllabi, content and structure, local planning of the syllabi for each subject and the organisation of the content into themes. Characteristics of the main levels - lower primary, upper primary and lower secondary - are underlined, and important ways of working, the use of different learning materials and evaluation strategies are presented.

3.3 Syllabi of subjects

The syllabus for each subject is divided into three parts, consisting of an introduction to the subject as part of a whole, ways of working and structure of the subject. Then there are main goals of the subject, goals of the levels (1-4, 5-7 and 8-10 classes) and, finally, the main elements of each class from class 1 to 10.

Until now curriculum guidelines in Norway have had the status of guiding frameworks for education. They only indicate the content and direction of teaching and upbringing. The local school authorities and, not least the teacher, could, to a great extent, decide what and how to teach. Main textbooks were authorised by national bodies. With national-elaborated exams and educational traditions the reality was that we had a standard national education plan.

L97 is changing the guiding status of the national curriculum. The consequence is that when L97 says that education will make sure that the students develop knowledge about, and insights and attitudes on, the development of the Information Society and Information Technology (L97) this must be done in order to fulfil the curriculum. If plans are not carried out, schools or municipalities can be sued by students or parents.

To understand the way L97 is designed and is supposed to work more details will be presented. The role of ICT, or ICT as conceived in L97, will be commented on along with a presentation of the curriculum.

4 AN OVERVIEW OF THE CURRICULUM AND THE ROLE OF ICT

ICT is to be integrated into all subjects through the new subject syllabi. New textbooks in every subject will include ICT, and some of the books contain multimedia CD-ROMs or other electronic learning materials. There are also references to Internet in texts and exercises.

The preface of L97 says the intent of the ICT curriculum have to be implemented gradually and that implementation should be adjusted to what is possible economically for municipalities - the school owners. It has been indicated that the place and significance of ICT in the guidelines was planned to be stronger but the Ministry of Finances found the plan to be too expensive. Educational gains were adjusted to economical realities. The result was that throughout the text plans for the use of ICT were modified. However use of ICT is obligatory in spite of the comments in the preface.

Reading L97 carefully we will find that ICT is not specifically mentioned in the general part. Technology is, but not ICT. The next part, on principles and guidelines, is included in the syllabus on the subjects - society and contemporary time, for example, where ICT is mentioned as an example of cross-curricular knowledge areas. A chapter about learning materials, for example, includes a discussion of ICT.

There are many statements that indirectly underpin the use of ICT. The most important sentence in this context, in my opinion, is the one stating that we shall prepare the students, making them able to cope with challenges in a rapidly changing world. It says the education will qualify people for productive participation in today's labour force and supply the basis for later shifts in occupations as yet not envisaged (L97).

4.1 Curriculum 97 - Syllabi

The elements of ICT are not strikingly emphasised in the syllabi but ICT is mentioned as an important part of the educational process that ought to be integrated, when useful, as a tool or learning aid. Using ICT to learn and learning to use ICT are included in the syllabi from the first years by directing that learning by playing should be an important part of schooling till the lower secondary level, when different kinds of software are to be introduced as well as use of Internet.

When goals and aims of the subjects are stated, ICT is included in discussions of the Norwegian, English, mathematics, nature and environment, and social science subjects. In discussions of ways of working, ICT is also mentioned. At the different levels use of ICT is described. Examples of selected curricular topics include:.

- Goals at the lowest levels 1-4 classes (6-9 year olds)
    - Norwegian: The students will be confident users of ICT .
    - Mathematics: The students will be confident about simple use of electronic learning aids.
- Goals of the 2 class - 7 years old
    - Norwegian: Students will play on the computer, and write and draw.

    - English: Students will read and write at their own pace by using text with pictures, and play with English software.
    - Mathematics: Students will experiment with numbers and symbols, examine methods of arithmetical operations and do calculations using a calculator and software.
    - Social science: Students will work with and discuss impressions and experiences gathered from magazines and comics, radio and television, video and computer networks.
- Goals at the lower secondary levels - 8-10 classes (13-15 year olds)
    - Norwegian: Students will be able to search for information using all kinds of information sources such as the library, archives and ICT , and will learn to use the sources critically and individually in their own work. They will know different media, and how different media make it possible to communicate orally and by written texts. Students will be able to evaluate the impact media has on the individual and the society.
    - Art and crafts: Students will be able to use different techniques of photo, ICT and video, and reflect on use of symbols and mass-media's visual messages.

Most of the subjects include similar descriptions of ways to use ICT at different grade levels.

5 COMPETENCE-BUILDING PROGRAMMES TO FULFIL L97

To make the new curriculum a reality in the classes every teacher is offered courses in one or more subjects. Courses emphasise new topics, ways of working/learning and other aspects of ICT use. Efforts are made to ensure that all teachers use cross-curricular ways of organising the syllabus. Teachers must also ensure that students work in cooperative learning situations throughout the planning and implementation of projects. ICT is supposed to be part of all subjects and working with projects should be integrated into instruction as a natural part of all subjects.

5.1 Competence building on ICT to support L97

The Ministry of Education has made an in-service training plan for ICT. The introduction states that L97 emphasises the need to meet the challenge of ICT and says that many teachers are personal users of ICT. The teachers are supposed to use ICT in their personal administrative work and in preparations for lessons.

The plan says that ICT is to be used as a integrated tool in learning, when useful to the learning process of the students. The plan also points out that ICT can open new ways of working and learning, and new areas of knowledge - especially in work on projects. A major statement in L97 says that ICT can be used for word processing in order to help students prepare for projects (brainstorming), in planning the project (formulating the goals of learning), in running the project (searching information, finishing and presenting the product), and in evaluating the projects. The plan says use of ICT can promote student-centred learning.

The plan says that at all levels adequate software should be used and that teachers must be familiar with the meaning of the terms 'use to learn', 'learn to use' and 'play to learn'. The aim of the courses will make the teachers reflective didactic users of ICT when planning and implementing classes. An important part of the courses is the new role of the teacher as facilitator, guide, advisor and team leader.

The teacher training programmes can be conducted as integrated parts of formal university grades, raising the importance of the courses and the significance of acquired knowledge, skills and salaries. The entire staff of schools can participate in order to strengthen the usefulness of the courses. Main goals of the in-service training are to make the teachers :

- become personal computer-users;
- be able to use ICT in education;
- develop reflective attitudes on use of ICT in education;
- be able to make use of ICT in personal competence development.

The plan also says that ICT users will know the relevant educational software for their subjects, know how the software can be used in learning activities and know the possibilities for the educational use of Internet.

According to the plan, to be a reflective ICT user it is necessary to be familiar with the experiences of others. Internet can provide access to educational networks and conferences. It is also recommended that homepages of schools be downloaded and discussed - both in teachers' own schools and on-line. Participation at ICT conferences is also viewed as useful.

To develop reflective attitudes the plan recognises that it is important to be aware of the possibilities and weaknesses of ICT, including ethical dilemmas in using ICT, legal laws and rights.

The plan also considers that it is important for teachers to become aware of the possibilities of using ICT in individualised adapted education, and for minority groups and students with special needs. Special equipment, switches and software developed for special needs should be known by teachers. For example, Internet offers new possibilities for language minorities to get in touch with their own language and culture by the World Wide Web.

A reflective ICT attitude also means being aware of and using new ways of organising and working in the classroom, both when learning to use ICT and using ICT to learn.

For courses to have the desired effect it is necessary to have access to a computer and time to get experience in using it. Self-instructing books/courses can be used in addition to the courses. The training then can alternate between instruction, self-training and new instruction. Exercises and tasks during the course can be related to the job.

Additional educational experience can be planned and run by mapping the participants' competence - offering basic modules for those in need and then mapping their level before going into more specialised courses related to their subjects and level of schooling. Finally, more advanced courses can be offered.

It is considered positive for teachers to use the equipment available at their schools and to group colleagues in networks. More advanced users on the staff can be guides to their colleagues. In this way experience developed through the courses will be more easily accessible later. Specialists can be engaged from outside the school for special purposes.

6 CONSISTENCY BETWEEN NATIONAL STRATEGIC ICT PLANS, CURRICULUM 97 AND PRACTICAL POLICY

There are comprehensive efforts to implement ICT in education in Norway nowadays. According to the national ICT plans, the new curriculum L97 and the supporting competence-building programmes for the use of ICT will be fully integrated to education by using ICT in the learning process, and in learning to use ICT.

There is a public focus and discussion on how to ensure equal opportunities and access to ICT in every classroom. No doubt great differences exist among schools and teachers, both for access to ICT and for readiness to use ICT. So even if there is some consistency between different national plans on ICT, the challenge in implementing ICT is to make every teacher and student personal users of ICT, and to make ICT an additional value for teaching and learning. The major bottleneck to the plan is access to computers.

It can also be questioned if the curriculum formulations on ICT will be considered obligatory by schools and teachers. It is likely that there will be continuously different levels in budgeting of ICT by school owners. This problem can be addressed by more national initiatives, financial support and/or more outspoken demands. Then, no doubt, the initiatives will be more effective. When access to ICT is solved in a proper way competence building can successfully support implementation of ICT to increase students' learning processes and society's need for competent citizens.

7 CONCLUSION

Reform '97 certainly does integrate ICT into the curriculum in a more pervasive way than previous plans. ICT is penetrating every subject and is supposed to be used as a tool where and when useful. Actions are taken, or planned, to make sure that ICT will be a real part of the curriculum by supporting national software development, by integrating ICT into standard learning materials, by offering ICT module courses and by integrating the use of ICT in the different subject areas.

So far though, the most obvious obstacle has not been dealt with in a proper way. Teachers' and students' access to computers is still poor. There are big differences from school to school and municipality to municipality, but mainly there is an overall lack of computers, not to say multimedia computers with Internet access.

If we are to cope with the challenges of the rapidly changing society and make use of new opportunities offered by ICT, plans have to be realised by giving teachers and students access to necessary equipment. If budgets do not include these resources, national plans and curricula will not be fulfilled, or may only be partly fulfilled. Only when schools have the needed amount of ICT equipment can competence building be successful. The most important competence building in this field is the development of pedagogical methods. That only can happen when long-term competence programmes can work along with real-life experiences where teachers and students are using computers in daily work and daily learning processes.

8 REFERENCES

The Royal Ministry of Education, Research and Church Affairs. (1996) IT in Norwegian Education. A plan for 1996-1999. (F 4033, English version). Ministry of Education, Oslo, Norway.

The main documents of Reform' 97, some in English, are available on Internet: http://odin.dep.no/kuf/

9 BIOGRAPHY

Sindre Røsvik has been chairman of the Norwegian Educational Computer Society (NPD) since 1987 and a member of IFIP's Working Group 3.5 (primary education) since 1987. Director of education in Giske municipality, Norway, he has over a range of years been actively organising courses on the educational use of IT, has presented papers at conferences and contributed to national IT plans through written contributions.

6

Development of Information Technology in Hong Kong education over the past decade

Alex Fung
Hong Kong Baptist University
Kowloon Tong, Hong Kong, China
Tele + 852 2339 5679; Fax + 852 2339 7894
E-mail: alexfung@hkbu.edu.hk

Abstract

In the early 1980s computer Eeucation was introduced in Hong Kong schools as a new subject in the curriculum. Almost all secondary schools now offer computer literacy to junior form students (ages 12 to 14) and computer studies to senior form students (ages 15 to 16). Computers have not been used across the curriculum nor in the area of CAL/CAI (computer-assisted learning/instruction). Hong Kong has advanced from a developmental to a popularization phase in the use of Information Technology to assist schools in administration and management. In the development phase of over a decade individual schools produced their own Computer-Assisted School Administration (CASA) software in an uncoordinated manner. Popularization began in 1993 when the Hong Kong government started a centralized approach to implement the School Administration & Management System (SAMS) in about 1300 schools. Schools will soon be provided with access to the Internet by the government. Whether there was conscious planning for capacity building for IT in Hong Kong is a matter of doubt. A major question is whether that path is unavoidable when developing countries are building their capacity for IT in education or if there could be quantum leaps bypassing the starts and fits of earlier implementers.

Keywords

Capacity building, computer-aided instruction/learning, management, regional policy

Capacity Building for IT in Education in Developing Countries
G. Marshall & M. Ruohonen (Eds.)

1 INTRODUCTION

Hong Kong's use of IT in education is primarily technology-driven. No proactive planning has occurred nor is there an IT policy for education. The strategy of introducing computers as a teaching subject in secondary schools followed by the introduction of the School Administration and Management Systems (SAMS) territory-wide has been driven by technology and some lessons can be learned from our experience. Other countries might ask if the way Hong Kong has used IT is unavoidable when they are building their IT capacity or if a shorter means to the ends could be found. Let's begin at the beginning.

Hong Kong's use of IT in education has increased over the past ten years. Though lagging behind business organizations, IT applications and developments are moving forward at all levels of education. Four different application and development areas of IT in education are ITEM (Information Technology in Educational Management), CAL/CAI (Computer-Assisted Learning/Instruction), Computer Studies and Teacher Support Systems (TSS). The Hong Kong Government introduced Computer Studies into the secondary school curriculum in the early 1980s but only started an Information System Strategy for computerized administration and management in 1993.

2 EDUCATION IN HONG KONG

Education in Hong Kong has expanded rapidly over the last decade. Compulsory education up to the age fifteen was introduced in 1978 and there are now approximately 900 primary and 400 secondary schools in the Territory. The school system is centrally controlled by the Education Department of Hong Kong. Over 90% of students who finish the compulsory stage of education continue to secondary schools or technical institutes that provide vocational training, and 18% of students have opportunities for further studies in university degree courses.

Computers have been used by the central Education Department since the 1970s for allocating school places to students at ages 6, 12, and 15. The Joint University Admission Scheme also uses computers to keep track of student admissions. The Hong Kong Examinations Authority, responsible for administering the public school leaving and advance level examinations, has had computerized administration.

Higher education institutes introduced computer science courses in the 1970s. Today IT-related departments and courses are common and popular in local universities. The Hong Kong Academic Research Network (HARNET), administered by the Joint University Computer Centre (JUCC), links the universities to share information and resources - library resources, for example. Computer courses in about thirty secondary schools began as pilot projects in 1981. Today over 90% of secondary schools offer computer studies in their senior grades and students can take public examinations in the subject in the Hong Kong Level Examination (HKCEE). Many schools also offer computer literacy courses to their junior secondary students but there is no government supported computer education in primary schools.

Teaching computers as a subject in secondary schools is the easiest and cheapest way to introduce the technology into an education system because it is not that difficult to put forward justifications to policy-makers to get resources but only a small percentage of the teaching force has an opportunity for staff development in IT.

Now a huge effort is required to train staff as the government is implementing the computerized School Administration & Management System (SAMS) project across the Territory. Putting computers into secondary schools for teaching has benefited teachers as many schools develop administrative uses for their computers. The less fortunate primary school teachers do not have such an opportunity and most of them are computer illiterate, if not resistant to IT.

3 APPLICATIONS OF INFORMATION TECHNOLOGY IN HONG KONG SCHOOLS

3.1 IT in educational management

Computerized school administration is common in Hong Kong secondary schools. According to Fung's (1991) postal survey over 85% of secondary schools were using some form of computer-assisted school administration. Word processing (86%) and student data - personal and academic data - administration (85%) were the most popular applications. The least applied area was library administration, where only 25% of schools had computerized systems. Other types of applications include teacher records (41%), timetable construction (39%), financial matters (40%) and coverage for teachers on leave (40%).

Usually each secondary schools adopted its own applications with no standardization or compatibility across different systems. No empirical data is available for primary schools' use of school administration software but use is much less than in the secondary schools.

The School Administration & Management System (SAMS) in Hong Kong

In September 1993 the Hong Kong government initiated the use of computers in educational management on a Territory-wide basis when it adopted an Information Systems Strategy (ISS) for the Hong Kong Education Department. This is a rare case, in terms of both the scale of implementation and investment, of a government taking a central lead in the development of a school information system. About 570 million Hong Kong dollars ($US 70 million) was budgeted to implement the ISS in the Hong Kong education system within five years.

It is planned that all schools in the public sector will be given a centrally developed SAMS package of computer hardware and software to assist in administration and management, and the schools can be tele-linked to the Education Department headquarters and the Examinations Authority for data communication.

The SAMS package has been distributed to about 600 schools and implementation should be completed by 1998. Design, development and implementation phases need to address issues of hardware, software, training and support (Wild and Fung, 1997). Integration and standardization with such a centralized system as SAMS, requiring sufficient built in flexibility to handle individual school characteristics and autonomy, is no easy problem to solve. Fung (1995) has said, 'It would be very wrong to assume that given the hardware and software, information technology can be implemented into educational settings with automatic success. Using information technology in educational management, ITEM, irrespective of scope or scale, is an innovative process which needs managing' (p. 37).

The government is facing problems because many secondary schools have developed their own CASA systems. Many schools say the government-produced CASA system is too standardized and does not meet individual school needs. At the primary school the low computer literacy level of teachers and staff in that sector presents additional problems.

3.2 Computer-assisted instruction and learning

A study by Gilmore (1995) reveals that teachers using computers in their teaching had increases in confidence and used IT to provide cognitive and social benefits for students. They believed that both Computer-Assisted Learning (CAL) and Computer-Assisted Instruction (CAI) are important in the learning and teaching process. Regrettably, the Education Department has no policy for CAL and this area is very much undeveloped in Hong Kong.

Lacking a government policy, the use of computers across the curriculum is virtually non-existent in Hong Kong schools. Individual teachers and students might be using imported CAI or CAL packages but, except for several CAI packages that come with textbooks produced by publishers, little CAI/CAL material is locally developed.

Perhaps the education market is too small in Hong Kong to attract commercial development of school products - a factor that developing countries must come to grips with. Recently there are small pockets of development which include a project supported by the Language Fund of the Hong Kong government to develop a CAL package for learning the Chinese language in primary school, and a collaboration between the Education Department and the Polytechnic University to produce a CD-ROM for secondary schools. A small market is also beginning to emerge with commercial production of CAL CD-ROMs for learning languages and mathematics.

3.3 Teacher Support Systems (TSS)

The concept of Teacher Support Systems (TSSs) - IT used to support teaching - is not new. About a decade ago, the Education Department of South Australia set up a trial project - NEXUS - as an electronic information service to provide information to teachers and students (Leonard, 1990). NEXUS has developed into a system of electronic mail, bulletin boards and information databases. Users of the system can now share ideas of common interests, access materials and obtain experts' assistance through the network. Leonard remarks that schools are even willing to pay for the telecommunication service to enhance the teaching and learning of their students.

In Hong Kong two TSS projects currently in development provide limited access to teachers from selected schools. TELENEX was started by the Teaching of English Language Education Centre of Hong Kong University in 1994 in support of English Language teaching (Tsui, 1994). CLTSS, for teachers of Chinese Language, began development in April 1995 at the SAMS T&R Unit of the Hong Kong Baptist University. Both projects are funded by the Language Fund of the Hong Kong government. Technical operations of the two networks are similar.

CLTSS - a two-year project to develop a computer-based information system network to support the teaching of the Chinese Language in local secondary schools - is simply a computer network with a server at the support centre that can be accessed by teachers with computers and modems at their schools. The system uses IT for sharing and disseminating valuable teaching resources. The content database in the server stores Chinese Language teaching resources for secondary schools - standard reading passages, teaching plans, teaching ideas, learning tasks, and test papers. The contents are not centrally developed by language experts but collected from teachers. In just one year 80 schools have become users of the system.

3.4 Preparing for the Internet

With the advent of the Internet and the World Wide Web a new era begins. The Hong Kong government will provide schools with one Internet access account each this academic year. Recent studies in America suggest that there are now more than 100 000 E-mail accounts in the USA on state educational networks and approximately 600 000 students networked through private and grassroots initiatives (Itzkan, 1992). Expert opinion estimates that by the end of the decade, there will be 3 to 5 million networked students in the USA.

The technology for building Chinese websites is growing more mature and, given time and resources, schools across the Hong Kong territory will be able to access a CLTSS website with hypertexts and multimedia capabilities. Similar websites for different subjects will be built in the future and teacher support systems will help to improve teaching and learning in many different subjects. We hope that the dominance of websites in English around the world will soon be balanced with websites in many different languages to the benefit of all.

3.5 Partnership with the other sectors

Given that Hong Kong's school system is overly centralized, the government must bear responsibility for resourcing all schools in the public sector with standard equipment. Financial implications always remain the first item on the agenda in any consideration of advancing technology in education. Partnership with business and commercial organizations is occasional, not the norm. The central development and supply of the Hong Kong SAMS to all schools, for instance, follows a different route to that in the UK or in New Zealand. In the UK, commercially developed packages such as the School Information Management System (SIMS) are available. In New Zealand, the University of Massey took a lead in developing and supporting the Massey University School Administration Computer (MUSAC) package for schools (Nolan, Ayres and McKinnon, 1997). Both the UK and New Zealand have contributions from the business sector and from higher education institutes in software development, and support serving the education community in a more efficient and effective way than Hong Kong is currently served. This is a strategy which developing countries should not ignore in building their capacity in IT.

4 CONCLUSION

Policy-makers need to be aware of the impact of IT on society-at-large and on education in general to prepare students for the 21st century. A vision must be developed and an integrated IT policy to support school management, teaching and learning must be implemented. National organizations such as the National Centre for Educational Technology in UK support schools and teachers in the advancement of individual IT policies. Without such support, effective capacity building for IT in Hong Kong will not reach maximum effectiveness.

An effective policy should not emphasize the provision of the latest technology but, instead, the development of the people's capacity to use IT for a wide range of educational applications. A secondary school head in Hong Kong had the foresight to put a few computers in the school office for free access by teachers in addition to computers dedicated to Computer Studies classes. The result was that most teachers became computer-literate without attending computer courses. Such a school would accept new technologies and other educational innovations more readily than the average school. Would it not also be the same when a country thinks about capacity building in IT? Well-designed policies must have a vision of the future. Without a grasp of the needs of our future citizens in the 21st century, we have no direction for preparing teachers to educate the next generation. Besides the commonly cited basic skills of the 3 Rs, a fourth one - skill in IT - has to be added for survival and competitiveness worldwide. The Lake Oswego School District, Oregon, USA (gopher://gopher.nrel.org:70/00/programs/technology/plans/lakeoswego_plan) plans to provide a learning environment in which the use of technology is just as natural to students as the use of a pen or pencil is to most adults. As teachers are the facilitators for preparing students, top priority should be given to teachers' staff development in IT use. Hong Kong's lack of teacher preparation leaves some, if not most, of its teachers ten years behind in technology readiness.

Countries seeking to build capacity for IT can learn lessons from many countries already using IT in education as well as from research. Bearing in mind the different contexts and cultures of different places, the Hong Kong experience can help to generate a few guiding principles: (1) a holistic IT policy in education is required that integrates the different areas of ITEM,

CAL/CAI, TSS and the subject teaching of IT; (2) staff development is a crucial element in such a policy, not than an add-on; (3) leadership by the central education authority is needed but decentralization and flexibility in management are necessary for effective implementation; (4) partnership and collaboration with business and/or higher education institutes are cost-effective in IT project development and support.

Working Group 3.7 of the International Federation for Information Processing (IFIP) TC3 is an international group of experts in Information Technology in Educational Management (ITEM) that welcomes networking. Developing IT capacity means developing networks of relationships across countries as well as policies within countries.

5 REFERENCES

Fung, A.C.W. (1991) Computer-assisted school administration in Hong Kong. *Journal of Research on Computing in Education,* **24**(1), 41-61.

Fung, A.C.W. (1995) *Managing Change in ITEM. Information Technology in Educational Management.* Chapman & Hall, London.

Gilmore, A.M. (1995) Turning teachers on to computers: evaluation of a teacher development program. *Journal of Research on Computing in Education,* **27**(3), 251-269.

Itzkan, S. (1992) How big is the global classroom? *Matrix News,* **2**(10), 1, 7-8.

Leonard, R. (1990) Nexus III - Telecommunications beyond the classroom, in *Computers in Education: Proceedings of the Fifth World Conference on Computers in Education (eds. A. McDougall and C. Dowling) Elsevier, Amsterdam.*

Nolan, C.J.P., Ayres, D.A. and McKinnon, D.H. (1997) An operational model for the implementation of computerized school information systems, in *Information Technology in Educational Management for the Schools of the Future* (eds. Fung, A.C.W., Visscher, A.J., Barta, B.Z. and Teather, D.C.B.), Chapman & Hall, London.

Tsui, A. (1994) The participant structures of TeleNex - a computer network for ESL teachers. Paper presented at the International Language in Education Conference at The University of Hong Kong.

Wild, P. and Fung, A.C.W. (1997) Evaluation of ITEM for proactive development, in *Information Technology in Educational Management for the Schools of the Future* (eds. Fung, A.C.W., Visscher, A.J., Barta, B.Z. and Teather, D.C.B.), Chapman & Hall, London.

6 BIOGRAPHY

Alex C.W. Fung received a B.S. in 1970 from the University of Hong Kong and Cert.Ed., Adv.Dip. Ed., M.Ed. in subsequent years from the same university. He received his Ph.D. in educational management and administration in 1992 from the London University Institute of Education. He was a secondary school principal in Hong Kong for more than twenty years before he joined the Department of Education Studies of the Hong Kong Baptist University as senior lecturer in 1994.

He is currently an associate professor and also Director of the SAMS T&R Unit at the Hong Kong Baptist University.

7

Fighting a lone battle for Computer Education in Nepal

Hari Gopal Shrestha
National Computer Centre
Singhdurbar Katmandu, Nepal
Tele + 227271; + 213252; + 271061; Fax + 977-1-220143
E-mail:glocom@mos.com.np

Abstract

Today in the Information Technology (IT) society computer technology is needed to accelerate the development of socioeconomic status in countries. This paper describes the introduction of computer activities in Nepal. The example of developing countries especially emphasizes the important role one person can play in introducing and managing computer education activities in his/her country. Without computer education you cannot handle IT use effectively. Hence computer education activities are needed in teacher education, secondary education and higher education. This paper also describes the critical need for textbooks written in the language of the country as well as the development of an IT education curriculum.

Keywords

Developing countries, resources, secondary education, higher education

1 INTRODUCTION

Nepal is a small Himalayan Hindu kingdom situated between India in the south , east and west, and China in the north. It has a population of 21 600 000 with a per capita income of US $190 and a literacy rate of 39%. The average life expectancy is 47 years. Nepal has an agriculture-based economy, with hydroelectricity and tourism as potential economical resources. The total area of Nepal is 147 181 square km.

Capacity Building for IT in Education in Developing Countries
G. Marshall & M. Ruohonen (Eds.)

2 COMPUTER ACTIVITIES IN NEPAL

At present Nepal has more than 300 private training centers, six foreign collaboration computer training centers and one National Computer Center (NCC), which is owned by His Majesty's Government of Nepal. There are about 15 software publishing companies and 20 private businesses selling hardware. Internet and e-mail are provided by the four private computer communications access providers. They have provided about 1500 links to the capital valley.

At the moment about 500 computer engineers are working on Information Technology in different ministries and departments as well as in the Nepal Electricity Corporation, the Nepal Telecommunication Corporation, travel agencies, airlines, hotels, banks, schools, universities and private institutes. Every year 100 to 150 students go abroad for computer study. At the moment, His Majesty's Government of Nepal has not managed for quality employment for the computer science graduates returning from study abroad. Therefore they go to foreign countries seeking jobs.

3 BEGINNING OF THE BATTLE

After serving five years as a lecturer of mathematics in Sanothimi campus, Tribhuwan University (TU) of Nepal, I joined the National Computer Centre (NCC), Katmandu in July 1975 and was trained in the Autocoder programming language for the IBM 1401 mainframe computer. As I worked as a systems programmer in those days, there was no awareness of computer technology. After working as a systems analyst programmer for NCC for eight years, through interactions with customers needing computers, I realized that they were seriously lacking in computer basics and knowledge.

In 1982 NCC gave me the responsibility to establish a computer training unit for the first time in Nepal. It was a big challenge for me. At the time I started organizing training regularly for data entry operators, computer operators, programmers, data supervisors, students and officers of different offices. There were no educational materials to distribute to the trainers. Then I was asked to design some notes for all of them.

Accordingly, in 1989, I decided to write an introductory book on computers (*Computer Paricharya*) in the Nepali language to fill the gap in others' computer knowledge, to share ideas and to solve the problem of bringing others to an awareness of computer technology. The book introduced computers, their history, types and specifications. It also discussed IT human resources, room design, data processing concepts, programming concepts, networking, systems analysis and design concepts, the DOS operating system and *Word Perfect*. This was the first computer book in Nepali history. It was a hot cake. Within one year the first edition was sold out. The book helped to generate an awareness of computers among the general public. The fifth edition is about to go to press.

In December 1988, on behalf of NCC Katmandu, I was lucky to get an opportunity to participate in a workshop and seminar in Bangkok, where an educational multimedia exemplar package was demonstrated and discussed. The seminar was organized by Asia Pacific Education Innovation of Development (APEID) UNESCO, Bangkok. There were 23 countries, including Nepal, participating in the seminar. Only Nepal had not started computer education in the schools and universities. Therefore, during the concluding session of the seminar, on behalf on Nepal, I requested the organizer, UNESCO, Bangkok, to help Nepal organize a national seminar to begin computer education in the schools. I requested that Dr. Mike Lally, senior lecturer in education at the Department of Education, University of Western Australia be a resource person.

4 CONTINUING THE BATTLE

4.1 National level Computer Education workshop

In September 1989, under my coordination, NCC, the Ministry of Education and UNESCO, Bangkok organized a national level computer education workshop - 'National training of teachers in the use of computers in education' for mathematics teachers, science teachers, curriculum experts, teacher supervisors, school principals, officers from the Ministry of Education, the Controller of Examinations of Nepal and NCC Katmandu. Dr. Mike Lally was the resource person for the workshop and seminar. There were 35 participants, who were divided into three groups. At the concluding session, each group concluded with a suggestion to begin a computer science course for the secondary school level students of 9th and 10th grade in Nepal. Due to our pressure, Honorable Assistant Minister of Education, Mr. Chhetra Pratap Adhikari, kindly announced the beginning of a computer science course for the 9th and 10th grade students as an optional subject from 1990 February in Nepal.

4.2 Computer curriculum development

Due to the lack of a curriculum the interested schools could not start the course. Therefore, on behalf of schools, I requested the Director of the Curriculum Department, Ministry of Education, Sanothimi to design the curriculum for computer science students in the 9th and 10th grades. As computer science was a new course, we have had no idea about how to construct a curriculum and nobody was ready to design it. Ms. Nani Hera Tuladhar, director general of the curriculum department requested me to design the curriculum. With the help of the multimedia exemplar package displayed at the UNESCO, Bangkok seminar I designed a computer science curriculum for the schools. In the team I was the only computer specialist. We completed the required curriculum within three months and submitted it to the Department of Curriculum in October 1990.

4.3 Computer textbook development

Due to the lack of awareness of computer education in Nepal, there was no author to write the computer textbook, a big problem. Therefore, the schools were in trouble since there were no textbooks for the Grades 9 and 10 computer course. Again, on behalf of secondary schools, we discussed the situation with Ms. Nani Hera Tuladhar, Director of the Curriculum Department, Sanothimi, Nepal. She requested me to write the textbook within three months, which was a big challenge for me. I was very happy to complete the computer science textbook in the Nepali language according to the requirement of the Curriculum Department, Sanothimi, Nepal. Now the textbook is in use in many different schools of Nepal.

4.4 Computer Science teacher development

Again, there were no qualified and trained teachers in computer science and no government teacher training centres. In university also there were no computer courses. Therefore, with the help of my friends, I registered the Alphaplus Computer Centre (a private computer training centre) at Katmandu, where a number of teachers were trained by me in 1991-1992. Also, I trained a number of teachers at the NCC from 1991 to the present time as the Chief Instructor of NCC. Thus, privately and officially, I was working as a computer science teacher trainer.

4.5 Computer course for teachers

Because there was a lack of computer teachers, I proposed a plan to the higher authority of the Education Faculty of the Tribhuwan University to arrange for the production of qualified computer science teachers. As a result, I was selected to be the computer specialist on a three-person task force and designed a computer curriculum for the three year bachelor's degree in Education (B. Ed). The three year Bachelor's degree of Education (B. Ed) curriculum was tested, checked and recommended by computer experts from IIT Delhi and Uni Jame Mili Islamia University, Aligadh, India, computer education consultants for World Bank, and approved by the Committee of the Education Faculty, TU, Katmandu in March 1994.

4.6 Computer curriculum for the Ministry of Labour

Similarly, His Majesty's Government of Nepal was trying to create the jobs for local youths. The Ministry of Labour wanted to prepare different skill-oriented courses to be run in different districts of Nepal for local employment generation. The Department of Labour requested me to design a computer course for the 75 district-wide local development offices. I was the main specialist of the computer science curriculum team. We designed the computer curriculum for the local youths and now it is running in Nepal.

4.7 Information Technology in Educational Management activities in Nepal

Two international seminars on Information Technology in Educational Management (ITEM) were organized by WG3.4 and were held in Singapore in 1992 and in Jerusalem in 1994 respectively. With the help of Geoff Fairall, Zimbabwe and Ben Zion Barta, Israel, I had an opportunity to participate and learned the basic ideas of ITEM systems. I shared the ideas, transferring the operations and concepts into Nepali schools.

4.8 The Computer Education Society of Nepal

I participated in both the Fifth World Conference in Computer Education - WCCE '90 - held in Sydney, Australia and the Sixth World Conference - WCCE '95 - held in Birmingham, UK. At both conferences I saw delegates from all over the world participating. So, when I returned to Nepal, I organized a Computer Education Society of Nepal (CESON) in December 1995 and became the founder president. It is the first Computer Education Society of Nepal of its kind. With the help of CESON, I am trying to prepare a qualified delegate to represent Nepal in the Seventh World Conference to be held in Copenhagen, Denmark in 2001. At present, the society is busy every year organizing a national level computer quiz and software competition in Nepal. We are also busy with computer teacher training and educational computer software development. Also, in December 1997 at Delhi, India, Nepal is going to participate in the South East Asia Regional Computer Confederation (SEARCC) software competition through the leadership of CESON, Katmandu. In the near future we are trying to organize inter-school education software exhibitions and demonstrations, and, with the help of INGO, run a project for international teacher and students exchanges. We are seeking funds to develop such kinds of computer educational activities through CESON and we would like to work together with international friends.

4.9 Establishing a computer course at Tribhuwan University

As an employee, I got a chance to work as a computer training unit chief and established a computer unit in 1982 at NCC. It was a good chance for me to play a good role in the country's development of computer technology. In those days, there was a lack of programmers, data entry operators, system managers, data administrators, data supervisors and computer engineers. The agencies, both governmental and nongovernmental, as well as private agencies were demanding trained manpower. Computer operators were badly needed too. Except for computer engineers, NCC trained all sorts of people and fulfilled the required human resources needs.

Therefore, on behalf of NCC, I proposed a plan to Tribhuwan University (TU) to start computer courses for the Bachelor and post-graduate levels. We had a two year-long series of discussions about the planning but it was not fruitful so I gave it up for the time being. Then, I switched to talking with the higher authority people of the Ministry of Education and the curriculum department. As I explained above, I was successful in starting computer education courses in schools of Nepal.

As many 10+2 passed students were going abroad to study computer science, once again, for a second time I started talking with TU higher-level administrators to start a three-year Bachelor degree in computer science in Nepal. But they said they had budgetary and other problems, and they were hesitant to approve and start the computer course in 1997. Then, I requested them to give permission to Australian universities or Banglore University, India to run computer courses in Nepal, if TU could not approve its own courses this year. We have been discussing about this for about eight months.

So I talked with and joined with friends at the Campion Academy Education group to start a private college for computer science. My friends were kind enough to establish Campion College for the three-year Bachelor's degree in computer science in 1997. The college is going to open on 16 September, 1997 at Kupondol, Lalitpur, Nepal. Similarly, I had talked to another group of friends as a member of the management committee of Viswo Niketan Science Campus. They also accepted my idea to open the National Institute of Technical Sciences (NITS) at Balaju, Katmandu. There we are going to start the same computer course designed by TU after about two months. For both the institutes Tribhuwan University is very kind to affiliate and give permission to start three year B.Sc. in computer science for the first time in Nepal after eight months long talks. Thus right now I am working in the management committee of both institutes.

I am working to develop computer education in Nepal as a curriculum designer, textbook writer, reference book writer, teacher trainer, computer science teaching advisor, computer local consultant and computer education initiator in Nepal. That is why people call it 'Fighting a lone battle in computer education in Nepal'. I am a happy and lucky man to contribute something to my developing nation.

5 CONCLUSION

This is a computer world. We are stepping into the 21st century. We must be ready to prepare quality IT human resources for that time. Therefore we must try to develop good computer education programmes everywhere. Without quality and skilled Ithuman resources, no country can accelerate the speed for all-round development. Therefore, let us share idea on IT, help and work together for it.

6 BIOGRAPHY

Hari Gopal Shrestha is the Founder President of the Computer Education Society of Nepal and the Chief Instructor of the National Computer Centre, Nepal. He has done pioneering work in developing computer education in Nepal. He started his work as a programmer and then worked as a training manager to establish organizations for computer education. He has made a number of international relationships in seminars and conferences, and he has developed the IT education curriculum for Nepal. In addition, he has provided computer education textbooks for his home country. He is a member of IFIP Working Group 3.7.

PART II

Building Skills in the National Context

8

Bridging the skills gap in Zimbabwe

Arthur Sithole
Courseware Development Centre
P. O. Box CY1912
Causeway, Harare
Zimbabwe
Tele + 263 4 756746
E-mail: asithole@zwe.toolnet.org

Abstract

The Zimbabwe education and training system, as is the case in any other emerging or developing nation, is experiencing problems and challenges resulting from changes in external factors such as technology, society's values and work structures. There is a need for justifications and mechanisms to build sustainable local capacities for the provision of an effective and efficient education and training system. An outline of core competencies and key qualifications required by the Zimbabwe Information Technology (IT) industry in order to empower individuals and organizations to realize their full potential is an essential ingredient for Zimbabwe's successful use of IT.

Keywords

Capacity building, competencies, skills, developing countries, national policies, professional development

1 INTRODUCTION

The scenario under which we are operating in Zimbabwe needs to be clearly articulated to ensure an understanding by the key stakeholders in education and training before we can discuss skills needs. There is:

- a call to empower industry and communities;
- a call for efficiency at higher levels;
- a call for outward-looking trade policies;

Capacity Building for IT in Education in Developing Countries
G. Marshall & M. Ruohonen (Eds.)

- a call for private sector initiatives to lead the economic development of the nation with government as a facilitator;
- increased pressure to promote indigenous efforts in the economic development of the country;
- diminishing resource provision for training by government, donors and the private sector;
- increased rate of change of technologies (locally and abroad);
- increased unemployment in the country (school leavers, retrenchers, retired personnel, *etc.*);
- increasing deaths as a result of the AIDS epidemic and other ailments;
- a critical shortage of skilled people in certain sectors of our economy, *e.g.* engineers;
- inefficient and ineffective utilization and misallocation of certain resources within education and training, *i.e.* personnel, equipment, software;
- increased changes in society's value systems;
- increased changes of work structures;
- inadequate training materials and resources for schools;
- placement of graduates in the wrong jobs;
- insufficient monitoring of graduates' progress and how they develop in the work environment;
- increased training costs difficult to justify over a short period of time;
- increased shifting of profiles or key qualifications on the job market, especially of our trainers, institutional leadership and support personnel, etc.

It is within the purview of the above stated problems, challenges and trends that I wish to discuss the need, justification and mechanisms to build sustainable local capacities through use of IT for the provision of an efficient and effective education system.

A discussion of capacity building for IT in developing countries provides a steppingstone for a discussion of our nation's truly becoming an Information Society.

2 DEFINITION OF KEY TERMS

In the context of this paper, 'policy' means a general guideline for decision-making; 'guidelines' could include standards, procedures and regulations; a 'procedure' is a detailed set of instructions that occur often or regularly, and 'regulations' are statements that specific action must or must not be taken in a given situation. Similarly, 'skills' refer to technological, methodological and personal/social competencies.

In all fields of working life the dynamic changes presented earlier, have meant that skills once acquired will no longer last a lifetime and will age if not constantly updated to keep abreast of current developments. In other words, lifelong learning replaces longlife learning. A skill also could mean proficiency, mastery, ability or capacity.

'NAMACO' stands for the National Manpower Advisory Council - a private body set up by act of Parliament to advise the Ministry of Higher Education and Technology on matters pertaining to education and training policy at a national level, *i.e.* occupational standards, accreditation, examinations, funding, curriculum quality and relevance, qualification frameworks, and access and management of the training processes. It is NAMACO's purpose to ensure the local skills base is strengthened, which will contribute to the increase in productivity, efficiency, effectiveness and competitiveness of our economy's formal and informal sectors.

3 THE ISSUES

Information Technology in education must be guided by an agreed-upon policy which outlines the purpose, aims and objectives of the education and training system of a nation. Such a policy could define prioritization criteria for education applications to be automated, technology acquisition, and maintenance and replacement procedures. It could also define security aspects, including use management and funding mechanisms for technologies in education. Responsible authorities and penalties could also be highlighted in such a document.

Zimbabwe has no official documented national Information Technology in education policy. The 'policy' currently guiding IT in education in Zimbabwe reacts to the needs now, and has a few mechanisms in place to predict and prepare for future IT- related needs for the country's education and training. Regarding IT use in education, several areas could be considered as important aspects of policy formulation and implementation.

Facilitate strategic planning, policy formulation and decision-making

A computer-based human resources information system has been proposed at NAMACO congresses. The existing systems haven't been very reliable and thus need capacity building. A labour market information system should be a high priority to facilitate planning based on fact, according to NAMACO.

Facilitate research

Our universities and colleges are being encouraged to use local industry problems as a source for projects. I cannot comment on the degree of achievement since those data are not readily accessible.

Stimulate efficient and effective IT training resource management

There is need to identify, allocate and use resources in an efficient and effective manner. A deliberate policy has been communicated on the need to ensure full participation of both genders for any meaningful economic development in the country. While this is a grand objective, there still exist cultural barriers which will take some time before they give way. The Affirmative Action programme in place is intended to ensure equity in student distribution for all national training institutions over a period of time. This has an effect of ensuring close to full utilization of the human resources in the country's economic activities of the future. Gender distribution is currently 51% to 49% in favour of women in Zimbabwe. An IT human resources deployment survey shows that males outnumbered females by

28%. The retired professionals are yet another untapped source to pursue via some policy framework. Technology can also be effectively used in this area.

Ensure accessibility to information technology education

Accessibility to IT education is threatened by the rising cost of living, which in turn creates or expands cultural disadvantages (classes, dropouts, etc.), thereby increasing delinquencies. Distance education approaches are being investigated to include the use of satellite technologies. Linkages between training providers is being encouraged through the infusion of private training institutions by the Ministry of Higher Education and Technology in order that they offer nationally-recognized programmes. Data communications can play a vital role to facilitate just-in-time learning, if exploited. There is need to ensure accessibility of education delivery material to all nationally-recognized training providers. There is also a need to control or facilitate bodies but the resources are not readily available.

Facilitate the development of training materials

The Curriculum Development Unit (CRADU) of the Ministry of Higher Education and Technology is driving the development of training materials, but due to inadequate resources, the development of syllabi, question banks, etc. has not been very satisfactory. This has contributed to a mismatch between certain curriculum and change demands. CRADU, in liaison with NAMACO, has formed curriculum development committees to facilitate in this regard. Technologies used include project management software, word processors and authoring tools.

Bridge or address the critical skills shortage area

The problem of critical skills shortages has been attributed to the rate of change of technology, and to the brain drain to other more lucrative markets such as South Africa, Botswana and other countries. A number of options are being pursued to address the problem, including foreign recruitment. However, this is a very sensitive area with high unemployment in the country such that NAMACO has proposed review of policy for foreign recruitment. An exemption system as well as revision of entry requirements and qualifications for programmes are being explored by CRADU in liaison with industry. Sectorial manpower surveys continue to be done for specific industries with the Computer Industry's Manpower Survey having been held in 1994 and already out of date in some ways. Industry trainers' placement in technical colleges is being encouraged on a part-time basis to ensure relevance of education delivery. Technology could be used here for maintenance of a database of experts.

Facilitate continuous professional development of users, including trainers

In order to keep pace with IT skill demands brought about by the fast rate of change of technologies, it is necessary that staff be trained continuously. Computer-based training and audio-based training could provide a more flexible method of keeping up-to-date, particularly with packaged software. The Computer Society of Zimbabwe (CSZ) has for the past years been running a pilot scheme called the Continuous Professional Development scheme (CPD) to address this problem.

Some CSZ functions, workshops and seminars were allocated a number of CPD hours, and society members attaining a minimum of 15 hours per society year were recognized as continuously developing themselves. Means are being investigated to incorporate other programmes which are not necessarily CSZ functions into the scheme and make attendance compulsory. In this regard we see the computer licensing scheme as a possible option whereby training establishments accredited with us could provide the training with CSZ testing the participants.

Facilitate ease of mobility, portability or progression within the IT profession

In 1994 a Career Path Model was developed by CSZ in liaison with NAMACO and is already being used for career guidance in schools. Also strides were made in 1990 by the Higher Education Ministry through a Rationalization Programme, which came up with a vocational education policy document with a Qualification Framework. This has ensured linkage between university education opportunities and training by technical colleges, which was nonexistent at independence in 1980 (in theory). The use of word processing and graphics packages is the major functionality of IT in this area.

Ensure the employability of products from the IT training institutions

Industrial training has been blended into nationally-recognized training programmes. Employers are being invited to participate in the running of the programmes and NAMACO, in liaison with CSZ and CRADU, are ensuring job-related programmes are in place. Also, entrepreneurship programmes as well as increased practical content in training have been introduced to facilitated self-employment. A labour market information system could be used to monitor demand, supply and use of human resources.

Guarantee the sustainability of the IT industry's human resources

Considering the AIDS menace, the rate of change of technology and general financial inadequacies, nothing of great significance has been recorded. This is attributed to the fact that the current capacity is far from meeting the demand. Now, maybe as a survival strategy, we may have to train and employ more than the anticipated need. College enrolment has been found not to match existing capacities and needs as reported at latest NAMACO congresses. This has been confirmed in our IT Manpower survey of 1994. We estimate that there may be over 400 organizations employing IT professionals in Zimbabwe.

Monitoring and evaluation

In Zimbabwe we have a Zimbabwe Manpower Development Fund (ZIMDEF) finance committee, a NAMACO/Government watchdog committee, a CSZ training institution accreditation committee, a CSZ IT industry code of practice/codes of ethics, complaints procedures and an IT Skills Requirements Model - all tools to facilitate monitoring and evaluating education practices. Technology is used for recording, financial analysis and other monitoring functions.

4 IMPLICATIONS

The big challenge posed to the training fraternity for capacity building are developing:

- distance education and lifelong learning tools and techniques;
- occupational analysis & skills needs identification methodologies and tools;
- qualifications standards or framework development;
- staff development, *i.e.* trainers, etc.; Teachers are the focal point of bringing a change in the education system. Expose them to IT pedagogy, emerging new technologies and other aspects of IT;
- institution management techniques and approaches;
- curriculum development methodologies;
- policy formulation and planning methodologies ;
- research on technology, the labour market and other social trends;
- access to technology and skills for materials development and skills;
- access to the technology and skills for courseware delivery. The potential for IT in enhancing quality of delivery of general education at the school level has not been fully recognized. Emerging technologies such as groupware, networking and multimedia can alter the way education is delivered;
- development of cooperation or networking;
- career guidance and counseling.

5 CONCLUSION

Most countries do not have policies IT in education - *i.e.,* few countries have formal, published official statements on the subject.

Many of the problems or challenges outlined in this discussion stem not from the absence of official policy statements or similar directives, but more from the fact that critical issues are either not being addressed or are being tackled in a half-hearted way. There is a lack of action, hence the need to concentrate more on acceptance and implementation issues. This is in line with not legally incorporating the policy items for fear of stifling innovation and creativity as changes to any legislation take long to effect.

The public need to be protected from misers; they need guidance on careers; they need to be able to access facilities for IT education and training even if it is just for familiarization. Social inequalities need to be considered in arriving at standards for sound education and training practices. There is need to sensitize education planners to the potential of IT through workshops and training programmes.

6 BIOGRAPHY

Arthur Sithole is the Chairman of the Zimbabwe National Manpower Advisory Council (NAMACO) and President of the Computer Society of Zimbabwe (CSZ). He is also Executive Chairman of the Courseware Development Centre (CDC) PVT Ltd, Zimbabwe and a representative in IFIP TC3 and WG 3.4. Previously he was the IT Field Consultant for the Eastern & Southern African Management Institute (ESAMI). Arthur has presented papers at many local and international forums, including conferences held in Singapore, Botswana, Lesotho, Malta and South Africa - the latest of which won him the Zimbabwean prestigious Carlisle Award last year.

9

Information Technology education and training initiatives - the Nigerian experience.

Uche Modum
University of Nigeria
Enugu Campus
Nigeria
Fax + 042 454 364; + 042 455 705

Abstract
Nigeria and its 100 million people have made some significant strides in IT education and training. This paper surveys the major efforts made by the Nigerian government and the Nigerian people over the last three decades to work with IT Education and training. Specifically, the paper will describe the two main phases in the collaboration and implementation of IT Education and training. Phase I dates from the early 1970s when Nigerians for the first time got to know about the existence and the potential of the computer. Phase II dates from 1988 when the Federal Ministry of Education, acknowledging the importance of IT, took the first bold step to formulate a national policy for IT education by setting up a committee. For a country as vast as Nigeria, with the well-known constraints and limitations of developing nations, the initiatives have been many but so have the problems.

Keywords
National policies, developing countries, informatics

1 INTRODUCTION

As the world assumes more and more the properties of a global village, the position of developing countries such as Nigeria appears more and more tenuous. Although it is now trite to say so, socioeconomic problems such as the absence of developed infrastructure, lack of funds for investment and the lack of well-trained

Capacity Building for IT in Education in Developing Countries
G. Marshall & M. Ruohonen (Eds.)

human resources are part of the burden that developing countries have to contend with.

While Nigeria and other countries are struggling to lay a foundation necessary for technological takeoff, and, hopefully, bridge the yawning gap that separates us from the advanced technologies of Western Europe, those countries appear to introduce newer and more sophisticated technologies every day. The gap we seek to bridge seems to grew wider every day.

But Nigeria, as well as every country that finds itself in similar circumstances, cannot afford to give up with regard to Information Technology (IT). The debate cannot be whether or not Nigeria needs IT but what should be the fastest path to take in the acquisition of the inestimable benefits that IT has to offer.

So while it is true that Nigeria is presently battling with the every basic necessity for modern existence - the provision of potable water supply for all its citizens, for reliable electricity supply, for telephones and good roads - it is also true that our polity and economy are presently going through very difficult times, and our public and private sectors are undergoing profound and traumatic transformations aimed at putting our political and economic structures on the path of sustainable growth and efficiency. The process of redressing national economies makes it imperative to embrace IT, which has been shown to enhance modern efficient management.

It is necessary to state the background of Nigeria's place in the world in order to present the importance of Nigeria's need for IT as well as the problems involved in planning and executing a viable programme of IT Education and training for my country.

2 EARLY STAGES OF IT EDUCATION IN NIGERIA (1970-1988)

Historically IT, like most modern technologies, took Nigerians unaware. When IBM entered Nigeria in the late 1960s, Nigeria was still very much a backward economy. However a few multinationals and financial institutions in the country considered it appropriate to adopt the computer for their organizations, which were essentially subsidiaries of European or American conglomerates. Nigeria had no time to prepare for the computer or to acquire knowledge about the technology. Intensive in-service training was given to some Nigerians (usually staff already serving in the multinational companies) to enable them to operate the systems.

Universities, especially the first-generation universities and the Federal Polytechnic, quickly responded to the computer invasion. A few of them bought and installed mainframes which they operated in their computer centres. A few Nigerians who had studied mathematics and computer science abroad came home to service the computer centers and, in most cases, establish the Departments of Computer Science. Thus, one observes from the foregoing that:

- The arrival of computer systems and technology in Nigeria preceded the availability of computer skills and knowledge in our educational system.
- The need for computer education came as a response to the demands of the public and private sectors of the economy.

- Computer education, coming after the need for it was manifested in the economy, was a latecomer and some gaps had to be filled. Nigerians were dabbling in an area they knew little about.
- The first-generation Nigerian universities and the four oldest polytechnics were the advance guard for Information Technology in Nigeria.

In the following years, the universities and polytechnics adopted individual staff training strategies aimed at building as speedily as possible sustainable human resources in IT.

Big companies quickly became the source of human resource development for the emerging market in IT in Nigeria. This state of affairs continued until the early 1980s when the explosion in IT occurred, thanks to the arrival of the PC, which meant that computers became cheaper and easier to acquire. The arrival of the PC was preceded by the period of the so-called 'economic boom'- with a general, if misplaced, feeling of well-being and buoyancy. Nigeria had become a major oil producing nation and the price of oil has risen sharply in the world market. Nigerians, demanding free education and the better things of life for the citizenry, had embraced modern ways - resulting in astronomical increases in school enrolment at all levels of educational system.

The quest for education translated into a sharp increase in the number of universities and polytechnics. In 1975, the Federal Government took over the funding of all existing universities and established seven new ones. State governments established five additional universities, bringing the total number of universities in the country to 18 - four of which were universities dedicated to technology.

Most of the new tertiary institutions established departments of computer science and/or computer engineering. But there was nothing that could be called a policy on IT Education and training at the national or state levels in Nigeria. Initiatives taken by tertiary institutions to establish and operate computer science and/or engineering departments were individual initiatives dictated by expediency. The initiatives were aimed at producing human resources in response to the rising demand for trained computer personnel by the ever-growing Nigerian economy.

3 GOVERNMENT STRATEGIES, POLICIES AND INITIATIVES (1988 - 1997)

Initiatives for secondary schools

It was not until 1988 that the Federal Government of Nigeria took the first bold steps to formulate a coherent set of national educational policies and strategies for IT. Then the Federal Ministry of Education set up an Advisory Committee to study the issue of IT's explosion as it affected Nigeria and to make recommendations to government on how best to harness the benefits of IT for the overall development of the country. The Committee was also to offer advice that would enable government to democratize computer literacy at the nation level. The committee submitted its final report, *National Policy on Computer Education*, to the Honorable Federal Minister of Education on August 27, 1988.

The report recognized the need to introduce/incorporate computer studies at all levels of the Nigerian educational system and recommended that computers should be introduced at all levels (including the primary schools), provided the necessary facilities and resources were available.

In spite of the report's optimism, the committee was sufficiently realistic to appreciate that Nigeria could not afford the enormous costs involved in the introduction of IT education in the nation's primary schools at that stage of our infrastructural and economic development.

One can infer from the foregoing that the Federal Ministry of Education had accepted in principle the recommendation of the committee to introduce computer education at the secondary school level and had immediately instituted a pilot programme in the nation's Unity schools, all the federal government-owned secondary schools established in every state of the federation at the rate of two per state. Consequently, the Ministry directed all the Unity schools to begin the teaching about IT from the 1989 session onward. Although it took three years, because of the difficulties that will be discussed later, for the directives on IT to be carried out, the fact remains that computer literacy programmes have permeated not only into Unity schools but also into a large number of other state and privately owned secondary schools.

Initiatives by tertiary institutions

Prior to 1988 the first-generation universities and polytechnics were the first to respond to the imperatives of IT Education and training in Nigeria - only the universities and Colleges of Technology were expected to teach courses in computer science and produce graduates in that discipline. The result was:

- Very few Nigerians had access to tertiary education and only a negligible number were admitted into departments of computer science. Thus only few Nigerians got to be trained in computer technology.
- Social demands for computer-literate Nigerians far outstripped the level of production.
- Since there was no exposure to IT prior to tertiary education, very few Nigerians were conscious of the career possibilities in computer science and very few got to embrace the discipline.
- There was no way Nigeria could achieve the objective of democratizing computer literacy while the policy lasted.

The situation changed following the report on the National Policy on Computer Education published in 1988. Part of the report highlighted the crucial role that universities were expected to play in leading the country into the IT age.

Perhaps it was in recognition of the crucial role of universities that the Federal Ministry of Education directed the National University Commission (NUC) to develop objectives for computer literacy. The directive led to the NUC issuing *Approved Minimum Academic Standards for Nigerian Universities* (1989). The *Standards* said, among other things, that all university undergraduates were required to take and obtain a pass mark in at least two basic computer courses - Introduction to Computers and Applications of Computers to X (where X stands for the student's field of study) before they could graduate. Although departments are given the option to choose which year of study to introduce the courses, it is noteworthy that the *Standards* are quite apart from requirements for both students from the computer science departments, and students enrolled in courses in computer engineering and the physical sciences, who obviously have to take many more computer courses for graduation. By the 1990/91 academic year, all 37 universities in Nigeria had started to implement the policy.

The effect of the policy has been phenomenal for IT education in Nigeria. According to the NUC Annual Report for 1996, approximately 60 000 graduates were produced by the 24 Federal universities in the 1995/96 academic session alone for regular programmes, while the 12 state universities produced about 19 000 graduates. If one adds another 12 000 graduates produced by the universities that operate 'Sandwich Programmes', we are talking about approximately 91 000 graduates produced in one year. At least, 4500 are single honours graduates of computer science and computer engineering. Although the figures are rather low for a country that has a population of about 100 million, they nevertheless constitute a significant step in Nigeria's march towards IT education acquisition.

The forward step is even more dramatic when you consider that the National Polytechnic Commission, which is to polytechnics as the NUC is to universities, is also striving to introduce computer courses into the curricula of all our polytechnics. The result will be an additional 50 000 computer-literate graduates produced annually by the polytechnics.

Since 1988 there have been genuine and concerted efforts by the Nigerian government to popularize IT Education and training in the country's educational system. Whether the efforts have been matched with the requisite funds to ensure high quality in the IT training that is dispensed in our education system is another matter.

The role of the informal sector

The story of IT Education and training in Nigeria cannot be complete without mention of the extremely active role which the informal sector has played and continues to play in this area. The informal sector is the hundreds of computer training companies which have sprung up all over in Nigerian cities. They are usually small- to medium-sized companies owned and run by individual businessmen and women. They have an average of three or four personal computers, a printer, a classroom and two instructors. They offer well-packaged computer training programmes to target groups of Nigerians. The programmes, which are divided into modules, take from 5 to 20 weeks depending on the requirements of the trainees. Programmes offered are mostly computer appreciation courses and courses devoted to word processing, the use of spreadsheets or the use of specialized application packages. The trainees come from every stratum of the society. They may be company executives who wish to catch up with the 'computer bug' because they fear they might lose out if they do not get computer literate, but most are young secondary school leavers who have completed their training as typists or stenographers and want to enhance their chances of finding good jobs by adding computer literacy to their qualifications. Through informal sector training a very large number of Nigerians who did not have the benefit of computer education during their school days are able to acquire competence in the use of the computer. It is estimated that at least 500 000 Nigerians receive such training each year from this sector.

4 PROBLEMS IN IT EDUCATION, TRAINING AND SOLUTIONS

Improper funding and lack of infrastructure

One obvious problem with which Nigeria has had to contend in her bid to achieve a viable IT Education and training programme is the debilitating state of her economy and infrastructure. Although she possesses the requisite potential for rapid growth and development - abundant human resources and unbelievable reserves of solid and liquid minerals - Nigeria suffers from the same inadequacies of other backward economies.

In an age of painful economic reforms dictated by international financial agencies, Nigeria, like most Third World countries, is going through very bleak times as our public and private sectors groan under profound and traumatic transformation aimed at supposedly leading our economy to the path of sustainable growth and efficiency.

In such a situation it is easy to appreciate that one of the setbacks to IT Education and training has been linked to the problem of allocation of available scarce resources. Where the managers of the Nigerian economy are faced with the choice between using the limited funds at their disposal to provide drinking water and electricity for the people or promoting computer education, they naturally settle for the former. The result is that over the years, one has had the impression that government has done little more than pay lip service to the development of IT education and training.

For example, since the 1988 government directive that computer courses should be introduced into the curricula of the nation's secondary schools that laudable objective is still to be fully realized, even in the Unity schools. And when it is known that the Unity schools, which are owned by the federal government, form only about one percent of the nation's schools one understands how computer training is faring at our secondary school level. The truth is that until now, most states, although they realize and appreciate the need for computer education, find themselves restrained by insufficient funds and cannot introduce computer studies into their secondary school systems.

Admittedly a couple of the states have adopted a few imaginative approaches to resolve their problems. For instance, two states have selected five or six schools for a pilot project in IT education while a third state has gone into partnership with the informal sector computer training schools to offer computer courses in its secondary schools at reduced costs. However innovative these measures may appear, the fact remains that our federal and state governments must realize that the present problems in our economy are largely related to the inefficiencies of the past. The process of redressing the national economy is largely related to the imperative for us to embrace IT, which has been shown to enhance modern efficient management. Money spent on acquisition of computer technology is money well spent so the Federal and State Governments must make up their minds to purse credible computer literacy programmes at the secondary school level. Once their minds are made up, they must, as a matter of priority, come up with the funds (even if it means seeking aid from international agencies and foreign governments) required for the implementation at the secondary school level. To fill the gap the following steps should be taken:

1. A computer literacy programme should be implemented, not only in our Unity schools but also into the nation's entire secondary school system. To allow sufficient time for states to prepare for the takeoff of the programme, a target date of 2001 should be adopted nationally.
2. Since a significant level of funding will be required for the implementation of the programme, only the senior secondary schools should be included in the first phase. Rather that dissipating the meager financial resources available to government by spreading computer education thinly on the ground, such resources should be concentrated on ensuring that the programme is successfully implemented at the tertiary and senior secondary levels.

The consolidation of computer education at the secondary school level (Nigeria's 6-3-3-4 educational system) will provide the much needed feeder for computer education at tertiary level.

General poverty

The problem of infrastructural deficiency is linked with the general level of poverty in the country. If one takes the example of a typical Nigerian university, one observes that not more than five to ten PCs are available for students' use in a university where as many as 8000 undergraduates are taking computer courses. The result is that most of the students are taught only theoretically and never have the opportunity of using a computer while they are enrolled in the university. Even with the few available computers, the unreliability of electricity supply makes it impossible to put them to maximum effective use. One would therefore imagine that if more money and more seriousness were invested into improving the nation's infrastructure, IT Education and training in Nigeria will be greatly enhanced.

Of course, if Nigeria is a poor country, it goes without saying that most of her citizens are poor. With galloping inflation, currency devaluation and public sector salaries that are grossly insufficient for subsistence, it can easily be imagined that most Nigerians are battling with the elementary problem of survival and can hardly find the money required for such capital intensive luxuries as the computer. The result is that today in Nigeria, what is normally known as the middle class has been financially emasculated and finds it almost impossible to embrace the use of computer. Where it is normal for middle class families in the developed world to have one or two PCs in the family, in Nigeria most of those who know the importance of computers cannot afford one.

Teacher education

Another vital factor in the effective implementation of the computer literacy programme in Nigeria is the obvious dearth of sufficiently qualified teachers who can handle computer courses at both the junior and senior secondary school levels. It is important to understand the magnitude of the problem in order to be able to suggest realistic solutions. It is calculated that there are at least 6000 secondary schools in Nigeria. If each of these schools were to require two computer science teachers to cover courses at senior secondary school level, one would need 12 000 qualified computer science teachers. If all existing universities, polytechnics and colleges of education in the country were well-equipped to teach computer science, and were to admit an average of 100 students a year, it would take about 3 years to produce the required number of computer science teachers. And it is assumed here that such computer science graduates produced by tertiary institutions will ignore the attractive offers of the private sector and accept teaching as a profession, which is not the case at all.

So it is clear that in order to meet the critical need for qualified teachers, without whom our national computer education programme would be meaningless, government should adopt a pragmatic and systematic approach to teacher education as follows:

- Deliberately fund universities, polytechnics and colleges of education to enable them to purchase equipment and employ staff necessary for the increased production of computer science graduates.
- Allow every secondary school to nominate two or three serving members of the staff to benefit from a specially-designed 'Sandwich Training Programme' aimed at preparing them for computer teaching. This is a most prudent approach since it will draw from the body of staff who are already teaching in the secondary schools and who can easily be bonded to ensure they continue to serve there.
- Provide incentives for teachers of computer science in order to motivate young graduates to take up teaching. As a matter of fact, the present trend is that conditions in the private sector (banks, oil industries) are so attractive there is growing fear that even the universities may not have any staff left to teach computer science in the very near future.

Continuing Education programme

Due to the strong job market for degree holders in computer science, fewer graduates continue with postgraduate studies in computer science. In fact, there has been a growing concern recently about an impending crisis brought about by a decrease in the number of computer science postgraduates produced. Fewer and fewer postgraduates go into teaching and an exodus of current faculty to industry is occurring.

As industrial applications become increasingly complex and require broader and/or deeper knowledge of computer science, students will find their undergraduate education increasingly inadequate. They will see a need for further education in the discipline. So it is important to stress the need for a well-designed continuing education programme for professional who are already in the field. Such professionals - be they lecturers in tertiary institutions or top executives in the public or private sectors of the economy - need to periodically update their knowledge in IT in order to keep abreast with developments in a fast moving IT world. We believe that a viable computer education programme for Nigeria must, apart from addressing the global developmental needs of all sectors of our economy, have an in-built mechanism to fill the gaps existing between sectors and within sector. A continuing education programme for professionals, who are already active participants in the economy, is an ideal instrument for this purpose. This can take the form of sponsorship to local and international seminars as well as conferences, other specialized short-term courses and symposia. Other strategies for continued education can also be employed.

Creativity

Another problem is the need for Nigeria to develop a real computer culture which goes beyond merely learning to use or even repair computers. A computer culture involves getting Nigerians to imbibe the values of the computer as a tool that can be used by all in problem solving, no matter their profession. Cultivating a computer culture means getting the entire populace to appropriate for itself the potential that the computer offers for problem solving. It is a process of internalization rather than mere learning. The fine line that separates computer culture from mere computer literacy can be likened to a man who knows how to solve difficult mathematical problems without knowing that he can use mathematics to solve everyday problems. It seems to me that IT Education and training in Nigeria lacks creativity.

This deficiency is most visible in our tertiary institutions where the computer science curriculum is straightjacketed. While computer science must include programming, it is not equivalent to programming. Similarly, while it is true that a computer scientist who can only program has no future, it is equally true that a computer scientist who cannot program has no present. Therefore, our IT curriculum must provide for both the present and the future.

5 CONCLUSION

One can say that IT education and training in Nigeria may finally be emerging from its first 25 years of difficulties and uncertainties stronger in its scope and penetration. Our governments are responding, albeit slowly, to the obvious need for computer technology acquisition for the overall benefit of our national development.

It is hoped that as the economy opens up in response to market forces and the awesome potential of the private sector is unleashed in the Nigerian economy, industry and other private sector players will take over from government as prime movers and initiators of the National Computer Policy. Then Nigeria will be a force to reckon with in IT education and training.

6 REFERENCES

Report on National Policy on Computer Education (1988). Lagos, Nigeria.

7 BIOGRAPHY

Uche Modum is a senior lecturer and the current head of the Department of Accountancy, University of Nigeria, Enugu Campus. She is a member of the Computer Professional Registration Council of Nigeria and is the chairperson of the Education committee of the Computer Association of Nigeria (COAN),

Anambra and Enugu chapter. She has published books in Management Information Systems (MIS), and over 20 journal articles in Information Systems and Technology.

10

Using applications programs in a university to build human capacity for Information Technology

D. Arganbright
Professor and Head Department of Mathematics
University of Papua New Guinea
PO Box 320, University PO, NCD 134, Papua New Guinea
Tele + 675 3267414; Fax + 675 3267187
E-mail: 100353.163@Compuserve.com

Abstract

To equip students and staff of the University of Papua New Guinea (UPNG) with technology skills needed in the workplace, and in school and university settings, UPNG's Mathematics Department is modernizing its curriculum to incorporate technology. The major vehicle for change is the creative use of Microsoft *Office,* and courses were developed not only to provide job skills but also to emphasize problem solving and critical thinking, mathematical applications and communication skills. Four components - computer literacy for students, spreadsheets for mathematics and statistics, community outreach, and staff development with word processing, spreadsheets, and databases - are important elements of the university's curriculum.

Keywords

Capacity building, developing countries, higher education, software, spreadsheets

1 INTRODUCTION

Papua New Guinea is a rapidly developing nation in the South Pacific. Like many other developing countries, it is grappling with the need to find ways to effectively expand its Information Technology (IT) capabilities in spite of

Capacity Building for IT in Education in Developing Countries
G. Marshall & M. Ruohonen (Eds.)

2 INTRODUCING UNIVERSITY STUDENTS TO COMPUTING

A primary goal of the Mathematics Department is to provide all university students with a good foundation in IT skills early in their university careers through the Introduction to Computing course. For several years the course emphasized programming but has gradually shifted to the use of application programs. Students now learn how to use *Windows 95*, *Word*, *Excel*, and *Access*.

Many students touch a computer for the first time in the course and so initial sessions concentrate on the techniques of using a computer, mouse and keyboard. Beginning sessions also stress the need for students to plan what they will be doing in a laboratory session before they sit down at a computer. Subsequent weeks are spent developing skills in the use of the application programs but the course has other educational purposes. For example, while learning to use *Word* students learn how to create documents that include graphics, equations and other significant features. Similarly, *Excel* is used to teach problem solving and analysis - skills that are often lacking in students' previous educational experiences. Spreadsheet examples are drawn from finance, population growth, epidemics, heat flow, mathematics and statistics, giving students insights into many different disciplines (Cartwright, 1993). Students generally find the course to be both interesting and useful, and become aware that they are acquiring skills that they can apply to their academic studies and to tasks they will encounter in the workplace.

Introduction to Computers is taught in two large 2-hour lectures and one 2-hour tutorial per week. Students are allocated at least five hours a week to work on computers in the laboratories. In 1997 improved staffing levels and the opening of a new central laboratory have enabled the department to use tutors to conduct small weekly hands-on laboratory tutorial sessions. The course is offered each semester to about 100 external students as well as 200 second and third year full-time students on the main campus. Forty second and third year Health Science students take a similar course. Future enrollments undoubtedly will increase since the university plans to make a similar course a requirement for all first year students .

3 INCREASING STAFF COMPUTING CAPABILITIES

The Mathematics Department has also provided instruction to the university's staff to assist them in increasing their computing capabilities through an introductory 6-session short course. Taught in the senior lab and meeting one hour a week, the class consists of one session on *Windows 95*, two sessions on word processing using *Word*, two sessions on spreadsheets using *Excel* and a concluding session where students learn to integrate the two programs. During the last two years the class has been offered frequently and over 200 staff members have attended. Both the lecturers and attendees participate on a voluntary basis.

The course provides staff with hands-on experience. Technology novices gain familiarity with computers and experienced computer users upgrade their skills by working in a Windows environment. Initially the sessions were conducted with two participants sharing a computer but that arrangement detracted from the goal of providing staff with intensive hands on experience. Now additional computers are placed temporarily in the lab so that each participant has his/her own computer. If the classes are to be successful staff must have adequate time to practice their new skills, so the department's senior lab is made available for staff at designated times.

Some classes are held after work hours, others at noon and others during work hours. Attendees include random cross sections of university personnel, with support, administrative and academic staff comprising each class. Although a heterogeneous composition of the classes has worked well, a few attendees say that it would be better to form homogeneous groups with participants having similar job functions and skill levels.

Staff members have requested additional courses and the department has been able to accommodate many requests. Two courses for advanced instruction in *Word* and *Excel* have been offered as well as an elementary five session course in *Access* teaching an introduction to database concepts. A two-session overview of *PowerPoint* is also a popular course.

The Mathematics Department also presents special short courses designed specifically for academic purposes. One course teaches the use of equations and graphics features in *Word* and *Excel* for the preparation of professional papers and classroom notes as well as the use of *PowerPoint* for classroom lectures and professional presentations. Other classes illustrate the use of *Excel* as an academic tool for mathematical modeling, research, classroom teaching and professional publications. Applications for a wide range of disciplines - physics, population studies, genetics, economics, epidemics, numerical methods, and operations research and computer visualization - are presented in the courses.

Microsoft *Office* provides the computing tools that support, administrative and academic staff require to perform their jobs, and the attendees appreciate the fact that the courses are offered on a voluntary basis. The extensive notes provided are well received by the university community and the Mathematics Department's efforts to present the short courses have been well received.

4 PROVIDING TECHNOLOGY RESOURCES TO THE PUBLIC

For many years the Mathematics Department advertised the Introduction to Computing and other computer science courses to members of the public. The external students comprise a significant component of the enrollment of the course. School leavers and university graduates need to acquire personal computing skills for their work, and the course provides them with an opportunity to resume their education, get started in a study of computing or bring their existing technology knowledge up to date. The university permits the Mathematics Department to use the fees generated to acquire and maintain the department's computers and software, enabling the department to establish first-rate facilities.

The department has also begun to design technology-oriented courses specifically for the general public. The spreadsheet is an excellent tool for the study of statistics (Arganbright, 1992; Middleton, 1997). Introduction to Statistics using *Excel* enables students to implement concepts from first principles much as they would do by hand but in a medium that affords them a natural way to experiment and investigate the resulting model. This approach can be supplemented by using a spreadsheet's statistical functions. *Excel's* statistical analysis tools provide students with a professional experience and many classroom teachers have taken the course to collect teaching ideas. The course also has been incorporated as part of a new postgraduate diploma in computing.

The statistics course was designed for team teaching. Initially a computer oriented mathematician was teamed with a national statistician who had never taught using computers. The procedure represents one way that lecturers lacking IT experienced can acquire computing skills while contributing to instruction.

5 INCORPORATING APPLICATIONS PROGRAMS INTO MATHEMATICS

The Mathematics Department had been slow to introduce IT into mathematics teaching - in large measure because few lecturers used computers. Now the situation is changing as technology-adept lecturers are hired and as a team-teaching approach is adopted to train existing staff. In 1997 computers will be used to teach the basic statistics course for the first time. The standard lectures will be presented by the statistics instructor while another lecturer demonstrates how technology can be used. *Excel* has been chosen because students will be familiar with the program. It provides a nonthreatening introduction to technology for the traditional staff members and is an exceptional tool for teaching statistics.

Practical Computing is an interesting course offered to fourth year students. Team taught by the Mathematics Department and the Director of Computing, the course provides students with practical hands-on skills in software and hardware maintenance coupled with a study of advanced features of Microsoft *Office*. The students' oral communication skills are strengthened as they research academic topics and make presentations using *PowerPoint*. As students learn *Word's* features they strengthen their writing skills as they prepare formal papers and, using *Excel*, they expand their problem-solving skills by creating mathematical models. *Access* is used to teach database skills and concepts.

At UPNG spreadsheets are used primarily in a special topics course and in a Numerical Methods course. The latter course employs *Excel* to study such topics as the zeroes of functions, numerical quadature and differentiation, interpolation, numerical linear algebra and numerical solutions of differential equations. At other universities spreadsheets are used in operations research, linear algebra, calculus, pre-calculus, combinatorics, statistics and probability.

Illustrative Spreadsheet Examples

Because the extensive use of spreadsheets is a distinguishing component of the curriculum at the University of Papua New Guinea, this section presents examples used for staff and student classes. Additional graphic examples may be found in the literature (Arganbright, 1993). In using spreadsheets, the primary focus is on developing problem-solving and analysis skills. Wherever possible the examples used involve Papua New Guinea settings.

The model of Figure 1 computes the growth of one-time deposit p (Cell B1) in a savings account at a fixed annual compound interest rate, r (Cell B2). Column A counts years. In Cell C4 the initial deposit is reproduced as the balance $p0$ at the end of year 0. The first year's interest $i1$ is determined in Cell B5 as $rp0$. The year's new balance is calculated in Cell C5 as $i1 + p0$. Similar results are computed for subsequent years by copying these formulas. The example becomes particularly interesting to students when they observe that it also provides an introductory population growth model. Often students are astounded by the implications of continued geometric growth at the nation's current rate of 2.5%-2.8%. Following this example, students can explore other growth models that assume there is a limiting capacity for growth.

	A	B	C
1	Initial =	200.00	
2	Rate =	12.0%	
3	Year	Interest	Balance
4	0		200.00
5	1	24.00	224.00
6	2	26.88	250.88

	A	B	C
1	Initial =	200	
2	Rate =	0.12	
3	Year	Interest	Balance
4	0		=B1
5	=1+A4	=B$2*C4	=B5+C4
6	=1+A5	=B$2*C5	=B6+C5

Figure 1 Geometric growth.

Virtually all of the techniques and concepts of elementary statistics can be implemented naturally on a spreadsheet. Figure 2 provides an example of a user-designed layout for a hypothesis test of the population mean. Sample statistics are computed in Cells B2:B4 and the hypothesized population mean and test level are entered in Cells D2 and F2. The computations for the conclusion are done by using built-in statistical functions. The chart of Figure 3 is created as part of the previous model and allows users to visualize the hypothesis-testing process.

	A	B	C	D	E	F
1	Parameters and Variables:					
2	smpl mean(x) =	51.5	Ho: μ =	50	α =	0.05
3	smpl sd (x) =	6.45	H1: μ<>	50	Crit: z<	-1.96
4	n =	100			Crit: z>	1.96
5	Conclusions:					
6	z =	2.326	Concl:	Reject	p-value=	0.02

Figure 2 Hypothesis test for population mean.

6 NEW ADVANCES AND FUTURE CHALLENGES

In 1996 the university's new Vice Chancellor established IT as a high academic priority and a new campus-wide fiber optic network was completed. In 1997 the initial phase of central laboratory construction has been completed and staffing levels in computing have been increased - events that should enable the Mathematics Department's efforts to reach a wider segment of the university.

The UPNG Mathematics Department's efforts to revitalize IT use has made a positive impact at the university. In a country where educational institutions cannot supply students with an extensive range of specialized software, Microsoft *Office* works well as a fundamental tool. While the university will continue to face difficulties supplying all of the essential IT knowledge and skills, a solid foundation provides students, staff and the public with fundamental IT skills. For each of the courses the department has prepared extensive notes, and the notes are being compiled into books that will be available for short courses and self-teaching at the university as well as throughout the country.

Nonetheless, more remains to be done. A national staff must be equipped to replace the overseas staff who are currently teaching IT courses. Many departments need additional training in IT. The university is looking for external funding to maintain and extend IT activities, and the daunting need to maintain staffs' IT competence must continue as technology changes rapidly.

7 REFERENCES

Arganbright, D. (1992) *Using Spreadsheets in Teaching Statistics, Statistics for the Twenty-first Century* (eds. F. Gordon and S. Gordon), Mathematical Association of America, Washington D.C., 226-242.

Arganbright, D. (1993) *Practical Handbook of Spreadsheet Curves and Geometric Constructions*. CRC Press, Boca Raton, FL.

Cartwright, T. (1993) *Modeling the World in a Spreadsheet.* Johns Hopkins, Baltimore, MD.
Middleton, M. (1997) *Data Analysis Using Microsoft Excel.* Duxbury Press, Belmont, CA, 1997.

8 BIOGRAPHY

Deane Arganbright is Professor and Head of the Mathematics Department of the University of Papua New Guinea. He teaches mathematics and computer science, and is Chair of the University Computer Committee. Professor Arganbright received his Ph.D. in mathematics (finite groups) at the University of Washington (USA), and is an authority on the use of spreadsheets for mathematical education, modeling and visualization. He has presented invited addresses at national and international conferences, and is the author of *Mathematical Applications of Electronic Spreadsheets* (McGraw-Hill, 1984) and *Practical Handbook of Spreadsheet Curves and Geometric Constructions* (CRC Press, 1993). He is currently developing mathematics and statistics material designed for use in Papua New Guinea.

PART III

Targetted Projects

11

Infrastructure issues for implementation of portable computer use in schools

Anne McDougall
Faculty of Education
Monash University, Clayton Victoria 3168, Australia
Tele + 61 3 9905 2790; Fax + 61 3 9905 2779
E-mail: Anne.McDougall@education.monash.edu.au

Abstract

It has been suggested that the use of battery operated portable notebook computers offers solutions for IT implementation in developing countries, especially where electricity supplies are not reliable. This paper raises a number of issues which need to be addressed when implementing portable computers in school settings and provides strategies based on Australian schools' experiences. The information should be useful to decision makers in developing countries.

Keywords

Developing countries, future developments, hardware, infrastructure, portable computers

1 INTRODUCTION

This paper looks at infrastructure issues in the implementation of portable computer use in schools. It is based on the introduction and use of portable computers in Australian schools and provides information for decision-makers in developing countries where this approach to school computing is under consideration.

The first projects involving extensive use of portable computers in Australian schools began in 1990. Now, although the proportion of schools using portable computers is still a minority of Australian schools, teachers and administrators

Capacity Building for IT in Education in Developing Countries
G. Marshall & M. Ruohonen (Eds.)

have considerable experience in the establishment and maintenance of portable computer use.

The experiences of a number of schools should prove instructive for educators in developing countries. After looking at the major reasons for adopting portable computers, the paper considers approaches to the provision and funding of portable computers for school use, the need for technical support, issues related to battery life and recharging, the need for additional desktop computers and other hardware in a school, and teacher support for integration of portable computers.

2 USING PORTABLE COMPUTERS IN SCHOOLS

Portable computers

The term portable computers refers to machines that are small and can be carried with one hand - in contrast to the large desktop machines. Portable computers run on power from batteries or with a mains power adaptor. The screen is an integral part of the case of the computer, not a separate monitor. Portable computers include the earliest laptop computers, the more recently introduced notebooks, smaller palmtops and some low cost dedicated word processors (NCET, 1992). Australian schools use notebook computers, machines roughly the size and weight of a telephone directory, and equipped with a full size keyboard and a screen contained under a folding lid.

Reasons for school use of portable computers

Portable computers were introduced into Australian schools because educators believe that students must be equipped for a technology rich future. Adopting schools, especially nongovernment schools where student tuition fees are the major source of income, are also cognizant of marketing issues. The motivation for most of the portable computer initiatives can be summarised by David Loader, Principal of the Methodist Ladies' College, the first school to introduce compulsory notebook computer acquisition by its students.

> 'The emphasis is ... on developing a new curriculum that is relevant in a culture that is being transformed by technology. ... The school is also mindful of the market situation that will determine enrolments'.
>
> (Loader, p. 9, 1993)

Where portable computers are being used extensively the resulting changes in curriculum and school culture have often been considerably greater than initially anticipated. For example, Grasso says,

> 'The new seemingly small and tentative step of introducing personal laptops into some classrooms in 1990 has mushroomed into the development of an entirely different school culture in which technology is not a novelty, but an all-pervasive influence. It has become a medium for constructing one's own learning which is taken for granted in much the

same way as pens and paper were previously. ... The school became a community of learners, where cooperative and collaborative learning became the norm'.

(Grasso, 1993)

Commenting on the benefits of portable computer use, Colin Potts, Director of Computing at Trinity Grammar School, Melbourne, lists the following advantages:

- Teachers know that their students will have ready access to the technology and can plan classes accordingly.
- Students can take advantage of the technology at the time it is needed and at the place it is needed.
- Students have access to the technology continually. Work started at school can be continued at home.
- Through regular use of the technology, students develop advanced skills in a meaningful context and through continual reinforcement.
- Student ownership of notebook computers relieves the school of the need to regularly upgrade and extend their hardware facilities.
- Mobile computers facilitate delivery of cross-curriculum computing (1997).

Potts's views would be shared by teachers in similar positions and by administrators and parents at most other adopting schools. In general the schools consider the benefits to be worth the costs of adoption of portable computer use.

Provision and funding of computers

In a considerable proportion of schools implementing extensive portable computer use, the students' parents are required to buy or lease their own computers. The school specifies the brand and type of computer and, in many cases, the software to be installed on the machine. A major advantage of this arrangement is that students can use the computers at any time, at school or at home. Standardisation of hardware and software facilitates maintenance, enables bulk purchase of software and makes teacher in-service training more efficient. A possible disadvantage for some students is that the machine required by the school might be incompatible with a computer already in the students' homes.

Although requiring students to provide their own computers does relieve the school of the cost of the actual machines, personnel with appropriate knowledge are needed in the school to arrange bulk purchases or lease agreements, install specified software, distribute the computers and keep records of maintenance, inventories and other transactions. In schools with extensive use of portable computers, where the curriculum is quite dependent on portable computer use, loan machines might be provided for students whose computers are away for repairs (Symes, 1997). Large monitors are also needed at schools for class display of work generated on the smaller machines regularly used by the students.

While some schools require students to purchase their computers, other schools provide the portable computers for students' use. Often these are in class sets for borrowing for limited times and, sometimes, for longer term individual use. The arrangement gives students greater access to computers and greater flexibility than is generally available with desktop machines but it requires some forward planning by teachers and does not provide the unlimited access that student machine ownership does.

Provision of portable computers for teacher use is important for successful adoption of a school portable computer programme. Generally the schools have provided either computers or financial assistance with computer purchase for staff members.

Insurance is another issue to be addressed as the situation for portable computers is more complex than is the case for desktop machines. Students' home use of the equipment must be covered. Transit between school and home must also be considered and transit is probably the time of greatest risk. Screen breakage has been a problem for some schools and special padded carry bags are used by some students. It is thought wise to avoid labels on the carry bags that identify the contents as computers, as this can invite theft or vandalism so some schools prefer students to carry their computers inside a bigger school bag for these reasons.

Technical support

All the schools adopting portable computers for student use have learned that technically-skilled personnel must be allocated time to provide technical support for students and teachers using the portable machines. The extent of this support varies - from the reduction of the teaching load of a regular teacher with appropriate skills through combinations of technicians on site to fix small problems and a courier service to the supplier for more major repairs (Fallshaw, 1993) to dedicated centres with several technical and administrative staff to handle repairs, maintenance, purchasing, software installation, distribution of machines, equipment bookings, classroom support and other services (Symes, 1997). Some schools with extensive portable computer use also provide a 'help desk' service for teachers and students. The schools say that personal and prompt assistance must be available if the technology is to support and not hinder the educational endeavours of the school (Symes, 1997).

Battery power for portable computers

Since the use of portable computers has been raised as a possible solution for school-based computing in developing countries where electricity supplies may be unreliable, the issue of battery power for portable computers warrants attention. While batteries can provide power for computing independent of mains electricity at the time of use of the machine, battery life is finite and the batteries do need recharging using mains electricity.

The batteries in the earliest laptop computers lasted only a few hours before needing recharging and ingenious systems for recharging during storage were devised in some schools. De Figueiredo (1991) described the construction of large boxes containing recharging plugs connected to mains power and used for storing and recharging class sets of portable computers. These 'computer coffins' were mounted on trolleys so they could be wheeled to classrooms where the computers were needed.

In other schools special storage lockers with recharging plugs have been built for the storage and recharging of individual students' computers when they were not needed in class. Schools may buy, and keep charged, supplies of spare batteries so that a student whose battery runs low in class can simply exchange the low one for a fully-charged spare battery.

Underlying all of these strategies is the need for a minimum level of reliability of mains electricity supply, at least for overnight recharging of batteries. As the technology develops the charged life of batteries is lengthening markedly; however battery-operated computers do not give complete independence from mains electricity.

Desktop computers, printers and other hardware

The adoption of portable computer use has not eliminated the need for schools to purchase desktop machines and other hardware. Many useful computing activities are not easily done on the portable computer. For example, relatively few schools have facilities in all classrooms for connecting portable computers to the Internet so this is more often done using desktop machines. Printers, scanners and other peripherals are generally provided in classrooms and in libraries or resource centres for use with the portable computers.

Teacher support

All of the Australian initiatives have been accompanied by staff anxiety, due either to technical problems or to stress from the increased workload and amount of change that seems inevitably to accompany innovation. This anxiety can be minimised by provision by the school of support for the teachers as the innovation is planned and implemented.

Support occurs in several ways - providing or subsidising teachers' purchase of their own portable computers, articulating the purpose and philosophy of the initiative, providing time to work with the new equipment and software before using it in classrooms, supporting classroom based technical problems, providing teachers with opportunities to attend workshops, courses and conferences, and facilitating the development of networks of people with expertise available to help (McDougall and Betts, 1996).

With good opportunities for professional development and adequate school and classroom support, it is clear that many teachers, including teachers who may have had relatively little confidence with classroom computing previously, can become creative and effective users of the technology. Conversely, implementation of portable computer use in a school without such teacher support is unlikely to be genuinely successful in terms of student learning.

3 CONCLUSION

Many issues need to be addressed in the implementation of portable computer use in school settings. Australian schools have developed strategies to address the issues and have accumulated experience in providing and funding of portable computers, devising ways to technically support the innovation, creating novel solutions for providing battery power for the machines, addressing the need for additional hardware in a school and meeting teacher support needs.

Another issue, which will be only briefly addressed in this discussion, is the question of what impact portable computer use has on schools' curricula. Although little research has been conducted on the long-term effects of portable computer use, two publications by the present author provide a preliminary analysis of the most recently observed outcomes (McDougall, 1995; McDougall and Betts, 1997). Reported outcomes include improved IT knowledge and skills, increased cooperative work and peer learning, more flexible approaches to problem solving, substantial changes in classroom organization and management, increased student responsibility for learning, and parental reports of improved attitudes to homework.

It is difficult for the writer to assess how directly the experiences of implementation of portable computer use in predominantly urban schools in Australia would transfer to the variety of school situations which exist in developing countries. Clearly there will be some major differences in contexts and settings, and it is expected that readers from different countries will respond to the ideas in the paper in different ways. However it is hoped that this account of the experiences and strategies used in Australia will provide information useful for those involved in relevant decision making processes in other countries.

4 REFERENCES

De Figueiredo, J. (1991) Selection, installation and use of laptop computers. Proceedings of the 1991 CEGV Conference. Computing in Education Group of Victoria, Melbourne, Australia.

Fallshaw, M. (1993) Using laptops in schools - the administrative implications, in *Reflections of a Learning Community: Views on the Introduction of Laptops at MLC.* (eds. I. Grasso and M. Fallshaw), Methodist Ladies' College, Kew, Victoria, Australia.

Grasso, I. (1993) Foreword, in *Reflections of a Learning Community: Views on the Introduction of Laptops at MLC.* (eds. I. Grasso and M. Fallshaw), Methodist Ladies' College, Kew, Victoria, Australia.

Loader, D. (1993) Reconstructing an Australian school, in *Reflections of a Learning Community: Views on the Introduction of Laptops at MLC.* (eds. I. Grasso and M. Fallshaw), Methodist Ladies' College, Kew, Victoria, Australia.

McDougall, A. (1995) Integration of portable computers into Australian classrooms: Issues and outcomes, in *Integrating Information Technology into Education.* (eds. D. Watson and D. Tinsley), Chapman & Hall, London.

McDougall, A. and Betts, J. (1996) Teacher professional development in a technology immersion school, in *Information Technology: Supporting Change Through Teacher Education.* (eds. D. Passey and B. Samways), Chapman & Hall, London.

McDougall, A. and Betts, J. (eds.) (1997) *Learning with the Media of Their Time.* Computing in Education Group of Victoria, Melbourne, Australia.

NCET (1992) *Choosing and Using Portable Computers.* National Council for Educational Technology, Coventry, U.K.

Potts, C. (1997) Laptops in schools. *TISP Online*, **2**(1), Technology in Schools Program, The University of Melbourne, Melbourne, Australia, 8.

Symes, E. (1997) Computer and audio visual engineers, in *Learning with the Media of Their Time.* (eds. A. McDougall and J. Betts), Computing in Education Group of Victoria, Melbourne, Australia.

5 BIOGRAPHY

Anne McDougall has worked as a secondary teacher in Australia and then as a computer programmer in the USA. In 1973 she took up a research fellowship in computer education at the University of Melbourne, developing software for use in undergraduate teaching. Her subsequent lecturing and research work has been concerned with computers and learning at secondary and primary school levels. She is now Associate Professor in Educational Computing at Monash University. Her recent publications include *Choosing and Using Educational Software* co-authored with David Squires and *Learning with the Media of TheirTtime* co-authored with Jenny Betts.

12

Capacity building with a difference

Sam Gumbo
Computer Educational Services
Box MP 139, Mt. Pleasant
Harare, Zimbabwe
Tele + 263-4-781022; Fax + 263-4-781022

Abstract

Information Technology (IT) has come to the classroom faster than most Ministries of Education in developing countries ever anticipated, resulting in ad hoc approaches to the implementation of IT in the school system. The major problems have been the lack of prerequisites to successful integration of IT in the school curriculum, for example a lack of qualified teachers, a lack of understanding of what curriculum to teach and whom to teach in the face of so many pupils in one school with limited equipment.

The Zimbabwe Midlands Information Technology in Education Project (ZiMITEP) is a pilot research project which is meant to lay a foundation for a systematic implementation of IT in schools in developing countries. The pilot project focuses on factors that have been identified as constraints to the introduction of IT in the schools' curriculum including: trained personal; technical support; and appreciation of IT in education. The pilot project seeks to: identify appropriate IT implementation strategies in developing countries; bring together, coordinate and harmonize IT activities in the schools; cooperate with other local and outside organizations for the purpose of exchanging ideas and share experience; promote and coordinate in-service training for teachers in IT education in Zimbabwe; provide possible solutions to problems experienced in the introduction of IT in developing countries; and provide a foundation for IT policy in schools.

Keywords

Case studies, curriculum policies, distance learning, resources, teaching materials

Capacity Building for IT in Education in Developing Countries
G. Marshall & M. Ruohonen (Eds.)

1 INTRODUCTION

Information technology (IT) has become a reality in developing countries. However, IT has come to the classroom environment faster than most governments anticipated, resulting in ad hoc approaches to IT's integration into the school curriculum. Schools that find themselves with computers donated or purchased by parents have been faced with numerous problems in their endeavours to introduce IT into the school system. Many of the problems are related to the shortage of trained teachers and technicians. The lack of adequate and appropriate hardware and software also creates difficulties. The situation is made worse by lack of national policies to guide schools in what to teach and how to teach.

2 IT IN ZIMBABWE

In Zimbabwe today only 1.6% of the 6187 primary and secondary schools have computers. The activities in the computer-equipped schools vary from computer clubs to formal examination classes. The three common syllabi being taught in the 'O' level classes are Pitman, Cambridge Computer Studies Syllabus or the Zimbabwe National Foundation Certificate, which is examined by the Ministry of Higher Education Examination Council (HEXCO). The choice of what to teach depends on the school, the availability of computer equipment and the qualifications of the IT teacher. One of the major problems in Zimbabwe schools is the lack of appropriate and adequate hardware and software.

Hardware

The number of computers in the schools ranges from one to 20 per school. Since most of the computers are donated, the schools do not have an opportunity to request computers which meet the requirements of the schools in terms of numbers, type and capacity. Some of the computers are not compatible with other computers in the same school. However, a few schools have the state-of-the-art computers.

Software

Most schools have application software. In addition, some schools have software for teaching the English language, mathematics, science and the social sciences classes. Most of the software was not developed for the African child and the African environment. More still needs to be done in this area.

Teacher Training

Zimbabwe has two teachers' colleges that train computer teachers. Other teachers' training colleges which have computers have not yet established a teacher training component into their curriculum.

Computer Educational Services, a private company has taken an initiative to provide an in-service Information Technology course for teachers called 'Computers in Education', which has been very successful. The first group of teachers trained, from all over Zimbabwe, graduated in 1997. This is a distance and open learning programme.

The University of Zimbabwe Centre for Distance Education also offers a component of Information Technology to the Bachelor of Education Administration students. The majority of students enrolled in the Bachelor of Education Administration programme are teachers. The University of Zimbabwe, the National University of Science and Technology and Selous University also produce computer science graduates, some of whom end up in the classroom teaching computer studies.

Human resources may not be a major problem but a national policy is required so that teacher training may be focused on relevant curriculum. It is critical that pilot projects be carried out to guide policy formulation and implementation strategies.

Technicians

One of the problems identified in schools is the repair and service of computers. Teacher training should include a basic understanding of how a computer works so teachers can acquire skills for first-line maintenance, be able to service the computers, and correct simple software and hardware problems. Major problems can be referred to trained technicians.

3 THE ZIMBABWE MIDLANDS INFORMATION TECHNOLOGY IN EDUCATION PROJECT

3.1 Project description

The Zimbabwe Midlands Information Technology in Education Project (ZiMITEP) is a pilot research project meant to provide solutions to many of the problems that inhibit systematic capacity building for IT in developing countries in education. The interests and contributions of all stakeholders in the field of education will be considered. Stakeholders include government, represented by the Ministry of Education, parents, teachers, the private sector, universities and teachers' colleges as well as the Computer Society of Zimbabwe.

The management of the project is flexible to allow schools to experiment with the independent, dependent, moderator and control variables being monitored to ensure the best result from the pilot research project.

3.2 Objectives of the project

In view of the situation in the sub-region in general and Zimbabwe in particular the project has been designed to:

- bring together and harmonize IT activities in the schools;
- promote and coordinate in-service training in IT in Zimbabwe;
- seek to cooperate with other local and external organizations for the purpose of exchanging and sharing ideas and experiences;
- provide some solutions to problems and obstacles encountered in the introduction of IT in developing countries;
- provide a base for the systematic implementation of IT in schools;

- provide the Ministry of Education with researched information for capacity building and national policy in IT.

3.3 Implementation and location

The ZiMITEP project is being implemented in the Midlands Province, which is the third-largest province in terms of the number of schools and enrolments. Midlands has 226 secondary and 640 primary schools for a total of 866 Schools - 13.6% of the 6187 schools in Zimbabwe. The 443 986 students in the province represent 14% of the total school population. The Midlands Province has a total of 12 579 Teachers - 13.6% of 92 554 teachers in Zimbabwe in 1996.

The Midlands is an ideal province for the pilot project because it is representative of Zimbabwe as a whole in terms of type of school environment. Urban, rural mining and farming communities are found in the province so it represents all the possible social, cultural, political and economic settings found in Zimbabwe. The Midlands Province is also unique in that it has the largest number of rural schools with electricity. The Information Technology project will also be used as a motivating factor for those schools without electricity.

Phase 1
Phase 1 of the project will include a minimum of 16 primary and secondary schools - government, mission and private - spread over the province. Each school's variables are being analyzed for the appropriate input and intervention.

Phase 2
Phase 2 will include more schools, including schools outside the province which have acquired computers. Radio and television broadcasts, and interviews on the project will encourage more schools to acquire computers.

Phase 3
Phase 3 will involve analysis of results from the pilot schools and the production of a report. The material that will be produced may be used for teaching IT at the national level.

3.4 Project management

The project will be managed at three levels - the school, the district and the provincial level.

School committee
The school committee is made up of the teachers and parents (students may be included), and the committee is responsible for the day-to-day running of the project.

District committee
Teachers from each of the pilot schools in the same district participate in the district committee. They hold regular meetings to share ideas and school experiences.

Provincial committee
Overall management and policy rests with the provincial committee which is responsible for planning implementation and research strategies. The committee has representatives from the District Office, Regional Office, Head Office, Curriculum Development Unit and the Computer Society of Zimbabwe.

3.5 Project activities

The project encompasses the following activities:

- identification of the sample schools in the project;
- curriculum research, development and diffusion;
- in-service teacher training;
- fund-raising for hardware and software;
- Internet and networking;
- establishing resource and service centres;
- popularizing Information Technology.

Production of support materials and basic materials has provided the required support materials resources.

3.6 In-service teacher training

Information technology is an innovation in our schools. Therefore in-service training should be viewed as an intervention to facilitate the diffusion of the innovation. Two models - A and B - will be used in the ZiMITEP project.

Model A has been used for teachers in the province who do not have computers at their schools. The teachers will be trained during school vacations and over weekends by going to a Resource Centre for their practical experience. They will receive learning materials for the theory part of the course to study during the term at their places of work. The model has been tried with over 300 teachers who have successfully completed the one year in-service Distance Education course which has proved to be a success. Urban teachers can attend lessons during the day or evening.

Model B has been used for schools which have or will have been given computers. The teachers receive their training at their schools at appropriate times. The teachers may sit for Certificate or Diploma Examinations to motivate them with recognized qualification. Training will include evaluation of educational software to take care of the differences in social and cultural values which are likely to be enshrined in the foreign-produced software.

The present in-service curriculum includes:

- Information Technology concepts;

- computer operations and packages;
- introduction to database management;
- Information Technology in education;
- curriculum development.

Curriculum development
The project will assist the Ministry of Education in the development of an appropriate curriculum for secondary and primary schools through the Research, Development and Diffusion (RDD) model. The basis of the curriculum will be computer literacy, the application of computer tools in other subject areas and the application of computers in professional areas.

The development of the curriculum will be done in consultation with other schools in the country teaching computers in conjunction with universities, commerce and industry. Innovation and creativity will be encouraged since the above suggestions were recommended by the International Federation for Information Processing (IFIP) Technical Committee on Education (TC3) Working Group (WG 3.1) sponsored by UNESCO (Tinsley and van Weert, 1994) to guide curriculum developers.

Internet Networking
The project will establish Internet connections so that schools can talk to each other and link with other schools outside Zimbabwe. This will be an instance of using computers as resources and communication devices.

3.7 Acquisition of hardware and software

The project will assist the pilot schools to acquire hardware and software through donors such as local companies. Schools are also encouraged to solicit donations through parents. Community commitment will be sought before schools can be given computer equipment.

Information Technology awareness
The project management committee will hold meetings with policy and decision makers to ensure their involvement so that they appreciate the value of IT in education. Meetings will be held with the parents so that they accept ownership of the equipment to ensure sustenance of the programme beyond the life of the project.

Establishment of IT Resource and Service Centres
Some of the schools that are centrally located and have separate computer rooms will be established as Resource and Services Centres where other teachers may utilize the facilities. Some teachers who are programmers will be encouraged to produce educational software. A joint venture will be encouraged between the private sector and the government in the production of the educational software.

3.8 Monitoring and evaluation

The Management Committee is using the Context, Input, Process, Product and Impact (CIPPI) Evaluation Model to control and monitor variables.

The context component has identified the number of teachers in the province qualified to teach IT and the number of schools with computers. Data has also been collected on the number and status of hardware in schools as well as data on the social, economic and political of environment of each implementing school.

Input includes the fact that the schools require state-of-the-art equipment in order to teach computers across the curriculum or be connected to other schools' resources.

Process evaluation occurs as every activity is being monitored to record the teachers' assessment and students' reactions, which are being shared by the teachers in the project.

Product evaluation means that at end of the project, the results will be measured to assess the replicability of the project.

4 CONCLUSION

It is expected that the pilot project will provide valuable experiences, knowledge and skills in the systematic implementation of IT in education in Zimbabwe and the neighboring developing countries. Some of the most important components of the pilot project relate to the involvement of all stakeholders in education to ensure sustainability and continuity of capacity building in terms of equipment and human resources training.

5 REFERENCES

Tinsley, J.D. and van Weert, T.J. (eds.) (1994) *Informatics for Secondary Education, A Curriculum for Schools*. UNESCO, Paris.

6 BIOGRAPHY

Sam D. Gumbo is the director of Computer Education Services, a company involved in the training of teachers through in-service distance and open learning activities. He is a member of various committees on IT in education, including the UNESCO committee on Inter-governmental Informatics. He is also on the Education Committee of the Computer Society of Zimbabwe.

13

Principals, Information Technology and leadership: coping with professional development despite isolation

William Newman
P. O. Box 1420
Alice Springs, Northern Territory
Australia
Tele + 61 8 89525044; Fax + 61 8 89527210
E-mail: wnewman@pobox.com

Abstract
Shaping the use and direction of Information Technology in a school is not an easy task. Since principals are the decision makers and driving force in educational institutions they must play a pivotal role but many lack the IT skills and knowledge to do so. The Australian Principals Association Professional Development Council project targets the changing of attitudes and work habits among principals via a self-paced learning program using the Internet. It is designed to provide a structure of security for all levels of ability and is a system-wide approach to professional development.

Keywords
Attitudes, distance learning, electronic mail, Internet, national projects, professional development

1 INTRODUCTION

How far have the developed countries advanced in terms of system-wide utilisation of Information Technology (IT) in education? I would suggest not very far at all. It is important to distinguish between what happens in individual schools and what is the norm. Some schools will excel in IT implementation but are a minority. They succeed as a result of individual vision and energy, and not as a result of

Capacity Building for IT in Education in Developing Countries
G. Marshall & M. Ruohonen (Eds.)

system wide sustainable initiatives. The sad reality of most Western education systems is that Information Technology is not integrated across the school curriculum in a pedagogically sound manner. There is no doubt that computers exist in schools and that they are being used, but how they are being used is often not addressed.

Even as we approach the next millennium too many schools are focused on the hardware and its costs without placing technology in the bigger picture. Costs cannot be ignored, but they must be considered in relation to the gains they provide and the human structures that must go with IT implementation.

Why, despite all the rhetoric, have systems not progressed in their use of the technology? It would be foolish to suggest that any one factor is responsible but from experiences in the Northern Territory of Australia one significant factor has been identified - the principal.

Why Target Principals?

Principals are the decision makers and driving forces in educational institutions. If they do not have an insight into the use of the technology, then its meaningful implementation will be limited. Traditional thinking is important but not necessarily what is required to implement IT in a pedagogically sound way into the learning process. It is easy for principals to simply do what has been done before and follow others in conservatism. The conventional wisdom within primary schools is to place computers at the disposal of students without ensuring that educators have the appropriate skills to use IT as a tool. Despite modeling being a recognised teaching/learning approach little exists within a classroom in terms of the use of Information Technology. Principals must be prepared to support staff in gaining skills and modeling behaviour.

In Australia the trend is for all education authorities to move to a self-managed or devolved management and financial model. This places considerable power and responsibility with the principal in terms of setting, supporting and maintaining any program involving the use of IT. The principal is the lynch pin.

Without adequate professional development principals will not have the IT knowledge, skills and, most importantly, the insight to initiate and support IT implementation in schools. Principals must provide support for real educational benefits and not be solely reliant on the views and advice of others. They must have a level of understanding that will enable them to make decisions based on information presented to them. Fundamental to this is an understanding of what IT in the school is for and what its role should be.

One of the common catch cries often heard in the school sector in Australia is 'Industry uses these types of computers therefore so should our school'. This can be a very powerful argument to the noneducationalists and one that has been very common over the years. Arthur Tatnall and Paul Jenner (1986) encapsulated the attitudes when they said:

> '... many people do not understand how and why computers are used in education, making the mistake that either they are used in the same way as in business or else just for drill and practice activities. This presents a problem that needs constant addressing'.

Keeping in mind that this was written in 1986 it is sad to think that it still rings true today. Not only that, it is an attitude that exists within education itself and the connection to business is one that can easily be used on IT-illiterate principals. Principals, above all others, must be aware of this attitude, and be able to combat it based on their own experience and knowledge. To do this requires a skill level and understanding that the majority of them do not have.

It is vitally important that developing countries focus on the human structure for the use of IT as much as they concentrate on the acquisition of the technology itself. IT in education is about people, not simply hardware. The hardware alone will never be able to provide improved learning outcomes for any education system. What is needed are educators and leaders with the insight to use IT as a tool within the school. Principals who can sort the hype from the reality and address issues in a proactive rather than reactive manner will be more than just managers, they will be leaders. To do this requires a human infrastructure of support and guidance.

Support for principals

The Australian Principals Associations Professional Development Council (APAPDC http//:www.edprog.tased.edu.au/apapdc/home.html) is a national body that represents all Australian principals regardless of the type and size of the school, and facilitates professional development among principals.

According to the APAPDC, 'In 1983, Professor Judith Chapman undertook significant research into the profile of Australia's school principals, on behalf of the Australian Schools Commission. No further research has been undertaken on the subject until the APAPDC commissioned a team led by Dr Neville Grady from the University of Tasmania at Launceston to undertake follow-up research'. This highlights that research on principalships has been few and far between.

From the work that has been done, Evans (1996) said principals must have the following competencies: Educational leadership, organisational management, organisational leadership, political leadership and reflective leadership. The competencies were created as a part of a strategy to identify the key areas in which principals must have skills and knowledge in order to prove successful as a principal.

The common thread through all of the profiles were the words 'interpret', 'vision' and 'communication' - interpret, vision and communicate in a world that can only be described as alien in comparison to most principals' own schooling experience. Where do they acquire the basic skill set in modern technology that will enable them to survive? It is of limited value to simply provide a resource as rich as the Internet to principals and assume that they then have all the answers. A number of informal trials facilitated by Roy Harvey of the Northern Territory Principals Association have taken place where principals were provided the tools and the location of 'useful information', but never obtained the information. Giving principals the tools without the skills, and without developing their confidence in the use of the tools and their own ability will not yield any positive outcomes. It cannot be assumed that just because children have a pencil and paper they will write meaningful passages of work.

One of the greatest difficulties facing the APAPDC is effectively reaching all principals. For this reason a project was established in the Northern Territory to find a model that could deliver professional development in an efficient and cost effective manner.

The Northern Territory covers a geographical area 5.5 times the size of the United Kingdom and 3.5 times the size of Zimbabwe. Despite its size it has a population of only 195 101 of which 112 845 are in the two largest centres separated by 1500 kilometres. The remaining 82 256 people are scattered throughout the Territory in small communities. Such communities often have small schools and are accessible only by four wheel drive vehicles. Some schools are up to 12 hours travel from their nearest support centre. Providing professional development in this context is extremely difficult.

The Internet was seen as a medium to deliver professional development, not only to principals in remote locations, but also those in urban centres. Many professional development programs exist on the Internet that cover a range of issues from Leadership to Behaviour Management but they all assume that the principal already has the skills to use the medium. The reality is somewhat different.

In order to tap into Internet resources principals need to have a basic skill set that was simply not there. The APAPDC project targets skill development via a self-paced learning model independent of geographical location. It is designed to provide a structure of security for all levels of ability. The results of the program thus far have been very impressive. Those completing the course have the skills to now use the wealth of resources that exist in the global community via the Internet.

Darling-Hammond and McLaughlin (1995) write that, according to Cohen, McLaughlin and Talbert (1993) the outlines of a new paradigm for professional development policy are emerging and the hard work of developing concrete exemplars of the policies and practices that model 'top-down support for bottom-up reform' has only just begun. The APAPDC project provides just such an approach.

2 THE PROJECT

The APAPDC project provides a course where principals get an individual professional development program that is completed in their own time at their own location. It is individual in the sense that they work at their own pace, and have a person who monitors their progress and provides tasks and feedback to those tasks.

The aims of the course are to:

- provide a professional development opportunity to principals who would not have otherwise had, or created for themselves, the opportunity;
- develop a model that would resist the itinerant nature of staffing in remote areas, and provide an ongoing mechanism for principals to acquire and further develop skills in the use of the Internet and information technology generally;
- ensure the skill set of principals was such that they could utilise the Internet as a medium for professional development on a range of topics not related to IT;
- enlighten principals about the educational value and issues associated with IT in a school environment.

The program was introduced during the 1996 calendar year. It was initially in two parts with principals being given the option to stop at the completion of part one. No one took this option.

The basic mode of delivery was to supply all participants with a booklet containing general information on the Internet and introducing them to the jargon. It also contained the first five tasks. The tasks involved the principal reading the information on how to do something associated with the Internet and then completing an activity.

Grady and Mulford (1996) point out that, 'There seems to be an understanding underlying the more highly-developed programs that success comes from following a developmental process, *e.g.*, one program is sequenced on the basis of what a principal needs for survival, then for control, then for stability, and then for taking initiatives'. The program is designed to achieve exactly that.

The program makes use of a mentor to work with the principal as a fundamental part of the course. The mentor in the early stages of the course was the original author of the course. Once the first group of principals had completed the course they then made themselves available as mentors for other principals. This has a two-prong advantage. Principals becoming mentors cements their own knowledge in the area and the project provides for a sustainable model -principals mentoring principals.

The complete course consists of three parts. Part one covers electronic mail, part two covers the World Wide Web (WWW) and part three puts the first two topics into a context by providing professional development on leadership. The focus for part three is not the technology and skill acquisition, but the content and issues of leadership.

Part one consists of 25 tasks and concentrates on e-mail using Eudora. Eudora was chosen for reasons outlined further on. The idea behind doing e-mail first was to ensure that principals had a set of basic skills that they could call on later in the program. It highlights the fact that the very nature of communication is changing. In addition, once e-mail is mastered all future problems for any professional development can be dealt with via e-mail.

Even though some principals had used e-mail they were generally unaware of the power and sophistication of a mail program such as Eudora. Part one presented a challenge for IT-illiterate principals as well as those who had used e-mail before.

Part two looks at using the World Wide Web and Netscape. There are only 16 tasks but they take longer to complete and are more conceptually challenging. People enjoyed and relished the challenge of this section.

Part three takes the skills associated with searching the WWW and using e-mail, and leads the principal through a course on issues associated with leadership in schools. This part is not concerned solely with IT in schools but a range of issues facing principals in the leadership of their school.

With all three parts participants cannot move onto the next task until their mentors have sent it to them. This has worked very well and provides for the following:

- It ensures a consistent use of the technology by principals.
- It allows the mentors to be convinced that the principals do understand the concepts and skills associated with the task they have just completed.

- It allows the mentors to monitor and, if necessary, contact the principals over their progress.

2.1 Tasks

For parts one and two of the program the tasks contain information and instructions on discrete skills. At the end of each of the tasks is an activity that principals complete and send to their mentors.

The tasks are written with two key factors in mind. First, each task has to cover a very small skill set. Second, each task has to be achievable in a relatively short period of time. Each task is written to take approximately half an hour to an hour to complete and constructed to be self-paced. Principals are very busy and need a structure where they can put something down for a month and come back to it without going over old ground.

The mentors ensure the principals have mastered the concepts and, once happy with the response, the mentors send, via e-mail, the next task to the principals. This means a principal cannot skim through the material but must master each small component on the road to completion.

2.2 Mentoring

Central to the model is the use of a mentor who provides feedback and monitors individual progress. If principals are not checking their mail the mentor will contact them and sort out any problems. The mentors are also responsible for sending out articles of professional interest to principals.

The success of the project stems largely from its use of mentors and their interaction with the participants. The use of mentors has been shown in a wide range of environments to be highly effective. This is highlighted by the work of Aubrey and Cohen (1995) who looked at where learning comes from and its relation to a principal. They found that in answer to the question, 'Where did you learn what is most useful to you in your working life?' the most often cited answers were a high pressure project, a major 'screwup', a career change or a nondogmatic mentor.

Other work by Grady and Mulford (1996) shows that 'the relatively widespread use of some form of mentoring system means that many inductees will retain a degree of control over the process'. The establishment of Professional Development Schools (PDS) in the USA further highlights the success of a mentor approach to learning.

The mentors spend considerable online time communicating with their principals on an individual basis to ensure they feel confident and secure in knowing help is there,and the mentor relationship is the fundamental cornerstone to the success of the project. It is important that the mentors respond to people quickly and in a meaningful way. The feedback associated with the use of a mentor has been exceptional.

2.3 Timing

From those who have completed the project it appears that the time required to complete both parts one and two is approximately 20 weeks. Part three is currently being trialed.

One of the strengths of the program is that principals can work on tasks when it suits them. If things are really hectic they may not complete a task for a month and then might do three in one week.

2.4 Resources

The key elements to the program can be divided into the model itself, the hardware, the software, access to the Internet and the mentor. The three that have not been previously mentioned are software, hardware and access to the Internet.

The software chosen for the program had to fit two essential criteria:

- It was legal. It is vitally important that only software that can be legally used in schools without cost be used in the program.
- It would run on most machines. The variety and power of computers that were and are to be used for this program is extreme. The software needed to be such that it would run reliably on lower-end machines as well as high-powered RISC machines.

In addition to the above criteria Eudora and Netscape were chosen because they are multiplatform. The hardware was not selected but was already in place, in essence whatever was already out there and could be connected to the Internet was to be used.

Internet access is the only infrastructure component that cannot be directly controlled by the principal or mentor. Quality and cost of access will vary from country to county.

3 BENEFITS TO PRINCIPALS

The change in confidence and attitude has been one of the most striking consequences of the program. In Alice Springs, for example, all urban principals are doing or have completed the program. All members of the executive of the Northern Territory Principals Association (NTPA) have completed or are doing the program. As a direct result of being involved in the program the principals have all placed IT as a priority area for their own future professional development as well as making it a priority for their schools.

An increased amount of electronic communication is now taking place. All correspondence for the executive committee of the NTPA now takes place electronically. Mailings of reading and association business are sent out electronically with no hard copy mailings occurring beyond 1997. If principals do not have their own account and connection to the Internet they will miss all mailings and association information that is being circulated. The time and cost savings of this approach is considerable, and has been made possible as a direct consequence of principals completing the APAPDC program.

On a local level principals now have computers on their desk with Internet access and are modeling IT use. The fact it is on their desks has prompted a shift of attitude, and principals are becoming more aware of the potential and the limitations of the technology. As a result of the program the majority of principals are now looking at how e-mail can be introduced at a school level to give electronic access to their staff.

The most significant outcome of the program is that principals are in a position to understand the potential and to ask the right questions when others present ideas or plans in terms of IT implementation at the school level. Confidence in not being seen as a Luddite has enabled principals to start down the track of genuine development.

4 CONCLUSION

Apart from the Internet infrastructure, concentrating on hardware and availability of computers alone will never succeed. Providing teacher training without having principals and decision-makers being conversant with the potential of the technology will be a slow and ultimately frustrating experience for teachers. For IT to be used as a tool in a pedagogically sound way requires an insight by teachers and decision-makers that can be best obtained by skill acquisition and, most importantly, modeling. If principals do not have skills and knowledge they are at the mercy of the techno-fix enthusiasts in the school, who are often keen on the technology for technology's sake. Even those who are keen to see the technology applied in a pedagogically sound manner often lack the skills and insight to ensure that it becomes a reality.

One step in the direction of sound, educationally valid uses of IT in schools is to ensure that the principal has the appropriate skills and insight. The cost of developing individual programs for all principals to achieve this is prohibitive. The model outlined here has shown itself to be a successful and economical way of providing professional development to all principals regardless of location and size of school.

It must be kept in mind that the project is more than just a professional development program on the Internet itself. It gives principals skills that can be used for a diverse range of noncomputing professional development and communication activities. It is providing a medium for the future delivery of a wide range of programs covering all aspects of leadership.

At the IFIP Fifth World Conference on Computers in Education no papers specifically covered the need for educational leaders to be conversant with issues relating to IT or the skilling of our leaders in this area. Without such skilling developing countries will follow the same slow and frustrating path followed by developed countries in terms of the pedagogical uses of IT within education. Grady and Mulford (1996) said 'management' is concerned largely with 'doing things right' and 'leadership' largely with 'doing the right things', and they thought that attention usually favours 'management' over 'leadership'. Until the balance is addressed principals will remain managers and not leaders of IT in education, and as such will struggle to develop and implement policy that will ultimately ensure improved learning outcomes of students.

Darling-Hammond and McLaughlin (1995) point out that 'What does need to be a permanent addition to the policy landscape is an infrastructure or web of professional development opportunities that provides multiple and ongoing occasions for critical reflection, and that involves teachers with challenging content'. This applies equally as well to principals. They explain that capacity building policies view knowledge as constructed by and with practitioners for use in their own contexts rather than as something conveyed by policy-makers as a single solution for top-down implementation. If such capacity is to be built then principals and decision-makers must acquire the basic skill set they need in their own environment with nonthreatening support.

Developing countries should not simply follow the trends of the developed countries believing they have the answers. There are no answers, just experiences. It is important for developing countries to look beyond individual schools and look at system-wide initiatives. By comparing and contrasting the two they will be in a far better position than many of our educational systems are today.

5 REFERENCES

Aubrey, R. and Cohen P. (1995) *Working Wisdom: Timeless Skills and Vanguard Strategies for Learning Organizations*. Jossey-Bass, San Francisco, CA.

Cohen, K., McLaughlin, W. and Talbert, J. (1993) *Teaching for Understanding: Challenges for Policy and Practice*. Jossey-Bass, San Francisco, CA.

Darling-Hammond, L. and McLaughlin, W. (1995) Policies that support professional development in an era of reform, *Phi Delta Kappan*, 597.

Evans, D. (1996) Leaders and Their Learning, APAPDC Publications, Canberra, Australia.

Grady, N. and Mulford, B. (1996) National Principals Induction Survey, Report to the Australian Principals Associations Professional Development Council.

Tatnall, A. and Jenner, P. (1986) How state education authorities recommend computer systems for use in Australian schools, *Computers in Education*, CEGV eighth annual conference.

6 BIOGRAPHY

Bil Newman has a Masters Degree in Applied Science (Artificial Intelligence) to complement his original degree and other postgraduate studies in education and mainstream computing. He is the only recipient of the Computer Association's Northern Territory Computer Educator of the Year award and was in the first group of 11 teachers in Australia to receive Master Teacher 3 status. To this day he remains the youngest ever recipient.

Bil is currently the senior computing adviser for the Operations South Region of the Northern Territory of Australia. Previously he worked in senior computing at Centralian College, has lectured for the Northern Territory and Swinburn Universities, and operated a consultancy business. Bil is currently listed in several international biographical references including *Who's Who of the World* and the *Who's Who in Science and Engineering*.

14

'Communicate and Learn' - a collaborative project

Zhang Ji-Ping
Department of Education Information Technology
East China Normal University
Shanghai 200062, China
Tele + 0086 21 62571257, Fax + 0086 21 62450731
E-mail: Jpz@guomai.sh.cn

Jef Moonen
Faculty of Educational Science and Technology
University of Twente
P.O. Box 217, 7500 AE Enschede
The Netherlands
E-mail: Moonen@utwente.edt.nl

Abstract
The 'Communicate and Learn' project is a collaborative project between East China Normal University, China and University of Twente, The Netherlands. The project is supported by the AT&T Foundation and the objectives of the project are to redesign and implement two distance courses in the field of educational technology for use in a networked learning environment in China. The background of the project, major objectives of the project, and organization of the project will be of interest to policy makers in developing countries. Current research results and some emerging problems of the project will provide guidelines for work on similar projects in other countries.

Keywords
Collaborative learning, communication, distance learning, networks

Capacity Building for IT in Education in Developing Countries
G. Marshall & M. Ruohonen (Eds.)

1 INTRODUCTION

In 1995, The AT&T Foundation announced an 'AT&T Global Distance Learning Initiative' program and called for project proposals from all over the world. The major objectives of the program were to encourage global distance learning programs using interactive communications technologies, and to encourage collaboration and technology-based distance learning projects between institutions, countries and continents. The announcement also provided the criteria for eligibility. The criteria included: participating institutions must be universities or institutions of higher education and they should have some experiences of using technologies in education; project proposals must involve at least two or more institutions - preferably from different countries; and proposals from some countries, such as Brazil, Canada, China, France, Mexico, and Japan, were strongly encouraged.

The Department of Educational Information Technology (DEIT), East China Normal University (ECNU), China and the Faculty of Educational Science and Technology (FEST), University of Twente (UT), The Netherlands have had a long and good cooperative relationship over the last decade. Both departments (DEIT and FEST) are cooperating on different educational research issues and have formalized their willingness to cooperate in the AT&T project in a 'Letter of Intent'. One main area of cooperation is the field of instrumentation technology - the use of media, computers, and telematics for education. That is why the DEIT and FEST agreed upon a more detailed 'Letter of Intent' in which both institutes provided more detailed specification of the cooperative activities in which they engage. The general objective of the latest 'Letter of Intent' was the development of a cross-institutional program to enable the FEST and the DEIT to further improve the design and use of instrumentation technology. A project proposal, 'Communicate and Learn', was developed by the two departments and was strongly supported by the AT&T Foundation.

2 OBJECTIVES OF THE PROJECT

By combining both developments in the project, each partner expected to strengthen the other. The general objectives of the 'Communicate and Learn' project are:

- to redesign and implement two distance courses devoted to educational technology and distance learning;
- to select ten key Chinese universities as network-users for testing and evaluating the two courses;
- to constitute a foundation for the further transfer of knowledge and skills between the DEIT and the FEST in the use of technologies for distance education;
- to gain insight in the use of communication technologies in order to design and deliver a distance educational programs about educational technology.

The two courses on which the project is based are Human-Computer Interfaces (HCI) and Authoring Systems. The redesign must lead to two distance courses that fit into context of Chinese educational networking. The redesign and implementation of the two courses is considered a foundation for the further transfer of knowledge and skills between the FEST and the DEIT, and from the DEIT to other Chinese universities. Finally, the redesign and implementation provides the two institutions use of communications technology in education.

3 ORGANIZING THE PROJECT

In the project, four major phases can be distinguished. If obligatory, a discussion of the phases will result in a report of activities.

First phase of the project

The first phase (January 1996 - December 1996) of the project was concerned with the redesign of the two courses - Human-Computer Interfaces (HCI) and Authoring Systems - with respect to educational technology. Two tasks were accomplished in the first phase:

- the first task involved requirement analysis, analyzing the context in which the course were going to be delivered, and course specification, analyzing the courses to be delivered. Tasks were carried out at the FEST by two educational researchers from the DEIT and one researcher from the FEST;
- the second task was related to the real design or coding of the two courses. The tasks were carried out at the DEIT by one educational researcher from the DEIT. During this step, support was given by research from the FEST using communication technology .

Second phase of the project

The second phase (January 1997- July 1997) of the project concerned the real implementation of the two redesigned courses by the Chinese Educational Network. Delivery was under the auspices of the DEIT, where students from the other key universities were invited to follow the course. In the first month, January, implementation at the DEIT was supported by a researcher from the FEST. Results will be described in two reports of activities. The DEIT is responsible for the production of the two reports.

Third phase of the project

The third phase (August 1997 - October 1997) of the project concerns the evaluation of the design and implementation of the two courses. A workshop in Shanghai will be held, in which representatives from ten universities will be involved. The data from the workshop will be collected on the following aspects of the project:

- the quality of the courses - including some usability aspects ;
- the number of students who follow the courses and the number of universities involved;
- the opinion of the teachers and students about the implementation of the courses.

- recommendations and guidelines for further (re-)design and implementation of distance courses in the Chinese Educational Network.

Fourth phase of the project

The last phase (November 1997 - December 1997) will be concerned with the evaluation of the entire 'Communicate and Learn ' project and will result in a final report.

Indicators of success will be:

- the successful design and implementation of the two distance courses;
- the experience in the use of communication technologies as a result of the (re-) design and delivery of the distance educational programs;
- the agreement between the Department of Educational Information Technology and the Faculty of Educational Science and Technology which will serve as a foundation for the further transfer of knowledge and skills.

The final report will describe the results of the project but will also describe the problems encountered during the project. The impact of the project on the two institutes directly involved will also be described.

4 CURRENT RESULTS

As of July 1997, the second phase of the work was completed and some current results can be described as follows:

- the redesign and development of the two distance courses (fully in a Chinese version) was completed and the two courses are accessible through the Chinese Educational Network or the Internet;
- the cooperation between the two departments was very successful - both learned a great deal from each other with respect to methods, technologies and even cultures -Western and Chinese;
- ten key Chinese universities are satisfied with the distance courses, and are using and testing the courses through the Chinese Educational Network;
- two workshops devoted to distance learning were held during last year, with over 60 universities involved, and this year ten key universities in China are participating. The project has stimulated many Chinese universities to start research on distance learning.

Emerging problems and future impact

Although the research and cooperation of the project was successful, there were several problems, which will be discussed in detail in the final report of the project. Several key issues are:

- copyright issues related to the knowledge transfer between different institutions;
- technical issues such as end-users' platforms, access speed for pictures or graphics;

- maintenance issues such as on-line service, hardcopy materials for learners and post-project maintenance of all aspects of the project after the project ends;
- the limited number of available Chinese - in Chinese versions - courseware for the Chinese Educational Network.

The impact of project on the two institutes involved is expected to be large. The project is expected to function as a catalyst for further cooperation between the DEIT and the FEST. Naturally, communication technology offers the opportunity to establish cooperation and, in addition, the technology enables the two institutes to present educational programmes at a distance.

Of course communications technology has functioned as a central topic of discussion in both departments recently. Clearly the central role of communication technology will have a large impact on the further cooperation between the two institutions. In general, the major role of the FEST in further cooperation is to transfer knowledge and experience to the DEIT about the use of interactive communications technology for educational purposes. The role of DEIT is to transfer knowledge and experience about the design and implementation of distance courses in China to the FEST. In addition, the DEIT is responsible for the transfer of knowledge and experience about the use of interactive communication technology for educational purposes to other key Chinese universities, who are interested in the use of interactive communication technology for educational purposes. Through the project, the DEIT will have gathered good experience and will be in a position to assume a leading position in the use of telecommunications for educational use in China.

5 BIOGRAPHY

Prof. Dr. Zhang Ji-Ping graduated from the Department of Physics at East China Normal University in 1977 and received his Ph.D. degree from the University of Twente, The Netherlands in 1996. His major research interests involve computer-based learning, multimedia-based teaching system design, distance learning, and instructional approaches and theory. He has published many papers and books about educational technology and computer use in education.

Currently he is the chairman of Department of Educational Information Technology and the director of the Modern Educational Technology Institute at East China Normal University. He also is a member of the board of the Society of China Computer-Based Learning.

15

The effect of network technology on education

Anton J. Knierzinger
Paedagogische Akademie der Dioezese Linz
Institut für Schule und Neue Technologie
Salesianumweg 3, A-4020
Linz, Austria
Tele + 43 732 772666 262; FAX + 432 732 772666 295
E-mail: Kna@mail.padl.ac.at
www.padl.ac.at/pers/kna/kna.htm

Abstract

Worldwide a rapidly increasing number of schools is connected to the Internet, which is a way of supporting teachers, students and school administrators. Although many teachers have great expectations in regard to this medium in terms of new didactic possibilities, many telecommunication projects with schools are mostly dealing with the technical infrastructure. Based on the results and experiences made in the Upper Austrian school-net 'Education Highway' project the following questions will be discussed: What are the wishes and expectations of teachers concerning networks in schools? Do we meet the needs of schools by doing Internet projects with them? What results can we expect if schools are connected to a network? What are the MUSTs which make a network project for schools successful?

Keywords

Telecommunications, distance learning, Internet

1 INTRODUCTION

We are now watching the transformation from the industrial to the information society. Industrial production in the world is rapidly changing. Many jobs in traditional areas are no longer necessary and new jobs are created, especially in the media sector and in media-related businesses.

Capacity Building for IT in Education in Developing Countries
G. Marshall & M. Ruohonen (Eds.)

But it is not only our work which is changing. New media are impacting the daily life of nearly everyone. The entertainment industry offers new techniques every year. Audio-visual media, communication technology and data processing are combined to a hyper-technique which is present all day every day.

Only learning in schools is still functioning nearly the way it did in the last century. Students still have to come to school, listen to the teacher and read the textbooks. The learning of students is still mostly controlled from outside. They cannot choose the place, time or even parts of the content they are taught, especially in vocational training where new methods and media are rarely used. Sometimes the use of new technology is added to traditional methods of teaching and learning, but this is not the revolution which we face in so many other areas. It is an interesting question why school is so resistant to change.

Looking back to the history of the past centuries we see that not every change of a paradigm in technology had great influence on the culture of learning. For example, the invention of the steam engine created a revolution in industry but it had no influence in schools, universities or other training institutions. Other inventions had a great influence on learning and teaching methods. The invention of printing books brought about the reading society of the last century, the invention of TV deleted it. What we see today is that not every technological invention has had a great influence on learning methods but every discontinuity in the media paradigm has made a difference.

Currently the development of the new digital Information and Communication Technology (NICT) is undoubtedly a radical change of the media paradigm. Therefore it will introduce a radical change in education. There are several reasons why we don't see the effects now, even if the technology is present.

The development in school is there, but it is very slow. It needs a critical mass to introduce radical changes in such a traditional system as the school. Even if many teachers are using technology today, it has not affected the overall picture of the school system.

Changes often need pressure from outside to take place. Now there is only little push from society to schools to use NICT. During the first phase of the introduction of a new technology we usually try to use it to solve conventional problems more efficiently. This is done now in schools with NICT and this is not very effective. In the next step a technology is used to solve new questions which have not been seen before.

The effects of networking technology on education will not only help us to solve known problems. Network technology in education will lead us to new challenges. It is my opinion that the effects on school systems of NICT will be evident when we stop integrating them into the established school system and when we are willing to adapt the school system to this new medium.

2 THE EDUCATION HIGHWAY PROJECT IN UPPER AUSTRIA

2.1 History

Our institute has been involved in telecommunication projects for schools since 1989. In the first phase of our project we established a local network for schools. As Austria has one of the highest telephone rates in Europe only schools and teachers of Linz and the surrounding area could take part. The second phase brought Internet connectivity and 50 schools were chosen to be integrated into the test, with student access featured in this phase of the project.

On November 18 1996 the Landeshauptmann (Governor) of our Bundesland (Province) announced phase three of the project - the expansion of the project to all schools in Upper Austria - and the funding was agreed upon. Our institute is responsible for the development of the project, for support to schools and for the provision of content. The technical infrastructure is under the responsibility of three companies.

2.2 Goals of the project

The main goals for us as the developers were defined as following:

- The 'Education Highway' should be a network that links all schools of all types in Upper Austria. Even elementary schools should have access to the network. It should serve administrative as well as educational needs.
- A full and unlimited access to the Internet should be possible.
- A high level of security is necessary, especially for administrative use.
- Not more then 40% of the overall sum of investment should go into technical infrastructure. The rest should be dedicated to fund and support projects and provide for the content of importance to Upper Austrian teachers.
- As teachers in our country spend many of their working hours at home, free access to the 'Education Highway' network from the teachers' homes should be possible.

2.3 Implementation

The 'Education Highway' networks consist of nine Points of Presence (POPs). Teachers can link into the POPs schools either by telephone lines, ISDN or via leased lines. To avoid too much traffic on the net in every POP you will find a proxy server. All POPs are connected to the central services in our institute and to a high band connection to the Austrian School Network (ASN). ASN is a project of the Austrian Ministry of Education and serves local initiatives in the different provinces of Austria as an Internet backbone provider. Figure 1 shows the configuration for the 'Education Highway Upper Austria and the POP-to-teacher/school.

You can consider the 'Education Highway' as a special type of intranet. For example, we are using an internal IP address scheme. The connection to the

Internet runs over a firewall. That allows us to implement special security features as well as to protect schools from content which offends the Austrian laws. We think that it is not possible to react to educational problems with technical solutions and therefore we are very cautious not be seen as a censor for schools. On the other hand many parents and teachers who are afraid that students might be influenced by unsuitable information should see that efforts in this direction are undertaken.

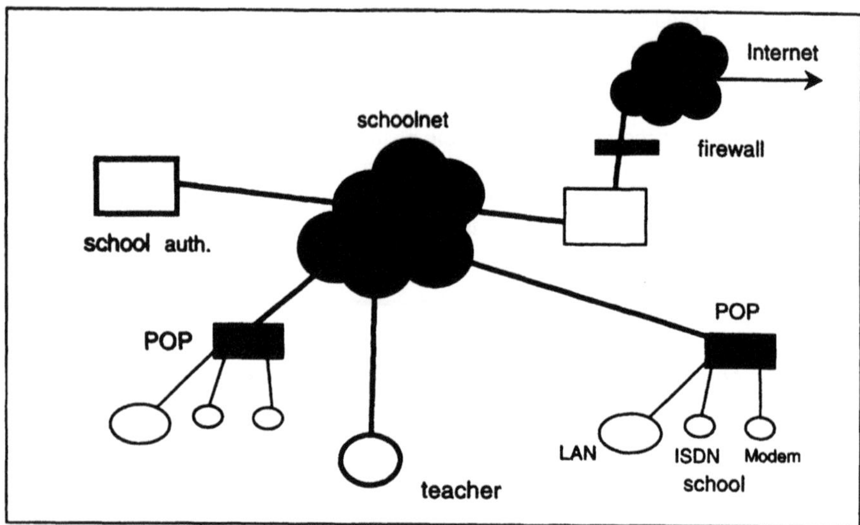

Figure 1 'Education Highway' connections.

3 WISHES AND EXPECTATIONS

3.1 challenges for our educational system

The implementation of a school network is far more then building a technical infrastructure. It is a challenge for the entire school system and therefore it should be measured by the current main goals for education. The goals might differ from country to country and should be adapted to the social and economical situation. For developed countries with a mid-European cultural background I see the following challenges for education (European Commission DGXXII, DGV).

Individualization of learning

The demands of individuals towards school and other educational institutions are much different than former times. Especially vocational training requires a better adaptation to individual needs. The whole education system is moving towards a better support of individual abilities and self-directed learning plays a much bigger role than in the past.

Lifelong learning
The need for lifelong learning in our rapidly changing world requires new strategies which can hardly be done by the traditional learning and teaching methods.

Efficiency of learning
Schools are under the close watch of society because education in every country requires a large portion of the budget. On the other hand, the measurement of success uses more and more the methods used in measuring the economy. We have to be very careful that the economical aspects of the school system will not become the most important factors in evaluation. But facing big restrictions in our budgets we cannot ignore the fact that the efficiency of learning and training is an important issue.

In addition, school as the most important institution for learning in our society now has many competitors. Commercial educational institutions are marketing their services and are willing to use new technologies. Audio- and visual-media show how NICT can be used for learning purposes.

The use of networks in schools can bring about many benefits and can help to meet the challenges posed by external-to-the-school resources.

3.2 Educational benefits

During the work with networks in schools in the last seven years we discovered many possible educational benefits by using network technology. They are include a desire to raise the desire for communication.

Raise the desire for communication
Schools in Austria up to now have had a low level of communication among themselves. Neither cooperation in projects nor communication between teachers to share their experiences has been very common until now. We consider network technology as a vehicle to raise the desire for communication and cooperation.

This might effect communication:

- between schools because schools can use network technology as a medium to carry out common projects. E-mail for communication and web technology for documentation offer new possibilities for cooperation. Trans-national projects often have not been possible up to now;
- between school and society because the easy access to information from outside and the possibility for a school to publish their ideas (*e.g.* via a school web-server) improves the communication between school and society;
- between teachers since our experiences show that readiness for communication between teachers is much higher in an electronic environment than without.

This will effect the efficiency of teaching and improves the quality of education.

The World Wide Web (WWW) is a service which originally was designed to improve the communication between high energy physicists and has become an educational forum for communication and information (Hobbs and Taylor, 1996).

Changes the nature of learning
Network technology introduces a big change in the nature of teaching and learning Schulz-Zander, 1997). Learning and teaching with networks will be more:

- project-oriented;
- problem-oriented;
- activity-oriented;
- open-minded;
- holistic (Weber, 1996).

Therefore the use of ICT in schools can be seen as a vehicle for the professional development of the whole school system, its content and its methodology.

Improves important personal qualifications of students
Many studies conducted around the world show that the use of ICT improves important personal qualifications of students - media competence, ability for problem solving and learning competencies in general. Therefore the use of network technology can be seen as a factor to prevent school failure.

Improves professional qualifications of teachers
The use of ICT has also greatly influences the professional qualifications of teachers. The personally-controlled access to information reduces reliance on textbooks and introduces more self-direction of the teaching process. Sharing of experiences between teachers and the exchange of materials for classroom teaching improves the quality of teaching in general.

Intercultural approach
The exchange of information between schools in different countries is also improved by network technology. Communication is now very quick and this leads to many joint projects done by schools which are far away from each other.

Access to information sources in other countries allows students of different cultures and countries to compare and exchange their opinions on a certain topic. This will lead to a better understanding of different cultures.

Improves the learning of children with special needs
There are many possibilities for how network technology can improve the learning situation for children with special needs. Communication among blind, deaf and dumb students is now possible (Cohen, 1994).

3.3 Organizational benefits

School administration is also expecting great benefits from the implementation of network technology. For example, improvements can be found in communication between school and administration on higher level; more information for headmasters can be easily exchange and data transfer between school and administration is much easier.

4 THE FOUR MUSTS

During our studies in the last two years, since the system was established for 50 schools, we identified four factors which are very important for the success of a school network. We consider them to be mission critical factors - meaning that the absence any one of them can bring failure to the entire project.

4.1 Time and motivation

Time
The design of a school network must include the time factor. There must be time reserved in the curriculum for the integration of network technology. Teachers and students need time to develop their abilities to cope with technical problems. There must be enough time for teacher training which allows teachers to reach a level of competence to master the technical issues and to adapt their teaching methods to the new medium.

Motivation
Many teachers in our project are claiming a lack of motivation to use the network in classroom. There are many reasons. Teachers who don't know the creative potential of ICT are not motivated to use it. Teachers who use ICT often claim that their efforts are not respected.

But there are many sources of motivation which can be identified. On one hand, the teachers themselves can take care of their own motivation and can try to motivate each other by cooperation. On the other hand, headmasters, school-administrators and parents can be a perfect source of motivation. Success stories which tell about successful projects and which are distributed to other teachers are one of the best ways to motivate.

What we need is the readiness of the whole school system to introduce ICT, not only a few volunteers fighting a lonely battle.

4. 2 Instruction and advice

Instruction
The introduction of ICT must be accompanied by in-service and pre-service teacher training. This must cover the following three areas:

- technical instruction must enable the teacher to work with the technical infrastructure provided by the school;
- technical instruction is not enough - teachers need also advice on how the new technologies can help them to make their teaching better, more attractive and more efficient (Van Lück, 1997);
- many teachers become frightened when they realize that the process of using NICTs will lead to a complete change of the role of teacher and learner. Teacher training in NICT, and especially in network technology, must always include help with how to cope with the situation.

Sources of advice
There are different sources of advice. It can come from fellow teachers, advice centers run by the school administration or through teacher training activities. In many cases, it has turned out, students can perfectly act as advisors for their teachers.

Evaluation and research
A culture of documentation and evaluation of projects must be developed, and this will produce success stories which will stand at the beginning of new successful projects.

4.3 Equipment and content

Equipment is necessary but is it not the dominating factor of a network project in schools. The use of a network often requires only technical functions which can be done by IT on a low technical level. Services such as electronic mail or text-based information services can also be used when high-level technology is not available.

For a schoolnet it is necessary to take care of the development and provision of content which is interesting for the target groups of the certain project. We always hear complaints about the USA's domination of the Internet and comments that there is no information in our native language available. At the moment this domination is a fact but in the case of digital networks this effect is not technology- but content-based. That means if we do not find enough information in our language, reflecting our culture and tradition on the web, it is undoubtedly our fault.

And as every country and culture has to take care of an adequate presence on the woldwide network, it is the duty of the school system to provide useful local information for the teachers. As content providers we see the 'Education Highway' as an umbrella project which, at the end, should encourage and support many local initiatives undertaken by schools, teacher training initiatives, companies and other organizations.

4.4 Local network with worldwide connections

The 'Education Highway' is a local network with worldwide connections. We think that 'surfing the web' has only a few pedagogical benefits. On the other hand, a school network without worldwide connections also only of little use (Van Lück, 1997). We face many problems when we offer schools access to a worldwide network and they can only be solved through a cooperation by network provider, school administration, teachers and parents. Among many other problems we see:

- the use of English and other foreign languages excludes a certain percentage of our students from the use of the majority of the existing information sources;
- different cultures and different laws in many countries result in the availability of material which might offend the children;
- technical progress in network technology is very fast and schools have difficulties keeping up with that progress;

- the nature of the Internet does not correspond with the nature of the school system - this causes problems, especially for the use of ICT in school administration.

5 CONCLUSION

Based on the experiences of several years' worth of telecommunication projects for schools I would say that the following recommendations are helpful for the design of a school network:

- Divide your overall budget into three equal parts and spend the same amount of money for technical infrastructure, for content provision - including support for projects - and for training and advice.
- Look for the enrichment of teaching and learning, and not for a substitution of existing methods (Tinsley, 1994).
- Try to show that your ICT activities are meeting the basic needs of the students. In Austria these might be the following questions: 'How can I be better employable?' or 'Does this technology help to solve our global problems?'

And at the end it is necessary to find a new pedagogical vision for schools in the world if schools want to keep their leading role in educating our society.

6 REFERENCES

Cohen, R., Pincemin, J. andTuillier, C. (1994) International communication as means to fight against school failure, in *Telematics in Education: The European Case.* (eds. W. Veem, B. Collis, P. de Vries and F. Vogelzang), Academic Book Centre, De Lier, the Netherlands.

European Commission DG XXII, DG V. (1996) Teaching and learning - Towards the learning society. European Commission DG XXII, DG V. Office for the Official Publications of the European Commission, Brussels, Belgium.

Hobbs, D..J. and Taylor, R.J. (1996) The impact of education of the World Wide Web, in Maurer Hermann, WebNET 96 - Proceedings of the World Conference of the Web Society. Association of the Advancement of Computing in Education, Charlottesville, VA.

Schulz-Zander, R. (1997) Lernen in netzen. *Computer und Unterricht*, **25**, Erhard Friedrich Verlag, Seelze, Germany.

Tinsley, D. (1994) Tele-learning in Secondary Education, in *Guidelines for Good Practice* (ed. T.J. van Weert), IFIP Working Group 3.1, Geneva.

Van Lück, W. (1997) Schulen ans Netz - Warum eigentlich? *Computer und Unterricht*, **25**, Erhard Friedrich Verlag, Seelze, Germany.

Weber, W. (1996) Vorschlag für die pädagogische Konzeption des NRW - Bildungsservers. Landesinstitut für Schule und Weiterbildung, Soest, Germany

7 BIOGRAPHY

After studying Physics and Mathematics at the University of Vienna, Anton J. Knierzinger worked for eight years as a school teacher in Linz. In 1996 he moved to the Paedagogische Akademie der Diocese Linz, where he is now heading the Institute for School and New Technology (IST). The main focus of his work is teacher training, distance learning and the introduction of IT into elementary education. He chairs the International Federation for Information Processing (IFIP) Working Group on IT in Elementary Education, WG 3.5.

PART IV

Classroom-based Initiatives

16

Technology and young children - new strategies to prevent illiteracy and create better chances of success for all

R. Cohen
72, rue de l'Est, 92100 Boulogne, France
Tele and Fax + 33 0148 25 03 19

Abstract
Research, both in France and in other countries, highlights the importance of the first years of life and the immense potential of young children. Educational policies need to recognize the importance of education from a very early age in order to eradicate illiteracy and allow better chances of success for all children. Young children, below age 6, can and do take pleasure in acquiring the written language if adequate conditions for learning are provided. New horizons have now opened up with the use of Information Technology and empowering results have been obtained in classes where children use computers for the simultaneous acquisition of both the oral and written language. This paper will focus on the new strategies used to implement such an educational policy - a policy of success for all should start in preschool!

Keywords
Capacity building, elementary education, equity issues, innovation, literacy

1 INTRODUCTION

In all countries, whether in the developed or developing world, educational policy-makers are faced with a major issue - how to create better chances of success for all children. It is essential to overcome the problem of illiteracy and school failure. Many solutions have been tried more or less successfully. Now two main research trends have opened new horizons: the importance of the first years of life and the breakthrough of technology.

Capacity Building for IT in Education in Developing Countries
G. Marshall & M. Ruohonen (Eds.)

Let us focus first on the following questions: why is early education important? Is a young child able to discover written language? Is a young child able to use a computer, not only for play but for learning?

2 THREE KEY PRELIMINARY QUESTIONS

2.1 Why is early education important?

Current theories say that young children have immense potential and that their learning abilities are far greater than was believed a few years ago. But in order to develop innate talents and potential, young children need a very rich environment, stimulating experiences and appropriate motivational encouragement. B. Bloom (1964), an American psychologist, speaks of 'exceptional levels of talents (that) require certain types of environmental support'. The same belief in the power of early learning is expressed by A. Jacquard (1978), a French geneticist who believes 'every child is a potential superman: what I am, I am by virtue of heritage: what I become depends on what I do with it'. Neurobiologists indicate that, in order to function, the neurological system has to receive optimal stimulation. Intelligence develops in interaction with the environment.

Therefore it is necessary to recognize the cognitive needs of young children, their wishes and their potential to learn. All children must be provided with a very rich and stimulating environment so that they may interact, explore and thus 'construct' their knowledge. Teachers must be careful not to merely 'teach' but to create conditions so that the child is able to learn for, according to Rogers (1969) 'the more the adult teaches the less the child learns'.

2.2 Is a young child able to discover written language?

It is no longer a question if a child should or should not, can or cannot, read before age 6. Research in many different countries has demonstrated that very young children enjoy discovering and using the written language (Cohen, 1977, 1982, Cohen and Gilabert, 1986). The problem is 'how' young children learn to read. Teachers using traditional methods often meet with little success with a number of students in spite of their efforts, professional skills and personal qualities.

The problem is a methodological one - not 'to teach reading' but to let the child discover the written language as s/he has discovered the oral language, in a natural way. In countries which have a long oral tradition of oral literacy, oral and written expression can thus be developed simultaneously.

It is not my purpose to develop the methodology of reading in this discussion but to explain that when we speak of written language we assume that it implies receiving messages (reading) and sending messages (writing). What has long prevented the acceptance that young children before age 6 are able to use the written language is the confusion between reading and writing capabilities. Of course, young children are not able to write readable messages because they lack motor coordination. But they love telling stories; their imaginations are active. They draw and scribble. But they are also ABLE to read, which means receive messages from the outside world! What if a special device should allow children to send messages in such a way that they are not hindered in their ability to express themselves and be read by others?

2.3. Is the young child able to use a computer not only for play but for learning?

Information Technology has been responsible for a breakthrough in the world of young children, particularly in the area of reading. International research has shown that, whatever the country, the language of instruction or the social environment, the use of new technologies by young children has brought about important changes in our perception of learning theories, of the process of acquisition of the written language and the development of capabilities considered unusual at such an early age. Bringing learning theories into question is a real challenge but preventing illiteracy, school failure and giving an equal chance to all children is an even greater challenge. This is what research into the use of IT for young children is all about.

Over the last ten or fifteen years, international research has demonstrated that young children are not only able to use a computer in play activities but also for working purposes (Cohen, 1987; 1992; 1993). One can argue that spending time and money to equip preschools and train teachers is not a priority, particularly in developing countries where emphasis should first be given to high schools. Research has shown that using computers allows young children not only to acquire fundamental knowledge for their future such as reading and writing but also develops mental abilities and basic skills which will transfer in other fields of activities thus preventing failures. Furthermore, being computer literate is easy for youngsters and allows them better school performances in the next years of their schooling. Thus spending time and money on young children means gaining time and money later.

The main questions are now: How should IT be used in a classroom for young children? What learning situations are likely to enhance creative and autonomous learning? What kind of new opportunities should we offer children? What is the role of the teacher ?

3 COMPUTERS IN THE CLASSROOM

It is clear that introducing IT to young children brings about important changes, not only in the type of materials offered to the children but also in the way these materials are used in a creative way. Traditional ways of teaching cannot fit into the new learning situations which integrate text, images, movement and voice, and which promote the autonomous search for information and communication with other children all over the world. Teachers must be prepared to face real changes in their role and must understand how much more effective learning is in the new conditions. It is as much a challenge for them as it is for the children.

Two excellent books (Downes and Fatouros, 1995; Casey, 1997) give a broad picture of new opportunities, areas and means for learning. They give precious practical advice for the use of IT in elementary classrooms. Casey shows the magnitude of the problem when she quotes Negroponte (1995): ‘Computing is not about computers anymore. It is about living. Schools will change to become more like the museums and playgrounds for children to assemble ideas and socialize with other children all over the world'.

It will not be easy to make drastic shifts in our educational systems and it is not the scope of this discussion to suggest how those shifts might occur. Nor can we give detailed practical advice, list the necessary equipment or suggest specific software programs that may be used. Instead, let's focus on using computers in preschools and elementary classes as we have experienced it over the years.

3.1. Organizing the environment

Even if teachers do not have high tech equipment or many computers, excellent work can be achieved all the same. Even one computer in the classroom, if used wisely, can make a major difference if considered as one among other opportunities to learn, albeit a valuable and selected one because of its high potential for motivating children to communicate. The 'computer corner' is one corner among the others - the painting corner, block corner, book corner and other spaces for enquiry - which children can choose freely, all during the day. Activities using the computer are integrated with other classroom activities and organized around a common topic or center of interest. In no way must we drive very young children to drill and practice activities nor drag them to a computer lab on a certain day and at a certain hour. Equipment should be available at all times if creativity is to be encouraged.

The classroom organization - and particularly the computer corner - should allow for independent and autonomous work as well as for group work and cooperative learning, which even young children are capable of assuming by themselves. Charts explaining the work to be done and rules to observe in the computer corner can be pinned on the wall. Children develop their own methods of work, share their experiences and become more and more efficient as a variety of settings are provided for them. Interactions between children - made easy around a computer because children can cooperate with one another as they work - enhances effective learning. The cooperative learning environment encourages self-learning and self-organization as well as self-esteem. In fact, a child should never face failure. Good software allows self-correction and the use of the delete key, and group learning will give all children opportunities to avoid and/or correct mistakes, thus leading them to successful results.

Thus the way the computer corner is organized as well as the materials offered should allow open exploration, experimentation and creativity (Vygotsky, 1978). Never should the teacher decide beforehand what the children are capable of doing, what they should learn, or when and how they should learn. Teachers should not set limits but open spaces in the classroom for the development of higher psychological processes (Papert, 1980). Who would have believed that young children were capable of using a keyboard at the age of three? Our findings, as well as others' research shows that this is not only possible but benefits their mental and social development (Lawler, 1985).

Let us take an example. The children, aged 4 and 5, went to visit the zoo this morning. On their return, they speak about their visit and the teacher writes down their sentences. They draw, paint the animals they saw and learn about each of them, finding information in dictionaries, books, films but also using the World Wide Web when the class is equipped for the Internet. They listen to stories such as the *Jungle Book* or *The Lion King*, or other stories and folk tales. But they can also, on the computer, draw and write about their visit or their individual stories. How to achieve this when one is 4 or 5 years old? Even if they do not know the alphabet yet our experience has shown that they can copy the sentences the teacher has taken down on a sheet of paper. Gradually they will learn the names of the letters and learn at the same time the spelling of the words. In doing this, they can help each other if they work in groups and/or copy what the teacher has written if their expertise in writing is not enough developed yet. Then they can print what they have written and thus make their own reading books.

A very important feature of children's computer use is that information is gathered in various forms - not only written information but also pictures and sound when available in the IT environment. The same is true of the different means the children will choose to express themselves. They should all have equal opportunities to use their talents so mastery is no longer in the hands of those who write well.

Information can also be obtained from different sources; some are remote but can still be reached easily. Hypertext reading is understood by young children and is great fun for them. They can also share their experiences with other friends all over the world by using network and telecommunications, which enhances curiosity for other countries and international understanding.

3.2 Organizing time

If space is to be organized, so must time. Children are so enthusiastic when they use computers that they tend to stay at the computer for long periods, forgetting that others are eager to have access. Individuals and/or groups of two or three children should be able to take turns. Even then, independent and self pacing activities should be organized by using a timer or some other strategy. In fact, as work develops, children's attention spans and concentration increases, and so does the speed of the learning process. We have observed children under 5 staying more than 45 minutes at the computer!

3.3 Work and play

When children are happy and take pleasure in what they are doing, when they concentrate and are attentive, is that play or work? In such situations the line between play and work is difficult to establish. What is certain is that if all activities are presented in a playful manner children will not show reluctance, especially if they are allowed to share their work with friends. Laughter and constant exchanges around the computer centre prove that this is a happy experience for the children, a major condition for stimulation and learning.

3.4 The role of the teacher

In self-learning situations the role of the teacher must change. His/her role is no longer to teach a class but to organize an environment where children can learn. The teacher provides the learning materials, organizes space and time, and sets out the storage spaces and rules in the classroom. He/she becomes a guide, a partner, a friend. Changes in the teacher's role do not mean the teacher loses authority. On the contrary, the teacher grows in the esteem of the children as he/she shares power with them. Thus the relationship with the students changes for it is they who have become the main actors in building up their knowledge.

The relationship with other colleagues also changes as teachers must cooperate. In many cases exchanges between different classes will take place as grouping by activities will replace grouping by age. The children might also go to different classrooms according to the different activities in which they are involved. Flexibility of time, space and grouping are useful rules to be observed.

4 USING COMPUTERS FOR THE ACQUISITION OF WRITTEN LANGUAGE

Now let us focus on the written language and ask ourselves what contributions and changes the use of computers bring about in the acquisition of written language by young children. If I use the words 'written language' in place of 'reading' and 'writing', it is because the terms highlight the idea that written language is a communication process and the computer offers young children very specific opportunities in this respect. First of all, their productions are neat, clear and readable by everyone. The children can correct their work but the text always looks 'pretty'. It can be printed and sent to others. Children do not read or write for their teachers but for themselves.

Computers lead children to important self discoveries in the use of written language - first, the direction and spatial structure of the writing becomes clear as the screen is filled from left to right, at least for languages such as French, English or German. Second, the use of spaces allows children to understand what a word is, and then the use of the letters on the keyboard, which allows them to learn the letters. In short, the written language is, from the very beginning, accessible to young children who are no longer prisoners of their motor skills and capabilities. Writing becomes very early a mode of self expression and communication.

Voice output is of special importance (Cohen, 1992; 1993). Some software programs allow children to listen to each letter or word they type. They can also listen to the whole text if they wish. In the case of 'speaking' software such as CD-ROMs, the story, text or pictures become self-explanatory. The children build their own stories by clicking on different objects, the story is written as the action appears on the screen and if they are unable to read the story, they can click on the difficult words and hear them.

The use of voice output enhances children's awareness of language and increases the speed of language acquisition. It encourages self -learning and acts permanently as positive feedback. More importantly, the voice output makes a fundamental contribution to foreign language learning and gives young children access simultaneously to the oral and written features of a second language. Here we raise a problem that, in classical education, has been approached quite differently and in so doing we are upsetting firmly-rooted beliefs. It is generally believed that young children should first learn to speak a foreign language before they learn how to write and read it. In our experience, many of our young children were nonfrancophone. For them French was a foreign language. But using a computer equipped with a voice synthesizer made them acquire both oral and written French simultaneously and without difficulty before age 6.

5 CONCLUSION

The joy and enthusiasm observed in computer-based activities leads us to think that computers may be a very 'good thing' for young children and that the written language can be acquired just as easily as the oral language without tedious repetitions or predefined progression. In our experience, children using computers have increased their language abilities and have become interested in sentences, spelling and punctuation much earlier than what is generally considered as 'usual'.

The pleasure of the children proves that what we are really providing is a response to a deep need of the child - learning - allowing for the development of many different kinds of personal strategies and creativity. Children will master the written language as they have mastered the oral language, by using it. What was considered difficult for children is within their reach! More than knowledge, what we are promoting is children's personal development to help them achieve all their inner capabilities and talents.

The results of international research in the field of computers and IT use by young children challenge what we thought were accepted theories of learning. More importantly, they open up new outlooks for all children, demonstrating that young children can acquire the written language at an early age in a constructive and fruitful way.

To equip high schools with IT is a good thing; to equip preschools and elementary classes is essential. But hardware and proper software are not sufficient. It is not easy to implement a policy of providing very young children with IT. Training of teachers, initially and then as continuous process, is basic to their successful understanding of their changing role and responsibilities. Knowing how to use the equipment is not enough. Teachers should be prepared to change their ways in a classroom. Not only should they be followed by a computer specialist during the first months to help them solving practical problems but group work should be organized among the teachers - exchange of experiences, documents and solving problems together. This practice has proved to be very beneficial and is essential to implement, promote and maintain such projects.

The new approach to education concerns all actors involved in the educational process - policy makers, educationalists, head of schools, counselors, teachers and parents. The goal is crucial and is the basis of a policy promoting equity among all children, creating for each of them better chances of success.

6 REFERENCES

Bloom, B. (1964) *Stability and Change in Human Characteristics*. John Wiley & Son, New York.
Casey, J.M. (1997) *EarlyLiteracy: The Empowerment of Technology*. Teacher Ideas Press, Englewood, Colorado.
Cohen, R. (1st ed. 1977; 5th ed. 1992) *l'Apprentissage Precoce de la Lecture, a Six Ans Est-il Deja Trop Tard*? Presses Universitaires de France, Paris. Translated into Spanish ,Italian, Portuguese, Bulgarian and Greek.
Cohen, R. (1st ed. 1982, 2nd ed. 1986) *Plaidoyer pour les Apprentissages Precoces*. Presses Universitaires de France, Paris. Translated into Italian and Spanish.
Cohen, R. and Gilabert, H. (1st ed. 1986, 2nd ed. 1988) *Decouverte et Apprentissage du Langage Ecrit Avant Six Ans*. Presses Universitaires de France, Paris. Translated into Spanish and Portuguese.
Cohen, R. (ed.) (1987) *Les Jeunes Enfants, la Decouverte de l'Ecrit et l'Ordinateur*. Presses Universitaires de France, Paris.
Cohen, R. (ed.) (1992) *Quand l'Ordinateur Parle*. Presses Universitaires de France, Paris.
Cohen R. (1993) The use of voice synthesizer in the discovery of the written language by very young children. *Computers in Education,* **21**(1/2), 25-30.
Downes, T. and Fatouros, C. (1995) *Learning in an Electronic World*. Primary English Teaching Association, Newton, Australia.
Jacquard, A. (1978) *Eloge de la Difference*. Seuil, Paris.
Lawler, R.W. (1985) *Computer Experience and Cognitive Development : A Child's Learning in a Computer Culture*. Chichester, Ellis Horwood, Ltd.
Negroponts, N. (1995) *Being Digital*. New York, Random House.
Papert, S. (1980) *Mindstorms: Computers and Powerful Ideas*. Basic Books Inc., New York.
Rogers, C.R. (1969) *Freedom to Learn*. Charles E. Merrill Publishing Co, London.
Vygotsky, L.S. (1978) *Mind in Society*. (eds. Cole , M., John-Steiner, V., Scriber, S., Souberman, E.) Harvard University Press, Cambridge, MA.

7 BIOGRAPHY

In spite of an MA in Philosophy and Psychology, Rachel Cohen started her career as a kindergarten teacher because of her great interest in early childhood education and strong belief in young children's potential. A full-time researcher at University Paris Nord, she explored the influence of early learning on children's development as means to prevent school failure and illiteracy. Her research includes the study of early reading, multilingualism, international education and the use of new technologies in education - both with young children using computers and adolescents using telecommunications.

She is the co-founder and first president of the European Institute for the Development of All Children's Potential (IEDPE), created in Paris, France in 1989.

17

Designing Logo-based microworlds for effective learning - a road to improving teacher education

Márta Turcsányi-Szabó
Loránd Eötvös University
Department of General Computer Science
1088 Budapest, Múzeum krt. 6-8.
Hungary
Tele/Fax: + 36-1 266 - 5196
E-mail: turcsanyine@ludens.elte.hu

Abstract

A discussion of Hungary's choice of Comenius Logo© also provides the framework for clarifying the role of computers in education. Methods for getting acquainted with Comenius Logo's programming environment and designing educational microworlds are examined. The benefits of Logo as a means of introducing computers to children and the use of Logo as a means of preparing teachers for their mission of achieving enhanced computer use in schools provide issues for developing countries to discuss.

Keywords

Constructionism, software, Logo, teacher education

1 INTRODUCTION

The Eötvös Loránd University, the largest university in Hungary, trains teachers in the field of informatics and prepares all teachers for the use of Information and Communication Technology (ICT) in education. Our educational policy, which has been oriented toward programming, is now shifting to use of ICT in subject

Capacity Building for IT in Education in Developing Countries
G. Marshall & M. Ruohonen (Eds.)

areas and moving towards the use of ICT across the curriculum - a move away from an emphasis on the learning of the technology and computer science itself. Students graduating from our university mainly teach at the secondary school level and, due to the reorganisation of many schools, also at the elementary level. So our teachers should be able to think about the overall role of education.

The university's undergraduate and in-service programs provide a strong basic computer science curriculum in:

- operating systems, application systems, and the design, installation and operation of networks;
- computer science subjects and programming in several languages with PASCAL as the main principal language;
- a strong foundation in mathematics.

Even though students take courses in pedagogy and psychology, the emphasis on computer science and mathematics is greater than the emphasis on pedagogy, and determines their approach to informatics for school use.

The long-term educational practice in Hungary has mainly been instructionism, with very few exceptions over the past few years. Today's teachers have experienced instructionist learning practices and so rely on the model for their own teaching. This is especially true for in-service teachers, who have adopted the method as a result of decades of educational requirements.

Considering the past experiences of teachers, it is not surprising that their vision of computers in education has two focal points:

- teaching the subject of computer science and all related topics;
- using computers with computer-assisted Instruction (CAI).

In developing countries the existence of any computers is much appreciated, even if the quality is low, and many different types of computers must be used in a single school setting. Under such circumstances standardisation can not be achieved and curriculum guidelines mainly start out from 'the computer' and what we can do with it, and not 'the pedagogy' and what we need to achieve through it. The moment the emphasis is allowed, by circumstances, to be shifted to pedagogy and its requirements, a basic question arises: 'For what reason do we intend to introduce computers into the educational process?' Seymour Paper gave an answer through constructionalism: 'The kind of knowledge children most need is the knowledge that will help them get more knowledge' (Papert, 1993).

2 FROM INSTRUCTIONISM TO CONSTRUCTIONISM

Instructionism focuses on the teacher and her/his improvement of instruction, while constructionism focuses on the learner and on improved ways to construct knowledge. Instructionism is a passive process in which the learner absorbs knowledge while constructionism is an active process in which the learner constructs knowledge. Constructionism is based in part on Jean Piaget's theories.

Teachers find it easier to just follow the guidelines of the curriculum by directly instructing using the required materials and then investigating the amount of learning acquired by students. They are reluctant to introduce open-ended activities. Lack of experience in dealing with open-ended learning activities and assessing possible outcomes also plays a role in teachers' hesitance to move to constructionist activities. Both tools and methods have to be shown to them and long-term engagement in the activities is needed for teachers to realise for themselves the value of learning that takes place during constructionist learning experiences.

2.1 Courses developed

In an attempt to change from an instructionist to a constructionist view of computers in education, several courses have been modified and new courses have been introduced at Eötvös Loránd University so that teachers can work directly with the concepts and actions required when teaching in a constructivist setting.

Application systems
This two semester course in the first year shifts the emphasis from the technical point of view to the user's perspectives, needs and goals; shifts the emphasis to the problem to be solved and the proper tool for solving the problem.

Informatics curriculum
This one semester course in the third year guides future teachers to develop an overall curriculum for teaching informatics; the emphasis is gradually shifting to the use of ICT in subject areas.

Computer modeling in mathematics
This block elective one semester course in third year demonstrates the use of programming languages in the acquisition of mathematical topics; the emphasis is on the need for students to construct models in order to understand the underlying theory.

Investigation of educational software
This block elective one semester course in the fourth year examines and analyses educational software for understanding its real values, asks whether it provides any benefit when used and if the method of application enhances the learning process. The approach is an expensive way to use computers in Hungary, since few schools have adequate financial resources for this type of computer use.

Computers in education
This block elective one semester course in the fourth year examines the National Curriculum and concentrates on topics other than informatics to analyse the educational benefit of the use of computers in the learning process. Research from other countries is analysed, K - 12 Web pages are investigated, and applications such as *Word* and *Excel* are studied for their potential to contribute to language and science education. Educational microworlds developed provide an economical way to develop tools and exploit software already available in schools.

Comenius Logo
This block elective one semester course in the fourth year uses the special environment of Comenius Logo as student teachers experience a Logo course in ways they can transfer to a school setting.

Designing educational microworlds
This block elective one semester course in the fourth year presents the advanced features of Comenius Logo. The design principles for educational environments are investigated and explored in individual projects.

These courses emphasize the changing view from 'teaching about computers' to 'teaching with computers'. On the other hand, they show examples of environments suitable for constructive activities in subject areas. Introducing the environments in education provides a variety of tools which enable students and teachers to solve problems the best possible way. The young generation has to be brought up conscious of their possibilities to produce a workforce that is open to environments and is able to function with the best available tools in hand.

2.2 Why Logo?

Teaching future teachers the educational use of computers can sometimes be a demanding job. After many years of studying PASCAL, programming methodology, data structures and other topics it is difficult for them to understand why they are not going to teach 'pure' computer science in ordinary schools. It is even more difficult to explain why they should teach Logo. Due to the scientific approach to computers and programming that has characterized IT's introduction to many schools, the Logo language has not been taken seriously. It has been considered a toy or, at most, the first programming language children should learn in order to get a brief introduction to programming. Teachers often say, 'I would introduce smaller children to Logo to let them believe they were programming'. 'But they are,' would be my answer, not taken too seriously by teachers.

To complicate the situation, fancy multimedia software obscures the necessity of teaching any kind of programming language. Creating educational software is better accomplished by multimedia authoring tools. Custom-tailored educational software has its own attractive appeal together with its limitations. Only an authoring tool can provide the flexibility of environment extension and the ease with which it can be done guarantees the possibility that the extensions can be made by the learners themselves.

Why Logo then? Logo is an easy-to-use, user-friendly environment developed especially for children. Moreover, some varieties are sophisticated enough to be used as an authoring tool. Authoring a project by students themselves permits trial and error in construction to attain an understanding of how things work within a system.

The approach of teaching Logo should involve direct strategies of problem solving in programming and the transfer of these skills to other subject-oriented problem situations. Investigations have reported positive results both concerning the development of thinking skills using Logo-learning environments as well as in the transfer of these skills into other subject domains (Clements, 1990; Swan, 1991; DeCorte, 1993)

3 THE COMENIUS LOGO ENVIRONMENT

3.1 Custom-tailored software vs. the Logo environment

Many computer games intend to convey knowledge about a specific theme and let students grasp important ideas without 'studying' but at the same time learning. By using Logo to produce educational games, the extension of a preprogrammed microworld becomes easier. Comenius Logo (© A. Blaho, I. Kalas, P. Tomcsanyi, Comenius University, Bratislava, 1994) is an easy programming language as well as a sophisticated authoring tool. So it has the most important properties for a good modeling tool - from simple drawing structures to complex problems of decentralised systems. It is easy enough to master without distracting attention from the problem itself and it has the power to act as a building block for constructing additional complexity. In addition the user-friendly environment provides effective tools to attain fast results.

'Hide and seek' in Comenius Logo

Logo allows children to create associations between words in several domains— such as 'square', 'jump' or 'flower' - and their meaning. The process of creation is in itself enlightening. After successfully using, and properly testing, a user-defined word it can be hidden to behave as any other predefined primitive. However the word must be defined properly - no more or less than needed, just exactly what the word means.

Every word (procedure) must contain a concise description of its function as general as possible. Then creating new words using previous primitives produces hierarchical structures of complexity, which can still be easily surveyed. The possibility of hiding and, if needed, seeking hidden words for understanding or modification allows the creation of models, which give us insights to the 'backstage' - how the program works. Predefined modules can be developed, exchanged and built in to enhance emerging systems, thus becoming expandable. (Turcsányi-Szabó, 1996) Microworlds containing words that are meaningful in subject areas *e.g.* 'speed', 'kick', 'bounce', 'temperature' and other words can be predefined, built-in yet hidden to function as normal primitives, expanding the original set of commands.

4 NATIONALISATION OF COMENIUS LOGO

4.1 Introducing Comenius Logo to Hungary and other countries

Realising the educational potential of Comenius Logo, the Hungarian Ministry of Education has financially supported the nationalisation of Comenius Logo in Hungary and also supported teachers as they learn to exploit it in the learning process. From March 1997 all schools are able to buy Comenius Logo for a favourable price that includes teacher education. Teachers are interested in Comenius Logo since our National Curriculum, issued in Fall 1995, clearly emphasises the educational use of ICT environments for benefit of learning and enhancing means of communication (Turcsányi-Szabó, 1997). With the emergence of compulsory informatics requirements and little time to fulfill those requirements, Logo's significant contribution to achieving curriculum goals increased. It also helped that teachers saw their students' motivation increase as they developed projects with Comenius Logo.

The Hungarian National Curriculum motivates teachers and researchers to develop environments and learning material to accomplish curriculum goals. Comenius Logo contributes because it can be used with young children while, at the same time, it enables older children, teachers and developers to produce sophisticated learning environments.

Comenius Logo has been introduced into many countries (Austria, Belgium, Brazil, Bulgaria. Czech Republic, Netherlands, Germany, Greece, Hungary, Poland, Portugal, Switzerland and the UK), producing a local version with the translation of the environment and the commands into each country's own language. Yet the environment leaves a common English command set for all versions to use as a choice. This allows a common platform for exchange of programs as a cross-cultural benefit. Comenius Logo is spreading worldwide and so has the potential of a common (yet nationalised) language for communication among children that breaks down boundaries and builds closer ties from one nation to another. The exchange of children's work can also bring teachers closer together as they compare educational strategies.

4.2 Teaching Comenius Logo to pre-service teachers

The Logo course was developed to be implemented as it would be in an elementary or secondary school classroom:

- toys and games prepared with Logo are introduced while teachers investigate their educational potential;
- Comenius Logo environment is explored as well as how commands can be introduced visually;
- bewildering animation programs are examined to show how amazingly few and easily understood commands make them work;
- little games are modified so users can realise the potential for control over the programs;
- new procedures - adding a new word to the vocabulary - deepen involvement with the programs and increase understanding of the functions of routines;
- variables are introduced to develop frequently used words;
- visual problem solving is encouraged, as discussed by Turcsányi-Szabó, and Senftleben, 1986;
- creating interactive animation occurs;
- conditional functions are introduced;
- music is created through a music add-on and recorded wave files;
- animated variables are introduced to explore the effect of change in inputs;
- functions are investigated;

- Cartesian and polar coordinates are explored in addition to Turtle Geometry and vector geometry;
- word games and text modeling are created, as discussed byTurcsányi-Szabó, and Senftleben, 1986;

Topics are investigated one at a time so teachers can create motivating problems for children that can be solved using few easy commands. Possible extensions are investigated to challenge fast-paced students or those in higher-level classes. The main motto of the course is 'Let's create games' while all the programming topics mentioned in the National Curriculum are covered at the same time subject areas such as music, visual arts, language, and mathematics are integrated into computer use. Computer-aided modeling has to be preceded by real-life experimentation and observation in order to understand behaviour and record properties. Modeling builds on the knowledge acquired and can be used as building blocks for more complex experiments in a safe environment provided that 'hands on' activities allow 'heads in' recasting experiments with 'play back' possibilities (Ackermann, 1993). The abstract knowledge attained by such experiments provides the basics for real- time constructions.

5 THE BENEFIT OF COURSES SHOWING HOW CHILDREN CAN USE COMPUTERS

5.1 Understanding that the point of interest is the child

The benefit of computers to children does not come by learning sophisticated topics of computer science, but by letting teachers understand the tools and how they can make use of them in their own world. My favourite appeal to student teachers is, 'Don't just notice the computers in class but the children who sit in front of them'.

5.2 Understanding the educational value of programs and necessity of computer use

The use of computers is not a must in any case. The value of a computer program should be thought of by investigating whether it contains virtues that could not be otherwise achieved. In other words apply the slogan, 'If something can be done as effectively, without the computer, then do it without a computer', which applies to a basic idea in the creation of educational software: programs should exploit the significant characteristics of computer power thus enhancing the form of educational environment created to be unique in this respect.

5. 3 The difference between using a tool and a procedural programming language

It is of vital importance to realise the difference between using a tool and a procedural programming language for modeling - one focuses on the end result while the other emphasises the process itself. The process of solving a problem - modeling a theory - is the process of learning how to do or learn something.

5.4 The motivation of creating a game

Children like to play all sorts of computer games and, after getting bored with the games, their dream is to be able to author their own games. Comenius Logo is a good environment for that type of authoring and, at the same time, children learn the compulsory topics in informatics.

5.5 Integration with subject areas

Learning to program should not be a final aim in itself. Problem-solving skills should be identified and transferred into subject content areas. Projects to be tackled should be motivating, deal with topics close to the children's world and benefit overall education.

5.6 Experiences of students

Future informatics teachers were highly motivated when they produced microworlds relating to other subjects. Developing microworlds was easy to do and the teachers found they could easily let their own students experiment and create models. Comenius Logo proved to be a highly sophisticated authoring tool in the production of environments for modeling, while many of its features could be well used in the experimenting process itself.

5.7 Cheap educational environment

Microworlds created with such authoring tools are easily developed and do not have a high cost effect like the purchase of constantly upgradable official educational software.

6 CONCLUSION

Hungary's future teachers are offered several courses on the educational use of ICT, the role of Comenius Logo in the learning process and strategies for designing educational microworlds. The use of Comenius Logo and the constructionist approach to learning is gaining ground and, although teachers might be reluctant to use such open ended strategies in their teaching, the existence of Comenius Logo and similar tools motivates teachers by motivating the children. The easy-to-use authoring environments help children develop their own ideas, and encourage teachers to observe children and help them as they work. By better understanding the learning process through observation of children at work in Logo environments informatics teachers can judge more realistically the value of educational software and can help their schools develop computer-based activities that enhance the learning process.

7 REFERENCES

Ackermann, E. (1993) Tools for Constructive Learning: Rethinking Interactivity. MIT Media Lab, E&L Memo No. 15.

Clements, D.H. (1990) Metacomponential development in a Logo programming environment. *Journal of Educational Psychology*, **82**.

De Corte, E. (1993) Towards Embedding Enriched Logo-Based Learning Environments in the School Curriculum: Retrospect and Prospect, in (eds. P. Georgiadis, G. Gyftodimos, Y. Kotsanis, C. Kunigos), Proceedings of the Fourth European Logo Conference, Doukas School S.A., Athens, Greece, August 28-31, 1993).

Papert, S. (1993) *The Children's Machine*. Basic Books, New York.

Swan, K. (1991) 'Knowing what': Declarative knowledge and the cross-contextual transfer of problem-solving skills, in (ed. E. Calabrese), Proceedings of the Third European Logo Conference, A.S.I.-Parma, Parma, Italy, August 27-30, 1991.

Turcsányi-Szabó, M. and Senftleben, D. (1986) The LOGO Programming Language. *Mûszaki Kiadó*, Budapest, Hungary.

Turcsányi-Szabó, M. (1993) Where to place LOGO in teacher training. in (ed. P. Georgiadis, G. Gyftodimos, Y. Kotsanis and C. Kunigos) Proceedings of the Fourth European Logo Conference, Doukas School S.A., Athens, Greece, August 28-31, 1993.

Turcsányi-Szabó, M. (1996) Learning through modeling with Comenius LOGO, in (eds. P. Bakonyi and M. Herdon), Proceedings of Informatics in Higher Education '96. Networkshop '96 Conference, Debreceni Universitas, Debrecen, Hungary, August 27-30, 1996.

Turcsányi-Szabó, M. (1997) Present role of informatics teachers in view of applications, in *Information Technology: Supporting Change through Teacher Education* (eds. D Passey and B. Samways), Chapman & Hall, London.

8 BIOGRAPHY

Márta Turcsányi-Szabó received B.S. and M.S. degrees in computer science from Eötvös Loránd University (ELTE) and started working on research at ELTE before graduating in 1979. Since then she has continued her work as an assistant professor, teaching teachers of informatics. She has been devoted to Logo since 1982, and has written several educational materials and programs on the subject. Her present research includes the study of application systems, the educational use of computers and the design of educational programs.

PART V

Research for IT-based Education

18

The needs and challenges of Information Systems education - the case of Nigerian Universities

Mikko Ruohonen
Associate Professor
University of Vaasa and Turku School of Economics and Business Administration
P. O. Box 110
FIN-20521 Turku, Finland
E-mail: mikko.ruohonen@abo.fi;

Olayele Adelakun
Turku Centre for Computer Science and Turku School of Economics and Business Administration
P. O. Box 110
FIN-20521, Turku, Finland
E-mail: olayele.adelakun@tukkk.fi

Abstract

Inadequate human resource capacity for IT development militates against effective IT adoption and utilisation in developing countries. Educational institutions play key roles in providing intellectual resources for society. Many of the organisational, management and development issues which are included in Information Systems (IS) education are not represented in the curricula of higher education institutions in developing countries. Our study examines the Nigerian perspective as one representative example of African IS university education, and examines the level and quality of IS education in Nigerian federal universities as well as the curriculum development challenges.

Capacity Building for IT in Education in Developing Countries
G. Marshall & M. Ruohonen (Eds.)

Keywords
Capacity building, curriculum development, higher education, informatics

1 INTRODUCTION

African countries need to plan sustainability of donor-funded IT projects. They also need to ensure that IT adoption and use should not only be geared to IT procurement but also to capacity building in IT, *i.e.*, indigenous IT industry and human resource development. In addition, research which supports the development of Information Systems that address the distinctive needs of developing countries needs to be addressed (Moyo, 1996). The design, use and management of IT need a carefully-planned educational infrastructure which should reflect the needs and opportunities of each developing country. Both the evaluation and development of IT/IS education curriculum towards more organisationally- and nationally-driven IT/IS courses and programs are needed.

Our study suggests that organisations will demand a cadre of IS professionals with knowledge and skills in technology, business operations, management and interpersonal skills to effectively lead organisational integration and process reengineering activities. Unfortunately, most universities in Africa do not educate students towards this kind of knowledge. There is a lot of effort put into computer science and other technically-oriented aspects of computer science - computer engineering for example, but little effort is put into the field of IS.

Lee, Trauth and Farwell (1995) noted recently that most of the lower-level IS jobs are rapidly disappearing and the requirements for IS professionals are becoming more demanding in multiple dimensions, particularly in the areas of business functional knowledge and interpersonal/management skills. They concluded that 'IS activities in organisations will require corresponding restructuring of IS curricula at universities'. Nigerian universities offering computer science degrees have been placing an emphasis on technically-oriented courses and mathematics.

Our objective is to investigate how much effort is put into the discipline of Information Systems in Nigerian universities, and find out if degrees in computer science or other closely-related disciplines have a minor in IS. The key research questions posed are: (1) What is the level and quality of IS education in Nigerian federal universities? and (2) What are the curriculum development challenges facing those universities?

Nigeria is the unit of analysis and one of its university computer science curricula (University of Lagos) will be used as a comparison with the well-accepted reference model IS '97 curriculum recommendations (Davis, Gorgone, Couger, Feinstein and Longnecker, 1997). We will also discuss our experiences with other Nigerian universities in the field of computer science or IS education. In addition, special characteristics of Nigerian organizations are discussed to reflect the needs of the organizational workforce.

Section 2 will discuss the field of IS education and Section 3 will introduce the IS '97 reference model for further analysis. Section 4 evaluates the African context and its implications for curriculum development. Section 5 concludes with recommendations for policies with international implications and backing.

2 INFORMATION SYSTEMS AS A FIELD OF STUDY

There are significant differences between computer science and Information Systems. 'The important differences are in the context of the work to be performed, the type of problems to be solved, the types of systems to be designed and managed, and the way the technology is employed' (Davis, Gorgone, Couger, Feinstein and Longnecker, 1997).

While the IS context focuses on an organisation and its systems, computer science focuses on algorithms and systems software. The nature of work in IS assumes that IS professionals are skilled in basic knowledgework software. The IS student should understand the relationship of systems to organisational goals. IS personnel are expected to understand IS functions and developments. The purpose of IS is to improve the performance of people through the use of IT.

Universities that have been focusing on the 'hard side' of computer science need to start looking into the 'soft side' (*i.e.* Information Systems) because there is a very high demand for the IS knowledge today. Davis, Gorgone, Couger, Feinstein and Longnecker, (1997) noted that 'a strong demand for IS professionals is forecasted to continue through the year 2005'. Their forecast points to the importance of IS as a discipline that might change our society, just as computers and medicine did in the past.

The demand for IS professionals is increasing as the functional areas of organisations seek to gain more capability in Information Systems. As organisations extend the use of IT to operational processes, decision support and competitive strategy, the academic field grows in scope and depth.

The different names used for the ISs discipline sometimes affects the meaning, which raises even more confusion in Africa. Aina and Mabawonku. (1997) reported that 'to an average, educated African, the information professional is synonymous with persons occupied with journalism, broadcasting, government propaganda, etc.'. It is time to start working towards the establishment of the discipline of IS within the African university communities.

3 AFRICA IN CONTEXT - KEY ISSUES IN DEVELOPING HUMAN RESOURCES

3.1 Selected approach for developing policies

Moyo (1996) describes two alternative approaches to formulating IT-related policies for developing countries. The first is the classical one of analyzing the conditions in developed countries, and then replicating and modifying them in developing countries. As Moyo (1996) and Korpela (1996) argue this approach may fail due to diverging socioeconomic and cultural differences in developing countries. They discuss an approach in which conditions in both developed and developing countries are analyzed, similarities and differences are assessed, and policies are formulated to transfer technology on the basis of local needs and capabilities.

The latter approach is used in this paper to discuss the reference model curriculum as presented by Davis, Gorgone, Couger, Feinstein and Longnecker

(1997). The model is compared against that of the University of Lagos's Department of Computer Science (CS) curriculum, which offers a Bachelor's and Master's degree in computer science. The department also offers a Ph.D. degree in three major areas - Computational Analysis and Applications, Computing Systems and Systems Science, and Operational Research.

Table 1 IS Model Curriculum vs. Computer Science curriculum from 1992 - 1994

Model Curriculum (Davis, *et. al.*), 1997	UniLag Computer Science Curriculum 1992-1994
Knowledge Work Software Tool Kit	Introduction to Computer Science
Fundamentals of IS	Principles of Computer Organisation
Personal Productivity With IS Technology	**Computer Programming I and II**
IS Theory and Practice	**Introduction to Data Structures**
IT Hardware and Software	Introduction to Information Processing methods
Programming, Data, File, and Object Structures	Operating Systems I
Networks and Telecommunications	**Structured H/L Languages I**
Analysis and Logical Design	**File Organisation and Processing**
Physical Design and Implementation with DBMS	Machine Language & Assembly Programming
Physical Design and Implementation with a Programming Environment	Introduction to Compiler Construction
Project Management and Practice	Algorithm Design & Analysis
Introduction to Statistical Processing	Comparative Programming Language
	Project

(Davis, *et. al.* 1997)

The curriculum of the degree programs in the University of Lagos (later UniLag) was selected because the department of Computer science of UniLag was among the first departments in the country to start a degree program in Computer science in 1973.

Table 1 shows the model curriculum and its recommended packaging of learning units for the IS major as well as the recommended sequence and the compulsory courses in the curriculum of the degree program in Computer Science (1992-1994) at UniLag. Some additional courses must be passed before a certificate in Computer Science can be awarded but these are referred to as electives. The courses that are represented in the model curriculum and the Unilag Computer Science degree curriculum are shown in bold. The UniLag curriculum is presented with its recommended sequence of advancement.

3.2 Human resource development and IS education

Human resource development strategies should be linked to many IT-related issues and problems such as national infrastructure development, general improvement of IT awareness in the respective countries, IT education curriculum development and IT industry support. As Avgerou (1996) says, the very common practice of developing countries to export software programming work is not a very long-lasting phenomenon while the real IS expertise demands skills and knowledge to analyze both organizational and business conditions, and the capabilities of IT to make effective Information Systems. Moyo (1996) recommends that managers be more responsible for mapping IT strategies for their organizations while the managers' lack of IT understanding seems to be a drawback for organizations in developing countries. This means that besides IT education curriculum development for long-term human resource development, universities and other professional institutions need also to develop Executive Education programs for African managers

Naturally the model IS curriculum discussed here cannot be transferred directly to African countries without changes because the model is developed to suit primarily organisations in the Western countries. However the curriculum can be used for guidance.

3.3 A case study of Nigeria in the African context

Nigeria is taken as a representative of an average African country because it has the largest in population in Africa and exhibits characteristics of most African countries (Korpela, 1994). Many companies - except for a few oil companies and banks - in Africa do not have an advanced data processing or IT department. That means that operations are manually carried out in most organisations.

The level of computer use in Nigeria is generally low and, to a large extent, the computers are under-utilised. Key activities are sometimes computerised but computer technologies are hardly used for strategic purposes. Management Information Systems are unknown in most organisations. Transaction processing systems are common but most organizations, including banks, seem not to have invested in a strategic use of IS.

The least computerized organizations are governmental institutions (Adelakun, 1993) - hospitals, primary and secondary schools, universities and ministries. It is not surprising to see a large set of hardware in some room used mainly for word processing or not at all. In governmental organizations transaction processing systems may not work efficiently enough. However most organizations are waking up - especially in the insurance business. They have began to understand the need for computer-based IS and are trying to move a step farther toward the strategic use of Information Systems. Most companies have realised that there is a need to invest in IT but the problem is how to do it successfully.

The problem of IS development is one of the key issues facing organisations in Africa. There is a significant lack of IT/IS professionals capable of developing suitable and appropriate ISs for organisations. For example, in 1993 it was very difficult for the second author to find a ready-made accounting system designed for Nigerian companies. Eventually an application developed for Western countries had to be purchased. In Nigeria most of the computer companies are hardware vendors. Over the period 1981-1986 Nigeria alone accounted for 20% of all computer imports in black Africa (Kluzer, 1990). The human resources are not capable of putting installed computers to effective use.

IS is not represented in many universities although the knowledge of IS is needed before the technical skills of computer experts can be converted into appropriate uses. There is a tendency for many organisations to look for applications used in the Western countries and transfer them to their organisations after some modifications. Many researchers have noted that this will not work; indigenous developers are required. (Avgerou, 1996; Korpela, 1994).

Telecommunications can not be over-emphasised. So it is important to develop an IS curriculum that will have relevance for organisations in Africa and that will not conflict with the value of their overall educational systems.

3.4 Course description and recommendations

Now we present our recommendations for the courses to be included in the Computer Science or related discipline curriculum in Nigerian universities. We suggest that since a degree in IS is not generally represented in Nigerian universities those universities could start by offering a minor in IS. Students studying for a major in computer science or computer engineering as represented in Nigerian universities could do a minor in IS if the courses recommended below are incorporated into the curriculum for a computer science degree.

Each course, though similar to the courses described in the model curriculum, has been analysed to suit the need of the organisations in Nigeria. Graduating students with minors in IS will be equipped with the resources needed to face the IS challenges in Nigerian companies.

Knowledge Work Software Tool Kit (IS '97.0)

Content: The course includes a basic understanding of software tools useful for knowledge workers. Examples include spreadsheets, databases, presentation graphics, database retrieval, statistics, word processing and electronic mail.

Analysis: The course seems not to be generally present as a whole in any Nigerian university offering a computer science degree. However computer science students are expected to study some of the topics in on their own. We recommend this course as a fundamental course for all students - even students studying non-computer-related degrees.

Fundamentals of Information Systems (IS '97.1)

Content: The course provides an introduction to systems concepts, IT and application software. It introduces students to how information is used in organisations, and how IT enables improvements in the quality and timeliness of information. Some of the other topics covered in the course include: design and reengineering of ISs; application vs. systems software; programming languages; functions and architecture; telecommunication systems and applications.

Analysis: The course is not well-represented in most universities in Nigeria. We recommend it as a fundamental course for students studying computer science as a major and those who will study IS as a minor. Most professionals working in industry today are missing the knowledge covered in this course and those professionals managing computer projects in most Nigerian companies have been trained in computer science or computer engineering, degrees that do not make provision for the fundamental knowledge of IS.

Personal Productivity With IS Technology (IS '97.2)

Content: The course enables students to extend their knowledgework and improve their skill in the use of packaged software in order to improve their personal productivity. The course topics include: end-user computing support; evaluating end-user requirements for tailored information needs; feasibility analysis; evaluation criteria for packaged software; database products; information retrieval; accessing internal and public databases; accessing shared software; groupware; data conversion and manipulation.

Analysis: The course does not seem to exist in any university in Nigeria at the moment. However parts of some of the topics are covered. It is recommended that the course should be considered mandatory for all students studying computer science, especially those who will take IS as a minor subject.

Information Systems Theory and Practice (IS '97.3)

Content: The course covers systems theory and concepts; decision theory and how it is implemented by IT; level of systems; strategic, tactical and operational; information systems strategies; roles of Information Technology; IS planning; human-computer interface and interaction.

Analysis: This is a very important course and it is recommended that it should be broken into several courses - each course addressing two or three of the topics mentioned above. The courses should be compulsory for an IS minor but not for pure computer science students. According to our experience, none of the selected universities is offering this courses at the moment.

Most organisations in Nigeria - governmental institutions and family-owned businesses - are still highly hierarchical in structure. The flat organisational structure is not very common and therefore the method for IS development used in the West might not work for many Nigerian organisations, which have no tradition of formal planning and little capacity for organisational reform on the basis of requirement analysis. Avgerou (1996) noted that 'Strategic decisions are either political, therefore not amenable to the analytical logic of organisational requirements, or intuitive based on the talent of the entrepreneurs and mistrusting formal management practices'. Therefore this course needs to be carefully designed from the viewpoint of the Nigerian organisation. We will personally recommend that this course should teach a mixture of the old classical approaches and the new methods to IS development.

Networks and Telecommunications (IS '97.6)
Content: The course provides an in-depth knowledge of data communications and networking requirements, including telecommunications technologies, hardware, and software. Emphasis is on the analysis and design of networks. Important topics are: Telecommunication devices; media systems; networking hardware and software; networking configuration; network application topologies and protocols; network performance analysis; security; and other topics.

Analysis: The course does not seem to exist in any university in Nigeria at the moment. Network devices are taught in some universities - Obafemi Awolowo University, for example - but only to such a very limited extent that we can assume that the course does not exist. We recommend the course as an optional course for pure Computer Science students but an IS minor must pass some of the topic mentioned.

4 CONCLUSION

We have raised curriculum issues to be developed in Nigerian universities to provide better management of the organizational needs of companies. In order to establish a well-grounded IS education infrastructure we need both to educate more IS-oriented students for companies but also set up Executive Education programs for managers in order to raise awareness of IS management (Ruohonen, 1992). Such a strategy demands collaboration between several stakeholders - governmental bodies, companies, vendors and professional organizations such as computer societies, consultants and agencies for development. It has been noted that the more challenging the IS development process is, the more stakeholders we need to include (Ruohonen 1995).

Although the involvement of international organisations in the computerisation process is not uncommon in Africa (Adelakun, 1993), the involvement of highly recognised universities in IS education is almost nonexistent. Meanwhile the development of human resources that will manage the developed Information Systems starts from the training of IS professionals in universities and other higher education institutions. Therefore it is recommended that African universities, Nigerian ones in particular, should establish collaborations with leading institutions in IS research and education abroad. The assistance given should be oriented more toward building capacities than toward financial aid for computerisation. The more adequately trained university graduates of IS enter into the industry in Nigeria, the more adoption and usage of IS will increase.

5 REFERENCES

Adelakun, O. (1993) Economic Problems in the Implementation of Hospital Information Systems (HIS) in *Nigeria: A Practical Experience*, (eds. S.H. Mandil, K. Moidu, M. Korpela, P. Byass, and D. Forster) Health Informatics in Africa -Helina 1993, First International Conference on Health Informatics in Africa. *Excerpta Medica*, Amsterdam, pp. 94-98.

Aina, L.O. and Mabawonku, I.M. (1997) The literature of information profession in Anglophone Africa: Characteristics, trends and future directions. *Journal of Information Science*, **23**(4), 321-326.

Avgerou, C. (1996) How Can Information Technology Enable Development Countries To Integrate into Global Economy?, in *Global Information Technology and Systems Management - Key Issues and Trends* (eds. P.C. Palvia, S.C. Palvia, and E.M. Roche), Ivy League Publishing, Nashua, NH.

Davis, G.B., Gorgone, J.T., Couger, J.D., Feinstein, D.L., and Longenecker, Jr., H.E. (1997) IS '97: Model curriculum and guidelines for undergraduate degree programs in Information Systems. *The DATA BASE for Advances in Information Systems*, **28**(1) .

Kluzzer, S. (1990) Computer Diffusion in Black Africa: A preliminary Assessment, in *Information Technology in Developing Countries* (eds. S.C. Bhatnagar and N. Bjorn-Andersen), North-Holland, Amsterdam.

Korpela, M. (1994) Nigerian Practices in Computer Systems Development: A Multidisciplinary Theoretical Framework Applied to Health Informatics. Ph.D. Thesis, Helsinki University of Technology, Otaniemi, TKO-A31.

Korpela, M. (1996) Traditional culture or political economy? On the root causes of organizational obstacles of IT in developing countries. *Information Technology for Development* 7, 29-42.

Lee, D.M.S., Trauth, E.M., and Farwell, D. (1995) Critical skills and knowledge requirements of IS professionals: A joint academic/industry investigation. *MIS Quarterly*, **19**(3), 313-340.

Moyo, L.M. (1996) Information Technology strategies for Africa's survival in the Twenty-first century: IT all pervasive. *Information Technology for Development* 7, 17-27.

Ruohonen, M.J. (1992) Hybrid Managers for the Corporation of the 1990s - Educational Implications, in *Professional Development of Information Technology Professionals*, (eds. B.Z. Barta, A. Goh and L. Lim) North-Holland, Amsterdam.

Ruohonen, M.J. (1995) Stakeholder Thinking in the Information Strategy Planning, in *Understanding Stakeholder Thinking*, (ed. J. Näsi, J.), LSR-Publications, Gummerus, Jyväskylä.

6 BIOGRAPHY

Mikko Ruohonen (D.Sc) works at the University of Vaasa as an Associate Professor and at the Turku School of Economics and Business Administration as a Docent in Information Systems Science. Dr Ruohonen's special interest areas are business strategy and information management, management participation in strategic information planning, strategic human resource management and IS education. He has published three textbooks, two chapters in international textbooks and more than 80 articles in the Information Systems research field. He is a full member and a vice chair of IFIP Working Group 3.4.

Olayele Adelakun (M.Sc) is a researcher at the Turku School of Economics and Business Administration. He received his B.Sc. (Computer Science) from the University of Lagos and his M.Sc (Software Engineering) from the University of Oulu, Oulu, Finland. He is presently working on his Ph.D. in Information Systems Quality and Quality Planning at the Turku Centre for Computer Science, Turku, Finland. He is also interested in research issues related to IS development in Africa. He has published articles on Information Systems quality and hospital information systems problems in Africa. He is a member IFIP WG 9.4.

19

Blame the technocentric artefact! What research tells us about problems inhibiting teacher use of IT

Deryn M. Watson
School of Education
King's College London
Waterloo Road, London SE1 8WA, UK
Tele + 44 171 872 3106; Fax + 44 171 872 3182
E-mail: deryn.watson@kcl.ac.uk

Abstract
Despite substantial resource provision and a number of national and regional strategies, the impact of IT in education is still relatively small. There is an apparent resistance by teachers to the use of IT within the normal pedagogy of the classroom. The confusion of purpose about the role of IT in schools is part of the problem. But more significantly teachers' reluctance is fueled by a complex intertwining of the technocentric focus associated with IT, real barriers to change and professional unease. The key to change, for both developed and developing countries, lies in addressing the concerns of teachers rather than imposing change upon them.

Keywords
Attitudes, case studies, developed countries, pedagogy, professional development

1 INTRODUCTION

Most countries espouse the role and value of Information Technology (IT) in education. Issues such as redefining the curriculum, new styles of teaching, empowering individualized learning and moving beyond the idea of a fixed location school are often discussed as if both the ideas and the power of IT to deliver them are incontestable. Yet evidence from developed countries, who have been 'using IT in education' for a number of years, suggests that the relationship

Capacity Building for IT in Education in Developing Countries
G. Marshall & M. Ruohonen (Eds.)

between IT and learning at all levels is complex and fragile. Indeed after so much resource provision, and so many national and regional strategies the impact is still relatively small. An examination of why is this so, with reference to research analysis and literature, may enable developing countries to avoid the same mistakes.

2 THE CURRENT SITUATION

Since 1973 the UK has been regularly promoting the use of computers in education through a number of national initiatives. There have been programmes for the purchase of hardware, the development of educational software and the training of teachers. A national agency has been in place for 15 years with the specific remit to promote the use of educational technology. Yet the recent independent McKinsey report (Stevenson,1997) stated:

> 'The UK has a higher ratio of computers per schoolchild than almost any other country, including the US. Yet despite this lead and the fact that information technology has been on the educational agenda for almost 30 years, it is not clear that IT has made a significant impact on educational standards.'

Pelgrum and Plomp (1991) reported in the IEA study, which covered 19 countries, that with the exception of the USA, only a small percentage of teachers in schools were actually using computers as part of their teaching. In the UK a series of government biennial statistics on the use of IT in schools has shown that despite a rise in the number of computers and a growing number of teachers reporting being confident with computers, the number who actually use them substantially in their teaching, rather than for administration or personal use, is still relatively small - at just under 10%. The figure has been consistent for some years. The most notable change since 1989 has been the growth of educational administration and the use of computers to teach IT skills in separate lessons.

The reasons for the apparent resistance to the use of IT within the normal pedagogy of the classroom needs further exploration. Evidence from three recent research projects, ImpacT - An Evaluation of the Impact of Information Technology on Children's Achievements in Primary and Secondary Schools (Watson, 1993), PLAIT (Pupils' Learning and Access to Information Technology) (Gardner, *et. al.*, 1992) and STAC (Supporting Technology across the Curriculum) (Ridgway and Passey, 1995) has shown that a number of factors appear to be involved. First the level and nature of IT depends upon resource provision, access and particular curriculum requirements. At the moment none of this infrastructure appears to support the majority of teachers and their current pedagogy in schools. Indeed all the projects focused on the role of the teacher, noting that the majority of teachers were unaware of or unwilling to explore the contribution which IT can make to their pupils' learning. It is clear that, as with other innovations, we need to focus on the role and perceptions of the teacher in order to understand why the take up of IT in education has been so resolutely disappointing.

3 A QUESTION OF THE CURRICULUM

It is clear that one major factor has been the confusion of purpose about the role of IT in schools, and how best that might be addressed (Watson, 1997). Van Weert (1986) has defined four interrelated roles of IT use in education.

1. Learning about IT, including programming and systems design; *i.e.*, IT as a separate subject;
2. Learning with the aid of IT, such as using a graphics calculator or CD-ROM, *i.e.*, IT as a teaching resource;
3. Learning by means ofIT, such as using simulations and modeling, *i.e.*, IT as an integral part of the learning;
4. IT to organize education, such as pupil records, *i.e.*, IT for educational management.

The last role is not of concern in this paper. But the first three have, in both the UK and elsewhere, been the subject of much debate. There has been a tendency to promote first one and then the other. Thus schemes to promote first computer science and now IT as a separate subject have been perceived as separate from and not related to the role of IT as a learning resource. The use of IT tools as a resource sits uncomfortably in the middle. The fault lies in the conception that the three roles are somehow distinct from each other, resulting in a dichotomy of purpose between a vocational and pedagogic agenda. Few schools have been able to incorporate all three. OFSTED, the UK's national inspection agency, reported that pupils were often practising low level skills and there were often insufficient opportunities to apply the IT skills, learnt in separate IT classes, to work in other subjects. As Ragsdale (1988) has noted, knowledge of IT skills does not mean the skills are always applied. He indicates that acquiring IT tool skills may be relatively easy but gaining wisdom to use them effectively is not. In reality not many teachers are using computers in their classes.

Thus there has been a lack of integration, a perception that IT has different identities and purposes within the same educational establishment. The McKinsey report (Stevenson, 1997) reflects on the 'lack of clarity of objectives' and argues for a more integrated approach. It also states that 'we need to be clearer about what we want children to learn (with IT) and whether learning should be about acquiring vocational skills or about learning for its own sake'. The focus on IT skills solely for vocational purposes has contributed to the rejection by most teachers, for whom pedagogic purpose and implementation lie at the heart of their professional concerns.

Recent further analysis of my case study research undertaken as part of the ImpacT project provides some further understanding of this phenomenon. In five schools, only one geography teacher in each department used computers; those teachers also failed to influence their colleagues (1993). Focusing on the reluctance of the colleagues helps identify further causes for their rejection - a complex intertwining of the technocentric focus, real barriers to change and professional unease.

4 SYMBOLIC FUNCTION OF TECHNOLOGY

Technology today appears to hold a major symbolic function in society, associated with imagery of the new, positive change and renewal, and of economic revival. From Logo to the Superhighway, education has been drawn into the confused notions of a technocentric society. As Bryson and de Castell (1994) state there are a wide range of policy documents that:

> '... urge educators to grapple with the implications of an 'explosion in knowledge, coupled with powerful new communication and information processing technologies' and therefore promote widespread 'technological literacy'. Arguments that enthusiastically promote the widespread implementation of educational computing typically predict that these technologies will (1) facilitate teaching processes, and (2) promote significant positive gains, both academic and vocational, for students.'

Evaluation studies such as Cuban's (1986) suggest that unreflexive and unabashed optimism about the necessarily transformative nature of new educational technologies is both naive and historically unfounded. Indeed Miller and Olson (1994) consider that 'the history of innovation in education should teach us to be cautious about predictions associated with new technologies. However there is something about computers that seems to negate this caution'.

It is clear that the conception of technology as an artefact, a desirable innovation that 'ought to be used', is itself part of the problem. The teacher colleagues in my case study were resisting partly because they resented the assumption, the value assumption, that IT 'should be done'.

The culture of technocentric mindedness can result in curriculum programmes that produce an alienation because they are perceived to have attitudes hostile to teachers' pedagogic culture. My reluctant teachers resented the intrusion upon their geography curriculum of IT. A technocentric culture distorts knowledge by focusing on it as information. Many teachers do not recognize this as part of their professional environment and so articulate barriers to use. In all countries, whether defined as developed or developing, IT must be perceived as an integral rather than separate and new transformational part of the curriculum.

5 BARRIERS TO CHANGE

It is important to see the role of the new technology through the eyes of the uncommitted classroom teacher. My case study teachers' colleagues articulated a number of reasons for not emulating their colleagues' use of IT. The rare in-service they reported had all the hallmarks of the failures recorded by Fullan (1991), who stated that 'in-service education or ongoing staff development explicitly directed at change has failed in most cases because it is ad hoc, discontinuous, and unconnected to any plan for change'. While both formal and informal attempts to share experiences had occurred within their schools they were hampered by lack of time for regular and ongoing reflection. Many reported poor experiences when using software both in an in-service context and in their classes, which I believe reflected their lack of professional confidence in the role and use of the resource. This poor experience coloured their willingness to explore further, even when the means were close at hand.

Problems with access also featured large. For teachers in the ImpacT study the location and control issues of the resource were simply too cumbersome, and lacked the flexibility and spontaneity which they needed and had in their own geography classrooms. Andrews (1992) has reported from a survey among mathematics teachers (75 replies from 40 schools) that booking in advance guarantees access for only half the teachers and spontaneous access granted to only one in ten. Wellington (1988) reported from a large survey that the advent of computer networked suites reduced both the amount and range of subject CAL that took place in schools. Even so the regular access to computers available in the PLAIT project (Gardner, *et. al.*, 1992) was found to be no guarantee that they would be used or the pupils' performance improved.

But questions of training, access and control were overshadowed by the problem of time - time to learn and explore, time to gain confidence and time to reflect on the potential for their pedagogy. This has been a common theme in the literature; teachers need time to reflect and consider the implications of the new. Drawing upon the longitudinal research project in Kingston Ontario, Olson (1995) raised the problem that teachers are not provided with enough time to reflect on practice and change. Indeed he believed teachers appear to be expected to take substantial risk in accommodating IT in their teaching that threatens their classroom ethos. He noted the value of computers in that they may help teachers to confront their experience; change is not just adoption and integration of the technology but involves personal reflection and adaptation as well.

Bliss, Cox and Chandra (1986) concluded from a study in one school that although the general attitude of staff towards computers was positive more than half had misgivings. They felt the change in their role occasioned by computers was unfavourable and they perceived their traditional role was threatened. Ridgeway and Passey (1995) considered that the advocates of computers, through overambitious claims and an underestimation of practical constraints, seed failure; computers challenged teachers' fundamental values and practices. Teachers have identified barriers as lack of full access to computers, lack of personal preparedness and the problem of unanticipated negative consequences of computer use. It appears that teachers in schools are less favourably inclined towards computers because they feel incompetent, because the facilities available are inadequate or because they are not yet convinced of their educational potential.

The large IEA international survey (Pelgrum and Plomp, 1991) confirmed that lists of barriers quoted by teachers consistently included difficulty of access and lack of time. I believe these barriers can be seen as the manifestation of a vicious circle in which these teachers feel trapped, unable to see a way forward or negotiate a route for exploring and adopting regular computer use in their classrooms. I believe that teachers used their articulation of time as a barrier in part to justify and reflect their overall unease with the innovation.

Many of the barriers to the adoption of computers in schools are simply specific examples of barriers to change in general. Willis (1993) in particular identifies a number of barriers common to all change but which may have a particular resonance for why 'efforts that involve technology may be particularly difficult to pull off'. The Williams and Williams (1994) study is based on the notion that the greater the number of conditions that are positive in any one scenario, the greater the chance of success. However identifying barriers to change still places the focus on the innovation as a construct, an artefact with characteristics teachers, in many different environments, have difficulty in accepting.

6 DEFICIT MODEL OF TEACHERS

One effect of this has been to maintain the long-standing association of the teacher as failure, the deficit model. Willis (1992) asks 'why do some teachers, when faced with an opportunity to begin using technology in their classroom, treat it more like a disease to be avoided than a promising aid to effective instruction?' His language indicates inadequacies of teachers rather than the innovation; he relates the inadequacies to whether teachers have Arts- or Science-based backgrounds. The PLAIT report, an evaluation of the use of laptops (Gardner, *et. al.*, 1992), was concerned to find that curriculum requirements alone do not sustain daily use. Laptops were distributed to all pupils; their relatively sparse use was attributed to:

> '... the inability of the wider teaching community to stimulate and extend the frequency of computer usage in the classroom. Indeed usage in some cases may not be frequent at all. Teachers are not felt to be sufficiently IT literate to easily and effectively integrate IT into their teaching.
> .... It is therefore unlikely that the frequency of usage will be greatly extended by innovations in teaching methods until teachers themselves are as literate in IT techniques as the pupils are expected to become'.

At no stage do the PLAIT evaluators address the possibility that the barriers perceived by the teachers may be sensible ones. As advocates of the technology they assume the artefact is desirable. PLAIT teachers were only offered three general purpose packages - word processing, data handling and spreadsheets - on the laptops. No indication is given of how frequently the use of such packages might fit into the subject curriculum concerns of the teachers. Ostlund (1974) highlighted the idea that attention must be placed on the characteristics of the innovation - characteristics such as relative advantage, compatibility with existing procedures, trialability, reversibility and risk. He noted that the same innovation does not have the same characteristics for all disciplines. So much of the advocacy of the use of computers in education has come from 'outside' agencies or national projects. Their stake in the technology could be said to have blinkered their analysis of such issues as compatibility, reversibility and risk that teachers in schools have faced. It is perfectly logical and sensible for teachers, when pressed for time in a busy schedule, to revert for the sake of efficiency, to routines and resources they feel comfortable with.

7 FOCUS ON PROFESSIONAL CONCERNS OF TEACHERS

The separation of the innovation from the classroom teacher and the idea that the teacher is at fault - that the teacher is an empty vessel into which this externally defined innovation must be poured - these notions have produced failure. Such perceptions focus on the innovation itself and in this focus its definition increasingly isolates it from the teaching and learning environment by locating it as something different and outside, an alienating artefact, that must now be brought within. The rhetoric to introduce Information Technology in schools has all the hallmarks of an imposed, mechanistic, top-down model of change, with a particular focus on the nature of technology within a wider national economic agenda. Many teachers have responded by articulating a number of barriers to using computers.

Excessive attention to the acquisition of hardware, a technocentric imperative that placed the desirability of the technology above its educational purpose and a confusion of how this should be translated into real IT use in the curriculum, have contributed to failure of substantial adoptions in developed countries. Thus the route taken by many developed countries so far would be a poor role model for developing countries. More attention is needed to consistent and appropriate pedagogic use with an infrastructure for support that includes ease of access and time to incorporate IT into a well-established curriculum. Time for teachers to reflect professionally is essential. Strategies targeting professional capacity building will have a greater chance of success. They need to be focused not on the technology but on pedagogy and on the delivery mechanisms to be contexted within, rather than superimposed on, the real professional environment of the teacher.

8 REFERENCES

Andrews, P. (1992) Teachers' perceptions of the availability of computer hardware. *Journal of Computer Assisted Learning*, **11**(2), 90-98.

Bliss, J., Chandra, P., & Cox, M. J. (1986) The introduction of computers into a school. *Computers and Education*, **10**, 49-54.

Bryson, M. and de Castell, S. (1994) Telling tales out of school: modernist, critical and postmodern 'true stories' about educational computing. *Journal of Educational Computing Research*, **10**(3), 199-221.

Cuban, L. (1986) *Teachers and Machines: The Classroom Use of Technology Since 1920*. Teachers College Press, New York.

Fullan, M. (1991) *The New Meaning of Educational Change*. (Second edition). Cassell, London.

Fullan, M. and Hargreaves, A. (eds.) (1992) *Teacher Development and Educational Change*. Falmer Press, London.

Gardner, J., Morrison, H., Jarman, R., Reilly, C., and McNally, H. (1992) Pupils' Learning and Access to Information Technology: An Evaluation. School of Education, The Queens University of Belfast, Belfast.

Stevenson, D. (1997) The Future of Information Technology in UK Schools. McKinsey and Company, London.

Miller, L., & Olson, J. (1994) Putting the computer in its place: a study of teaching with technology. *Journal of Curriculum Studies*, **26**(2), 121-141.

Olson, J. (1995) Classroom ethos and the concerns of the teacher, in *Integrating Information Technology into Education*. (eds. D. M. Watson and D. Tinsley), Chapman & Hall, London.

Olson, J. (1995) Classroom ethos and the concerns of the teacher, in *Integrating Information Technology into Education.* (eds. D. M. Watson and D. Tinsley), Chapman & Hall, London.
Ostlund, L. (1974) Perceived innovation attributes as predictors of innovatedness. *Journal of Consumer Research,* **1**, 23-29.
Pelgrum, W.J. and Plomp, T. (1991*) The Use of Computers in Education Worldwide.* Pergamon Press, Oxford.
Ragsdale, R. (1988*) Permissable Computing in Education: Values, Assumptions and Needs.* Prager, New York.
Ridgway, J., & Passey, D. (1995) Usin g evidence about teacher development to plan systemic revolution, in *Integrating Information Technology into Education.* (eds. D. M. Watson & D. Tinsley), Chapman & Hall, London.
van Weert, T (1986) A model syllabus for literacy in information technology for all teachers, in *Information Technology and Education: The Changing School* (eds. R Ennals, R. Gwyn and A. Zdravchev), Ellis Horwood, London.
Watson, D.M. (Ed.). (1993). The ImpacT Report: An Evaluation of the Impact of Information Technology on Children's Achievements in Primary and Secondary Schools. Kings College London, London..
Watson, D.M. (1993) Do enthusiastic users inhibit change?, in *Informatics and Changes in Learning.* (eds. D. C. Johnson and B. Samways), North Holland, Amsterdam.
Watson, D.M. (1997) A dichotomy of purpose: The effect on teachers of government initiatives in IT, in *Information Technology: Supporting Change through Teacher Education* (eds. D. Passey and B. Samways), Chapman & Hall, London.
Wellington, J.J. (1988) Computer education in secondary schools: an electronic survey. *Journal of Computer Assisted Learning,* **4**(1), 22-33.
Williams, J.C. and Williams, J.B. (1994) Change at the chalk face: A case study of the factors affecting the adoption of curriculum innovation. *Journal of Curriculum Studies,* **26**(2), 201-216.
Willis, J. (1992) Technology diffusion in the 'soft disciplines': Using social technology to support Information Technology. *Computers in the Schools,* **9**(1), 81-118.

9 BIOGRAPHY

Deryn Watson is a Senior Lecturer in Educational Computing at King's College London. Since the mid-1970s she has been actively involved in the research and development of CAL materials in the humanities and languages, writing both on models of software development of CAL materials and the potential for interactive learning. She has conducted research into the effects of the location of computers and the impact of IT on children's learning. Her current research is on the role of ICT in teacher education, an examination of IT national policies and the reality of IT use in schools.

20

Measuring success in the global village - resources for conducting systematic and comprehensive evaluations in IT settings

Gail Marshall
Gail Marshall & Associates
2393 Broadmont Ct., Chesterfield, MO 63017, USA
Tele + 314 230 6613; Fax, + 314 230 3609
E-mail: 74055.652@Compuserve.com

Abstract

A well-designed evaluation plan is essential if decision-makers are to assess the problems and prospects for Information Technology. In designing the evaluation plan the resources in the community, the point of view guiding teaching and learning, and lessons from previous attempts at innovation must all be taken into account. Many models for conducting evaluations exist. Tests, measures and alternative assessment strategies currently in circulation can be adapted for IT settings. The dissatisfaction with attempts to use IT successfully in education, voiced by many commentators around the world, could be countered with data on the powerful impact IT on schools if all the relevant data were collected, analyzed and used in successive cycles of policy making, program improvement and program evaluation.

Keywords

Assessment/testing, case studies, evaluation, policy, culture

1 INTRODUCTION

Every society has been 'technological'. Across Africa, for example, many different technologies supported life. The inhabitants of the Olduvai Gorge had spatial techniques for mental and physical map making and direction finding. They

Capacity Building for IT in Education in Developing Countries
G. Marshall & M. Ruohonen (Eds.)

developed implements suitable for a wide variety of animal and plant husbandry. Gold mining and cattle farming contributed to the economy long before machines and microchips began to mesmerize societies around the world. Villages have traditional ways of assessing how well they are operating and we should be careful not to abandon village ways that provide valuable information as we try to collect data on the impact of Information Technology (IT) on schools.

Developing countries, now beginning to implement IT in many schools and seeking to assess IT's impact, should be cautious about adopting the pre/posttest model of evaluation to the exclusion of other data collection techniques. Adopted as part of the 'efficiency' movement in American education, the pre/posttest model, if used at all, should only be used as one data collection strategy near the end point of an evaluation cycle. At the beginning of the cycle many more strategies must be employed - strategies that will describe and analyze the match between what was anticipated, what was accomplished and what went wrong. Every village storyteller knows how to capture the essence of a situation and so, in the global village, we should be relying on a wide range of skills and strategies to convey the essence of successful endeavours and point out where we went wrong.

Both early and recent IT adopters face a variety of implementation, assessment and institutionalization challenges - among them the question, in the case of early adopters, of whether current national, local and classroom IT policies are appropriate; in the case of recent adopters the question is whether other countries' IT policies and practices will meet their own needs. In establishing national policies and local projects both groups of countries must consider the importance of early, frequent and targeted evaluations of IT planning, implementation and impact. Resources, used in evaluating a wide range of pre-IT innovations, can be adopted and adapted to provide answers to all the questions that must be asked before we ask, 'Did it make a difference for the students?'

2 NECESSARY AND SUFFICIENT CONDITIONS FOR EVALUATING IT'S IMPACT

2.1 The need for systematic and comprehensive evaluations

Evaluations of IT in educational settings must be systematic and comprehensive. Successful IT use changes the dynamic at all levels of use (Rowe, 1996); unsuccessful use introduces dislocations and disaffections across the organization. Evaluations must look at a wide range of activities and events - the planning process, the initiation process and the implementation process - and evaluations must occur for several cycles before any pretest/posttest comparisons between student groups occur. The evaluator must be a full partner in the innovative effort. A wide variety of measures must be used and several different types of reports must be prepared - each addressing specific facets of the innovative process.

2.2 Defining goals for IT use

Very early in the life of the innovation it is important to ask, 'What are our goals and how will we know we have achieved them?' Answering such a question is not easy because each participant in the innovative process may have, especially at the early stage of the project, only partially-formed ideas about what should be done and how success will be defined. The problem of differing ideas held by members of the innovation group has been especially true with many technology-based innovations where the content and processes are often so novel that many decision-makers are unaware of or do not understand the implications of curricular choices. Database and telecommunications use, for example, have often been poorly understood, even by educators well-versed in other aspects of technology. So the introduction or evaluation of these aspects of technology has been problematic.

An important, although often lengthy, part of the development of an evaluation plan is the negotiation of what will be evaluated and how it will be evaluated (Smorodin, Marshall and Brooks, 1981). Such negotiations are often ignored or curtailed but at the risk of finding, at the end of the evaluation cycle, that each participant had a different vision of IT and that few, if any, of the participants' real questions have been answered.

2.3 Recognizing different epistemological viewpoints and different educational objectives

Another neglected dimension, the epistemological point of view, must be discussed before, during and after evaluation activities begin. At the present time the question of which point of view should determine the design and delivery of instruction is hotly debated (Marshall, 1995). For example, the introduction of Integrated Learning Systems (ILSs) in the United States, the United Kingdom and Australia has been welcomed by some educators and resisted by others. A major reason for the debate is the irreconcilable difference between educators with a behaviorist view of learning and educators with a constructivist view of learning (Reese and Overton, 1970). The worst-case scenario for an evaluation is that teaching and learning based on constructivist principles is evaluated within a behaviorist framework - and only that framework - or vice versa. Important questions that flow from one theory will be ignored while other questions, which may not be germane, are asked instead. Benzie (1995) stresses the importance of understanding how the questions we ask about IT use determine policy for good or ill.

Different historical foundations for the design and delivery of instruction also mean different designs of instruction, which call for different measures of success. For example, a school or a country may choose from among one or more of the following foundations of instruction - each with its own goals and objectives: (1) learning in the classical tradition, which emphasizes the Western canon of literature, history and science; (2) learning as a socialization process, which emphasizes the historical forms of interactions within a village or community; (3) learning as a vocational activity, which mimics the actions and goals of industry and commerce; (4) learning as a political activity, which seeks to inculcate the ideas and values of the ruling (or, in some cases, the wishing-to-be-in-power disenfranchised) class.

IT, while it appears to be value neutral, can be applied to any one of these goals for learning. Evaluating IT's impact on students can only be accomplished when the evaluators decide which point of view is actually being espoused at the school and/or classroom level. Lengthy sessions may be needed until all parties agree on the central themes and the interesting questions related to the themes. Failure to spend time at this critical point may lead to failed evaluations as implementation progresses since the evaluator's questions may focus on aspects of the project ('Have students' keyboarding skills improved?') that conflict with others' visions ('How much more fluent have students become in writing via computer?').

3 RESOURCES FOR EVALUATING IT

3.1 National policies, individual strengths and cultural traditions

It is perfectly acceptable if one of the greatest resources for planning, implementing and evaluating a country's IT use is its own history of innovation and implementation. Strategies that have worked for other innovative efforts may lend themselves to the IT endeavour. Peoples' experiences, both positive and negative, in attempting other change processes are invaluable assets for supporting the IT revolution. Similarly, the country's culture and traditions must be carefully considered when IT policies are established. For example, while factions in the highly industrialized nations may call for classroom-based IT use to support large doses of drill and practice because the tradition of the 'school as factory' is widely established as cultural currency, other factions may cite pedagogical and cultural traditions that dictate very different ways of using IT resources.

Resources from other countries and from international organizations, in terms of policy statements and practices for determining effectiveness, may provide models that should be considered as evaluations of IT are framed. Many countries' professional bodies - the National Council of Teachers of Mathematics in the USA and the Association of Mathematics Teachers in UK, for example - are also valuable resources. The publications of the International Federation of Information Processing (IFIP) may also facilitate the evaluation of IT use.

It is especially important for countries to learn from one another, both with respect to failures as well as successes. For example, the rationalist model of policy-making assumes that a carefully planned series of decisions will lead to a coherent set of practices but the reality of many innovative efforts prior to the IT revolution shows us that change is not straightforward, and is often compromised by individual and collective activities that deform and derail plans (House, 1975). Policy-makers in different countries should analyze their own efforts against the yardstick of other countries, asking how what works in one country is transferable to other countries and how problems in some situations might prove instructive for the design of future policies and practices.

People who have played an active role in all prior educational activities and innovations are significant resources for evaluating IT's impact. Administrators, teachers, students, parents and other community members have long memories. They will remember previous attempts at innovation. They will be able to offer their analyses of what went wrong and what went right. At this and all other stages let tradition play its proper role. In some communities storytelling is a hallowed and powerful way of transmitting data. Data from stories told about innovative failures and successes may be far more useful that data collected via surveys and questionnaires.

Throughout the innovative process there are at least two contexts in which the innovation is being conducted and judged. On the one hand there are national and local education authority goals deciding school inputs and processes. Those national and local bodies also set criteria for judging outputs; on the other hand the family, the students and the community-at-large have goals, and provide their own inputs (student motivation to work with the innovation or parents' satisfaction or dissatisfaction with the goals and processes, for example). A well-designed evaluation will use community resources to assess the impact of IT implementation at all levels of the country and community.

3.2 Models for evaluations

When it comes to evaluating IT use in schools we seem to have regressed to a primitive stage of evaluation. Far too many evaluation designs are conducted in a small number of classrooms using a pretest/posttest experimental design. As Rowe (1996) points out, we should be looking for differences in patterns - how teachers in IT settings do what they do differently and how those differences bring about differences in students' learning - and not patterns of differences. Many sophisticated but uncomplicated techniques have been used in pre-IT days and should be studied as models. For example, *Federal Programs Supporting Educational Change Volumes I - VIII* (Berman and Pauly, 1975) describes a complex design for evaluating four federally funded change projects in the USA.

The Rand researchers conducted a nationwide survey of 293 sites - including interviews with project participants at all levels of responsibility. Then 29 field studies - at sites with different characteristics and goals - were conducted with observations, interviews and analyses of the change process as a major part of the evaluation effort. Volume I of the Rand Corporation's report contains a lengthy bibliography of change-oriented efforts prior to 1974.

The Eight Year Study, an analysis of attempts to modernize the curriculum in selected American high schools during the 1940s, remains a classic of its kind. Tests, inventories, questionnaires, checklists and student logs in 30 high schools were used to see if planned changes in curriculum actually occurred (Smith & Tyler, 1942). More recent analyses of curriculum innovation can be found in Fullan and Pomfret (1977).

The case study model provides crucial data for deciding how the early stages of IT implementation are proceeding. The case study should be an important way to ensure that plans are proceeding on schedule, that goals have been specified, and that problems are being identified and addressed. As the implementation process begins, the evaluator observes the decisions and actions of all participants, and interviews them frequently. Interviews are especially useful during the staff development phase and early stages of classroom implementation. Cooley and Lohnes (1976) have published examples of several case studies, including an analysis of guidance counseling programs, an evaluation of bilingualism and a study of primary education in Ireland. Such models will be useful for IT-based evaluators.

A variant on the case study is the Action Research approach to collecting data. Teachers and others work together to discuss and analyze patterns of teaching and learning, looking for generalizable trends. However one does not embark on an Action Research approach without taking the time to fully acclimate all participants its methods and without recognizing the demands for data collection that it places on teachers (Jaworksi, 1994).

For many policy-makers and community members the experimental design model is the only one considered appropriate for evaluating the impact of an innovation. It is regarded as 'scientific' and 'value free' - both designations assumed to legitimize the use of the experimental design above all other designs. In fact, the model is often misused. It is often used to the exclusion of other more necessary data collection activities and the results are often interpreted inappropriately. Other techniques and evaluation models are far more appropriate. For example, Worthen and Sanders (1973) have collected many different models of evaluation, including Provus's discrepancy model and Stufflebeam's call for evaluations as decision-making tools.

Evaluation should be a long-term endeavour. Way before the classic pretest/posttest design is used all sorts of data should be collected. It is important to know that staff development occurred and was deemed satisfactory; that classroom instruction occurred and was managed in such a way that students could be seen to be using IT as well as applying skills and concepts gained from IT use. Only when all questions about implementation have been answered is it appropriate to ask, 'Does using IT make a difference?'

3.3 Models for reporting

The design and intent of the interim and final reports should be one of the first items on the evaluator's agenda. S/he must discuss with the rest of the innovation group the goal of the information to be collected through the evaluation. Shipman (1989) cites Bastiani's discussion of models (1978) as a useful way to frame reporting. The models are:

- the 'Basic Information Model' where only factual information is transmitted - the number of computers purchased, the student-to-computer ratio, etc.;
- the 'Public Relations Model' where persuasion or the attempt to avoid conflict by describing what has been accomplished is the goal;
- the 'E.P.A. Primary Model' where an attempt is made to convince one constituency of the value of the innovation while trying to convince another constituency of the need for resources;
- the 'Academic Recruitment Model' which seeks to recruit adherents or participants - either recruiting teachers to participate or urging parents to support the program by enrolling their children;
- the 'Developmental Model' where information is provided to support participants as they go through the early stages of implementation;
- the 'Involvement Model' where the information is used to create a deeper involvement of all participants.

In fact, each of these models may be used at key points in the process of initiating and sustaining IT use.

3.4 Instruments for observation and analysis

There are time-honored methods of collecting data, including storytelling. But at times other methods are called for, including the use of easy-to-scan-and-score instruments. Instead of devising instruments, the evaluation team should consider using instruments that have served other innovators, either by using the instruments as designed or modifying them to fit the situation. *Mirrors for Behavior* (1974) is a compendium of classroom observation instruments ranging from the Adams-Biddle instrument that enables educators to analyze the sociology of a classroom to the Wright-Proctor instrument designed to assess the extent to which teachers were using new pedagogical methods in 'new math' classrooms.

It is often that case that the most successful implementations can be undone by choosing inappropriate measures. For example, if students work steadily at problem-solving software in their mathematics classes and are then tested with an instrument that merely measures basic computational ability we should not be surprised that the test results show no difference between computer-using and noncomputer-using students. Most basic computation tests are too limited to assess the range of problem solving skills acquired through the use of problem-solving software.

Fortunately several resources are available for choosing well-designed and well-targeted tests. The Buros *Mental Measurements Yearbook* series lists tests in subject areas ranging from achievement tests in English and other languages to tests that measure clerical and mechanical ability. Descriptions of the tests, analyses of their psychometric properties, and information on how to order and administer the tests can be found in the Buros collections.

Once again, professional organizations around the world have developed curriculum frameworks and assessment strategies that lend themselves to IT settings. The State of California, for example, has a wide range of publications devoted to assessment. Stenmark's (1989) presentation of alternative assessments is only one example.

4 CONCLUSION

Data provide the power for decision makers to continue or refine policies and practices. In the absence of data implementation may falter, aspirations may wither and dreams for the future may die. It is essential that technology use at all levels, from the national to the student level, be assessed in order to determine problems, generate solutions and drive further IT development. Carefully assembled, the wealth of evaluation resources can highlight difficulties and identify successes.

5 REFERENCES

Benzie, D. (1995). The Impact of Our Questions on Information Technology Policies and Practice, in *Proceedings of the World Conference on Computers in Education VI: Liberating the Learner* (eds. J.D. Tinsley and T.J. van Weert), Chapman & Hall, London.

Berman, P. & Pauly, E. (1975) *Federal Programs Supporting Educational Change*. Rand Corporation, Santa Monica, CA.

Buros, O. *Mental Measurements Yearbooks*. Buros Institute, Lincoln, NE.

Cooley, W.W. and Lohnes, P.R. (1976) *Evaluation Research in Education*. John Wiley and Sons, New York.

Fullan, M. and Pomfret, A. (1977) Research on curriculum and instruction implementation. *Educational Researcher*, **47**(2).

House, E. (1975) *The Politics of Educational Innovation*. McCutchan, Berkeley, CA.

Jaworksi, B. (1994) *Investigating Mathematics Teaching: A Constructivist Enquiry*. Falmer Press, London.

Marshall, G. (1995) The ABC's of today's technology decision-making in Australia, the United Kingdom and the United States. A paper presented at the WCCE '95 World Conference Computers in Education, Birmingham, UK.

Reese, H.W. and Overton, W.F. (1970). Models of development and theories of development. In *Lifespan Developmental Psychology: Research and Theory* (eds. L. R. Goulet and P. B. Baltes), Academic Press, New York.

Rowe, H. (1996) I.T. is failing to revolutionise the curriculum, because to date we have failed to evaluate its benefits in context. Proceedings the Australian Computer Society, Canberra, Australia.

Shipman, M. (1989) *Assessment in Primary and Middle Schools*. Routledge, London.

Simon, A. and Boyer, E.G. (1974) *Mirrors for Behavior III: An Anthology of Observation Instruments*. Research for Better Schools, Philadelphia, PA.

Smith, E.R. and Tyler, R.W. (1942) *Appraising and Recording Student Progress*. Harper and Row, New York.

Smorodin, C., Marshall, G. and Brooks, T. (1981) Point of View: A Critical Variable in Program Development and Program Evaluation. A paper presented at the American Educational Research Association meeting, Los Angeles, CA.

Stenmark, J. (1989) *Assessment Alternatives in Mathematics: An Overview of Assessment Techniques that Promote Learning*. Regents, University of California, Berkeley, CA.

Worthen, B.R. and Sanders, J.R. (1973) *Educational Evaluation: Theory and Practice*. Charles A. Jones Publishing Co., Worthington, Ohio.

6 BIOGRAPHY

Gail Marshall evaluates projects for local, state and federal agencies. She was a Divisional Assistant in the Division of Research and Evaluation for the St. Louis Public Schools, a member of the evaluation team for the Comprehensive School Math Project (CSMP) and the Midwest Regional Exchange at the Central Midwest Regional Laboratory She was also the coordinator of the IBM Model Schools Project 1983-1984 for the St. Louis Public Schools. A graduate of Marymount Manhattan College, New York, she has an MA and a Ph.D. from Washington University, St. Louis, where she studied child development and psychometrics.

A member of IFIP's WG 3.5, Gail Marshall is also a member of the Computer Using Educators, based in California, USA, the International Society for Technology in Education (ISTE) and she has been listed in *Who's Who in American Education.* The international editor for ISTE and the software review editor for *Education Technology Monitor*, Gail raises irises and many different varieties of artemesia.

PART VI

Resource Acquisition, Allocation and Utilization

21

The role of educational and professional bodies in guidance towards capacity planning

Peter Juliff
Professor and Head of School of Management Information Systems
Deakin University
Burwood VIC 3125, Australia
Tele + 61 3 92446266; Fax + 61 3 92446928
E-mail: pjuliff@deakin.edu.au

Abstract
This paper examines the rationale for an Information Technology (IT) education policy for developing countries and suggests contributions which IT professional bodies may make towards its development. Areas covered include raising of the level of public awareness of IT, the need for a technical infrastructure and commercial expertise, the development of academic curriculum development and accreditation, the formulation of professional standards of practice, and the creation of joint training schemes with industry.

Keywords
Curriculum policies, professional development, accreditation, industry training

1 INTRODUCTION

The aim of this paper is to examine the respective roles of educational institutions and professional societies in the process of IT capacity building. It will address the levels at which IT education may be delivered and some rationales for each of those levels will be presented. In particular, it will emphasize the need for teacher education as a foundation for all other levels.

Capacity Building for IT in Education in Developing Countries
G. Marshall & M. Ruohonen (Eds.)

The paper will suggest activities which might be undertaken by computing professional bodies to provide constructive assistance to this process. Some of the activities are able to be pursued in their own right and others will be in collaboration with the providers of IT education.

The need for informed public opinion

Information Technology has an ever increasing impact on society. It is a significant determinant of business practice, manufacturing efficiency, levels of employment, available public services and global communication. It may be regarded with enthusiasm or with suspicion but, in either case, public opinion should be well informed lest a Luddite mentality develop due to ill-founded fear and resentment. Computing technology has moved into the realm of consumables. The general community need not understand the principles of the computer's internal operation any more than they need to understand the principles on which the telephone or electricity work but, as with these other technologies, there is a need for a general appreciation of the capacity for its application in everyday life.

The news media often present a view of the technology which is emotionally biased either for or against a particular issue such as employment or privacy. It is virtually impossible for the general public to form an independent opinion on such matters when the technology concerned seems to be beyond their comprehension. The situation can only be remedied by education.

The need for technical infrastructure

As with all technologies, an educated and skilled workforce is required for the installation and maintenance of IT, if not for its manufacture. A manufacturing capacity provides independence as well as employment but may be difficult to justify in a developing country due to the high cost of initiation and the rapidity of changes in the technology. Developing countries' primary concern in planning educational policy should be the establishment of facilities to educate and train engineers and technicians to support installed technology in the workplace.

The need for commercial expertise

It is trite to say that technology has no purpose of itself and that its value lies in how it can be used to assist human endeavours. Despite this, much of the IT education currently found at all levels would seem to ignore this principle. IT is an enabling technology helping many commercial - using this term in its broadest sense - organizations work more effectively. For many other organizations it is an essential factor in their continued existence.

The driving force behind the majority of IT education initiatives in any developing country, arguably in any country at all, is the training of a workforce capable of using technology to foster the country's progress. Information Technology supports business and manufacturing efficiency and largely determines the level of services available to the general public. It provides a step rather than a curve in the level of production of goods and services in the same way as the steam engine aided manufacturing and mechanization aided agriculture.

2 ACADEMIC CURRICULUM DEVELOPMENT AND ACCREDITATION

Education for a career in IT or education in IT for a career? The question provides a useful focus for considering the general issue of IT education. While it is obvious that every student won't want to study for a career in IT, it is becoming increasingly true that all careers - especially professional careers - will demand competence in IT. The last thirty years' history of IT systems in developed countries has failed to produce a specific IT manager career classification in any significant numbers. The management of the Information Technology resource continues to be the responsibility of the general business management.

Despite the emergence of information as arguably the most important asset possessed by any organization, its management is still largely left in the hands of end-users. The implication of this on the education programs offered to business managers in general is that a significant 'major' study in IT is a desirable component of all other professional education.

The levels of education needed encompass primary/secondary education, postsecondary and vocational education, tertiary education and postgraduate education.

Primary/secondary education

IT education at the primary and secondary levels should encourage familiarity with technology and dispel fear and mistrust. Technology should be neutral to gender, culture and school subject. The use of the technology should be encouraged in as many educational areas as possible and certainly not only in mathematics and science. Technology should be seen as an enabler, helping in tasks such as the retrieval of information and developing the basic skills of reading, writing and arithmetic. Given the preponderance of English language software products, the development of native language-based software is likely to be a desirable priority in many countries. China, for example, despite a language which is not friendly to screen and keyboard operations, has made significant progress in this area.

Postsecondary and vocational education

Contrasted with tertiary courses, those offered at postsecondary level are normally shorter in their duration and more limited in their scope. Despite these limitations, such courses train a paraprofessional level of IT employees able to develop systems from standard application software and to liaise between user groups and professional computing staff in an organization. The courses also offer a means whereby all staff whose daily work involves considerable interaction with computer-based systems may obtain a level of knowledge sufficient to understand the implications of dealing with the technology. The courses may lead to a certificate or diploma, or may be shorter and offered with no academic credit for attendance.

Tertiary education

Two key areas are required in tertiary education to support the growth of an IT infrastructure in a developing country and to contribute to the use of IT in the growth of commerce, industry and services. A cadre of engineering and technical support personnel must be trained to develop a local capacity for producing professional and technical staff who can install and maintain the hardware and communications resources needed to allow the widespread use of the technology.

A cadre of business information systems personnel must be trained who can integrate business, management and IT skills essential to business, manufacturing, government and service provision. The emphasis in the development of tertiary computing courses must move away from viewing technology as an end in itself and must concentrate on its use in adding value to commercial processes.

Postgraduate education

In addition to courses at an undergraduate level, IT studies need to be offered at a graduate diploma level to train graduates already in the workforce who want to upgrade their knowledge and skill in order to make an informed contribution to IT systems being developed within their organizations.

3 PROFESSIONAL DEVELOPMENT RESPONSIBILITIES

The need for teacher education

One of the prime requirements the widespread use of IT in education is the supply of educators who are qualified in IT. Expertise is needed at all levels of education. Policy makers responsible for teacher training and employment must be committed to provide funds, time release and recognition of achievement for those taking part in IT training. IT needs to be seen as a specialist area in education, along with the traditional specialties such as languages, science, mathematics and other school subjects. Too often IT has been seen as something which mathematics teachers do in their spare time. Such a limited view of IT use perpetuates the myth that IT is only for the mathematically-inclined and restricts the application of IT to technical areas.

It is significant that much of the ongoing contribution to IT education in the workplace is being undertaken primarily by professional bodies outside of the IT communities. National engineering, accounting and law societies have established educational programs and publications for members whose interests have become focused on IT. In addition, most countries have one or more IT professional societies whose main aim is the advancement of knowledge of their members. In Australia, and I suspect in other countries, the growth of membership in computing societies has been less than the growth of IT specialist areas in other professional bodies.

The educational role of IT professional bodies

Computing professional societies may make a number of specific contributions to their communities. For example, most IT professional societies engage in significant programs of ongoing education for their members. Much of this is done on a noncredit basis but the Australian Computer Society's (ACS) Certification Program, a formal course of study comprising two general and two specialist units administered by Deakin University and providing advanced standing in that university's MBA program, might be worth replicating in other countries.

The raising of IT awareness in the general community.
In the early days of IT development and its permeation through the general community in Australia, the ACS conducted public programs such as 'Computer Week' or a similar title. The activities provided information to the general public about IT, its likely effect on the general community, the possibilities IT could provide through increasing the level of services offered to the public and the longer term implications on employment and education. The events were conducted to combat the often ill-informed and emotional portrayal of those issues by the popular press and consisted of a number of public forums in which speakers from the IT profession presented information in a format easily digestible by the general public together with an opening to the general public of the computing facilities of tertiary institutions.

Assisting in the dissemination of IT awareness.
Professional bodies can also assist in spreading IT awareness among the general community. For the past 25 years, the ACS Victorian Branch has conducted an annual Careers Night attended by up to 500 secondary students, teachers and parents. The event explained to students the variety of IT-related careers which they could pursue and the types of academic or vocational courses which they would need to complete in order to attain their goal. In addition, speakers visit secondary schools and universities to tell local groups of students about the increasing importance of IT in business and industry. The activities have had a significant influence on providing a body of high school leavers who are aware of the employment opportunities in IT and able to make informed choices about the path of education which will lead them to careers of interest to them. Developing countries might do well to adopt such outreach activities.

Examination-based criteria for membership.
The Australian and British Computer Societies conduct their own examinations as an alternative path to membership for those who have not completed a tertiary or post-secondary IT qualification. But such a policy should be seen as a short-term expedient to be employed in the earlier days of the growth of a viable IT profession and should be phased out in the longer term in favour of a requirement of tertiary qualifications for IT professionals.

Accreditation of academic courses.
Professional bodies play a significant role through the accreditation or certification of educational curricula. This may be done by the independent development of sample syllabi to be used by the educational institutions and/or by the inspection of syllabi developed by the institutions in the light of current best practice and state-of-the-art technology and methodology. The accreditation process may be carried out on an advisory basis or may be given 'teeth' by requiring prospective members to complete an accredited course of study as a prerequisite for membership. The latter policy has long been followed by accounting, law, medicine and engineering professions but has been a source of contention among computing professionals due to the difficulty which IT has always had in viewing itself as a profession, let alone encouraging that view among the general public.

In addition to the more direct formulation or accreditation of academic curricula as referred to above, professional bodies can play a secondary role as advisors to other groups developing IT-related curricula. Tertiary and post-secondary institutions typically appoint advisory boards or panels to provide input into the curriculum development process. Government education departments also develop curricula for use in primary and secondary schools, and require advice and expertise from various sections of the community in doing so. Professional bodies can play a significant role by providing members for the advisory bodies.

Codes of professional practice and ethics

The Achilles heel of the IT profession has been its difficulty in coming to terms with its professionalism. Accounting, law, medicine and engineering professional bodies have no qualms about enforcing the skills and knowledge which must be acquired before membership is granted. They have long standing codes of ethics and professional behaviour which - if breached by members - lead to loss of membership. The community has come to expect that professionals display a level of knowledge and behaviour that provides a climate of self-perpetuation of the professions' status. In contrast, the IT community has grown - as did the more hallowed professions in times past and now conveniently forgotten by their members - by recognizing those with a demonstrable talent for doing the work regardless of their background, education or standards of behaviour. Attempts to influence employers to undertake a policy of selective recruitment of employees who are demonstrably educated in the requisite skill and knowledge for IT has proven to be a dismal failure. The professional IT bodies have a duty to the public-at-large to continue to promote a code of professional practice and ethical behaviour which may result in the acceptance of IT as a profession and not merely as an occupation.

The Computer Industry Training Program (CITP)

A description of a training program which was successfully conducted by the Australian Government and the ACS over a number of years could serve as an example to countries wishing to accelerate the development of an IT infrastructure.

The CITP was active in two Australian states - New South Wales and Victoria - over a period of approximately five years. The program was undertaken with to boost the number of trained IT employees available in the marketplace and reduce the number of unemployed. It was a 'sandwich' program consisting of periods of formal education and on-the-job training and experience.

Applicants could apply for the program in one of three intakes during the year. The program was open to all with an interest in an IT career and was actively encouraged among those who were currently unemployed. Encouragement was given by staff in the Commonwealth Employment Service, who tried to find employment for job seekers. No IT qualifications or prior experience were necessary for entry into the program.

Applicants were given an aptitude test to determine, as far as possible, their suitability for employment as trainee programmers. Those achieving what was deemed to be a suitable level in the test were then interviewed by a panel of industry representatives to determine their attitude to IT employment, motivation and likely employability at the end of the training. Those selected as a result of the interview were interviewed by prospective employers, who had agreed to participate in the scheme.

The inducement to employers was that the government agreed to subsidize the salary of the employee for the period of the trainees' academic studies. In order to progress to the education phase of the scheme, the prospective trainee had to find a sponsor employer who had to agree to employ the trainee for a two year period following the completion of the initial education phase - subject to a right of dismissal for incompetence or dishonesty.

The sponsored trainees then attended an eight-week full-time program organized to produce trainee programmers and conducted by a postsecondary education institution. At the end of the eight-week training, the trainees went to work for their sponsoring employers for two years. In the second year, the employers were obliged to release the trainee for a further 2-week training course designed to equip them with more job skills.

The scheme was jointly administered by the Commonwealth Department of Employment and the ACS, and worked well over a number of years. It provided an opportunity for hundreds of trainees to enter the IT employment arena who would not otherwise have had the chance and encouraged employers to expand their employee base at minimal cost and risk.

4 CONCLUSION

One of the advantages of being a follower rather than a leader is the ability to avoid the pitfalls into which others have fallen. Countries wishing to build their IT resource capacity should give serious consideration to their policy of IT education and training at all levels. The IT professional bodies are well placed to assist in the process by proactive policies of accreditation and advice to educational institutions as well as playing a role in the education of the public at large. By pursuing a wide range of activities, the professional bodies have created a body of well-informed and well-educated IT practitioners to swell their own ranks. They will also have the opportunity to influence the level of professional behaviour and competence exhibited within their community.

5 BIOGRAPHY

Peter Juliff is Professor of Management Information Systems at Deakin University, Melbourne, Australia. He has spent the last 34 years working in the IT profession, over 20 of which have been as an academic. He is the Chief Examiner for the Australian Computer Society and the Chair of IFIP Working Group 3.4 on Vocational and Professional IT Education. He is the author of several books on computer science and software design, and has conducted professional development courses throughout Australia, Malaysia, Singapore and China.

22

The European computer driving licence

Dudley Dolan
ECDL Foundation
2, Blackglen Court, Sandyford
Dublin 18, Ireland
Tele + 353 1 294 1997; Fax + 353 1 294 1996
E-mail eddf@cs.tcd.ie

Abstract

The European Computer Driving Licence (ECDL) is an international standard of competence for computer users. The ECDL establishes standards for everyone who uses a computer in either a professional or a personal capacity. It is a certificate that verifies competence, declares computer skills and makes the holder readily mobile within business across the European Community. The challenge is to introduce a credible skill certification scheme covering a wide geographical area while still retaining its relevance and quality to local populations.

Keywords

Accreditation, assessment/testing, competencies, skills, standards

1 INTRODUCTION

The ECDL is promoted by the ECDL Foundation and has a number of objectives:

1. To raise the level of IT competence within the workforce in industry, commerce and public services throughout Europe;
2. To provide a basis for certifying computer skills in all levels of the education sector and provide a basis for certification of skills for lifelong learning;
3. To reskill the unemployed so that they may re-enter the workforce;
4. To provide an incentive for the disadvantaged to bridge the gap between the haves and the have-nots in the Information Society;
5. to provide an incentive for those outside the workforce, not unemployed, to develop computer skills.

Capacity Building for IT in Education in Developing Countries
G. Marshall & M. Ruohonen (Eds.)

The ECDL is a basic skill test of the competencies required to perform basic tasks using a personal computer. It provides a documentation that the holder can use a computer in practice and has some background knowledge about IT. The ECDL consists of seven modules covering all major uses of IT in practice and reflects the needs for individuals, small and large companies, and the teaching profession.

Individuals prove their proficiency by passing a test in each module. Progress is registered on a European Computer Skills Card. An ECDL is awarded once all seven module tests have been passed successfully. Except for one theoretical module, the tests are task oriented. The tests are independent of both machine and software vendors and products. The many possible tests within each module, along with a syllabus, constitute an integral part of the ECDL and define a norm for practical IT competence.

The initial geographical extent of the ECDL market is defined as 31 European countries with a total population of about 500 million. Based on generic statistical information, a target group of roughly 60 million may be assumed under current demographic conditions. This is an estimate of the number of individual who employ IT at a level where it constitutes a necessary element in their working activities. The long-term goal for the ECDL efforts is to reach about 10 million of the 60 million by Year 2005, corresponding to a 17% penetration of today's target group. It is assumed that the public education system will supply the workforce with another 15-20 million skilled entrants. For the business plan period ending in 2001, the goal for the initial phase is about 1.8 million European Computer Skill Cards or Driving Licences issued.

In the short term, the main distribution channel of the ECDL is the body of existing course vendors within each country. Course vendors will see the ECDL as a positive enhancement of their services, being able to market their courses as conforming with and leading to the ECDL. Course vendors will have to be authorized to ensure proper quality of the end product. Authorized course vendors will utilize the ECDL test base in their actual testing. In the longer term Internet will become a major distribution channel, necessitating automation of ECDL testing.

2 THE ECDL AND THE INFORMATION SOCIETY

> 'The emergence of an Information Society in Europe will affect everyone . . . the European Union is well placed in comparison with the USA and Japan in public availability of the new generations of digital communications infrastructures. However, Europe is falling behind in business investment in IT and communications equipment for employees, notably office workers, and there are worrying disparities in purchase and use of information technologies and services for personal and home-use between Northern Europe and Southern Europe'.

Arising from the above statement it is recommended that:

- 'greater efforts must be made in our schools, to prepare the next generation to participate and benefit fully;

- greater efforts must be made to stimulate European citizens to create content for new services whether education, entertainment or business;
- continued efforts must be made to keep Europe at the forefront of technology and infrastructure development and deployment for everyone;
- sustained efforts must be made to increase the public awareness of the benefits of active participation in the information society;
- new collective efforts are needed to realize broader social benefits, particularly at local and community level.'

(Bangemann, 1996)

The above extract from the forward by Commissioner Bangemann to the report on *The Information Society and The Citizen* (1996) raises many points and the European Computer Driving Licence addresses most of the issues and will contribute significantly to the successful development of an all inclusive Information Society.

Over 40 million European households owned a PC in 1994, up from 23 million in 1990. However, the proportion of European households with a PC, and particularly with a networked multimedia PC, is significantly lower than the USA.

Information technologies have already substantially changed the work place in Europe. Over 72% of office workers have a PC or equivalent on their desks and use it as an integral part of their work.

Varying use of the computers across Europe

In addition to the above statistics it can be seen that the speed of adoption of the new technologies highlights cultural and linguistic differences between Northern and Southern Europe; more Swedish families bought PCs than TVs in 1995, while fewer than 7% of households in Spain had a PC in 1994. This situation may well show differences between Western Europe and the CEE Countries when the European Union expands after the new century.

Changes in the workplace

Each year, on average, more than 10% of all jobs disappear and are replaced by different jobs in new processes, in new enterprises, generally requiring new, higher or broader skills. There is a much slower pace on the supply side in the acquisition of new skills. Ten years from now 80% of the technology we operate today will be obsolete and replaced with new, more advanced technologies. By that time, 80% of the workforce will be working on the basis of formal education and training more than 10 years old. The workforce is aging and the technology is getting younger.

Unemployment

The area of unemployment is of vital importance and leads to a need for re-training rather than de-skilling. Instead of having 9 million people in long term unemployment and de-skilling, the most expensive form of public spending with the lowest return to the economy or the individual, and many more millions on their way to long term unemployment, the member states of the European Union should have 9 million involved in upgrading, maintaining and improving their skills in literacy, numeracy and IT.

The Green Paper, *Living and working in the Information Society: People first* (1996), says 'It should be a right, an obligation, for all unemployed to maintain and develop basic skills for the Information Society and have them imbued with relevance to the real, dynamic labour market.'

All of the above helps to make the case for lifelong learning. The concept of the ECDL with the European Computer Skills Card to record the acquisition of skills will play a significant role in encouraging people to keep up to date and acquire new skills throughout their lifetime.

3 FROM FINNISH IDEA TO EUROPEAN PROJECT

The Computer Driving Licence concept was developed in Finland and was introduced in January 1994. It consists of seven modules and is the model on which the ECDL is based. It was introduced with the support of the Ministry of Education, the Central Organization of Finnish Trade Unions, the Confederation of Finnish Industry and Employers, the Finnish Information Processing Association and the Ministry of Labour.

The first Computer Driving Licences, where the candidates passed all seven modules, were awarded in 1994 and 25 000 have been issued as of June 1997.

CEPIS (The Council of European Professional Informatics Societies) set up a task force consisting of representatives from ten countries - Norway, Sweden, Denmark, Finland, Netherlands, Ireland, France, Austria, Italy and UK - to consider the increase in competence required for the European workforce. The User Skills task force looked for a suitable model and examined the Finnish CDL in detail. After thorough study it was concluded that the basic Finnish concept was widely applicable throughout Europe, however changes and updates were required.

In order to assess the amount of changes required and the modifications needed to have the ECDL meet the requirements of a wider marketplace a series of pilot tests were carried out in Norway, Sweden, Denmark, France and Ireland. As a result of these tests and a thorough evaluation of the concept, modifications were agreed. A new European Computer Driving Licence Syllabus and European Question and Test Base were developed to meet the newly defined requirements.

The pilot tests gave an opportunity to evaluate the concept from a number of viewpoints. The pedagogical aspects were considered from the point of view of the breadth of knowledge required and the depth of detail needed. The need for the theoretical module was the subject of considerable debate. In the end it was retained.

A method for administering the tests automatically was researched in Sweden and is under extensive evaluation at the moment. It satisfies many requirements and an enhanced version will be introduced in the near future.

In addition to evaluating the tests themselves a period of time was used to establish what the market response would be to such a concept. The response was uniformly optimistic although the numerical forecasts vary considerably due to the different levels of penetration of PCs in the different countries.

It was clear from our research that industry felt a need for some sort of certification to ensure that their investment in training was worthwhile. Individuals welcomed the opportunity to show that they had acquired some skills, which they perceived to be vital in the current information society.

Course vendors were happy with the concept as it gave them a focus for their course offerings. Government, employers and trade union organizations in many countries found the concept attractive. In particular, the Irish Congress of Trade Unions (ICTU) was very supportive. Ministries of Education in a number of countries gave active support. In Denmark a government-supported regional initiative was undertaken.

The ECDL project has been funded by various sections of the European Commission. These include the DGIII ESPRIT programme, DGV European Social Fund and DGXXII LEONARDO programme.

The ECDL Foundation is involved as a partner in a number of other proposals submitted to the ESPRIT programme. In addition to support from the European Commission and National Government departments the project has created great interest in many large multinational organizations, including ABB, Ericsson, IBM, Microsoft, Rank Xerox and Norsk Hydro.

The establishment of the ECDL Foundation in Ireland in January with a small staff created the platform for the development of the ECDL and the implementation of the ECDL concept throughout Europe. The ECDL Foundation will monitor the quality and ensure the adherence to standards throughout Europe.

4 DESCRIPTION OF THE ECDL PRODUCTS

There are four basic components which comprise the ECDL:

1. The European Computer Driving Licence (ECDL)

This is the document which indicates that the holder has satisfactorily completed all seven modules of the European Computer Driving Licence. The document will have a similar format throughout Europe. It will bear the name 'European Computer Driving Licence' in English and also the name by which it is known in each individual country.

2. The European Computer Skills Card (ECSC)

The ECSC is a document which is used to record the progress of the candidate and the dates on which each of the seven modules were completed. When all seven modules are completed the candidate will return the completed European Computer Skills Card to the National European Computer Driving Licence Centre and a European Computer Driving Licence will be issued.

The modules can be taken in any sequence and the tests can be taken in different test centres and indeed in different countries.

3. The ECDL Syllabus

The ECDL Syllabus describes the objectives, content and guidelines for assessment of each of the seven modules of the ECDL. The ECDL

Syllabus version 1 was published in October 1996 and represents one of the outcomes of the work of the ECDL Task Force during 1996.

The Syllabus will be updated on a continual basis and new versions will be issued at least once per year. The Syllabus represents the norm for IT skills requirements throughout Europe and as such it will be used as the basis for both conventional and Computer-Based Training, which will lead to the attainment of the ECDL.

4. The European Question and Test Base (EQTB)

The EQTB is the set of questions and tests which candidates must pass in order to attain an ECDL. There are some 100 questions for module 1 and approximately 20 tasks for each of the practical tests. The EQTB sets a test norm which may be implemented by a number of systems including manual, semi-automatic and fully automatic.

The time allowed for each of the test modules is 45 minutes.

In addition to the four components listed above there will also be a number of associated products and services including the authorization of organizations wishing to conduct tests for the ECDL. Also assistance and consultancy services will be offered to intending licensees.

Income will be generated mainly from licence fees from the sale of European Computer Skills Cards.

The tests are carried out using a PC. Tests can be for individuals, or more typically, for groups consisting of from 5-20 persons. The results are recorded in electronic form and the candidates actually carry out real tasks. The tests and exercises ask the candidates to do something rather than asking do they know how to do it.

5 QUALITY ASSURANCE

The tests for ECDL will be conducted by authorized test centres. These centres will be validated by the licensee in each country using guidelines provided by the ECDL Foundation. The test centres are expected to be operated by course vendors, educational establishments, and large organizations or companies.

It is the intention that authorized test centres should provide facilities to test not only their own pupils but also persons who wish to take a test without undergoing formal courses.

Quality will have a high priority and quality assurance procedures will be instituted in the ECDL Foundation, the licensees and sub-licensees and the test centres. The quality assurance procedures will include use of rigorous implementation of standard authorization guidelines.

The results of the tests across Europe will be monitored on a statistical basis and any unusual patterns will be investigated by the ECDL Foundation. Strict adherence to the syllabus and the use of approved EQTB's will also ensure that the tests will be of an even standard. The ECDL Foundation will perform an audit function to ensure that standards are maintained and that the quality of the product is ensured.

Development and updating

The ECDL Foundation will ensure that the ECDL Syllabus and EQTB are updated on a regular basis to ensure that they always reflect the needs of the marketplace and the persons who are taking the tests. This updating will ensure that the product reflects the latest developments in the software available by modifying the existing modules, and will also cater for new developments by introducing new modules if and when required. Integration of existing modules could also take place if market forces so demand.

There will be a Members Forum which will give a platform for licensees, sub-licensees and test centres to share experiences and to suggest any developments which they feel are appropriate. This will ensure that the products are updated and developed in line with market requirements.

Automation

A priority in 1997 will be to ensure that the testing process is automated to the fullest possible extent. This is seen to be vital in the light of the volumes of persons to be tested, which should be some hundreds of thousands initially and ultimately will be millions. The feasibility of taking tests over the Internet from work or home will also be investigated as will diagnostic tests which will point to the areas of weakness of each candidate rather than the current pass/fail testing process.

6 CONCLUSION

There is a window of opportunity for this product at the moment. It is essential that it quickly gains acceptance as **the** test of skills in Europe. There are already optimistic signs that this will be achieved. The support of the European Commission through funding from the ESF, DGIII, DGXXII gives the ECDL considerable credibility. In addition, the fact that it is included in the *Information Society Action Plan* prepared by Commissioner Bangemann for Central and Eastern European Countries adds to this.

Acceptance by the large employers and support from the Ministries of Education, Labour and Industry in many countries has greatly added to the credibility of the European Computer Driving Licence and its associated products.

7 REFERENCES

Bangemann, M. (1996) Foreword, in The Information Society and The Citizan: A status report on the availability and use of information and communcation systems. A report by the Commission Services, Brussels, Belgium.

Commission of the European Community. (1996) Living and working in the Information Society: People first. A Green Paper of the Commissin of the European Communities, Brussels, Belgium.

8 BIOGRAPHY

Dudley Dolan was educated at Trinity College Dublin and graduated in 1962 with an honours degree in Production Engineering. He joined IBM on graduation and spent twenty years working in the computer industry in various positions. He joined the staff of Trinity College in 1983 and has been responsible for a B.Sc. Degree in Computer Science since then. In February 1997 he commenced two years leave of absence from Trinity College to act as a Managing Director of the ECDL Foundation.

He is a past President of the Irish Computer Society and he was a trustee of IFIP from 1989 to 1996. He was a Vice President of the Council of European Professional Informatics Societies (CEPIS) from 1992 to 1995.

23

Information literacy - the missing link in education, with special reference to developing countries

James R. Isaac
NIIT Ltd. National Institute of Information Technology,
NIIT Ltd., 8 Balaji Estate
Kalkaji, New Delhi, 110 019, India
Tele + 91-11-6203210 (direct); 6203300; 6482054
Fax + 91-11-620333 or 6475892
E-mail: isaac@internet.niit.co.in

Abstract

In their efforts to leapfrog into the Information Age, developing countries often attempt to catch up with the technologies and developments in the West. The only possibility of leapfrogging would be in the more effective exploitation of Information Technology towards human development. Such an exploitation can only be achieved through strategic initiatives concerning the very nature of information itself.

That exploitation is the information opportunity for developing countries. The paper identifies information understanding and information literacy as prime human resources if Information Technology is to be effectively exploited in developmental processes. For this opportunity to be seized, education and training, and not technologies, hold the key.

Keywords

Information handling, literacy, skills, industry training

Capacity Building for IT in Education in Developing Countries
G. Marshall & M. Ruohonen (Eds.)

1 TRADITIONAL INDUSTRIAL AGE EDUCATIONAL SYSTEMS

The Industrial Age was concerned with the production of material goods. Those goods were essentially concerned with the conversion of materials yielded by the earth and transformed into commodities for human use. Due to the very nature of materials, the production paradigm had to resort to the divide-and-rule policy in order to attain higher productivity and efficiency. Using the concept of the span-of-control and the span-of-coordination the management (or social) pyramid structure can be derived and explained. The strategic, control and operational levels fall into perspective with the top management mainly handling external information - implied uncertainties and complexities, heuristic - while the lower levels handle internal information - structured and organised, algorithmic. It is these aspects of information that are going to be fundamental to future educational concerns.

While the divide-and-rule policy certainly paid dividends in the Industrial Age, the paradigm was unfortunately carried over into other human activities. For example, offices adopted various forms of bureaucratic procedures and associated support staff structures resulting in various forms of gross mismatching, *e.g.*, a lower division clerk is expected to be an expert typist and when s/he is promoted to the next hierarchical rung is too senior to just type so the upper division clerk turns into a decision maker. As a consequence, s/he does not type in the new job But perhaps the greatest harm of the divide-and-rule policy has been in education. This led to compartmentalisation and isolation as indicated in Figure 1.

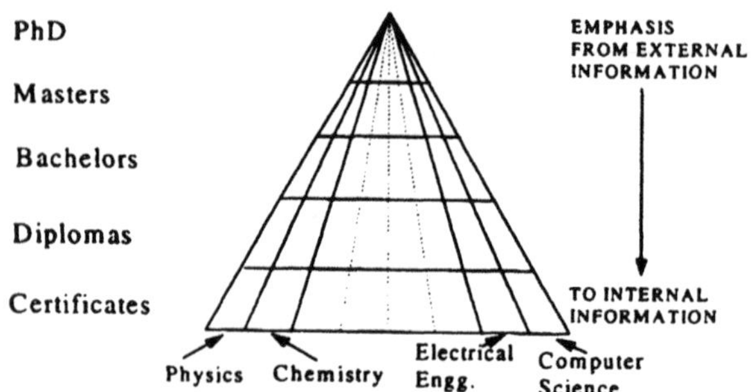

Figure 1 Divide and rule policy.

The figure indicates cells of specialised activities which are almost deliberately designed to work in isolation. It is this isolationist educational strategy that has led to unforeseen problems of pollution and environmental degradation and raised questions - not just the efficacy of education - but even of its very need in its present form. Ayn Rand (1971), for example, was caustic in her criticism of schooling, likening it to the process by which children were kidnapped, maimed, disfigured and trained to entertain European royalty. The modern tendency is to ignore the warnings of people such as Illich but it would be wise to recall the notion of his 'Learning Webs' which forecast Internet opportunities long before Internet was even conceived. However, even modern studies do conclude that education, as it is, should be reconceptualised, restructured and revitalised.

Understanding the problems of the Information Age and its technologies - especially in the context of developmental issues

The Information Age quite obviously evolves around the notion of information (Machlup and Mansfield, 1983; Wright, 1988). However, this is unfortunately not the case - and the central theme of this paper is that information understanding and information literacy offer an immense opportunity to developing countries that should not be ignored. The usual thrust in most developing countries has been to attempt to leapfrog only in a technological sense. The aim has been to attempt to absorb technologies, especially the latest and the best. However this can be an exercise in futility. For example the educational systems' response towards technological needs has been to proliferate computer science courses at a time when even in the most advanced countries, the role of computer science is under question.

This should be more so in the case of developing countries which are resource restricted. Computer science as such aims at creating inputs for advanced developments in hardware and software, and needs high capital intensive research environments for actually delivering results. Such environments are not available in developing countries. No wonder then that computer science students from these regions seek greener pastures, causing an enormous burden on the countries' already restricted resources. The main issue is whether developing countries should plan for technology innovation or whether they should work towards technology absorption.

Table 1 Technology innovation and creativity versus technology absorption

PARAMETER	TECHNOLOGY INNOVATION	TECHNOLOGY ABSORPTION
Base education and training	Computer science & computer technology	General education, information literacy and skills plus computer skills
Focus of education and training	Computer theory, extensive knowledge of hardware/software; computer applications not taken seriously.	Basic education on potential application areas - not computers; computer and

	Tools almost completey ignored.	information skills acquired through training in problem solving and tools
Student attitudes	Prefers computer R&D environment, shuns computer applications.	Amenable to application-oriented training; prepared for a wide range of applications.
Leads to	Innovation and creativity in capital intensive R&D environment	Wide range of computer applications
Resulting overall productivity (in general)	Low, even could be very low	High, cost effective and in wide spectrum
Significance	Innovation in a technological environment	Technology absorption into society in any environment

Table 1 clearly indicates that the strategy for rapid development, particularly of society, must obviously aim at technology absorption.

Problems of the Information Age

While there is much said about the opportunities of the Information Age little is done to even understand the Information Age (Machlup and Mansfield, 1983). Why is this? Basically, the problem lies in understanding fundamental economic principles. In place of material goods and commodities we now have to contend with information goods and commodities. The fundamental acceptance of the barter principle is challenged. When a material good was sold, it exchanged hands for money paid and all was well. But an information commodity, when it is sold, still remains with the user, thus upsetting all previous notions of value. Consider Table 2 shown below.

Table 2 Material commodities versus information commodities

Parameter	Material Goods	Information Goods
Type	Tangible	Intangible
Natural resource required in production?	Yes	No
Replicability	Difficult, costly	Easy, very low cost
Durability	Low	High
Transportability	Difficult, expensive	Very easy, very low cost
On usage. . .	Gets depleted	Does not deplete
Number of consumers	Restricted	Infinite number (theory!)
Life cycle	Single	Single or multiple
Appropriability	More-for-me, means less for you, exchangeable	Usually public good, shareable but not exchangeable
Special features	Nothing specific	Expandable, increases with use, compressible, summarisable, integratable, value over time - unpredictable
Utility	As originally intended, or as-is	Value add to all phases of human activity

This study clearly indicates the dilemma of understanding information economics and is the start of acquiring information literacy. This is the fundamental reason why studies on information and its use become fundamental to the problems of the Information Age. Despite the formidable view presented of information value being very difficult to pinpoint there are studies that show that effective information usage does convert to money and productivity. In fact, with the concept of globalisation hovering over even developing nations the need to be competitive in production can become crucial. Hence they must use the earliest opportunity to become information sensitive.

2 THE EDUCATIONAL SHIFT FROM THE INDUSTRIAL AGE TO THE INFORMATION AGE PARADIGM

The problem is exacerbated when we consider fundamental educational paradigm shifts that take place when we move into the Information Age. So it would be worthwhile to make in-depth studies on the implications of the shifts. Let us first take an in-depth look at the changing educational drives that result.

The table clearly indicates the radical changes that have to be made in educational planning for the future and here lies the real opportunity for developing nations. The educational systems of some developing nations are still in a transitional stage, and, unlike technological leapfrogging, educational leapfrogging can become a reality with proper planning.

Table 3 Educational drives and paradigm shifts

Item/characteristic	Industrial age	Information age
Duration, time spent,	Preparatory for life, early in life, one time	Lifelong, goal continuous
Stress, focus	Science/Technology orientation	People, management, organisation oriented
Brain Focus	Left hemisphere	Right hemisphere
Societal Models	Factory model, centralising	Information model, distributive, dispersive,
Driving Strategy	Atomization Divide and rule	Aggregation Integrate, collaborate
Goal of Education	Degrees, diplomas	Knowledge, experience capability

Knowing/doing relationship	Knowing (knowledge) isolated from doing (practice); knowledge for its own sake.	Knowing and doing integrated; knowledge redefined as knowledge + practice
Scope/Effectiveness of skills	Restricted to physical activities, task specific skill saturates, low returns	Information skills at all levels of management, wide range, very high returns
Use of Information tools	Data collection, storage processing	Conversion of data to information to knowledge
Nature of computing	Task oriented	Organisational computing, synergistic
Transition	From corporate hierarchies	To corporate networks

What are the resources for such an educational shift?

Due to the perpetual resource crunch in developing nations whenever any change for the better is mentioned resources come to the forefront. However, when we wish to leapfrog into the Information Age through education there is no need for extensive technological expenditures. What is required is a deep study of how education can sensitise entire populations into understanding the use of information as an economic tool. This can be done only through understanding the role of information sensitivity in the educational process and this calls for an understanding of information skills and information literacy.

Identifying core information skills

Fortunately much work has been done on understanding information skills but educational systems prefer to ignore these studies. Core information skills have been identified by Vockell and van Deusen (1989):

- Focusing skills: Defining problems, setting goals;
- Information gathering skills: Observing, formulating questions;
- Remembering skills: Encoding, recalling;
- Organising skills: Comparing, classifying, ordering, representing;
- Analysing skills: Identifying attributes, components, relationships and patterns, main ideas, errors;

- Generating skills: Inferring, predicting, elaborating;
- Integrating skills: Summarising, restructuring;
- Evaluating skills: Establishing criteria, verifying.

It is an interesting exercise to compare these with the *Taxonomy of Educational Objectives* (Bloom, et. al., 1956) - knowledge, comprehension, application, analysis, synthesis and evaluation - and then attempt to order them into the Bloom pattern.

A practical example of teaching and applying information skills

The company I belong to is among the world's largest computer training endeavours. Annually they train over 150 000 students on computer skills. Formal education basically undertakes to teach 'only-what-it-knows'. This may seem rather obvious but 'What is it that the student has to learn?' is a far more serious question. Yet it usually remains unanswered.

If students are to become computer professionals how can they be helped during their studies? Computer professionals, or for that matter any other professionals, are not filled with only technical knowledge. They must acquire world knowledge. Usually when a student moves into the world of the professional, s/he feels like a fish out of water - there seems to be so much that s/he doesn't know. The reason is that formal studies stick to logical, science-based approaches while real life does not.

To remedy this we brought out an innovative integrated monthly magazine *IT-Digest*, an abstracting and classifying service. However, we added a novel element. Usually abstracting services are confined to well-defined boundaries of what they cover and they restrict themselves to one field and level of source documents. *IT-Digest* violates this principle by abstracting and classifying from three levels of sources: daily newspapers (general and financial), magazines and journals (Indian and international). The sources vary from informal to the formal and yet they are classified in the same way. This is where the integration of information takes place. For the students' world view it is not sufficient for them to stick to just technical topics. They must understand, especially in developing countries, how the policy of the government is reflected in the process of technology absorption and this is better understood through newspaper articles than through journals. The processes enables one to put oneself into a total information environment in the business of information technology.

The next step was to identify how the various information skills could be woven into a learning structure. This opportunity was offered to the student through a course titled Information Search and Analysis Skills (ISAS). The student was exercised through the process of using *IT-Digest* as an information laboratory in which to find solutions to fairly open-ended professional questions that would never find a place in formal education. The course clearly proves the power of such a methodology in getting students to be information sensitive and to acquire information skills. This experience gives us the feeling that this methodology can be extended into other fields of educational activity though information technology serves as an ideal base.

3 LEAPFROGGING THROUGH THE ACQUISITION OF INFORMATION SKILLS

The absorption of IT into the developmental processes though extremely promising has its pitfalls. The tendency is to do it through the acquisition of technology into a population that is information insensitive. Developing countries would open up new opportunities for themselves if they stop putting the cart before the horse and turn their educational systems into a conscious acquisition of information skills. The ISAS methodology could be initiated at a much lower level of education. Information skills also can be honed through a conscious training of students to make use of libraries in an effective manner. In fact, the library can take the place of the *IT-Digest* as an information skill learning environment.

If students are trained in information skills on a large scale then the absorption of IT into the developmental processes takes on an entirely new shade of meaning. It is only then that the true power of IT can be released into effective developmental strategies.

4 REFERENCES

Bloom, B.S., Engelhart, M.D., Furst, E.J., Hill, W.H. and Krathwohl, D.R. (1956) *Taxonomy of Educational Objectives, Handbook I: Cognitive Domain.* David McKay Co., New York.

Hills, A. (1991) Teaching information networking. IEEE Spectrum, October, 1991.

Isaac, J.R. (1997) Information Systems: Changing Paradigms in Society, Management, Education andTraining. Proceedings of SCI/ISAS Conference, Caracas, Venezuela, July 7-11, 1997.

Jonscher, C. Information resources and economic productivity. *Information, Economics and Policy*, **1**(1), 1983.

Machlup, F. and Mansfield, U. (1983)*The Study of Information: Interdisciplinary Messages*. John Wiley, New York.

Rand, Ayn. (1971) *The New Left: The Anti-Industrial Revolution*. Signet, New York.

Vockel, E. and van Deusen, R.M. *The Computer and Higher Order Thinking.* Mitchell Publishing Co., Watsonville, CA.

Wright, R. (1988) *Three Scientists and Their Gods: Looking for Meaning in an Age of Information*. Times Books, New York.

5 BIOGRAPHY

Prof. J.R.Isaac completed his engineering studies in Bangalore, India and at the Carnegie Institute of Technology (now Carnegie Mellon University) in Pittsburgh, PA, USA. He worked for two years at the IBM Research and Product Development Labs in Poughkeepsie, N.Y. From 1958 until 1990, he taught electronics and computer science courses - the last 29 years at the Indian Institute of Technology (IIT) at Bombay, India. On retirement from IIT-B in 1990, he joined

NIIT (National Institute of Information Technology) Ltd., New Delhi as an advisor and he is also Director of the Institute for Research in Information Sciences (IRIS), a division of NIIT. He is the editor of a monthly abstracting and indexing service, *IT-Digest*. He also heads a project to create an 'Interactive Learning Environment' for disabled persons who cannot use a QWERT keyboard. His current research interest lies in studying information age impacts and paradigms.

24

Maximizing the benefits of aid for Information Technology

Ian Mitchell
President, The New Zealand Computer Society
Director, The iE3 Group Ltd.
78 Godden Crescent
Mission Bay, Auckland 5, New Zealand
Fax + 64 9 521 1316
E-mail: ianm@ie3.co.nz

Abstract

In this paper the author examines critical success factors for aid projects. Many anecdotes about aid projects were told to the author by donor personnel, recipient personnel and the economists responsible for analyzing the projects - especially successor projects which built on previous projects. The successor projects often revealed inadequacies in completed projects. The resulting success factors may be of value to recipient countries in ensuring that the aid they receive will deliver its full potential benefits.

Keywords

National policies, government, culture, developing countries, infrastructure

1 INTRODUCTION

This paper is based on the author's experience in South East Asia and the Pacific. The author prepared an Information Technology (IT) strategy for a small Pacific country and provided technical assistance to the Ministry of Finance and Economic Planning. The assignment included building a methodology for prioritizing the allocation of national expenditures. Because a substantial proportion of funding came from aid donors, the methodology needed to be extended to cover the evaluation of aid proposals because they required local senior public sector policy advisors to be involved. Some projects required related expenditures from the

Capacity Building for IT in Education in Developing Countries
G. Marshall & M. Ruohonen (Eds.)

national resources. Many activities which were considered for national funding were satisfied through donor aid funding.

2 PLANNING FOR AID PROGRAMS

2.1 What aid do you want?

The aid that a country may want needs to be identified by a well-reasoned methodology - similar to the method used to allocate national resources. In general there is a surplus of ideas that warrant further examination - these will usually require feasibility studies. From such studies there will be many which need funding in the implementation phase and unless 'user pays' they will also require ongoing funding during the operation phase of the project.

Because all aid projects should be of value to the recipient country and because they will usually lead to ongoing funding drawn from the national budget the same criteria as those applied to national expenditure decisions should be applied to such projects. Only the source of funding should be different - the donor's instead of the nation's budget. Indeed, aid requests should really be for those items which cannot be funded nationally but are the next priority for expenditure - those at the 'margin'.

2.2 The national budgeting process

A methodology for the national budgeting process should be clearly defined. Revenues arise from taxation, duties, user fees and fines.

- If taxation levels are set too high there will be little foreign investment and local investment may move off shore. General economic activity may be depressed. In a subsistence economy there may be only a small tax base.
- If only a small section of the population benefits by a service then it is appropriate that the user pays unless the general population accepts that the service should be subsidized.
- Duties are tied to the movement of goods and generally inhibit trade.
- Fines rarely offset enforcement costs and may have significant compliance costs.

Thus revenue is limited.

Having determined the revenue, public expenditure will be divided into social, defence, environment, infrastructural and economic. Expenditure is clearly constrained by revenue and debt considerations. Many operational expenditures and project opportunities will be promoted by ministries and lobby groups as well as politicians. Therefore the possibilities must be ranked and prioritized.

A clear and well-enunciated policy of national priorities will ensure that potential donors have a clear understanding of projects which will be valued. This will also reassure them that the recipient country can plan and act over intermediate time frames.

It should be noted that there will be feasibility projects and implementation projects as well as ongoing operational outputs, and that some projects lead to improved infrastructure rather than to direct outputs.

Thus a developing country can develop a clear national strategy and look to aid to build on this strategy. The band of projects which fall just below the cutoff in funding available from national sources become the prime candidates for aid projects.

2.3 What aid can the donor give?

A New Zealand view of 'foreign' aid is one of offering to do what we can do well - agriculture, horticulture and animal husbandry - and to do it 'on the ground' alongside local people. Alternatively aid is given as work assignments and training in New Zealand, particularly for civil servants. As citizens in a multicultural society New Zealanders recognize that other cultures have different values arising from fundamentally different world views, and critical comments must be limited by mutual respect and a moral obligation to listen and learn first.

New Zealand has a policy of asking the recipient country what it would like. Aid can clearly make a major difference to the economic well-being of least developed countries. But to ensure success we must identify the essential ingredients of success.

3 INGREDIENTS OF SUCCESS

3.1 Getting the right aid

The motivations of donors need to be understood. They can be: generosity and compassion, mutual benefit or trade, or factors internal to the donor (for example supporting an ailing local industry) and, in the worst cases, simply dumping.

Asking for what you really want requires knowing what you really want. Even governments must do their homework to identify their real needs. Openness and consensus in the political process will ensure support and guarantee that objectives are not subverted. Policies must be clear and enabling to gain the support of nationals and of donors.

Adopting a strong methodology to prioritize development projects will ensure that donors (and particularly agencies such as the Asian Development Bank (ADB) and the International Monetary Fund (IMF)) can readily assert that their contributions are really valuable, are appropriate and free of questionable motivations.

Your need for aid must be 'sold' so how you to put your case is important. This means preparing a well-documented case and presenting it in a way which appeals to potential donors and is aligned to their criteria for aid.

Giving the donor choice is important as it provides the donor with flexibility and may lead to a better fit between donor and recipient.

Donors should be offered a 'choice from your choices'.

3.2 Writing the brief

Ensure that any feasibility studies conducted by outsiders are examined for appropriateness. Many external 'experts' bring ideas which have been formed in a different social and cultural milieu. They may not understand local competencies and may not be aware of even such apparently straightforward factors such as climate, vegetation and local natural resources. Worse, they may not be aware of infrastructural issues such as limited electrical power, water or fuel.

Ensure that the projects fit your priorities. Quietly asking for the right things first is best. It is critical to ensure that you get aid for all three phases of a project: feasibility, implementation and operation. Failure to get aid for subsequent phases can lead to 'rusting monuments' - factories built but not operational; machinery idle for lack of spare parts.

Most cultures are hesitant to place demands on aid agencies and fail to include requests for fine-tuning projects after they have been agreed in principle. Western cultures often expect you to ask for what you want and to be clear about it. If this is not your usual way to seek what you want you may have to respond anyway.

Being able to understand and develop such evaluation techniques as Economic Internal Rate of Return (used by ADB and IMF) means that your priorities can be requested with substantial justification already prepared. By setting appropriate values on local economic costs such as the value of education, the value of preventative health measures, the value of elder care and so on the EIRR techniques will help you focus on projects which will deliver the desired benefits to your country. The objectives of your requests will then be clearly understood by the donor, who may be able to think through aid planning and respond more innovatively. A better fit may be achieved.

3.3 Cultural sensitivity

Cultural sensitivity is essential for a successful working relationship. A poor experience while aid personnel are present will leave the nationals on the project with a poor image of its values. Local recipient 'ownership' is required if the project is to continue to work successfully or be further developed.

The most helpful document I received was one briefing me on the culture of the aid-requesting country. Westerners sometimes need to be reminded of the values of other cultures and that there are older cultures than Western culture. Westerners may need to be reminded that not all cultures appreciate the individualism of the West.

3.4 Doing your homework

Mother knew best when she said you must do your homework. I have seen:

- abandoned fish farms built through aid in a country with the richest oceans in the world - an agenda brought in by a consultant;
- electrical devices installed which were drawing more current than the local generation capacity - a project designed without local knowledge;

- complex engineering projects affecting tidal and river flows - projects needing the same careful planning and modeling as any such major project would receive in the West;
- an ear surgeon flown in to help when the children swam in a polluted lagoon - a project conceived because donors could not acknowledge that a previous failed project had resulted in pollution that needed expensive resolution.

The projects should not have been started without straightforward questions being asked before any commitment to proceed was made. The questions should have been asked by both parties.

Within your own (recipient) government you may need to remove inhibitors such as structural issues and colonial leftovers. Excessive regulation is expensive in all economies. Poor legislation can lead to expensive administration. Bureaucracy has been spread like a disease in the last century but may be thinned down in today's world. Rules controlling the promotion of civil servants may hinder the deployment of local expertise and leadership on short term projects. Government can rarely retain experts in the face of remuneration offers from private enterprise. You may need to accept that your local experts need to be contracted from private enterprise

3.5 A fit to local conditions

Projects need to fit local conditions. While there may be a belief that governmental systems should be sophisticated in mature economies, the Business Process Reengineering (BPR) belief in simplification should be emphasized. The best form of simplification is obliteration - does it really need to be done at all?

An unreliable infrastructure will not support sophistication. Thus the following statements may be made about computing:

- Small distributed computer systems not linked in real time but through store-and-forward messaging may be sufficient.
- Local staff skill levels may be low so focus on small simple systems. This may imply using only PCs and simple languages such as Visual Basic and databases such as *Access*.
- In developing the software a local competency must be left behind - the technology should not push the envelope. Software needs to be well-documented in the local language.
- Local conditions may require some attention to the hardware. Clearly power conditions may be marginal so uninterruptable power supply units may be required. It may not be appropriate to run computers unattended. It may be necessary to ensure that they will shut down cleanly on power failure. You may need to discuss these issues with your suppliers.

Local conditions may also give problems with rats, insects and moulds. In New Zealand, in some areas, we need protection from sulphur fumes. Be proactive - point these issues out to your prospective donors.

3.6 Basic competencies

In many under-developed countries there is a small cadre of well-educated people but they may not be able to meet all the time demands of systems support staff.

The development of local information systems skills - software installation and upgrades, monitoring disk utilization, back-up procedures and elementary problem-resolution - is essential.

The project must leave behind a mechanism which enables local competencies to continue to build towards self-sufficiency. A train-the-trainer regime may need to be created. This will require that leadership opportunities are identified, created and nurtured.

As with any management activity it is necessary to ensure the competencies of your external advisers and to quality-assure their advice. If sensitive, this may have to be done informally. Use all your networks - previous consultants, university contacts from your past, acquaintances. Seek out other success stories.

3.7 Keep projects small

In the new Silicon Valley 'execution' model the emphasis is on handling projects which have early deliverables. A target is often stated as 'deliver something within six weeks which the user can exploit immediately'.

This 'Just do it' attitude enables the recipient user to evaluate the task deliverable and implement it. The user can then ask more precisely for the next deliverable and define what it should contain. This leads to learning so that the next deliverable is more focused. The long-term strategy is to continually adapt to experience and to the learning that is inevitably occurring for the users.

3.8 Ownership being left with nationals

When the consultant moves on, local staff must support the project in the operational phase. A mechanism for on-going advice must be established. The Internet now provides access to advice through low priority e-mail and the World Wide Web. Provided the telephone system is up once a day or so, messages can be moved to international centres of expertise but especially to the original consultant, who can continue to provide liaison and information source references. Such forms of low priority but expert support encourage local staff to take responsibility which they may otherwise avoid because they feel they have insufficient skills.

4 SUPPORT ACTIVITIES

The Internet gives new opportunities for developing countries in several key ways.

4.1 Scientific support

If scientists have participated in an aid project they will have a better understanding of local conditions and competencies. Using the Internet then enables the local staff to remain in contact with the experts. The experts can devise solutions and, because they understand the local competencies and infrastructure, they can give advice that can be implemented locally by recipient nationals.

Centres of excellence with ongoing international electronic links will ensure that best-in-class knowledge remains available to locals working in the field. Thus the advice available to the recipient should be no less than to staff in a developed country.

4.2 Transfer of data for complex analysis

Data requiring complex analysis can be forwarded to a research institute in the donor country where it can be analyzed, the results interpreted and quality advice returned. Such analysis projects are likely to be funded under scientific research grants rather than through aid projects.

Empathy and rapport can be built between recipient field workers and the donor country scientists.

4.3 Software support

Software enhancements and general support can be provided over the World Wide Web. They can be self-installing, reducing the need for expertise at each computer site.

4.4 Computer-based training

CBT courses can be delivered over the World Wide Web. Because they often require long time periods online it may be best for such material to be distributed on CD-ROM rather than only over the Internet. This is an effective way to keep staff with basic skills in touch with current developments or with changes in the current knowledge base.

Such courses need to be developed using examples which are within the experience of the recipient user and which are culturally appropriate. Indeed such distance education may be the dominant method of all professionals keeping their competencies and knowledge up-to-date in the future.

4.5 Peer support

The Internet allows staff to maintain contact with their original trainers who might be university staff or peers in the donor country. Most of us have the benefit of ongoing contact with our teachers and peer group. Such people networks need to be maintained.

5 A NATIONAL INFORMATION SYSTEMS STRATEGY

A national strategy may be needed to develop information systems competencies. The first need is to develop an extensive base of software developers competent in simple tools such as *Access* and Visual Basic.

Even in the West less than 2% of users of Microsoft *Office* have formal training. Therefore promote wide-spread preliminary training in software products and then form support groups so that the more talented may increase their ability to exploit the software more extensively. Those people can then be available as support staff to others.

It is possible to gain aid for projects in order to set up full training facilities and to staff them with experts for the initial year. Naturally the teaching examples must be suitable and within the experience of local staff for learning to occur.

I believe that courses delivered by experts made available through aid need to focus on finding the best local talents and to build their competencies. It should matter little that they are in the public or the private sector. Indeed a healthy flow between the two sectors builds a pool of competent staff who can be retained on any one project in the public sector. A centre of expertise may need to be established to continue to build on such expertise

6 SUMMARY

Nationals of the donor country charged with concluding aid agreements should endeavour to do the following:

- Take the initiative.
- Ask for what you want.
- Give clear justification for what you want.
- Use the donor's rules.
- Ensure that what you want fits with overall government priorities.
- Ensure that every project enhances local competencies and capability.
- Do not be too concerned whether it is 'public' or 'private' good.

These actions will each improve the likelihood of gaining the maximum benefit from the aid. Finally, if you can publish the success stories, especially back in the donor country, you may receive ongoing aid, and a bonding between your nationals and the donors leading to more trade, more transfer of skills and knowledge.

7 BIOGRAPHY

Ian Mitchell completed a Master of Science in Nuclear Physics in 1964 and joined IBM as a systems engineer. He has 35 years of experience in information processing and management consultancy. He has supervised large software projects, taught postgraduate courses in software engineering, information systems strategy, management awareness and the management of information technology. He has expertise in public sector software, including financial management software. He has consulted for the Asian Development Bank and has delivered papers in several Asian countries. He is the President of the New Zealand Computer Society, and has been a member of TC 3 and WG 3.3.

25

Building capacity for Information Technology in educational management in developing countries

Adrie J. Visscher
University of Twente
Department of Educational Science and Technology
P. O. Box 217
7500 AE Enschede
The Netherlands
E-mail: Visscher@edte.utwente.nl

Abstract
Information Technology has important benefits for the administration and management of educational institutions. Important aspects of School Information System (SIS) planning and implementation are the approaches used for analyzing the school from an information processing perspective, the implementation process itself, and the degree to which the SIS matches essential school organizational characteristics. In this paper each aspect is elaborated and the importance of its relation to the use and effects of SISs for developing countries is explained.

Keywords
Developing countries, systems design, management, information handling, capacity building

1 INTRODUCTION

Experience gained through research and development activities in Hong Kong, Australia, New Zealand, Great Britain, Israel, the USA and The Netherlands over the last ten years (Visscher, 1991; 1992; 1994; 1996) shows that Information Technology and Educational Management (ITEM) is a valuable tool for developing countries. ITEM, the use of technology for the support of clerical and management

Capacity Building for IT in Education in Developing Countries
G. Marshall & M. Ruohonen (Eds.)

activities in educational institutions, may improve the efficiency and effectiveness of school staff. Efficiency is the relation between the input for and the output of data, resulting in savings for educational institutions. School effectiveness, the degree to which the school goals are realized, may also be positively influenced. A discussion of school effectiveness as well as important factors in the design and introduction of SISs will be discussed to help developing countries determine a strategy that will enable them to benefit from computerized data management.

2 THE NATURE OF SCHOOL INFORMATION SYSTEMS AND THEIR POTENTIAL BENEFITS

A computerized SIS is an information system based on one or more computers with a database and one or more computer applications. Together the system enables computer-assisted storage, manipulation, retrieval and distribution of school data.

The contents of the SIS and the support it can provide depends, among other things, on the number of applications (*e.g.* student registration, personnel registration, timetable construction, etc.) it includes. The nature of the applications can differ considerably. Sometimes they only support clerical and school office activities; in other cases they also assist school managers in their work.

Registering data leads to a database with data concerning the organizational environment. Clerical staff retrieve and manipulate data from the database. An SIS framework is presented that was constructed on the basis of an analysis of Dutch schools for secondary education. The framework consists of seven registrational (Figure 1) and four management (Figure 2) school information subsystems.

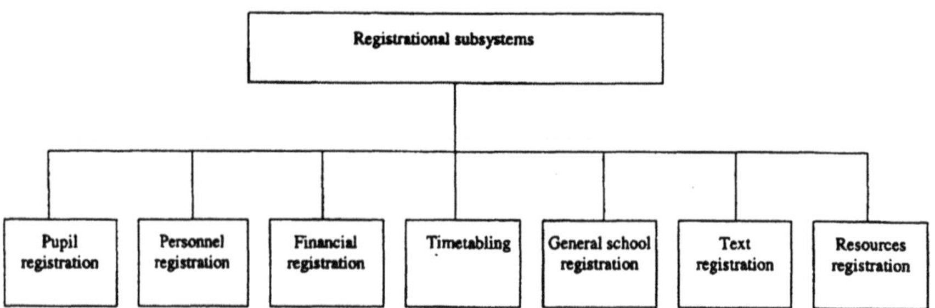

Figure 1. Registrational subsystems

The registrational subsystems support the use and manipulation of student, financial, personnel and other data. The student registration subsystem concerns the heart of the school office - student data with regard to enrolmnt, absenteeism, student counseling, testing and deletion.

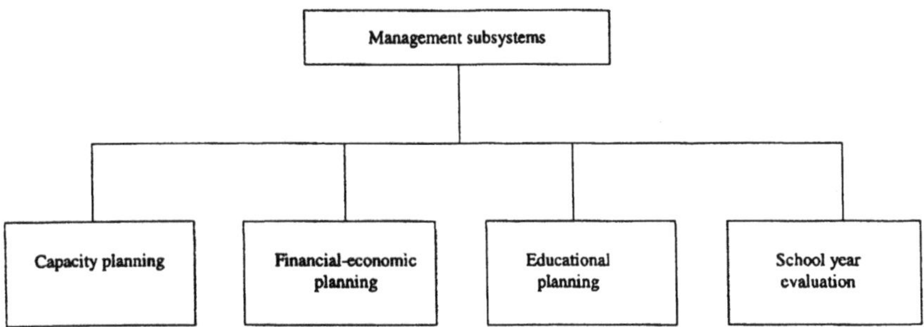

Figure 2. Management subsystems

The four management subsystems shown in Figure 2 support different types of activities:

- capacity planning: planning physical facilities, staff and technical facilities. The computer can assist the development of plans by providing reports regarding the current situation, computing the number of staff needed and providing information on the effects of alternative capacity-planning measures;
- educational planning: allocating the number of lessons to staff members and constructing the timetable;
- financial planning: estimating the expected revenues and their proposed allocation;
- school year evaluation: evaluating what has been planned. The subsystem uses financial, social and educational data to answer pertinent evaluation questions such as, 'What percent of students move to other schools?' 'What are their grades and did they pass the final examination?', or 'What budgets have been exceeded over the past five years and how many times has this occurred?'

2.1 (Expected) effects of system use

The use of SISs is expected to improve school efficiency and effectiveness. Efficiency may be influenced positively as a result of:

- single entry and multiple use of school data; in the pre-computer situation data were registered several times at different locations;
- computer-assisted transfer of data on various internal and external forms;
- computer-supported data manipulation;
- computer-assisted data exchange with external bodies and institutions.

Although it is very difficult to prove time and human resources savings through educational research, the above mentioned benefits are plausible. More effectiveness may be possible in schools for a number of reasons:

- improved efficiency enables the carrying out of activities that, in former days, were impossible because school staff were occupied with registrational activities;

- staff can find better solutions for structured allocation problems (*e.g.* timetables) because the computer can now show alternative solutions from which the best one can be chosen;
- SISs enable better process control; in case certain standards are exceeded (*e.g.* the number of times a student is allowed to play truant, a student/class achievement level, department budgets, etc.), the computer can observe that something is going wrong and requires the attention of school staff. A more timely reaction may help schools function more effectively;
- policy development and evaluation. If school data are registered in a database that enables investigating the relationship between variables (*e.g.* between truancy and student achievement) and more informed school policy making becomes possible. Moreover, it becomes easier to study the effects of policy measures (for instance whether the number of truants has been reduced or not).

Just as it is very difficult to prove efficiency improvements empirically, more school effectiveness as a consequence of the use of SISs is surrounded by obstacles. However, the fact that the majority of schools using an SIS would refuse to return to the old manual system confirms our positive opinion on the impact of SISs. Schools are especially enthusiastic about efficiency improvements; effectiveness improvements have not yet been demonstrated.

3 A PROPOSED WAY TO ASSIMILATE SISS IN DEVELOPING COUNTRIES

In the design and introduction of computer-assisted management information systems many variables and relationships between the variables play a role. In the discussion about this topic Figure 3 may be helpful.

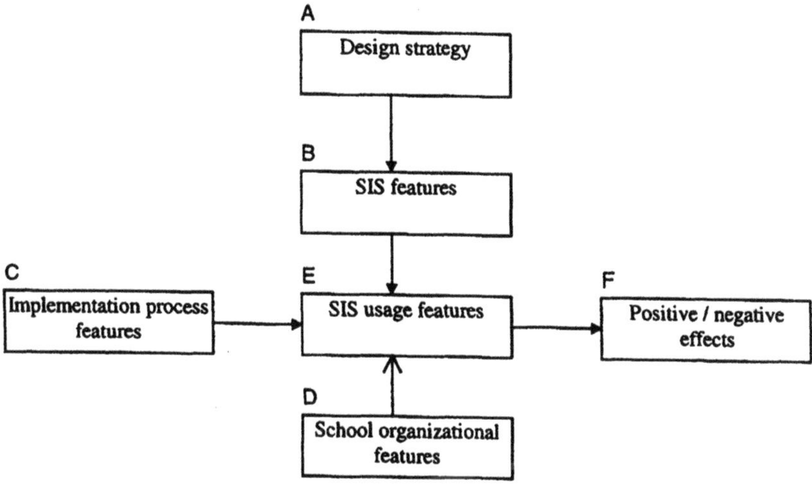

Figure 3. The variable groups influencing school information system usage and its effects

Figure 3 consists of six groups of variables: the design strategy, the SIS features, the extent of SIS use, the features of the implementation process, the school organizational features, system use, and the positive and negative effects of system use. The arrows between the variable groups show that system use is supposed to be determined by information system quality features - which result from the chosen design strategy - as well as from the nature of the implementation process (the training users receive), and of the organization into which the SIS is introduced. The (un)planned effects are considered to be a function of the intensity with which and way in which a SIS is used at various school levels.

With respect to the central question of this paper, what is a good SIS design and implementation strategy for developing countries constitutes, Figure 3 shows the interrelatedness of many factors - each of the six variable groups consists of many variables. Neither the information system quality nor the implementation process, or the school features alone can fully explain how the SIS is used and which impact system usage has. The impact of the system depends on system usage features, which are dependent on the variables in the blocks A, B , C and D. The combination of variables is decisive for what happens.

Although much more empirical research on the contents of the blocks and desirable combinations of variables is needed some know-how regarding variables 'that matter' is available. Each block in Figure 3 is discussed now.

3.1 Design strategy

The history of ITEM shows an evolution in the strategies for designing SISs. Important elements of the strategy concern the automation goals strived for, the way in which the organisational analysis that forms the basis for the SIS definition is carried out and how the standardisation/flexibility problem - to develop an SIS that is standard but flexible enough to be used in as many schools as possible - is addressed.

In the first stages pioneer teachers developed one or a few computer applications to improve the efficiency of school office activities. System analysis and design were not very professional at that time. Their strategy may be labelled a 'first things first' approach. One started with developing the first application (*e.g.* student registration). When it had been realised the search for another application started and so on. The software was designed for use in a small number of schools and was tailor-made for that school.

In the next stage software vendors entered the arena, developing more clerical applications with the goal to sell their standard SISs to as many schools as possible. Although designers operated more professionally than before, still no profound analysis of the school has been carried out as a basis for system development. Though complete integration of the SIS modules was still distant there was more attention to the relationships between the various applications.

The third and last group of SIS designers strived for sophisticated comprehensive systems. In addition to the efficiency of clerical work, increased school effectiveness became an automation goal. Designers became aware that SISs can support managers in their work in valuable ways, and the goal is to determine all useful forms of support for clerical and management school staff. To accomplish this goal a fundamental design strategy (Visscher, 1994) is chosen to draw a picture of the entire school in terms of the information demands at various school levels, the information flows between these levels, and between the school and external organisations.

Once the overview is available and the architecture - modules and mutual relationships - of the entire SIS is known, the modules it consists of can be developed in a stepwise manner. User participation in system design to balance the role of computer science experts is important. Realising quality systems also requires extensive formative evaluation of prototype-SISs in the intended implementation situation.

Such an evaluation of the match between user-context characteristics and SIS features must start early and not stop before the iterative test-redesign cycles have led to an SIS that is appreciated by designers and users. In other words, the cycles ideally do not stop before the high-perceived SIS quality equals the high-actual quality. Too often too little time is spent on analysis, design and the systematic collection of user feedback as a basis for SIS development. As a result resources are wasted to a certain degree, users complain, become frustrated and do not benefit fully from the SIS.

The SISs designed in the third stage are meant to be used in as many schools as possible. However, although the SIS is standard, wherever possible it has been tried to achieve a compromise between standardisation and the specific features of each school, which asks for flexibility. Schools can choose the modules they need and in the modules user options are created. The use of relational databases in combination with query languages, enables users to determine for themselves which specific information they retrieve from the SIS.

The fundamental approach of the third stage can be observed in countries that have started early with ITEM. If a developing country plans to build capacity in this area it definitely must start with the fundamental, participative, centralised - develop one system for all schools at a central level - design approach. It will be expensive but the cost and effort invested will return the investment by important school efficiency and school effectiveness improvements, It also avoids the loss of capital that would result from developing SISs in less profound ways, which after some time will prove to be unsatisfactory and cannot be optimised.

3.2 SIS features

Although there is little empirical research on which SIS features influence SIS use some ideas on factors 'that matter' can be presented. Systems that from a technical point of view are very sophisticated may neither be appreciated nor used by the target group because the systems do not consider the essential features of the user context and are therefore perceived to be inadequate.

Important quality aspects of SISs are the extent and quality of the support they offer to school staff in terms of the information handling activities supported as well as how the information handling has been accomplished. Other SIS quality aspects concern the ease-of-use of the SIS for the average user (how easy it is to enter, retrieve and output data), the transparency of the SIS and the difficulty of navigating through it. System reliability (does it always work?), accuracy and speed also influence the extent of system use. The appeal and added value of the SIS information in comparison with other ways of data handling are also important considerations. If the analysis of computer data consumes a lot of time and effort but does not help much users probably will not use the SIS intensely.

3.3 Implementation process features

'People variables' prove to be crucial in the process of introducing SISs. The motivation of users for the innovation influences the success of the introduction of the SIS into schools and should therefore receive the required attention from those who support users in implementing the system. Related to this are opportunities for users to influence system implementation. A project champion encouraging the innovation and solving problems also seems to increase the chance of successful implementation (Fung, 1991). Limited resources to innovate frequently overload those involved in the innovation process. A careful management of the innovation process is crucial: clear innovation goals and a feasible innovation pace are essential. Schools need time to assimilate a SIS module into their organisation.

Visscher (1994) says a school-based project team, consisting of a group of school staff with the relevant SIS know-how should be convened and dispersed throughout the school. Thus, if one staff member leaves the school this will not cause big problems for the continuation of ITEM.

Support during the innovation process is also very important for quick answers to user requests for information that rise when they invest in this new, uncertain activity. Clear manuals can also help users when direct support is impossible.

Though user-training is essential, it usually does not receive the attention it requires. The training is often too technical (the use of software and hardware) and neither focuses on computer-supported management activities nor on how the system output must be interpreted and used in school decision-making. If schools are not coached on such problems matters the probability that powerful SISs with management supporting capacity are only used as automated card-trays supporting clerical school staff increases.

3.4 School organisational factors

The extent to which the school leader supports the innovation is probably influenced by what s/he knows about the potential of these systems and his/her skills and experience in this field is decisive for the success of introducing SISs into schools. An enthusiastic school leader stimulates system use, takes and supports initiatives in this area, allocating resources (hardware, software, time) to it.

The readiness of schools to benefit fully from the SIS, especially for higher-order management activities, will also influence the extent of system use. In schools that do not meet the conditions for this form of system use rather drastic organisational development work is necessary to move to that level of system use.

School managers receive information from a variety of sources and their work consists of many short activities. Profound problem analysis is rare; the use of quick, informal, verbal information, matching with their own views and triggering actions is very common. Moreover, they are not experienced in using quantitative data. Such characteristics of the school organisation do not fit with the features of SISs very well. So attention has to be paid to the perceptions of school managers who must learn to value the power of SISs and to experience how they can benefit from SISs in addition to the informal sources they use.

Organisational problems are not taken away by introducing a SIS. To enhance the successful introduction of SISs at clerical and management school level serious organisational problems need to be solved before the SIS is introduced into the school.

Teachers usually operate autonomously in the teaching-learning process which, because of its unpredictability and complexity, asks for professional discretion. More management information on how teachers function in the primary process may, for that reason, not result in fundamental changes in their activities.

3.5 System use

System use can differ with respect to the degree to which users transform their old activities and procedures into new ones. In many cases the innovation remains restricted to replacing old manual procedures by the same, but computer-assisted, ones or by adapting old operations a bit. The degree of innovative system use is influenced by:

- the degree to which the SIS enables substantial new ways of operation;
- the type of system use the school is aiming for and capable of;
- the degree to which the required implementation support is given.

SISs are until now mainly used for clerical work; computer-supported school management remains very limited. In some countries this may be due to the fact that the available SISs can not support school management work substantially. However in countries with powerful SISs it does not happen to a large extent either! Probably the use of the SIS in solving complex allocation problems causes less problems than benefiting from the computer's assistance in solving ill-structured problems. The former does not ask much from the user since the data are entered and the SIS generates alternative solutions from which the manager can choose the one /she likes most. The latter type of system use requires much more since the users must:

- determine which information one would like to retrieve from the SIS;
- retrieve the information;
- interpret the output correctly;
- use the information in school decision-making;
- evaluate the results of the decisions taken.

The second and third skills are more or less technical, and managers can be trained to acquire them without great difficulty. The others are harder to acquire. To critically evaluate how a school functions, to detect problems and causes, and to design and evaluate remedies will require organisational development in most schools. That may well be a lengthy procedure and demand a great effort from schools and their managers. Nevertheless, the added value of sophisticated SISs is such that not trying to bring schools to this level of system usage would be a great loss.

3. 6 Effects of system use

Research on the impact of system use is limited. Actually, large scale empirical research on its impact has just started in a number of countries - Hong Kong, The United Kingdom and The Netherlands.

Although user perceptions concerning the effects of system use are positive (a better quality of registration, available information and decision-making, more efficiency, and better allocations) strong empirical evidence for SIS effects is lacking. Although most users hate the idea that their SISs would be taken away and few users perceive negative effects, the quality of schooling until now is not considered to have improved as a result of SISs. The benefits are probably especially gained in the school administrative area.

4 CONCLUSION

Developing countries can benefit from the experience gained in developed countries in using a strategy for designing SISs, and implementing them with a high probability of SIS acceptance and use by the target users. Crucial elements of such a strategy are:

- the careful analysis of the school concerning its information demands and information flows;
- a definition of the SIS framework, containing a complete definition of all required capabilities that can be obtained from the SIS;
- the step-by-step participative design and development of prototypes for the modules in the SIS architecture in iterative design-test-redesign cycles, until it supports users widely in valuable and user-friendly ways, and system designers and users are happy with them;

- the attention paid to the planning and managing of the innovation process (*e.g.* clear goals, feasible planning);
- the allocation of sufficient resources for the innovation and the dispersal of expertise among school staff;
- the stimulation of users by explaining, showing and letting them experience the potential of SISs;
- the preparation and training of users for system use at clerical and managerial level;
- the ensuring of the probability that users will experience success during the first innovative activities;
- the support for users during the introduction of the SIS by answering questions, by helping to solve problems and by developing support material they can refer to if problems occur.

Since individual schools do not have the expertise and resources to operate in the proposed way and commercial enterprises would have to invest too much in relation to the potential revenues, an active government is needed. The government must combine the required resources and expertise, and coordinate the entire process of design and implementation. If this condition is not fulfilled a waste of resources is unavoidable and school staff will not be able to work with professional SISs that can help them to enhance the quality of schools and schooling.

5 REFERENCES

Visscher, A.J. (ed.) (1991) Computer-assisted school administration and management: an international analysis. Special issue of the *Journal of Research on Computing in Education*, **24**(1), 1-168.

Visscher, A.J. (1992) *Design and Evaluation of a Computer-assisted Management Information System for Secondary Schools* (doctoral dissertation), University of Twente, Enschede, The Netherlands.

Visscher, A.J. (ed.) (1996) Information Technology in Educational Management. Special issue of the *International Journal of Educational Research*, **25**(4), 289-390.

Visscher, A.J. (1994) A fundamental methodology for designing management information systems for schools. *Journal of Research on Computing in Education*, **27**(2), 231-249.

Fung, A.C.W. (1991) Computer assisted school administration in Hong Kong. *Journal of Research on Computing in Education*, **24**(1), 120-145.

6 BIOGRAPHY

A.J. Visscher has been an assistant professor in the Faculty of Educational Science and Technology of the University of Twente since 1983. He received his Ph.D. for his doctoral thesis *Design and Evaluation of a Computer-assisted Management Information System for Secondary Schools.* In collaboration with others he designed and evaluated an integrated school information system (SIS) for secondary schools. Among the articles he has published on computerised SISs are special issues in the *Journal of Research on Computing in Education* and the *International Journal of Educational Research.*

26

Information Technology resources for education in developing countries

Marsha R. Williams
CDP Professor of Computer Science
Director of Project MISET (Minorities in Science, Engineering & Technology)
Department of Computer Science, Tennessee State University
3500 John A. Merritt Blvd. McCord Hall, Room 5
P.O. Box 9604
Nashville, TN 37209-1561, USA
Tele + 615 963-7039 or 615 963 5852; Fax + 615 963 5099
E-mail: WILL002@ACAD.TNSTATE.EDU

Abstract

Information Technology (IT) resources include not only equipment, particularly computers, but also software and experts as well as students, teachers and parents. Resources are provided by government, industry, education, associations and collaborations. Developing countries, which are often rich in people, land and natural resources, are, in many cases, poor in even the traditional educational resources (teachers, schools, desks and books). They are especially poor in IT resources. In this paper, IT resources for education in developing countries are reported from available statistical data and from related literature. IT resources have the potential for making education accessible and enhanced for many, even over great distances - which is a critical need in many developing countries. A hierarchy of IT resources is described, which, if considered as a whole, and applied appropriately and respectfully, could play a key role in building the capacity of a developing country for improving not only education but also government, business and the quality of life for all.

Capacity Building for IT in Education in Developing Countries
G. Marshall & M. Ruohonen (Eds.)

Keywords
Informatics, resources, developing countries, elementary education, secondary education, higher education, vocational education

1 INTRODUCTION

Information Technology (IT) is a means of communication and telecommunication over large distances, involving a combination of computers, networks, satellites, telephones, radio, television and other electronics (Stover, 1984). IT resources involve not only equipment (hardware) but also software (programs), people, education, government and association/collaboration resources. The consideration of the many resources required for the application of IT to education involves many disciplines related to computers in the handling, processing, management, automation and communication of information in the broader cultural and economic context of a society. The discipline, which is called informatics, is a new and modern form of communication (Stover, 1984)

The commonly-referenced terms, developed countries and developing countries, were not found to have standard international definitions and there will be exceptions to the descriptions used herein. Developed countries (*New Encyclopedia Brittanica*, 1980) are generally high-income, industrialized countries with high per capita gross domestic product (GDP - the value of goods and services produced within a nation in a year; the gross national product (GNP) is the GDP, plus income earned abroad, minus income earned by foreigners from domestic production.), high literacy rates and low rates of population growth. Countries such as the United States, Japan and the United Kingdom are considered as developed countries.

Developing countries (*New Encyclopedia Brittanica*, 1980), underdeveloped or less-developed, 'Third World' countries are generally low-income, agricultural countries with low per capita GDP, low literacy rates and high rates of population growth. At the top (in terms of development) of the group of less-developed countries are the newly-industrializing economies (OECD, 1992) or advanced developing countries, whose economies have experienced rapid industrialization, including Brazil, Hong Kong, Mexico and Singapore. At the bottom of the group of developing countries is a group called least-developed, or undeveloped, countries with no significant economic growth, very low per capita GDP and low literacy rates.

Much of the data on IT resources for education in developing countries reported here will use the format of the UNESCO (1997) grouping of countries into developed countries and developing countries. UNESCO further subdivides the developing countries into six sub-groupings (Sub-Saharan Africa, Arab States, Latin America and the Caribbean, Eastern Asia and Oceania, Southern Asia and the Least Developed Countries). The UNESCO groupings will be used in this paper's tables with selected data from some of the UNESCO tables (1997), along with data and calculations from a number of other sources. Although data on the status of IT in developing countries is limited and not the latest, it nevertheless shows the big picture of IT resources in a few developing countries from each of the major world sub-groupings in comparison to two major developed countries.

2 IT EQUIPMENT AND SOFTWARE RESOURCES

Key resources for the use of IT in education are equipment resources such as the computer, television and radio. Table 1 shows the radios, televisions, phones and computers per 1,000 inhabitants in selected developing and developed countries (for comparison). The criteria for selection were simply the availability of pertinent data, particularly on computers in these countries.

According to *The Computer Industry Almanac* estimates (1994), there were approximately 173 million computers in use worldwide by the end of 1993, with nearly 43%, or 74 million computers, in use in the USA alone. Another 40% of the world's computers were used in 17 other large industrialized, developed countries such as Japan, Germany, UK and France, which accounted for just over four-fifths of the world's computers. This left less than one-fifth, or approximately 29.4 million computers, in use in the nearly 200 other countries of the world, including less-developed countries (more than three-quarters of the world's population). If all the 29.4 million computers were in developing countries (and they are not), there were roughly 7 computers per 1000 inhabitants in less-developed countries at the end of 1993. As is shown in Table 1, the computers for the selected developing countries are near this rough estimate. Hong Kong, which is one of the newly industrializing economies, shows a much higher number of computers.

Radios, televisions and telephones are much more plentiful than computers in the selected developing countries but are still far less available in the developing countries than in the developed countries. Table 1 also gives some indication of the amount of educational programming on TV and on radio in a few countries.

Television broadcasting in developing countries has presented a number of problems, such as technician training on appropriate technology, expensive, advanced broadcasting equipment and lack of frequency/line standardization for sharing programs. As seen in Table 1 there are many more radios in developing countries than televisions, which vastly outnumber computers, at least for the selected countries.

Though cost-prohibitive for most developing countries, satellite technology has offered a means of delivering distance education to remote locations in Mexico, a number of Southeast Asian nations (Sussman and Lent, 1991) and India (Stover, 1984). Volunteers in Technical Assistance (VITA, www.vita.org on the World Wide Web), a private organization that provides technical assistance and information to developing countries, has developed a global communications system (VITAcomm) which consists of VITASAT (low-earth-orbiting system, LEO, for messages and files), VITAPAC (independent terrestrial digital radio systems for low-cost radio communication with computers) and VITANET (electronic message delivery system, mailer and bulletin board, using existing telephone networks). VITAcomm technologies can be used anywhere in the world, even if telephone and electricity resources are not available, which can be the norm in rural areas of a developing country, though the use for education is presently unknown.

Table 1 IT equipment resources

	Radio[a c] per 1000	TV[a] per 1000	Phones[b] per 1000	Computers [b] per 1000	Education al program[a] hours Radio	TV
Developing Countries		104				
Sub-Sahara Africa	152	28				
Zimbabwe	71	27	12[c]		9.9	
Arab States	251	104				
Saudi Arabia	217	255	160	24	2.0	
Latin America	354	171				
Mexico	233	163	91[c]	17		
Eastern Asia Oceania	197	156				
China	172	189	12	9		
Hong Kong	588[d]	291	570	101		
Southern Asia	88	35				
Pakistan	402	77	19	13[c]	6.6	7.0
Least Developed Countries	98	10				
Kiribati	161	192	23[c]		88.7	
Developed Countries						
USA	2000	817	965	287		
UK	1111	439	615	162		
World	357	195	155	31		

[a] UNESCO Statistical Yearbook, 1996 [b] Computer Industry Almanac, 1994
[c] World Almanac (individual nation), 1997 [d] Brittanica Book of the Year, 1997

An International Connectivity Table (Version 15, June 15, 1996) is available on the World Wide Web that shows the network connections of nations around the world (ftp.cs.wisc.edu). From that table, the selected developing countries in this paper were found to have 1-3 network connections. Most of the cited developing countries showed all three connections - International IP Internet links, UUCP sites and FIDONET sites for e-mail only, with some sites not being widespread. Developing countries with less than all three connections were Hong Kong (IP, FIDONET), Pakistan (IP, UUCP), Saudi Arabia (IP) and Kiribati (minimal UUCP). A related connectivity map of Africa showed about one-third of Africa with no network connectivity at all and about another third with e-mail only as of November 1995. E-mail connections in Zimbabwe, for example, are provided through the nationwide FIDONET and the University of Zimbabwe's Zimbix network with Internet connection through Rhodes University in South Africa (Buxton, 1995). CD-ROM is used to search databases, and several schools in Harare communicate about the environment and climate with other schools around the world in the Global Laboratory program. One Harare school participates in the Global Student Village program, receiving meteorology satellite signals and connecting via e-mail to USA Global Student Village schools.

In addition to the equipment, or hardware, requirements for the use of IT in education, there must also be software, or programs and applications, to direct the hardware in producing information that is educationally useful. Such software resources can range from simple games, word processing, programming and drill-and-practice to sophisticated programming, computer-assisted instruction (CAI), computer-managed instruction (CMI), computer-aided learning (CAL) and simulations in support of education. For example, the Korean Educational Development Institute developed a collection of CAI software for improving the teaching/learning process in the late eighties (Hebenstreit, *et. al.*, 1992). Various computer media - interactive videodisc players and the newer compact disk (CD-ROM) drives in microcomputers - are being employed in education, but no statistical data specific to their use in developing countries was found.

3 IT GOVERNMENT, PEOPLE AND EDUCATION RESOURCES

A group of nine small countries, most with populations less than or near 5 million, were recently reported as major IT producers or sophisticated users (Dedrick, Goodman and Kraemer, 1995), including two developing countries that are newly industrializing economies - Hong Kong and Singapore. The other countries were Denmark, Finland, Ireland, Israel, New Zealand, Norway and Sweden. The report looked at the factors that determine a small country's IT success, or lack thereof. Environmental factors included a minimum development level (more than a few thousand GDP per capita), a good basic educational system and high literacy rates or specialized skills. In all the small countries there are communities well-connected to the international IT community (Internet, conferences, journals) with advanced telecommunications infrastructures. The report noted that an open government policy towards foreign trade and investment is a key factor, as well as government promotion of IT production and use.

While very few developing countries fit this profile, the report suggests the critical resources needed to begin to approach such a level of IT achievement, even for a small country. Though IT data and its use in education are not available for many developing countries, Table 2 is a compilation of data that indicates the status of such IT resources as government spending in areas related to IT, and education and literacy levels. The countries cited are the same ones that appear in Table 1 for continuity and consistency.

For the developing countries R&D expenditure as a percentage of GNP (1997) is low in comparison to that of developed countries, as is the GDP per capita, with the exception of the newly industrializing economy of Hong Kong, whose GDP is comparable to that of the United States and higher than that of the United Kingdom! 1990 IT spending estimates in billions of 1990 US$, as reported by the Organisation for Economic Cooperation and Development (OECD) (OECD, 1992), are available for only a few developing countries, where the estimates are all low, compared to the cited developed countries.

Using data from the International Data Corporation (1990) the 1990 world IT spending on products and services is $305 billion (US$). The growth rate of the world IT market (1989-90) is estimated to be 12%, with software accounting for the majority of this growth (17%). The IT spending breakdown (1989) was 60-70% for hardware (90% for China), 20-30% for software, 1-5% for data communications and 5-10% for data services. As expected, hardware is a major investment for IT users. Only six developed countries accounted for 80% of the world IT spending - USA, Japan, Germany, France, UK and Italy. Ten developing countries (newly industrializing economies) accounted for 5% of world IT spending in 1989.

Table 2 shows that public education spending (1994 US$) per capita in developing countries (UNESCO, 1997), from which would likely come IT educational spending, is very low for least-developed countries, Asia, Oceania and Africa. As expected, per capita education spending in developing countries is far less than in the developed countries. Literacy rates, as indicated by the percent of literate of persons over age 15 as shown in Table 2, are low for Sub-Sahara Africa, the Arab States, Southern Asia and the least-developed countries. It is the literate population that would be potential first trainees in the use of IT and could then assist in bringing literacy to the rest of the population with the help of IT!

Katz (1988) reported politics (growth of government) as the decisive variable in the transition of developing countries to information societies. For example, in a developing country the government may operate the existing communication industries and impose tariffs to protect the industries from new information technologies. Earlier researchers showed that the growth of information occupations and the diffusion (adaptation and use in society) of IT in developed countries are mainly determined by the growth in markets/economy (production of goods and services), influenced by politics.

Table 2 IT government/people/education resources

	GDP per Capita[a]	Literacy % over age 15[d]	R&D expenditures as % GDP	Higher Ed R&D personnel	Public education spending per capita
Developing Countries		70			45
Sub-Sahara Africa		57			28
Zimbabwe	1.6				
Arab States		57			112
Saudi Arabia	9.5				
Latin America/ Caribbean		87			152
Mexico	7.9	20.9	0.3	10,988	
Eastern Asia/ Oceania		84			31
China	2.5		0.6	141,100	
Hong Kong	23.1[b]				
Southern Asia		50			13
Pakistan	1.9		0.9	5580	
Least Developed Countries		49			8
Kiribati	0.80				
Developed Countries		99			1179
USA	27.6			2.4	128000
UK	18.0			2.2	66000
World	5.9		77		244

[a] World Almanac, 1997 [b] Brittanica Book of the Year, 1997 [c] Billion US$ (OECD, 1992) [d]UNESCO, 1996

From a 1988-89 study of the educational use of computers in developing countries, Hawkridge, Jaworski and McMahon (1990) address the critical issue of computer training, especially for teachers, as a major factor on the success or failure of IT in education. They emphasize that training is needed, not only for teachers, but also for indigenous teacher trainers, school administrators, revisers of curriculum to integrate computers, software evaluators, specifiers and developers, hardware selectors, and maintainers and policy-makers. Developing countries may seek educational consultants, as resource persons, from developed countries but should be aware that what they propose in hardware, software and training may, or may not, be appropriate for a particular developing country. Input from teachers, students and parents, as important resource people in a developing country, could help insure that what is implemented is appropriate. In addition, a support system needs to be readily available on the use of IT for education.

4 IT ASSOCIATIONS AND COLLABORATIONS

Professional associations related to IT exist in a number of developing countries and are resources for training, personnel, seminars, conferences, consultations as well as the promotion of IT in education, government, business and in society. A number of international organizations also exist, involving multiple governments, multinational corporations and professional societies in the promotion of IT in education through the exchange of information, and the sharing of expertise, experience, mutual support and cooperation.

UNESCO recently convened, with the cooperation of the Government of the Russian Federation, the Second International Congress on Education and Informatics (EI '96) - Educational Policies and New Technologies - held in Moscow, July 1-5, 1996 (Khvilon and Patru, 1997). At EI '96, declarations and recommendations were adopted by UNESCO, the UN Development Programme, the International Labour Organization (ILO) and the World Bank committing support for the use of IT in education, particularly in developing countries.

In the mid 1980s UNESCO sponsored the Intergovernmental Informatics Programme (Hebentreit, *et. al.*, 1992) in support of training, infrastructure building and national policy development. During the same period, the developed countries cooperated in the use of IT in education through the Commission of the European Community (CEC) and OECD's Centre for Educational Research and Innovation (CERI). A number of collaborative projects between institutions of higher learning that emphasize the use of IT in education has been reported. For example, the Africa Informatics Research Project (Buxton, 1995) involves UNESCO, the African Academy of Science (AAS) and the Association of African Universities in developing the regional cooperation of university informatics research centers and others in solving regional problems.

This paper proposes an association, or 'hierarchy', of countries, regions or schools (in terms of level of IT development only) that might facilitate the sharing of IT educational resources, where the 'development distance' (and perhaps also the 'physical distance' and 'cultural distance') between participants is not great. This is not to suggest that existing relationships between nations nor new linkages between any nations be restricted, but that such a hierarchy could facilitate easier/better understanding and the more appropriate application of IT in education in developing countries. Developed countries could be viewed as resources for developing countries with newly industrializing economies, which could be resources for other developing countries with growing economies, which in turn could be resources for least-developed countries.

Schools and students in developing and developed countries, or in urban and private schools, with IT experience could be resources for those without, or with less, experience. Higher education institutions, professional associations and businesses could be resources for government, vocational and secondary level schools, which could assist primary schools, and all should be resources for their respective communities. Such a movement has already begun, as evidenced by existing collaborations and associations. Its implementation would involve a large (world) distributed database system with some components likely already in existence. However, it remains for us to identify these components, and to expand and complete the big picture of IT resources around the world and then use them appropriately and respectfully for the good of all.

5 CONCLUSION

IT resources for capacity building in developing countries have been presented from available statistics and by the example of the many uses of IT in education around the world. The resources include equipment, software, media, databases, government, people, education, associations and collaborations. The developed and developing countries can work together, as examples have shown, for the good of all, but expanded collaborations hinge on a willingness to cooperate, based on mutual respect, benefit and understanding - all of which rests on the foundation of communication, not just for some, but for all.

Communication, whether by old, traditional means or by new, modern IT must be a two-way, honest, respectful process, which is the foundation of peace. The process must recognize the worth and dignity of both communicating partners - no matter how rich or how poor. There is a richness and a poorness perspective of every nation in a complete view of things. Upon a solid foundation of respectful communication can be built cooperation and trust, out of which comes collaboration, or working together. Collaboration and cooperation are not possible without prerequisite communication. Even in the poorest of countries in the remotest areas, there is a natural hunger for knowledge, 'an abiding faith ... in education as a means of advancing economic and social well-being' (Sagahyroon, 1995). A hierarchy of IT resources, applied respectfully and appropriately, can help to satisfy that hunger and begin to build, at the most fundamental of levels, the capacity of even the poorest of nations to educate and prepare present and future generations, whether rural or urban, for more effective and efficient production and service to society and for a better quality of life for all.

6 REFERENCES

Buxton, T. (1995) Networks & CD-ROMs aid research, development and education in Zimbabwe. *T.H.E. Journal*, **22**(6), 67-71.

Dedrick, J.L., Goodman, S.E. and Kraemer, K.L. (1995) Little engines that could: computing in small energetic countries. *Communications of the ACM*, **38**(5), 21-26.

Famighetti, R. (ed.) (1996) *The World Almanac and Book of Facts 1997*. World Almanac Books, K-III Reference Corporation Mahwah, NJ.

Hawkridge, D., Jaworski, J. and McMahon, H. (1990) *Computers in Third-World Schools: Examples, Experience and Issues*. St. Martin's Press, New York, NY.
Hebenstreit, J., et al. (1992) *Education and Informatics Worldwide: The State of the Art and Beyond.* Jessica Kingsley Publishers, London, England; UNESCO, Paris, France.
Juliussen, E. and Petska-Juliussen, K. (eds.) (1994) *The Computer Industry 1994-95 Almanac*. Computer Industry Almanac, Inc., Dallas, TX.
Katz, R.L. (1988) *The Information Society*. Praeger Publishers, New York.
Khvilon, E.A. and Patru, M. (1997) UNESCO's mission in the promotion of international cooperation, *T.H.E. Journal*, **24**(6), 58-60.
McHenry, R. (ed.) (1997) 1997 *Brittanica Book of the Year*. Encyclopaepedia Brittanica, Inc., Chicago, IL.
New Encyclopaedia Brittanica. (1980), *Micropaedia, **vol. X***, 15th Edition, Encyclopaedia Brittanica, Inc., Chicago, IL p. 255.
OECD. (1992) *Information Technology Outlook 1992*. Organisation for Economic Cooperation and Development, Paris, France.
Sagahyroon, Assim A. (1995) Computer education in developing countries: the Sudan case. Proceedings of the sixth IFIP World Conference on Computers in Education (eds. J.D. Tinsley and T.J. van Weert), Chapman & Hall, London.
Stover, W. J. (1984) *Information Technology in the Third World.* Westview Press, Boulder, CO.
Sussman, G. and Lent, J. A. (eds.) (1991) *Transnational Communications: Wiring the Third World.* Sage Publications, Inc., Newbury Park, CA.
UNESCO, (1997) *UNESCO Statistical Yearbook, 1996*. United Nations Educational, Scientific and Cultural Organization & Lanham, MD: Bernan Press Paris, France.

7 BIOGRAPHY

Dr. Marsha R. Williams is a tenured professor of computer science at Tennessee State University, where she teaches and conducts research on Project MISET (Minorities in Science, Engineering & Technology). She has worked for the University of Mississippi, Memphis State University, IBM and the National Science Foundation. Dr. Williams holds a B.S. degree in physics (Beloit College), M.S. degree in physics (University of Michigan), M.S. and Ph.D. degrees in computer science (Vanderbilt University). She is a Certified Data Processor (CDP) and a member of ACM, AITP (DPMA) and the Tennessee Academy of Science. Her biography appears in *Who's Who in the World, Who's Who in Science and Engineering* and *Who's Who in American Education.*

PART VII

A Curriculum for the Future

27

The need for a new perspective - creating learning networks for African teachers: change, professional development and ICTs

David Berg and Jeannette Vogelaar
UNESCO, Learning Without Frontiers
7, Place de Fontenoy
75352 Paris 07 SP
Paris, FRANCE
Tele + 33 1 456 80498/81142/82061; Fax + 33 1 456 80828
E-mail: d.berg@unesco.org, a.vogelaar@unesco.org
URL: http://www.education.unesco.org/lwf

Abstract

The dynamics of today's world require a new approach to learning. Rather then tinkering with the current educational practices aimed at improving the situation, we should approach the current crisis of schooling from a completely different perspective. The need to learn how to learn and to provide multichannel learning opportunities through a variety of flexible delivery mechanism forms the basis of the new perspective. How can we teach teachers how to learn? Ongoing professional development through the establishment of collaborative learning networks promises to provide incentives for change not perceived before. An important driving force behind the professional networks is Information and Communication Technologies, around which UNESCO is developing and implementing a project in Africa,
with a pilot in Zimbabwe.

Keywords

Program development, evaluation, lifelong learning, teacher development

Capacity Building for IT in Education in Developing Countries
G. Marshall & M. Ruohonen (Eds.)

1 INTRODUCTION

'Creating Learning Networks for African Teachers' is a project currently being implemented in the framework of UNESCO's Learning Without Frontiers (LWF) initiative. The project aims to benefit from the emerging powers of modern Information and Communication Technologies (ICT) to stimulate processes of change within the broader objective of rethinking education and learning. The rationale for the project and the opportunities and challenges we are facing with the implementation of pilot activities in Zimbabwe should be of interest to other practitioners.

2 LEARNING AND TEACHING IN A CHANGING WORLD

2.1 Lifelong learning - learning to live

Today's world is rapidly moving towards a more open and global society, bringing opportunities for economic growth, peace, human rights and international partnership but also creating new sets of problems related to changing patterns of labour, multicultural societies and environmental disruption. Knowledge is dynamic - what is true today may have no value tomorrow. At the same time, access to information is perceived to be vital to economic development and power. The increasing variety of media sources and growing amount of accessible data create a situation in which the individual or community at the receiver end is increasingly becoming responsible for the selection of relevant, useful and accurate information - a responsibility requiring critical media awareness. While Information and Communication Technologies more and more allow many people to generate and disseminate information, thus playing an active role in the processes of interaction between professionals, laymen, learners, policy makers, peers, etc. - it requires skills, knowledge and access to resources to effectively do so.

Pressures of the contemporary age require people, communities and institutions to continually develop and utilize different kinds of knowledge frameworks, value systems, intelligences and skills in order to make sense of, adapt to and contribute to change in constructive and nonviolent ways. There is a need for people to learn how to deal with the changing demands of our society and, at the same time, develop the capacity that allows them to change in order to take control. Learning has become an essential condition for personal and societal growth and development. For example, the Delors Commission report defines the vision of the coming century as one 'in which the pursuit of learning is valued by individuals and by authorities all over the world, not only as a means to an end, but also as an end in itself' (UNESCO, Delors, 1996).

2.2 Building flexible and open learning environments

During the second half of this century education received more and more attention as a major factor contributing to development, mainly driven by the thinking represented in the emerging human capital and modernization theories (Fägerlind and Saha, 1983). The attention resulted in expansion of school enrolment and increases in educational expenditures in absolute terms on a global level. Such actions have been stimulated and reinforced by international conferences such as the World Conference on Education for All held in Jomtien, Thailand, 1990 and the mid-decade meeting of the International Consultative Forum on Education for All (UNESCOa, June 1996). While these actions have to be applauded for the achievements in achieving higher enrolment figures, we see at the same time how schools increasingly fail to provide the learning opportunities required in today's communities.

Both human capital theory and modernization theory have been criticized for their weak argumentation regarding the role of schooling in development. Fägerlind and Saha (1983) argue that schooling is mostly adaptive in nature and reproduces existing social and economic systems rather than triggering change and development. Apart from theoretical critiques we can observe now, in the late 1990s, that reality has proven us wrong in our belief in the expansion of the school system as such. In the 1970s and 1980s Africa had the highest growth figures in educational enrolment at all levels as well as the highest expenditures for education as a percentage of GNP (UNESCO, 1995). In the 1990s the figures have stagnated or even declined. In Africa more than 200 million adults are illiterate (44% of the adult population) and the gross enrolment figures in sub-Saharan Africa are 73,1% for primary level, 23.1% for secondary and 3.3% for tertiary level education. We also see increasing numbers of dropouts and alarming high unemployment figures among educated youth. Furthermore, the rapidly increasing enrolment during the 1970s and 1980s has resulted in ongoing excessive pressures on school systems through increased need for training and retraining of teachers, for more schools, for adaptation of curricula, for more textbooks and learning materials, and for improved communications and administration systems.

The Africa example teaches us that society's learning needs cannot be addressed only by expanding the formal education system but require new ways to look at both access to, and quality of education and learning. Rather then only aiming at the building of more schools and training more teachers to allow for higher enrolment figures, a new perspective is required in which we look at how we can create more open and flexible learning opportunities for all. We argue that it is not so important to have as many people as possible in the classroom. Instead we believe that the focus should be on the creation of learning environments as the Amman Affirmation (UNESCO, 1996a) states:

> 'Given the trend toward more open societies and global economies, we must emphasize the forms of learning and critical thinking that enable individuals to understand changing environments, create new knowledge and shape their own destinies. We must respond to new challenges by promoting learning in all aspects of life, through all institutions of society, in effect, creating environments in which living is learning.'

The Amman Affirmation provides the basis for shaping a new learning environment and provides us the opportunity to present three interrelated principles underlying UNESCO's Learning Without Frontiers programme.

The need to learn how to learn

We are living in a world that is dramatically different from the world of just six years ago - the time it takes an individual to complete primary school. The rate of change is so dramatic that it no longer suffices to teach our children what we think is important. Rather than us preparing our children for their life tomorrow, we have to place this task in the hands of the coming generations themselves.

> 'Whereas in the past, change could be managed through generational processes, each generation preparing the conditions for the next generation to adapt to change, this process has now become an intra-generation one'.
> (Visser, 1997b).

The capability to cope with change requires the capacity to learn. It is essential that each person develops a concept of 'self-as-learner'. Learning to learn involves developing oneself to engage in critical reflection and creative thinking. Such processes can be stimulated through approaches that are learner-centred, self-directed and focus on problem- and activity-based learning. A big challenge lies in stimulating the learners' abilities to build and enhance their own knowledge structures that are flexible and adaptable.

Multichannel learning approaches

People are part of different communities with diverse social and cultural backgrounds and are, at times, exposed to different situations from which one can learn. Children only spend a part of their time in the classroom. In developing countries and also in urban areas of less developed countries, they are watching 3-4 hours of television per day. Teachers often feel they are competing with modern media for children's attention and interest.

Rather then trying to compete, we believe that the teacher can very much benefit from such 'outside' influences in a constructive way. In order to create effective learning opportunities, learning process facilitators should build on experiences and stimulate the development of an integrated model of learning that involves classroom teaching as well as interaction with other learning channels such as family members, others in the community, social experiences, other learners and a variety of media (Anzalone, 1995). Within this framework, teachers should be encouraged to link up more actively with the communities they belong to and build a multichannel learning approach. At the same time, teachers should assist learners in developing a critical eye in judging the varying, and sometimes conflicting, information that the different channels provide.

Flexible delivery mechanisms

Learning can no longer be viewed as a ritual that one engages in only during the early part of one's life with an occasional refresher course. Instead learning is a continuous necessity and opportunities for learning need to be provided that are more flexible and open to the specific needs of individuals or groups of learners. People should have the opportunity to engage in learning whenever and wherever required without being hindered by barriers such as age, distance, time, social, economic or cultural circumstances.

The three principles imply an approach to learning that promotes the constructive and active contribution of individuals to their dynamic environments. But the principles also reflect an approach to learning that is able to continually adapt itself to the needs of the learners.

2.3 Educational reform and teacher development

If we take the existent school establishment and look at the opportunities there are to really do things different rather then tinker with ongoing practices or, worse, try to do more of the same, we see that teachers are the actors who really are in the position to make things happen, given their central role in the current practice of education. The idea of teachers as change agents is key to many education reform programmes that emphasize the importance of improved teacher training. But such programmes never seem to have the expected results.

Teachers constitute the 'largest single group of trained professionals in the world' (UNESCO, 1996b) - a tremendous challenge when we realize that they are also often considered the largest force against change (Visser, 1997a). Fullan describes teacher training as society's missed opportunity:

> 'Teachers and teacher educators do not know enough about subject matter, they don't know enough about how to teach, and they don't know enough about how to understand and influence the conditions around them. Above all, teacher education - from initial preparation to the end of the career - is not geared towards continuous learning'.
>
> (Fullan, 1993)

Teachers often operate in isolation. They mostly have no opportunity to reflect on their own practice or to exchange experiences and ideas with colleagues due to high work pressure and/or the necessity to have more than one full time job. At the same time, those teachers who are enthusiastic, capable and highly motivated are frustrated with their contribution to change and their chance to have a lasting impact since a supporting and understanding environment often seems to be lacking.

Triggering teachers to initiate processes of change should not involve the imposition of measures by the school management but should be the result of self-motivated processes of learning by the teachers themselves.

Fullan, Bennet and Rolheiser-Bennet (1990) identify four aspects of the teacher as learner which are crucial in the improvement of classroom practice and functioning of schools as a whole. We would like to go further and argue that the following four aspects promote a process of opening up the classroom as learning environment, merging the activities that take place in surrounding communities with what is happening in school:

- development of the instructional repertoire in teachers - the range of instructional strategies and capability to put to work a variety of learning channels;
- development of reflective practice that facilitates clarity, meaning and coherence for teachers in regards to their functioning and role in the learning process;

- stimulation of research activities to develop an attitude of investigation and exploration, widening the horizon of the teaching practice beyond the constraints of the classroom;
- promotion of collaboration with colleagues nearby and across long distances to enable teachers to exchange experiences, receive and give ideas, feedback and assistance.

It is not so much the four activities that Fullan and his colleagues see as important which concerns us as it is the fundamental underlying attitude:

> '... not just being good at cooperative learning, but at an array of instructional models; not just being involved in a reflective practice project, but being a reflective practitioner; not participating in a research investigation, but conducting constant inquiry; not being part of a peer coaching project, but being collaborative as a way of working'.
>
> (Fullan, Bennet and Rolheiser-Bennet, 1990)

Rather then trying to mould teachers' attitudes along these lines, we should seek for opportunities to let teachers become learners, to challenge them in a process of professional development in order to develop those skills and practices that are most constructive in the learning communities they are part of (*i.e.*, the school and the school's environment). Such processes should not be seen in isolation, but rather as an integrated approach to professional development and educational reform. Teacher development should aim at strategies that stimulate collaboration and partnership between teacher educators, teachers, specialists as well as learners and their parents.

2.4 ICTs as a catalyst to change - providing opportunities for learning

Communication and Information Technologies (ICTs) have become an integral part of society in many countries - not only in industrialized countries but more and more on the African continent (Janssen-Reinen and Vogelaar, 1997). Technological developments are contributing to expanding opportunities for engaging in teaching and learning at individual, community and society levels.

Through their potential to facilitate communication and access to information, ICTs can contribute to collaboration and partnership. They are key ingredients in professional development and educational reform. Using applications such as e-mail, computer-mediated conferencing, discussion lists, bulletin boards and the World Wide Web, the new technologies have been shown to create opportunities for:

- collaboration among teachers and their partners to break through their traditional isolation - see, for example, Dimauro and Jacobs, 1995; Lieberman and McLaughlin, 1994; Huberman, 1995; Fullan, Bennet and Rolheiser-Bennet, 1990;

- partnerships across the globe among children, parents, teachers for international peace and understanding of global issues related to cultural diversity and environmental health - see, for example, international learning projects promoted through Kidlink <http://www.kidlink.org>; the Globe Programme <http://www.globe.gov>; MajaQuest <http://ed.info.apple.com/education/MAYA/index.html>; Intercultural E-mail Classroom Connections <http://www.stolaf.edu/network/iecc>);
- access to nearly unlimited resources on the Internet and to locally stored information (graphical, audio and text) for the manipulation of materials retrieved or locally produced by users in a variety of ways for presentation purposes, for experimentation purposes, for exploration purposes, herewith enhancing the development of locally relevant learning and teaching materials;
- learner-centred and self-directed learning approaches - see, for example, the Apple Computers of Tomorrow <http:www.research.apple.com/go/acct>).

We don't believe in ICTs as such. We believe in the creative power of collaborative networks combined with easy access to learning resources which are possible through ICTs. It is in this context that UNESCO has developed the project 'Creating Learning Networks for African Teachers' linking teachers through electronic networks to stimulate educational change.

3 CREATING LEARNING NETWORKS FOR AFRICAN TEACHERS

3.1 A description

The project 'Creating Learning Networks for African Teachers' (<http://www.education.unesco.org/educprog/lwf/doc/IA1.html>) aims to improve the quality of education and learning by connecting teacher training colleges in Africa to each other and to the Information Highway. Specifically the project seeks to enhance their capacity to respond to new challenges to teaching and learning by facilitating and stimulating innovative experiences such as:

- opening up teacher training colleges to the communities by becoming information, communication and learning resources for educational planners and researchers, for teachers and for specific learning communities;
- changing perceptions among educational planners and policy makers, researchers, teacher educators and teachers, to begin seeing themselves as lifelong learners and agents for transformation in multifaceted environment;
- involving teachers and others as learners in a process in which they are not passive receivers of education, but, instead, actively contribute to the definition of their learning needs, the planning and execution of their learning and as such participate in the ongoing process of constructing knowledge useful to themselves and their communities.

The project, still in its pilot stage, will connect a number of teacher training colleges (four to six in twenty African countries) to the Internet in order to develop local, national and regional networks to initiate activities that focus on:

- enhancing dialogue between teacher training colleges, educational planners and policy makers, researchers and practising teachers on issues related to learning and teaching;
- accessing and assessing information on latest concepts, developments and experiments in the field of learning, teaching and education to enhance professional development, build local knowledge structures and stimulate processes of change;
- stimulating the development of locally adapted and relevant
- curricula, appropriate teaching and learning materials, including print based materials, through group work and groupware by using locally relevant images and sounds (including otherwise inaccessible 'artifacts', in close collaboration with the relevant national education authorities);
- promoting the development and implementation of learning projects targeting different learner groups of the communities.

Through the development of these activities, providing room for creative initiatives of teacher trainers and other parties, the project aims at opening up the school system and developing an approach to learning which is more in line with the needs and requirements of today's African society.

3.2 Pilot activities in Zimbabwe

Before implementing the project on a large scale, pilot activities will be initiated in a limited number of countries to assess the feasibility of the proposed activities and to further develop the specific modalities and requirements for hardware, software, connectivity arrangements, networking partners, training, etc. Zimbabwe was selected as a first country for the pilot project and it is currently experimenting with the first phase of the project. The choice of Zimbabwe was based on its advanced connectivity plans and current attempts to improve the overall quality of its educational system.

So far, a team of enthusiastic educators comprising a selection of members of teacher training colleges, the teacher education department at the University of Zimbabwe, and the audio-visual and curriculum development unit within the Ministry of Education have received basic training in the use of the Internet. They have also received computers, which have been installed and connected by specialists from the country. Currently, an electronic discussion group is being set up for thematic discussions on education issues relevant to the specific Zimbabwean context and a national web site is being prepared that will facilitate access to learning resources for Zimbabwean teachers. More advanced applications and collaborative learning projects are expected in time when the users have gained some experience with handling the new technology.

4 CONCLUSION

We would like to end with the following conclusions and observations based on our current experiences with the pilot project in Zimbabwe and other experiences around the world.

An expanded vision on lifelong learning requires a perceptual change among teachers, who must see themselves as learners as well as facilitators of learning processes that focus on developing capacities among learners to construct their own knowledge base for future development. Teacher development programmes should focus on professional growth and educational reform, rather than on knowledge transfer and skill training.

Teacher development could be stimulated through networking and collaboration among peers, researchers and learners. The emerging powers of modern communication and information technologies to enhance communication and facilitate access to information could play and important role in building such partnerships.

Past experiences taught us that introducing ICTs in education is a complex process and success depends not only on the technology itself but also on sets of attitudes and expectations of the different actors involved, as well as on the organizational and managerial context in which the technology is being introduced.

In most developed countries, academic research formed the basis for electronic networking. After its growing success, the commercial sector came in and took over. In most African countries, however, the development and growth of the Internet is a process driven by commercial interests, and specific policies and programmes will be required to ensure democratic participation of the public sector and, in particular, the poorly resourced educational institutions.

The introduction of networking technology in industrialized countries followed the introduction of computers in education. In Africa, however, the processes take place simultaneously, offering both an opportunity to have access to the latest equipment - computers in most Dutch schools, for example, are too old for access to the World Wide Web - and a challenge to address the general lack of basic computer skills among teachers as well as learners.

5 REFERENCES

Since the World Wide Web continually expands and changes, we cannot guarantee that at the time of publishing and reading this article the URLs provided here are still valid.

Anzalone, S. (1995) The case for multichannel learning, in *Multichannel Learning: Connecting All to Education* (ed. S. Anzalone), Education Development Center, Washington, D.C.

Delors, J. (1996) Learning: The Treasure Within. Report to UNESCO of the International Commission on Education for the Twenty-first Century. UNESCO, Paris.

Dimauro, V. and Jacobs, G. (1995) Collaborative electronic networkbuilding. *Journal of Computers in Mathematics and Science Teaching*, **14**(1/2), 119-131.

Fägerlind, I. and Saha, L.J. (1983) *Education and National Development: A Comparative Perspective*. Pergamon Press, New York.
Fullan, M. (1993) *Change Forces. Probing the Depths of Educational Reform*. The Falmer Press, London.
Fullan, M.G., Bennet, B. and Rolheiser-Bennet, C. (1990) Linking classroom and school improvement. *Educational Leadership*, **47**(8), 13-19.
Huberman, M. (1995) Networks that alter teaching: conceptualizations, exchanges and experiments. *Teachers and Teaching: Theory and Practice*, **1**(2), 193-211.
Janssen-Reinen, I. and Vogelaar, J. (1997) Educational change and the role of ICTs. Paper prepared for the workshop on Information and Communication Technologies to Change Education, Zimbabwe, 7-11 April, 1997. Paris, UNESCO.
Lieberman, A. and McLaughlin, M.W. (1994) Networks for educational change: powerful and problematic. *Phi Delta Kappan*, **63**, 673-677.
UNESCO, (1995) World Education Report. UNESCO, Paris.
UNESCO (1996a) *Education for all. Achieving the Goal*. UNESCO, Paris.
UNESCO (1996b) Strengthening the role of teachers in a changing world: Issues, prospects and priorities. Working paper prepared for the 45th session of the International Conference on Education, 30 September - 5 October 1996, International Conference Centre, Geneva, Switzerland. UNESCO, Paris.
Visser, J. (1997a) Elements for a vision of where the world of learning is going, in *Learning Without Frontiers: Beyond Open and Distance Learning* (ed. J. Visser), UNESCO, Paris. UNESCO.<http://www.education.unesco.org/educprog/lwf/doc/icde/icde.html>
Visser, J. (1997b) *Multilingualism in a Pervasive Learning Environment*. Paris, UNESCO. <http://www.education.unesco.org/lwf>

Any opinions expressed in this paper are those of the authors and not necessarily those of UNESCO. The mention of specific companies or of certain manufacturers' products does not imply that they are endorsed or recommended by UNESCO in preference to others of a similar nature that are not mentioned.

6 BIOGRAPHY

David Berg works as Associate Expert with the Learning Without Frontiers Coordination Unit in UNESCO. After graduation in 1992 from the University of Twente, Department of Educational Science and Technology, he was self-employed, and produced videos and did consultancy work in the Netherlands. Before joining UNESCO, he worked two years with the World Health Organization in Amman, Jordan. In the multicultural context of international cooperation, David Berg specializes in the design, development, production, evaluation and implementation of materials for learning - from print based materials to interactive computer applications.

Jeannette Vogelaar graduated in 1989 from the University of Twente in The Netherlands, Faculty of Educational Science and Technology, after which she spent time as a consultant in projects in Indonesia and Pakistan, focusing in particular on the professional development of teachers and extension workers. Since 1992, Ms. Vogelaar has been working with UNESCO, first in the sub-regional office in Harare and, since 1995, at the UNESCO headquarters with the Learning Without Frontiers coordination unit.

28

Informatics for secondary education - the UNESCO/IFIP curriculum as a resource for developed and developing countries

Tom van Weert
School of Informatics, Faculty of Mathematics and Informatics, University of Nijmegen
P. O. Box 9010, 6500 GL Nijmegen, The Netherlands
Tele + 31 24 3652084; Fax + 31 24 3653450
E-mail: tomvw@cs.kun.nl

Abstract
Countries currently beginning to use Informatics and Information and Communication Technology (ICT) in any major way should be able to benefit from the newest technological developments. Fundamental concepts and results of Informatics are independent of any computer platform or software environment. A cadre of professionals with a sound informatics background must be developed and supported. Advantage can be gained by capacity building through international cooperation, by using the similarity in the diversity of earlier experiences elsewhere and by concentrating on stable concepts. The UNESCO/IFIP secondary informatics curriculum - adaptable to specific cultural, educational and technological environments - can be implemented by countries and communities for the education of both computer literate and Informatics professionals at the secondary education level. But also elementary school materials, as well as materials for pre-service and in-service training of teachers, and for the preparation of teacher trainers can be based on the curriculum.

Keywords
Developing countries, informatics, infrastructure, secondary education

Capacity Building for IT in Education in Developing Countries
G. Marshall & M. Ruohonen (Eds.)

1 INTRODUCTION

Taking advantage of international cooperation
With respect to Africa Fatima Seye-Sylla concludes in *Education and Informatics Worldwide* (1992) that computers are still expensive for developing countries but Africa cannot remain indifferent to the technological revolution. To follow, one by one, the steps of the developed countries would, however, be the best way to remain the slave to the tool, rather than its master. She questions whether Africa should deny itself the efficiency of computers and their profits in use, because it is poor. Since Africa is poor in natural resources, she thinks that the best way to improve the economy is to develop and use human resources. The African Region may be poor but objectives can be achieved if the political will exists. As Seye-Sylla says: 'If African countries want to develop the human resources through education, which is a factor of sustainable economic and social development, they will have to put their maximum efforts together to achieve this goal'.

That concern about technology and development is supported by the International Federation for Information Processing Working Group on Secondary Education (IFIP WG 3.1). In this group international specialists work together; individual members are appointed by peers, not by national governments, on the basis of their expertise. Human resource development, both of its members and others, is the key in the work of IFIP Working Groups.

Informatics is a science dealing with theory, methods and techniques. Methods and techniques from informatics are the basis of the development of informatics technology: word processors, information systems, technical systems and other components. Informatics technology is often combined with other technologies; the resulting combination is often called Information Technology (IT) or Information and Communication Technology (ICT).

IFIP WG 3.1 members share their growing expertise not only with each other, but with other agencies, organisations and countries as the Information Revolution accelerates. IFIP's work has an international orientation and is based on international experience at the 'state of the art' level. On the one hand, this experience shows that there is not just one best solution to problems related to informatics and information technology in education. Solutions depend on local circumstances. On the other hand, this experience makes it possible to predict developments and identify needed processes of change. For these reasons nonmembers are able to benefit from the IFIP WG 3.1 experience and move forward more quickly by avoiding costly, but non-essential steps in development. With this in mind IFIP WG 3.1 has developed a set of *Guidelines of Good Practice* (Ruíz i Tarrago, 1993; Taylor, Aiken and van Weert, 1992) and the UNESCO/IFIP secondary curriculum on informatics (Tinsley and van Weert, 1994).

Taking advantage of similarity in diversity
There are important economical, social and cultural differences between countries, but also important similarities. Take the introduction of Information Technology into education as an example. All industrialised countries and quite a few developing countries have tackled this problem in much the same way - 'Computer Literacy' for all. While approaches may differ from one country to the other and

while the content of educational materials may differ, the problems encountered turn out to be much the same. IFIP members identified common problems and suggested solutions in *Guidelines of Good Practice*. The development of the *Guidelines* showed that similarities exist notwithstanding local differences and that the identification of common problems provided a basis for practical international cooperation. But in each case an application of theory in good practice must take into account local circumstances.

Taking advantage of earlier experiences

Some people argue that when starting late, you have to go through the same development processes as the early starters. This is not IFIP's view. Starting late you can take advantage of early experiences; you may go through the same stages of development, but you will be able to go a lot faster, and cheaper, because you know where you are going. Starting late one should leap to the forefront of development, aim at 'state of the art' policies and practices as well as emerging trends, and bypass obsolete ideas and technology. This leap is possible if based on the fundamental concepts and results of Informatics which are independent of any specific hardware or software environments.

Taking advantage of stable concepts

Multiple changes, quantitative and qualitative, have occurred in computer and software technology. Technological knowledge may rapidly and easily become obsolete. At the same time fundamental concepts and results of Informatics are as independent of any specific computer platform and software environments as ever. Capacity building should therefore be based on stable concepts and not on the technology of today - which may be antiquated by tomorrow. To take part in the newest developments countries currently beginning to use Informatics and Information and Communication Technology in any major way should build up a cadre of professionals with a sound Informatics background.

2 CRITICAL ASPECTS OF CAPACITY BUILDING

The need for Informatics education

There is a clear need for Informatics and Information and Communication Technology in secondary education. Data in Table 1 show the need for qualified personnel in developed countries and give a clear demonstration of the need for effective Informatics learning at all levels

The need for professionals skilled in ICT operations and application of informatics concepts will, in most countries, far exceed current levels. Secondary education has an important role to play in closing the gap.

Table 1 Need for training

Year	1970	2000
Professionals with ICT qualification	5%	65%
Professionals in other disciplines with Informatics qualifications	1.5%	20%
Professional informaticians	0.5%	4%

Schul Computer Jahrbuch, 1993 (p. 15)

Different phases of Informatics development
To get a grip on the very fast developments of Informatics, these may be grouped into three phases:

- automation: information technology is used to automate simple, standard processes, such as business accounting;
- information: software tools support the professional at the work place, empowering the individual. Information Technology is used as an umbrella term for these tools;
- communication: powerful personal computers are integrated in local area, wide area and global networks as personal (and sometimes) intelligent communication agents. Information and Communication Technology is used as an umbrella term in this situation.

Countries or communities will find themselves in one of these phases of Informatics development.

Different levels of technological and human resource development
The different phases of Informatics development are paralleled by different levels in technological and human resource development:

- automation: essential infrastructures are still being developed. Informatics is the sole responsibility of technical personnel;
- information: personal use of computing tools grows, with a strong influence of the user on the adaptation of systems;

- communication: computer use is characterised by collaboration between users, and Informatics and Information Technology form part of the essential infrastructure of the organisation, institution or country.

In secondary education the Informatics curriculum in its implementation must aim at the appropriate level of technological and human resource development in countries or communities.

Required competencies are changing

Technological developments have resulted in changes in work and the organisation of work. This is very apparent in countries which have passed through the information and communication phases of Informatics development. As the changes occur, required competencies, which secondary education has to provide, change. In the information, and especially in the communication phases, inductive thinking, generalist informatics competencies enabling expert work, decision-making, handling of dynamic situations, teamwork and communication competencies become increasingly important.

To take part in the newest developments countries currently starting to invest heavily in Informatics and ICT must take account of the changes in required competencies. Their secondary Informatics curriculum should contribute to the building up of a reservoir of professionals with the required competencies.

3 THE ROLE OF INFORMATICS IN SECONDARY EDUCATION

Learning to use and become proficient with ICT are basic necessities in secondary education. Currently, in developing or developed countries, the ability to use ICT is a necessity, as has been illustrated by the need for ICT competent professionals shown in the *Schul Computer Jahrbuch* study (1993).

Everyday use of ICT cuts across all aspects of economical and social life and across all disciplines in secondary education so ICT should be integrated in all disciplines of secondary education.

Where does this leave the discipline of Informatics? Technological developments in ICT are very rapid. This creates two problems. First of all, technological knowledge quickly becomes obsolete and new technology has to be frequently mastered. To allow a smooth adaptation to new technology and intelligent use of current ICT, secondary education should offer its students an understanding of ICT based on invariant, stable concepts. Since ICT is built on the foundation of Informatics, understanding Informatics concepts is indispensable.

Secondly, countries need to educate students who can immediately obtain employment in ICT-supported companies. In economic life tools of ICT have to be developed, sometimes from scratch, but most of the time by adaptation of existing tools (software packages). Students must learn the basics of development and adaptation, which in turn are based on concepts, methods and techniques of Informatics.

Finally secondary schools must teach Informatics to prepare their students for further education.

Implications for an Informatics curriculum for schools

Current and future needs should be reflected in an Informatics curriculum for secondary education, both in developing and developed countries. This curriculum should address:

- computer literacy - the competent use of basic ICT tools;
- the competent use of special, problem- or subject-oriented ICT tools;
- problem solving with Informatics - application of methods and techniques of Informatics to problems in other subject areas;
- solving professional problems with Informatics - application-oriented Informatics, aimed at application of methods and techniques of Informatics to business or industry problems.

The use of ICT should be integrated in any discipline in secondary education where the student must have access to the same personal computer support as professionals in business and industry find on their desks (Ruíz i Tarrago, 1993). Like the professional, students must use the personal tools in an integrative way.

Informatics aims to solve problems in an increasingly more complex world. Special purpose conceptual 'programming' environments in which microworlds of reality can be modeled and problems from this microworld solved provide a setting for working on complex problems. Everyday examples of this type of conceptual programming are the building of macros for text processing and the building of formulas in spreadsheets. More advanced examples are the creation of simulation models in simulation software tools and problem solving in mathematical tools such as *Maple* and *Mathematica.*

The backbone of ICT and conceptual programming is Application Oriented Informatics. It includes modeling methods and techniques, design of conceptual data structures and program design in high level as well as conceptual programming languages. As 'Informatics for a few' it may be offered in preparation of specific jobs or specialised further studies. It may also include more advanced topics such as software engineering and design of human computer interfaces.

4. THE UNESCO/IFIP CURRICULUM FOR SCHOOLS

The UNESCO/IFIP Secondary Informatics Curriculum has been designed to reflect the competencies required for today and tomorrow , and allows adaptation to local circumstances by school book authors and publishers. Table 2 provides an overview of the curriculum.

The curriculum is built from units which are grouped in modules designed for different educational levels - Foundation level modules and Advanced modules. Depending on local circumstances these units, designed for one level, may also be used at another level.

Table 2 An overview of the UNESCO/IFIP curriculum

Secondary education	Level	Topics
General education	Foundation	A. Computer literacy B. Application of ICT tools in other subject areas C. Informatics in other subject areas (optional)
General education	Advanced	B. Application of ICT tools in other subject areas C. Informatics in other subject areas
Vocational education	Advanced	D. Informatics in professional areas

In the curriculum the units are described according to: Objective and sub-objectives, context, content, description of student activities, resources needed and optional resources, links to other units, and teaching methodology.

Topic A. Computer literacy
Objectives - Handle basic software and hardware facilities of a computer; apply application oriented software tools (spreadsheet, database, etc.); solve routine problems in algorithmic form (*e.g.*, by building macros); social, economical and ethical consequences.

Modules and units - the units covering this topic can be found in the Core Module, the Core Elective Module, the General Options Module and the Optional Programming Module as shown in Table 3

Table 3 Computer Literacy

Core Module	Core Elective Module	General Options Module	Optional Programming Module
Hardware	Database design and use	Keyboarding skills	Introduction to programming
Systems software	Spreadsheet design and use	Desktop publishing	Top-down programming design
Computing trends	Careers in Informatics	Communication	
Using a computer		Creating graphics	
Text processing		Working with multimedia	
Working with a database		Computer-aided design	
Graphics		Modelling/simulation	
Social and ethical issues		Expert systems	
Choice of tools		Robots Music Statistics	

Topic B. Use of ICT tools in other subject areas
Informatics and Information and Communication Technology tools may be of considerable value in teaching many subjects at Foundation and Advanced levels. By integrating the use of computers within subject areas, most of the computer literacy objectives can be met without the need for a separate computer literacy course. UNESCO/IFIP's curriculum offers examples of integrated computer use in Natural Sciences, Mathematics, Languages, Social Sciences, Art and Music.

Objective - students should be able to use ICT tools to solve problems in other subject areas. Units which contribute to the integrated teaching of computer use are for the most part found in the Core Elective Module and the General Options Module as shown in Table 4.

Table 4 Use of ICT tools in other subject areas

Core Elective Module	General Options Module	Optional Programming Module
Database design and use	Keyboarding skills	Introduction to programming
Spreadsheet design and use	Desktop publishing	Top-down programming design
	Communication	
Core Module	Creating graphics	
Text processing	Working with multimedia	
Working with a database	Computer-aided design	
Working with graphics	Modelling/simulation	
Choice of tools	Expert systems Robots Music Statistics	

Topic C. Informatics in other subject areas

In this module , shown in Table 5, relatively complex problems will be solved with the help of methods and techniques of informatics. These problems are either solved using general purpose, high level programming environments or using special-purpose, conceptual 'programming' environments in which microworlds of reality can be modelled and problems from this microworld solved. Everyday examples of this type of conceptual programming are: the building of macros for text processing and the building of formula in spreadsheets. More advanced examples are the creation of simulation models in simulation software tools by clicking and dragging, and problem solving in mathematical tools such as *Maple* and *Mathematica*.

Objective - students should be able to methodically model and solve relatively complex problems in other subject areas.

Prerequisite - Topic B. Use of ICT tools in other subject areas

Modules and units - units which contribute to the solving of problems in other subject areas using informatics are found in the Core Elective Module, the Programming Module and the General Advanced Module as shown in Table 5.

Table 5 Informatics in other subject areas

Core Elective Module	Programming Module	General Advanced Module
Database design and use	Introduction to programming	Foundations of programming and software development
Spreadsheet design and use	Top-down programming design	Advanced elements of programming
		Applications of modeling

Topic D. Informatics in professional areas
The topic presented in this module, shown in Table 6, is relatively simple professional problems to be solved with the help of methods and techniques of Informatics. The problems are solved using methods and techniques of Informatics which are in professional use.

Objectives - students should be able to methodically plan, design, realise and implement relatively simple application systems with the aid of problem oriented software tools and identify problems involved in project management.

Prerequisites are Topic B. Use of ICT tools in other subject areas, Units P1 and P2 from the Optional Programming Module

Modules and units which contribute to the solving of problems in professional areas using Informatics are found in the Vocational Advanced Module.

Table 6 Informatics in the professional areas

Vocational Advanced Module	
Business Information systems	Students methodically plan, design, realize and implement relatively simple information systems with problem-oriented tools
Process control systems	Students methodically plan, design, realize and implement relatively simple process control systems with problem-oriented tools

Project management	Students deal with variables influencing progress and success, and plan team activities for small projects.

5 IMPLEMENTATION OF THE CURRICULUM

How can this curriculum be implemented, especially in developing countries? The experience, gained in both developed and developing countries, of the members of the working party which has designed the curriculum, shows that implementation is dependent on different stages of technological and human resource development in any community or country, and in the secondary education systems of those communities and countries. In their experience the following stages can be discerned:
Stage 1: insufficient hardware, few experienced teachers;
Stage 2: more hardware, teachers receive some in-service training;
Stage 3: more hardware, a larger percent of teachers receive training and some achieve degrees in computer science;
Stage 4: sufficient hardware, almost all teachers are computer literate and many achieve degrees in computer science.

The technological and human resources in each stage define boundary conditions for the implementation of the curriculum. From the IFIP/UNESCO curriculum those parts can be selected by education authorities which can be realised under the boundary conditions at the appropriate level of education. When the boundary conditions change, new parts of the curriculum can be implemented. In such a way implementation is possible quickly and at a minimum cost. Other experiences, for example gained in Russia (van Weert, 1996), have shown such an approach to be viable.

In stage one, when there is insufficient hardware and few experienced teachers, it is advised to start implementation of the curriculum at the Advanced General level (ages 16-19) with Computer Literacy core units for most students and core elective units as an extra for a selection of students.

In stage two, when there is more hardware and teachers receive some in-service training, it is advised to move the Computer Literacy core units to the Foundation of General Education (ages 12-16) for all students, to extend the core elective units to all students at the Advanced General Education level, to offer most students at this level Computer Literacy option modules and to offer selected students optional programming units. In this stage optional programming units may also be offered to students in Advanced Vocational Education.

An overview of which units to choose for implementation at which educational level in which phase is given in Table 7.

Table 7 refers to units which come from the Core Module (units C1-C10), the Core Elective Module (units E -E3), the General Options Module (units Op1-Op11), the Optional Programming Module (units P1-P2), the General Advanced Module (units GA1-GA3) and the Vocational Advanced Module (units VA1-VA3).

Table 7 Phases in development

Phases in development	Initial	Second	Third	Advanced
Educational level				
General Education Foundation Ages 12 -16		all students: literacy core units C1-C10	all students: literacy core units C1-C10	all students: literacy core units C1-C10
			all students Electives E1-E3	all students Electives E1-E3
				selected students: optional programming
General Education Advanced Ages 16 - 19	most students: literacy core			
	selected students: electives E1-E3	all students: electives E1-E3		
		most students: options Op1-Op11	all students: options Op1-Op11	most students option Op1-Op11
		selected students:	selected students:	selected students:
		optional programming P1-P2	optional programming P1-P2	optional programming GA1-GA3
Vocational		extra for vocational students:	extra for vocational students:	vocational for vocational students:

optional programming P1-P2	optional programming P1-P2	optional programming P1-P2
		vocational students: vocational vocational advanced units VA1-VA3

Obtaining copies of the UNESCO/IFIP curriculum for schools

The curriculum is available, free of charge, through your regional UNESCO office or through the UNESCO headquarters in Paris. The curriculum has been developed in English but through the efforts of many Informatics professionals translations in French, Spanish, Russian, Chinese, Japanese, Polish and, lately, Portuguese are available. The website address <http://www.ge-dip-etat-ge.ch/cip/unesco/frwelcome.html> gives access to the English and French translations of the curriculum.

Addresses

Adresses of regional UNESCO offices can be found on the World Wide Web: <http://www.education.unesco.org/unesco/educsect/offices.html>

UNESCO Headquarters
7, Place de Fontenoy
H. G. 435
75352 Paris 07 SP
France

UNESCO office Harare
P. O. Box

Highlands, Harare
Zimbabwe

Acknowledgment

The UNESCO/IFIP Informatics curriculum for secondary education was prepared by a working party of the International Federation for Information Processing Working Group on Secondary Education (WG 3.1):

Ulrich Bosler, Germany
Charles Duchateau, Belgium
Sam Gumbo, Zimbabwe
Raymond Morel, Switzerland
Harriet Taylor, USA
Peter Waker, South Africa
Zoraini Wati Abas, Malaysia

Chair & Joint Editor: Tom van Weert, Netherlands
Joint Editor: David Tinsley, United Kingdom

6 REFERENCES

Ruíz i Tarrago, F.R. (1993) Integration of Information Technology in Secondary Education: Main Issues and Perspectives, in *Guidelines for Good Practice*, (ed. T.J. van Weert), IFIP Working Group 3.1, Geneva, 7-15.

Seye-Sylla, F. (1992) Current restraints and prospects: Regional examples, in *Education and Informatics Worldwide, The State of the Art and Beyond.* (eds. Hebenstreit J., *et. al.*), Jessica Kingsley Publishers/UNESCO, London, 196-202.

Schul Computer Jahrbuch (1993), Ausgabe '93/94, Metzler Schulbuch Verlag, Stuttgart, **15**.

Taylor, H.G., Aiken, R. M., van Weert, T.J. (1992) Informatics Education in Secondary Schools, in *Guidelines for Good Practice* (ed. T.J. van Weert), IFIP Working Group 3.1, International Federation for Information, Geneva.

Tinsley, J.D. and van Weert, T.J. (eds.) (1994) Informatics for secondary education, a curriculum for schools, UNESCO, Paris. The curriculum may be obtained free of charge through regional UNESCO offices.

van Weert, T.J. (1996) Analysis of UNESCO/IFIP documents, published by UNESCO in 1994-1995, in: Proceedings of the Second UNESCO Congress on Education and Informatics, in press.

7 BIOGRAPHY

Tom J. van Weert is Director of the School of Informatics (Computer Science) of the Faculty of Mathematics and Informatics of the University of Nijmegen, Netherlands. The School of Informatics educates Masters in Informatics and also provides informatics courses for other departments. Tom van Weert also teaches the management of large software projects to Informatics students who develop real software applications in multidisciplinary teams. Previously he worked in teacher education teaching Mathematics and Informatics and prior to that as a computer system engineer in an academic environment. His background is in applied mathematics. He has been active in several IFIP Working Groups and is currently Chair of IFIP Working Group 3.2 on university education.

PART VIII

Workshop Presentations

29

Teaching informatics as a subject

Peter Hubwieser
Fakultät für Informatik der Technischen Universität München
D-80290 München
E-mail: hubwiese@informatik.tu-muenchen.de

Steffen Friedrich
Fakultät Informatik der Technischen Universität Dresden
D-01062 Dresden
E-mail: sf2@inf.tu-dresden.de

1 INTRODUCTION

The following theses concern the teaching of informatics, which is synonymous with the teaching of the basic concepts of Information Technologies. We are not discussing the use of Information and Communication Technologies (ICT) across curriculum.

2 WHY SHOULD WE TEACH INFORMATICS?

Modern information and communication (particularly Internet and multimedia) technologies (ICT) are more and more dominating our private spheres as well as our social and working environments. They are changing the way we think, the way we talk and the way we watch our world. Shortly, they will be affecting the foundations of our society.

Therefore the schools are facing the task of enabling their students:

1. to make use of the technologies in economical and efficient ways;
2. to control and to judge the consequences of using technology.

Capacity Building for IT in Education in Developing Countries
G. Marshall & M. Ruohonen (Eds.)

The teaching of user skills meets some serious obstacles as there are:
1. a broad variety of different user interfaces and different systems often expect very different sequences of actions to perform the same work routine. It is not possible to train on all possible systems;
2. the design and operation of the systems is changing very fast; what fits today is not working tomorrow. Nobody can foresee which user interfaces will be the fashion in the coming year.

To control and judge the consequences of the rapid evolution of IT means to understand, at least in principle, the way IT systems and operations are constructed and the way they work because such understanding is equivalent to the ability to assess their inherent possibilities (Friedrich, 1995).

Thus we have shown that we have to teach the basic concepts of modern ICT. As a result the students should learn:
1. to build proper mental models of the systems that explain their peculiarities (Brauer and Brauer, 1989);
2. to look at the systems as universal complex tools that feel no emotions and suspect no mysteries.

This has to be done by teachers who are carefully and specifically educated in Informatics, which means that they have completed a special course of studies at university (Friedrich, 1996). This is impossible to guarantee in the case that Informatics is taught in other subjects.

3 WHAT SHOULD WE TEACH IN INFORMATICS ?

The raw material of all ICT is information. Every treatment of information follows the same process pattern:
1. The first requirement of any operation is a suitable representation of the information - a proper model of a real life situation or a proposed system is formed and described by adequate means; data structures are constructed and realized, and a message is encoded following the rules of an communication protocol.
2. Once there is such a representation, it is possible to change it (information processing) or exchange it (communication); a system model is improved by refinement or abstraction; data structures are changed by an algorithm that has to be constructed and encoded to make it runnable; datagrams are exchanged.
3. After (ex-) changing the representation has to be interpreted in order to produce information that is entirely new or that is not yet known at this particular place or by this particular subject; the system model is interpreted by a programmer; the state of a data structure causes some output on the screen; electronic mail is read.

The described pattern induces the range of contents we propose to teach - techniques and concepts of representation, processing and interpretation of representations.

Not every subject is teachable in schools: following Bruner (Bruner, 1960; Bruner, 1966; Schwill, 1997) we have to observe at least three principles:

- generality - the concepts should be applicable or observable in multiple ways and different areas;
- durability - what is taught today should be relevant at least for some years in the future;
- teachability - of course we have to take into account the students' abstraction level and specific abilities related to their particular age.

The result of these reflections is a set of concepts that form the skeleton of our proposed curriculum (for details see also Hubwieser and Broy 1996; Hubwieser, Broy and, Brauer, 1997):

1. Modeling techniques - precise descriptions of complex systems by diagrams concerning decomposition, subsystems, data flows, message sequences, states and transitions, causal relationships;
2. typical data structures as objects of information processing - atomic types, sequences, records and variant records
3. typical applications of the structures - representation of arrays, relations, graphs, trees and typical data structures of standard software;
4. fundamental strategies of problem solving - 'divide et conquer', top-down, bottom-up, algorithmic, rule-based, object-oriented strategies;
5. algorithms and their description through programming languages - atomic structures of algorithms handling sequences and trees, searching in networks (graphs), fundamentals of programming languages;
6. local and global networks - description by graph, typical topologies;
7. basic concepts of communication - addressing techniques , protocol stacks, services of computer networks;
8. synchronisation of parallel processes - common data structures (semaphores), monitoring, handling of deadlocks, problems of consistency;
9. assessment of representations, systems and solutions - borders of computability, basics of cost-benefit analysis, manipulation of data;
10. problems data protection - legal situation, management of data access, encryption techniques.

4 HOW SHOULD WE TEACH INFORMATICS ?

We base our methodical approach on the psychological concepts of cognitive flexibility (Spiro and Jehng, 1990) and cognitive networks (Anderson, 1985). Above all we demand to arrange the lessons around larger project sequences.

We propose to follow the process of modeling and simulation, using adapted methods of modern software engineering (Broy, 1995; Broy, Facchi, Grosu, Hettler, Hussman, Nazareth, Regensburger, Slotosch and Stoelen, 1993; Booch, 1994; Jacobson, Christerson, Jonsson and Övergard, 1991; Rumbaugh, Blaha, Premerlani, Eddy and Lorensen, 1991):

1. The teacher selects a problem to be solved or a real life system to be simulated. It should be as close to the students' experience of life as possible in order to illustrate the concepts. The complexity has to be high enough to prevent solutions by naive, intuitive means. This will motivate the students to learn and use new techniques.

2. The starting point of the real project forms an informal description of the problem. Hereby the students are forced to make their own reflections on the problem.
3. This step represents the most important learning process - we construct a (as much as possible formalized) model of the situation, using adequate description techniques.
4. Based on that model we construct a realization of our solution, a simulation of the system, aiming to illustrate and check our model. According to the students' interests this will be the most popular part of the project.
5. At the conclusion of the project we review all our work - the correspondence between informal description; model and simulation is inspected; the cost-benefit analysis is performed; the consequences of our solution are judged; and we think about possible improvements.

5 REFERENCES

Anderson, J.R. (1985) *Cognitive Psychology and Its Implications*. Freeman & Co., New York.

Brauer, W. and Brauer, U. (1989) Better Tools - Less Education?, in (ed. G.X. Ritter): *Information Processing 89*. Elsevier Science Publishers B.V. (North-Holland). IFIP, Amsterdam.

Booch, G. (1994) *Object-Oriented Analysis and Design*. Benjamin Cummings, Redwood City, CA.

Broy, M. (1995) Mathematics of Software Engineering. Invited talk at MPC 95. In Möller, B. (Hrsg.): Mathematics of Program Construction, July 1995, Kloster Irsee, *Lecture Notes of Computer Science* **947**, 18-47, Springer.

Broy, M., Facchi, C., Grosu, R., Hettler, R., Hussmann, H., Nazareth, D., Regensburger, F., Slotosch, O., Stoelen, K. (1993) The Requirement and Design Specification Language SPECTRUM. An Informal Introduction (Version 1.0). TUM-I 9311, Technische Universität München.

Bruner, J.S. (1960) *The Process of Education*. Harvard University Press, Cambridge, MA.

Bruner, J.S. (1966) *Toward a Theory of Instruction*. Harvard University Press, Cambridge, MA.

Friedrich S. (1995) Informatik-Didaktik, ein Fachgebiet im Aufbruc. *Innovative Konzepte für die Ausbildung*. Springer.

Friedrich, S. (1996) Ausbildung gefragt. *LOG IN*, **16**.

Hubwieser, P., Broy, M. and Brauer, W. (1997) A New Approach to Teaching Information Technologies: Shifting Emphasis from Technology to Information, in *Information Technology: Supporting Change through Teacher Education* (eds. D. Passey and B. Samways),Chapman & Hall, London.

Hubwieser, P. and Broy, M. (1996) Der informationszentrierte Ansatz, ein Vorschlag für eine zeitgemäfle Form des Informatikunterrichtes am Gymnasium. Institut für Informatik der Technischen Universität München, Technischer Bericht TUM-I9624, Mai 1996.

Jacobson, I., Christerson, M., Jonsson, P., Övergard, G. (1991) *Object-Oriented Software Engineering - A Use Case Driven Approach*. Addison-Wesley, Reading, MA.

Rumbaugh, J., Blaha, M., Premerlani, W., Eddy, F., Lorensen, W. (1991) *Object-Oriented Modeling and Design*. Prentice-Hall, Englewood Cliffs, NJ.

Schwill, A. (1997) Computer Science Education Based on Fundamental Ideas, in *Information Technology: Supporting Change through Teacher Education* (eds. D. Passey and B. Samways), Chapman & Hall, London.

Spiro, R.J. and Jehng, J.C. (1990) Cognitive Flexibility and Hypertext, in *Cognition, Education and Multimedia: Exploring Ideas in High Technology* (eds. Nix, D. and Spiro, R.J.), Lawrence Erlbaum & Associates, Hillsdale NJ.

30

Using hypermedia and the Internet in the teaching of mathematics

Karen S. Norwood
North Carolina State University
326 Poe Hall
Box 7801
Raleigh, North Carolina 27695
E-mail: Karen@poe.coe.ncsu.edu

Hypermedia documents contain links or connections to one or more other media. The advantages of hypermedia over traditional instruction are:

1. appeals to different learning styles;
2. provides a variety of means of expression for students;
3. gives students more real-world presentation experience;
4. taps into students' creativity;
5. prepares students for the 21st century;
6. has entertainment value;
7. has storage capability.

Many educators are exploring the possibility of using the World Wide Web, not only as an information and discovery medium, but also as a tool for publishing educational material and delivering them to other educators and students in an inexpensive and efficient manner. Using the Web, educators can create maps and guide their learners through the various domains of knowledge. The Internet has two real advantages over other media. It combines the advantages of other media so that it conveys video and sound better than a book, is more interactive than a video, and, unlike CD-ROM, it can link people around the world cheaply.

Using hypermedia and the Internet enables mathematics educators to explore areas of mathematics that, without the use of the technology, would be too difficult to tackle. Secondly, it allows students to demonstrate their understanding of mathematical knowledge in creative ways through presentations and projects instead of traditional term papers. The use of these tools allows the mathematics to come to life right before students' eyes.

Capacity Building for IT in Education in Developing Countries
G. Marshall & M. Ruohonen (Eds.)

31

Information Technology and problem solving in mathematics education

G. Dettori, S, Greco, E. Lemut
Instituto Matemetica Applicata, C.N.R.
Via de Marini 6
16149 Genova, Italy
E-mail: Dettori@ima.ge.cnr.it

1 WHAT IS IT?

Several slightly different definitions of IT can be found in the technical literature: basically all of them state that IT:

- is the confluence of informatics with other technologies;
- is aimed at the processing and communication of information;
- has many social, economic and individual implications.

The rapid development of IT and the permeation of its use in almost any field of human activity have brought about profound cultural and social changes which require corresponding changes in educational systems.

2 INTEGRATION OF IT WITH TOPIC EDUCATION

IT influences education in several ways: it influences knowledge and the need for knowledge. When technology was first introduced into education, the focus was mainly on technology itself; since then, the focus has been more and more shifted from technology to the knowledge to be taught and learned; and technology is viewed more and more as a means to mediate learning. This does not mean that IT should not be studied also as a discipline by itself; in fact, basic competencies should be taught to students independently of other disciplines - as general knowledge that can be useful outside school or as a tool for learning.

Capacity Building for IT in Education in Developing Countries
G. Marshall & M. Ruohonen (Eds.)

3 COMPUTER LITERACY

When microcomputers became widespread in schools, preoccupation with computer literacy began and mathematics courses started including a self-standing informatics module, aiming to become familiar with the computer. Over the years curricula have been modified more and more in order to integrate IT into teaching school subjects. This implies that computer literacy is becoming less a subject in itself and more a practical way to understand potentialities and limits of computers, finalised to its application. Students gain experience with computer systems while using them and, at the same time, learn to appreciate them as a tool which helps in solving problems, in fomalising ideas and in investigating.

4 WHY PROBLEM SOLVING?

Problem solving has been a field of study in cognitive psychology for years, as concerns general learning, not just in conjunction with mathematics or other scientific disciplines. At present, the name 'problem solving' indicates an active processing of information, which involves more than a set of general strategies; problem-solving ability is domain-dependent and cannot be easily generalised to a wide range of domains.

When teachers want to emphasise problem solving in a curriculum, they must play the role of mediators of learning rather than transmitters of knowledge. This entails adopting a cognitive view of learning in which students construct meanings through their experiences, rather than barely teaching algorithms and finding learning environments that facilitate experiential learning and support problem solving activities.

Concerning mathematics, problem solving does not mean simply to assign students some problem, asking them to find a numerical solution. It is an approach to learning where theoretical concepts are introduced during the solution of a problem. This is useful from three points of view:

- it motivates the introduction of theoretical points, showing that they have an actual applicability;
- it eases the introduction of new topics, since they are learned 'by examples' and 'by doing' hence making them more concrete;
- it makes teachers and students aware of preconceptions, which sometimes hinder learning (cultural obstacles).

Moreover, to make problem solving even more motivating and stimulating, particular attention should be paid to the choice of problems that should be related to some problematic situation somehow familiar in the students' context.

For all these reasons, problem solving should be proposed, including not only standard problems containing a complete problem description and all data, but also problems without numerical data and open or semi-structured ones, from which students must develop mathematics. These situations help them open up their minds and look deeper into problems and offer occasions to connect mathematics education with other disciplines, in particular with developing good expressive capabilities.

Hence problem solving is an application-based approach to mathematics and this has been found a necessary condition for a mathematics education program to be emancipatory and empowering, tuning students' learning with society's needs. On the other hand, a formal and theoretical mathematics program is often used as a way to discriminate and marginalise some sectors of society.

5 WHY IT AND PROBLEM SOLVING?

Several reasons motivate the application of IT in education at all levels of mathematics learning:

- the need to support the processes of abstraction;
- the need to mediate learning by means of representations;
- the need to relieve students of work-intensive technical operations (such as graphing or heavy number computation.

As concerns representation in particular, the research in mathematics education has highlighted its importance both in problem solving and to mediate the introduction of abstract concepts. It has also been pointed out that using in parallel different representations for the same topic can be even more fruitful if they are correctly and strongly linked, since this allows one to emphasise different aspects or properties of the concepts under consideration hence leading to a deeper understanding and to a better capability to apply the learned concepts to new situations. Several representations of a concept can co-exist in somebody's mind, complement each other and eventually get integrated into a single, more general representation of that concept. This process of integration is the base of abstraction (that is, the ability to shift attention from instances of objects to their structure, properties and relationships), which is an essential component of mathematical thinking and, in general, of mature cognitive capabilities. From this point of view, the computer appears an excellent tool since it represents a fundamental advance in our representational capabilities. In fact, it makes it possible to represent mathematics with an amount of structure not offered by any other tool.

Moreover, using IT to promote activity-based learning brings about a change in students' learning style, making them more involved and responsible for their mathematics education. This also brings about a change in students' beliefs about what doing mathematics means. Hence this use of IT and problem solving in math education favours the transformation from a passive leaning style based on copying and memorising to a learning style based on action and direct experience.

6 POTENTIALITIES FOR IT IN EDUCATION

Lab activities in mathematics education can exploit, either for introducing and for deepening concepts, the characteristics of software of different kinds, such as educational software, commercial software or programming languages.

Computers are very particular tools with characteristics different from any other used in school. Their potentialities stem from their capabilities of interaction; their limits from the fact that their way of interacting can follow only fixed schemes, depending on the running program, without any personal possibility of changing the thread of discussion.

Computers allow fast computations, visualisations of two- and three-dimensional objects, simulation of casual events with several advantages:

- to discuss a mathematical concept under different points of view, which usually leads to a deeper understanding and a better mastery of concepts (for instance, geometrical transformations can be completely described by means of equations but using a graphical representation clarifies better the concept);
- to change the presentation order of some concepts, based on their relative degree of difficulty (for instance, the resolution of equations can be introduced graphically before completing the study of algebraic manipulation rules);
- to focus on resolution strategies rather than on performing calculations which can improve problem-solving activities;
- to emphasise the meaning of math concepts before being able to formally handle them (for instance, derivatives computed by some software can be used to find minima and maxima of a function based on their meaning, before learning to compute them).

This approach implies a redefinition of a teacher's role and a revision of curricula in order to give more space to non-routine activities apt to stimulate the student's creativity. Moreover, learners usually have different background and experience, and this influences the impact of IT on their learning.

7 EDUCATIONAL USE OF IT HAS BEEN CHANGING

The first attempts to introduce IT in education were made at the beginning of the 1960s with systems whose design and aim was strongly influenced by the hardware and software at the disposal at that time (only mainframes, usable in timesharing; few programming languages for the construction of systems; little application software). A change of approach and use over the past 35 years is due also to the availability of new hardware and software tools which are cheaper, more ductile user friendly, and with a range of features.

Technological development has produced a growing distance between the basic functioning of computers and the way computers interact with users. It has produced new, more intellectual and virtual ways to use them.

This evolution has been influenced by the research in education; it has gone in parallel with a different conception of teaching and learning, underlined by changes in the official school programmes.

8 AN OVERVIEW OF APPROACHES TO USING IT IN EDUCATION

It is not our purpose to give a history of IT in education. However, summarising general trends can help us understand the present and prepare for the future.

A precise classification of software tools which have been used in education over the years is rather difficult since often one kind of tool evolved into another, so that several tools belong to more than one group we are going to mention.

Systems have evolved under several respects: focus, structure and interface. As concerns focus, it has shifted from seeing the computer as a tutor to using it as a tool to giving a central roles to students' activity. As concerns structure, software has evolved from rigidly organised systems to more and more flexible ones. As concerns interfaces, they are becoming more and more articulated and user-friendly, supporting communication in different forms, as is the case of multimedia systems, where the concept of interactivity acquires a new dimension by focusing on individual strategies during the learning process and encouraging the exchange of knowledge in various forms between the system and the learner.

8.1 CAI/CAL system

The attempt to use technological tools in education began in the early 1960s with the design and implementation of computer-assisted instruction/computer assisted learning systems, which offered individualised pacing, provided reinforcement and evaluated performance. They were generally limited to present some topics. The didactic path was very rigid, based on a 'stimulus-response' model, with a one-way teaching interaction. A system posed some questions and/or problems and evaluated the student's answers based on a rigid predefined schema. Hence the behaviour of the system was not adaptable to the different needs of students. The merit of CAI/CAL is that they have been a first attempt to use technology to mediate learning in a period when the use of computers was mainly based on programming with languages which required one to adapt one's own thinking to the way computers worked.

8.2 Intelligent tutoring systems ICAI/ILE

The need to get over the limits of CAI encouraged studies in cognitive psychology and artificial intelligence, with particular attention to the interaction between teacher and student. These researches led to the development of new educational systems called ICAI (Intelligent Computer-Assisted Instruction) or Intelligent Tutoring Systems (ITS). In an ITS a student can exploit a two-way dialogue, somehow personalised to his/her needs. Some ITSs give students a well-defined didactic path; others let students free to choose their own paths; other mix the two approaches. An ITS is a collection of expert systems (that is, systems planned to emulate the behaviour of human experts on some determined topic), suitably designed to interact with each other, such as (at least):

- an expert module, experienced on the topic to be taught (this module is needed to analyse, understand and solve problems on that topic either proposed by the student or by the system itself);
- a tutoring module, experienced in some didactical methodology, able to handle problems related to the learning process;
- a student module, that is, a knowledge base concerning the learning status of the students as gathered by the system through a dialogue (a qualitative model, dynamically improved and increased, which allows the system to personalise the teaching dialogue, and, in some way, to direct the learning path);

- an interaction module to make the system easy and pleasant to use, and to allow both the system and the student to take the initiative in the dialogue.

ITSs have been objects of research for many years and have evolved towards more and more flexible configurations in order to adapt them to the behaviours of the users. This has gradually led to design software structured more as learning environments where the user has freedom to explore the topic under consideration and to pay more attention to the design of interfaces based not only on text but on different media, used not simply to make the system more appealing, but actually as dialogue tools. These changes opened the way to the creation of microworlds and multimedia.

8.3 Microworlds - learning through exploration with constraints

The concept of microworld was first formulated in 1971 by Marvin Minsky and Seymour Papert within the Artificial Intelligence community in order to communicate the idea of problem solving in a simple and constrained domain. Since then the goal for microworlds has shifted - from teaching computers to solving problems to designing learning environment for the acquisition of knowledge, making personal discovery a part of mathematical education. Microworlds explicitly intend to develop an investigative attitude towards mathematical enquiry.

Their basic features include:

- providing the user with a visual language which allows the generation and manipulation of objects in order to produce visual representation of a problem's situation or solution step;
- offering several different ways to achieve a goal;
- allowing a direct manipulation of objects;
- embodying a model of an abstract knowledge domain of visual, manipulable representation mediates between the concrete and directly manipulable on one side and formal and abstract on the other side.

A free exploration of a microworld (or other system) offers learners a rich experience but does not guarantee that specific learning occurs. Hence the system requires a suitable using environment organised by the teacher.

The best-known and most widely used examples of microworlds are the Logo programming environment and the graphic system Cabri-geometre. Cabri-geometre is a direct manipulation system designed and implemented for educational purposes, in particular for the study of Euclidean geometry, Euclidean geometry represents a synthetic view of geometry and is usually more difficult than analytic geometry. It is still controversial which of the two approached should be presented first at school. Cabri gives a contribution to smooth and make appealing this approach to geometry, The system is available for both Macintosh and PC computers and is used in many schools of different kinds at different levels. It offers pure drawing primitives - for lines, points, polygons, geometric primitives to build geometric objects with some given properties and in relation to other objects already drawn, and it allows a high degree of interaction by moving the constructed objects yet preserving the original properties and relations. It has a user-friendly interface and is easy to learn. A problem with its use is that it does not have the possibility to choose or produce random elements.

8.5 Hypertexts, hypermedia and multimedia

These terms refer mainly to the structure and operating mode of systems.

Hypertexts breaks the traditional sequentiality of texts, subdividing materials into modules variously connected with each other to form a graph structure so that users can create their own personalised reading path.

The term 'multimedia' refers to systems that combine information in different formats (texts, images, sounds, video and animation) to communicate more effectively. Multimedia achieve a high degree of interactivity between user and the system since non-textual input/output is not used simply to make the interface more pleasant but is strictly part of the handled knowledge.

Hypermedia systems combine the non-linear structure of hypertext and the variety of interaction forms of multimedia, giving rise to a new concept of interactivity where the user is a fundamental component determining the starting point, the aim and the form of the interaction.

As concerns content, multimedia systems often, but not necessarily, include some microworld with excellent results since these two approaches are both learner- and activity-centred.

8.6 Perspectives - cooperative learning by means of Internet

The current trend is to add communication technologies to IT and to realise systems that allow a meaningful and complex exchange of information, ideas, solutions and materials, by using the facilities of Internet. This long distance, real-time, structured communication will probably be a good way to overcome the isolation of off-centred locations, allowing students to share learning outside their school environments. This approach can increase motivation, foster group work and discussion, stimulate writing and communication skills, and open up minds with the acquaintance of different social and cultural contexts.

Other kinds of software, mainly developed for commercial purposes, have undergone a parallel process of evolution and have been successfully applied in mathematics teaching.

8.7 Software packages - professional and educational

Spreadsheets and other tools

Software packages, both professional and educational, are often successfully used in school, in particular spreadsheets, symbolic manipulators, graphics systems, statistics packages, and ad hoc systems with mixed capabilities. From an educational point of view, the increased use of general purpose commercial software has put an emphasis on the information handling aspects of students' work. Their use requires from the teacher a working out of educational approaches in order to avoid using them to find numerical results rather than as learning tools.

Spreadsheets have been created as professional tools. They are table builders with a labelling systems for rows and columns and facilities to draw graphs based on the constructed tables. Their most salient feature is the facility to express formulas making reference to cells' addresses and using them to fill a table based on input or previously computed values. Other facilities are the possibility to insert, delete and move columns or sets of cells, hence adding a dynamic aspect to the produced tables. It is clear that they are a generic tool as concerns mathematics education, which makes them suitable for numerous topics - from a first approach to algebra to the introduction of function, to statistical analysis of data, etc. Due to their nature, problem solutions based on them are essentially numerical computations based on a trial-and-error strategy, rather than formal solutions based on some mathematical theory. The two best-known, *Lotus* and *Excel*, differ only in a few features in the interface, and are essentially equivalent as concerns their use.

Computer algebra systems are mostly general-purpose mathematical manipulation systems. offering the possibility to perform symbolic manipulation, calculus, number theory, linear algebra, statistics and differential equations. In high school teaching usually only symbolic manipulators (such as *Derive* or *Theorist*) with a restricted range of operations and graphing capabilities are applied since they are easier to learn and do not require big memory occupations. Richer systems, which require more memory space and offer programming possibilities, *Maple* or *Mathematica*, for example, are used more for professional purposes or at the university level. Despite their use in school in several countries, computer algebra systems as cognitive technology for mathematics are considered to be still a field with great potential for evolution.

Graphical and geometric software

Among graphical programs that have been successfully used in school for supporting geometry learning the most widely-known are *Cabri-geometre*, *Geometer Sketchpad* or the graphical part of Logo. All these systems differ from drawing tools (*MacPaint*, for example) where the process of construction of a drawing involves only action, in that they require an explicit description of figures in terms of their geometric properties, either by selecting a menu item or by writing a list of commands. This is valuable from an educational point of view since the description of a drawing is strongly related to the deep structure of geometry. In them a construction task aims not simply to produce a drawing but to produce a description resulting in a drawing. Moreover they offer facilities to modify a drawing yet preserving the intended properties.

Proramming

Computer programming has been present in education for many years. The initial absence of appropriate high-level programming environments resulted in the widespread use of teaching students some very limited programming. At present, though languages are usually embedded in better operating environments which may stimulate their educational use, the use of programming in math courses is not as popular as it was years ago. One of the reasons is that attention is now more on what computers can do to help us solve problems than on the inner-working of computers themselves.

Programmable environments have been often regarded as superior to ready-made software packages since students can learn that they can construct and modify working tools. However programming is a difficult discipline that cannot be learned in a few weeks. It is impossible, in the limited time that a mathematics teacher can dedicate to teaching programming, that students can gain such a mastery to be able to develop anything more than simple exercises, which makes programming a suitable topic only if complemented with other environments.

9 TOPICS FOR DISCUSSION

How much awareness of the historical evolution of technology should students and teachers acquire? Is it necessary that developing countries go through all steps developed countries have gone through?

Compare national situations:

- How diffused are computers in schools? What kinds of hardware and software are available?
- How extensively are computers used? For what kinds of activities?
- What is planned by official programs?
- How are teachers trained and supported to carry out activities?
- Is teaching based on a problem solving approach?

32

Appropriate research in IT in emerging countries

Paul Nicholson
Deakin University
Burwood
VIC Australia 3125
E-mail: Pauln@deakin.edu.au

1 INTRODUCTION

Much of the research about IT in education is essentially Western, reflecting the Western research paradigm, models of education and culture. It is essential that the embedded influences that permeate the research in undefined and intangible ways are recognised as essentially cultural artifacts.

Within the research literature itself, there is no one preferred methodology that suits all circumstances. Instead a number of competing paradigms are often represented as being 'better' or 'more reliable' or even 'more valid' than others (*e.g.*, Lynch & Tarson, 1984). The debate about methodologies is much more significant than the debate about specific models and methods of quantitative research, and is very difficult to engage.

The purpose of this workshop session is not to directly engage in the debate, other than to acknowledge it. You will be presented with two 'alternative' models of research that appear to have much to offer educators in many countries. Together they can facilitate effective research in implementation and in planning for IT in education (along with many other issues).

The workshop will briefly discuss action research, and engage with its essential methodological components, before moving on to examining the use of scenario-based research as a means of planning and positioning educational computing in a changing cultural, social and political milieu. It is a kind of 'action research for the future'.

Capacity Building for IT in Education in Developing Countries
G. Marshall & M. Ruohonen (Eds.)

2 ACTION RESEARCH

Action research is research that is embedded in the experience, context and (frequently) workplace of the researcher. Its focus is on the 'practitioner as researcher' with the outcomes being realistic understandings and solutions to practitioner-level problems. It provides iterative solutions to real problems through an ongoing cycle of research, reflection and then application of strategies derived from the research. Its major strength is the localisation of the research with the practitioner and the consequent development of increased understandings.

Action research is good for solving problems that require strong local knowledge, give flexible and adaptable outcomes, allow for localised solutions, and involve community values and attitudes to be incorporated as valid parameters.

Often action research is not valued because it is such a simple approach to solving many educational problems that it does not require the theoretical constructs that define and constrain most other models of research.

3 SCENARIO-BASED RESEARCH

Scenario-based research is action research for the future. It is 'future-proofing' education and business. It is a rapid response plan, an informed, researched action plan to meet future challenges in policy, economic or political factors.

Most of us must make a decision now! Anything that can help make a decision in the confusion of uncertainty will be valuable. Scenario planning is one such tool.

The primary driving forces of scenario-based research are:

- social dynamics - quantitative, demographic issues;
- economic issues - macroeconomic trends and forces shaping the economy as a whole;
- political issues - electoral, regulatory and litigative;
- technological issues - direct, enabling and indirect.

After identifying the predetermined elements of the driving forces, a number of uncertainties remain. Are they critical uncertainties - an uncertainty that is key to our focal issue?

Determine the set of scenarios that focus on our uncertainty:

- Realize that there is more than one possible future.
- Understand that it is important to identify the most likely possibilities.
- Accept that the 'solution' that applies across the widest range of possible futures is probably the best and most robust.

4 GETTING TO WORK WITH SCENARIO-BASED RESEARCH

Now we will work through the process of scenario planning. Realize that there will only be enough time to develop one scenario. The workshop is about understanding the process!

WORKSHOP TIMETABLE

Phase 1: Where am I now?
60 minutes

Review of current situation
Identification of assumptions
Small group presentation
Writing task

Phase 2: What can change?
60 minutes

Identification of issues
Articulating and prioritising the impact
Small group presentation
Writing task

Phase 3: Planning for change
60 minutes

Short and long term reactions
Small group presentation
Writing task

Phase 1: Where am I now? (60 minutes)

In this phase it is essential to identify 'where you are' now.
This includes identifying the assumptions that are embedded in your current situation and thinking, and a listing of all of the factors that have led to the present.

- Briefly describe your current situation:

- In the following box, make a list of the **KEY** assumptions that you believe underpin 'where you are now' in regard to the situation you want to consider.

- In the following box, list the **KEY** factors that have led to the present situation.

- List the THREE MOST satisfactory features of the present situation.

1.
2.
3.

- List the THREE LEAST satisfactory features of the present situation.

4.
5.
6.

- Now you can give a 5 minute presentation on your work to your group. This will help you to ensure that you have covered the key issues. At the end of the group session, you should add/revise your items above based on feedback from the group. You should then have a clear idea of where you are starting from, or at least as seen by others.

Phase 2: What can change? (60 minutes)

The whole point about scenarios is that they confront the future. Therefore there are no certainties.

In this part of the process, it is important for you to identify issues and trends that could subtly or significantly alter the way in which you now go about your business. Some of this will come from your professional understandings of the area you are working in; other ideas will come from hunches and gut feelings.

This is a key part of scenario planning - getting your expert, intuitive ideas on paper where they can be reacted to.

- List at least 6 things that, **in your opinion**, could alter the present situation.

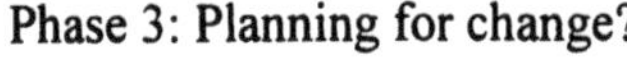

Phase 3: Planning for change? (60 minutes)

For each of the three issues that you listed in the table, suggest at least two appropriate ways in which you could react to them, if they became reality.

Issue 1

response 1

response 2

Issue 2

response 1

response 2

Issue 3

response 1

response 2

- Present a 5 minute summary of your proposed responses to your group. Use the feedback to refine them to your satisfaction.
- Now, take the issue that you consider to be the most significant and develop your response to it in two ways:

1. As a short term response (1 - 3 months) so that you address its immediate concerns.
2. As a long term response (1-3 years) where you:
    - show how you expect it to develop over time,
    - describe how you anticipate it might change,

- Prioritise these in order of 'most likely' to 'unlikely'.

1
2
3
4
5
6
7
8

Take the three top items and explain them to your group. To do this well, you will have to clearly identify the potential issue and explain its likely impact to the other members. The group will give you advice about the issue, and what might need to be explained or explored further. At this stage, you should be able to clearly identify exactly what the issue is and what its origins are. To make sure that you have thought this through, complete the following self-check table.

Issue	Details	Comes from	Reason for its existence
1			
2			
3			

- the KINDS of institutional, social or economic resources that might be needed,
- social, cultural, economic and political considerations.

SHORT TERM STRATEGY:

LONG TERM STRATEGY:

At the end of the session, you will have the opportunity to present your work in a 10 minute presentation to the whole group involved in the workshop.

5 REFERENCES

Lynch, P. and Tarson, M. (1984) Research on Educational Planning: An International Perspective, in (ed. E. Gordon) *Review of Research in Education*, **11**, American Educational Research Association, Washington DC.

PART IX

Discussion Group Recommendations

33

Discussion Group 1 - IT in curriculum and courseware development

Chair: Peter Bollerslev (Denmark)

Rapporteurs: Margaret Niess (USA), Paul Nicholson (Australia), Márta Turcsányi-Szábo (Hungary)

Participants: Olayele Adelakan (Finland), Deane Arganbright (Papual New Guinea), Ben Awuah (Botswana), Ann Baillie (Zimbabwe), Rachel Cohen (France), Klaus-D Graf (Germany), Jacqueline Grierson (Zimbabwe), Hildigunnur Halldorsdottir (Iceland),Anne McDougall (Australia), Richard Simango (Zimbabwe), Matti Sinko (Finland), David Squires (UK)

GROUP 1A

1 IT IN ELEMENTARY EDUCATION - REVIEW OF THE CURRENT SITUATION

1.1 International Experiences

Psychology shows that access to new media at this age is easy. Children do not yet build resistance to new media and are not biased. International research shows that small children can use and love to use computers, and take benefit from this.

Why it is important to start early:
1. Develop literacy;
2. Develop personal skills (thinking process, creativity and communication);
3. Learn to use technology and develop basic skills;
4. Integrate of application software.

Numerous countries have started as early as kindergarten with unexpected and encouraging results.

Literacy

- Computers facilitate writing, illustrating stories, listening to stories on CD-ROMs.

Capacity Building for IT in Education in Developing Countries
G. Marshall & M. Ruohonen (Eds.)

- Specific programs and word processors can be used by young children. Many are available on the market but if no funds are available, experience has proved that standard software that comes with the computer is as good.

Developing personal skills (thinking process, creativity, and communication)

- Problem solving programs help develop reasoning with computers.
- Children are able to use spreadsheets and databases. Easy ones are available (in Denmark, England, Netherlands and the USA) particularly used in environmental studies, science and mathematics.
- Use Logo environment for visual problem solving.
- Programs such as 'Writer's Helper' assist in the development of creative writing.
- Use standard drawing programs (create pictures, illustrate text).
- Use multimedia for creative purposes (*e.g.* creating stories, animation, music).
- Use Internet for communication and information retrieval.
- Use application programs in subject areas.

Learn to use technology

Through literacy programmes and programmes designed to develop personal skills children learn to use technology and these approaches are integrated into everyday life.

Integration of application software

Application software can play a vital role in the education of young children:

- applications in the different subject areas (such as packages that are created for curriculum use);
- integration of IT across the curriculum;
- multidisciplinary projects carried out using IT, multimedia and Internet.

1. 2 Local conditions

Each country should analyze (a) the local situation and availability, (b) determine goals, and (c) identify the useful application and priorities, taking into account the traditions, cultures and existing strategies.

(a)The local situation and availability:

- situation of schools: electricity, etc.
- equipment available, hardware and software.
- human resources: support of local administration and principal of school; motivation and willingness of teachers; technicians, involvement of parents.

Courseware
In Zimbabwe:
- There is very little courseware development.
- Most (all) books are of UK origin - textbooks related to examination syllabuses.
- Most curriculum materials are locally made.

Software
In Zimbabwe:
- Older versions of conventional applications software (DOS 5.0 *WordPerfect*, *Lotus*, *dBase*, etc.) are the most common.
- There is little funding for software development.
- There is very little subject-specific software.

Collegiality
In Zimbabwe:
- User groups and links to computing associations are not well developed.
- Very limited forums for discussion are available.

Hardware
In Zimbabwe:

- Many schools do not have computers.
- A small number of state and private schools do have computers - this contrasts strongly with developed countries, *e.g.*, European countries typically have pupil/computer ratios of about 7:1

2 PHASE 2 - WHAT CAN CHANGE?

Curriculum
The examination system is an inherent part of the education system. Parents and students expect courses to be certificated; in particular, computing courses are expected to be certificated as they provide vocational qualifications. It is very unlikely that this situation can change in the medium-term future and formal examinations in computing will remain an established feature of the curriculum. However, some changes in other subject areas through the use of Information Technology (IT), *e.g.*, data logging in Physics, can result in curriculum changes through the use of IT across the curriculum.

Hardware
There are three possible ways in which hardware provision may be changed:
1. The price of computers may be reduced. Possible approaches here include increased use of cloned machines and a reduction in duty paid to foreign imports.

(b) Determine goals.

(c) Identify the useful application and priorities, taking into account the traditions, cultures and existing strategies.

2 RECOMMENDATIONS

- Educational policy should define the goals before actions such as choosing hardware and software are taken.
- Introduction of IT into education should start as early as preschool, when available, in order to enhance development of children's potential, prevent illiteracy and school failure, and enhance computer literacy
- In elementary schools no definite curriculum should be designed in IT; IT should be integrated into all subjects.
- The use and enrichment of IT skills should be continued throughout schooling to provide a continuous involvement with technology for everyday life.
- Resources should be converted to standardized equipment to facilitate training and exchange of experiences.
- Special attention should be made in the choice of existing software, taking into account the local conditions and culture as well as the educational potential of software. Creation of software, national and/or regional, and cooperation between nations should be encouraged.
- Computers should not be introduced into schools unless they comes with appropriate teacher education and technical support. In certain countries it has been a fruitful solution to organize mobile computer classes, where computers are installed in busses and move around a region together with an experienced teacher.
- Promising schools should be encouraged and supported to serve as models for other schools. Concentrating supporting in such model schools would become a consulting and resource center for other schools as well.
- Schools should be encouraged to find partners in other countries to exchange ideas, software, literature and experiences.

GROUP 1B

1 WHERE ARE WE NOW?

We shall use the framework presented by Paul Nicholson in his workshop on scenario planning to consider issues under four headings: curriculum, hardware, courseware and collegiality.

Curriculum

In developed countries (*e.g.*, UK, Denmark and Australia) the prevailing rationale is to integrate IT into the curriculum. In Zimbabwe IT/computing is conceived of as a separate subject: *e.g.*, computer literacy courses and examination courses in computing.

2 WHAT CAN BE CHANGED?

Teacher educators have to adopt, implement and model the appropriate use of IT (Underwood, 1996). This is critical as research also shows that teachers often 'teach with, and what, they were taught'.

Currently, many teacher educators and university staff see IT as either a tool for learning computer science, or as a support for social and economic progress. Little consideration is given to its value in education. Often the technology leads the learning process (learning about the technology) instead of learning with the technology. A lack of emphasis on software evaluation and associated pedagogy, and access to model classrooms is common.

There are a number of critical factors which can be changed in order to help to develop a suitable environment for the adoption of IT in education:

- Develop organic, flexible, responsive plans that allow for both local concerns and national priorities rather than centrally imposed models.
- Develop regional consortia to plan for curriculum and infrastructure projects as this may result in reduced costs.
- Upgrade the competencies of teacher educators in the use of IT in education.
- Make ongoing teacher education a key focus of the implementation process.
- Change the culture of teachers from being deliverers of imposed curricula to reflective, action-research focused practitioners (Elliot, 1981), who can develop localised, contextually and culturally relevant materials.

3 HOW COULD CHANGE BE IMPLEMENTED?

The aim of this plan is to develop an organic, flexible, collaborative and responsive system that allows for both local concerns and national priorities to be addressed by local communities or government as appropriate.

Short term (1-2 years)

- Identify and clarify relevant national priorities in IT in education.
- Identify prospective funding and development partners, and commence planning.
- Identify and train a core of teachers to design and implement short-term 'cascade model' professional development programmes based on the UNESCO curriculum (Tinsely and van Weert, 1994) guidelines.
- Design and develop the materials for the short-term professional development programs.
- Mandate minimum IT competencies for newly-graduating teachers.
- Invest more heavily in teacher education programmes.
- Plan dissemination processes for sharing ideas, materials and projects on IT - *e.g.*, conferences, journals, newsletters, etc.

2. More money may become available: overseas aid, increased government expenditure, donations. (Note that the donation of old equipment causes severe problems - maintenance is expensive or impossible, configurations are inadequate to support appropriate software and shipping costs are often prohibitive.)
3. Reconsider hardware configurations, *e.g.*, the use of palmtops and the use of lower configuration desktop machines in networked environments.

Courseware

Locally-produced material offers a chance for producing more courseware, courseware which is directly relevant to local needs. As IT is used in other subject areas, *e.g.*, data logging, the content of published courseware such as textbooks will change. Syllabi will also change to reflect the use of IT.

Collegiality

This may be increased by the formation of local and national teacher groups and groups sponsored by international organisations such as IFIP. The Internet provides opportunities for virtual peer group interaction and continuing professional development programmes also offer opportunities for collaboration.

GROUP 1C

1 INTRODUCTION

Many international research articles show that teacher education plays a critical role in the successful adoption of educational innovations such as the use of IT in education. This has significant implications for planning for IT in education. Planners often think that teacher professional development is not needed because it is assumed that normal classroom pedagogy can be transferred directly to the technological medium. This is incorrect. Teacher change is gradual, and requires a change of knowledge, teaching strategies and beliefs as well as the addition of IT skills (Fullan, 1991).

The Concerns-based Adoption Model (Hall, Loucke and Rutherford, 1977) also shows that teachers will only be effective change agents if the change addresses their immediate concerns. In many developing countries, teachers and schools face significant problems in regard to IT - including little, if any, exposure to or experience with computers. They also face the lack of specialist IT teachers to work with and to learn from, lack of essential infrastructure and little awareness of appropriate models of use.

Planners must accept these findings and include them in their thinking about planning for IT as well as accepting the idea that teachers will be the people who will bring their plans into reality. They will have to start to invest in people as well as hardware and software.

Medium term (3-5 years)

- Develop localised cross-disciplinary teams to identify local priorities, needs and concerns.
- Develop mentor links with teacher education institutions.
- Develop localised, contextualised materials for teachers and students.
- Identify and develop culturally-relevant models of use.
- Develop localised professional development models and materials - *e.g.*, modify the 'cascade' model materials for local conditions.
- Develop the infrastructure for all schools to be able to incorporate computers into their curriculum.
- Develop the infrastructure for widescale networking.

Long term (ongoing)

Use computer networks to establish widescale professional development programmes and curriculum development projects.

4 REFERENCES

Elliot, J. (1981) *Action-Research: a framework for self-evaluation in schools.* Cambridge University Press, Cambridge.

Fullan, M. (1991) *The New Meaning of Educational Change.* Teachers College Press, New York.

Hall, G., Loucke, H. and Rutheford, W. (1977) Measuring stages of concern about an innovation. University of Texas Research and Development Center for Teacher Education, Austin, TX.

Tinsley, J.D. and van Weert, T.J. (eds.) (1994) Informatics for secondary education, a curriculum for schools. UNESCO, Paris.

Underwood, J. (1996) Teacher education for primary and secondary schools, in (eds. Samways, B & van Weert, T.) IFIP: Window to the future. WCCE95. Postconference report. Aston University, Birmingham, UK.

34

Discussion Group 2 - Policies, strategies & initiatives of ICT in education

Chair: Sam Gumbo (Zimbabwe)

Rapporteur: Pieter Hogenbirk (The Netherlands)

Participants: Walter Chakuzira (Zimbabwe), Peter Hubwieser (Germany), Geoffrey Kiangi (Namibia), Olivia Magaya (Zimbabwe), Marshall Mlambo (Zimbabwe), Joanna Marivara (Zimbabwe), Rudo Mataranyika (Zimbabwe), Simon Mphisa (Zimbabwe), Hajime Ohiwa (Zimbabwe), Charles Nherera (Zimbabwe), Sindre Røsvik (Norway), Simon Satumba (Zimbabwe), Obert Sifile (Zimbabwe), Enock Tinofirei (Zimbabwe), Lorraine Tafira (Zimbabwe), Marsha Williams (USA)

1 INTRODUCTION

Discussing the theme of policies, strategies and successful initiatives for Information and Communication Technology (ICT), one has to consider first the objectives. From these objectives, policies can be derived to meet the goals. Policies still are general statements, which have to be worked out in elements of strategy. In the last stage of elaborating on this theme the elements of strategy need to be made operational into activities and actions which might be the most successful to achieve the originally formulated objectives. We actually decided not to split up the discussion into the three levels of education - primary, secondary and tertiary education - in order to get a framework that could apply to all of these levels. So it was agreed to structure the discussion in the following four stages:

- definition of the targets, needs, objectives or goals one wants to achieve with respect to ICT in education - (the 'why');
- development from this of various aspects of policy making (the 'what');
- development of the strategy elements fitting to the policies (the 'how');
- implementation of the strategies by activities that might be most successful.

The framework we used made the discussion very clear and fruitful. Nevertheless we should make one remark at the beginning. We should not bother too much about whether something is a policy, an objective, a strategy or a down-to-earth activity. It is very important that policy makers are aware of the choices to be made in strategies and easy-to-implement activities. At the same time the educational community should recognize the fact that innovations and changes have a need for support and approval of the politicians and the industry. By understanding the

Capacity Building for IT in Education in Developing Countries
G. Marshall & M. Ruohonen (Eds.)

mutual interests stakeholders and participants in the process could be involved to a level needed for making the innovation a success.

2 OBJECTIVES

Objectives could be defined from different perspectives. They could be social, applying to the needs of the society; they could be vocational, aiming at professional development; they could be pedagogical, affecting the actual teaching process; and they could be catalytic, stimulating other innovations and changes to occur. We established the following list of objectives which involve the four categories. All of the objectives apply to the pupils, the teachers, the administrators as well as the teacher trainers - the whole of the educational community.

- You should be able to use the computer as a tool for your personal functioning.
- You should be able to use ICT for communication and information retrieval.
- You should know the potential and implications of ICT.
- You should achieve ICT-abilities for future professional development.
- You should be able to participate actively in the global society, not widening the gap between the 'haves' and 'have nots' any more.
- The use of ICT should catalyze and improve the quality of the learning process.
- There should be more capacity building on ICT-use and research in the local language, culture and national programs.

3 POLICIES

To achieve these objectives we need to have policies - not only written papers but actual statements that could be translated later into strategies for achieving the policies. We came up with the following policy statements:

- Every child and teacher should have access to the use of ICT. This policy is often referred to as the issue of accessibility.
- Males and females should have equal opportunity in using ICT. This policy is often referred to as the equity issue.
- There should be a development of national curriculum aspects for ICT, short-term and long-term. These elements cover ICT in separate subjects as well as ICT integrated in other subjects.
- All relevant stakeholders (government, industries, educational community, local communities, parents) should be involved when that is relevant and essential for the strategy.
- There should be an intensive program for teacher training going along with curriculum development and technical development.
- A basic infrastructure of hardware, software and connectivity should be defined and implemented, which enables all kinds of activities and projects to work together.

- There should be set up a system for the accreditation and certification of the ICT programs as well as for the assessment of ICT objectives in the curriculum.
- There should be a thorough financing programme for achieving the objectives. The plan of actions should be defined in terms of feasible outcomes, depending on the budgets available.

4 STRATEGIES

Still the policies are phrased in a rather general way. They have to be translated into strategic actions and ideas to make them work. Note that the strategies could be streamlined along various aspects, *e.g.* national, regional and school level. We did not do so because the list will not be exhaustive. Yet we can divide the strategies into two categories. At first we state a preliminary idea (A). The first set of strategies (B-I) applies to ideas and actions to be taken for elaborating on the policies. The second category (J-O) consists of actual activities, in general terms, to be undertaken. This leads to the following list:
A. The strategy should have both top-down and bottom-up elements. This will provide a balance for responsibility and involvement of the relevant participants in the process.

To implement the policies the following actions could be taken:
B. A major effort should be made to influence policy makers and politicians. They are the key persons when it comes to making up the general policy statements and the funding of the process.
C. Plans of activities should be tied up firmly to national development programs and perspectives for the necessary governmental support.
D. The involvement of administrators is needed to back up the teachers, the parents and the local communities.
E. Collaboration between public and private sectors should be established by appealing to their mutual responsibilities and abilities.
F. To stimulate such collaboration we should create and enable an environment with incentives for industries and major representatives of the public sector to get involved and take responsibility.
G. The development of educational software is very expensive. So one should try to use existing software when possible and at the same time have some good examples of software that fit the national language(s) and culture.
H. To narrow the gap between developed and developing countries there should be investigated the development of research centers for assembling and manufacturing ICT tools.
I. To be part of the global society and participating members of the world community we should network all schools to public offices, to other schools and to the Internet.

Some strategies can be formulated much more as general activities. In the next phase these could be translated today to start initiatives. We thought of the following list:

J. We should define a syllabus for ICT as a subject and integrate it (as a catalyst) into other subjects.
K. We have to define and start experimental projects that are provided with all resources needed.
L. We have to start pilot projects in which the main objectives have to be to investigated to see if they are replicable and to see how experiences gained from them could be multiplied.
M. Most important is the development and orientation of the human resources, synchronized with the technical equipment and the curriculum development, and giving people time to change and to adapt to the new situation. So an integrated and step-by-step approach will be necessary. Human resources imply:

- M1. the administrators,
- M2. the teachers,
- M3. the technicians,
- M4. the teacher trainers.

N. Especially in developing countries it is very important to get the local communities involved so they should be mobilized.
O. There should be given preferential treatment to disadvantaged schools, *e.g.* by divising the means in a way they got more than the more privileged schools.

5 SUCCESSFUL ACTIVITIES FOR IMPLEMENTING STRATEGIES

The strategic elements have to be translated into 'on-the-floor' initiatives. The discussion group brainstormed about activities with a low threshold, strategies which could be started today. Added to each of these activities is a reference to the list of strategies above. The order of these activities is just coincidental.

- Industrial parties should invite politicians to influence their thinking and views (B, D).
- From successful sites there could be organized demonstrations and sessions for training ICT skills for administrators and teachers (C, M1).
- All participants involved have to share responsibilities for project and their outcomes, *e.g.* by signing a mutual agreement and by all contributing financially (C, M).
- Professional networks of teachers and technicians - via the Computer Teacher Association (CTA) - should be established (M2, M3).
- It was emphasized that a flourishing ICT Teachers Association should be built.
- Schools should try to get used equipment from industry and from abroad (N, D). National and international organizations have to take the lead for that.
- Stakeholders must organize community outreach (M).
- Schools and training institutes can make use of parents, teachers, assistants, school development associations, computer associations, etc. for giving good examples and helping in capacity building (M).

- Research projects on assembling and manufacturing computers and software can be initiated (F, G).
- As in the European countries the European drivers licence could be introduced, including keyboard skills (L).
- Software could be developed that fits the local cultural environment and is written in the national language(s) (F).

6 CONCLUSIONS

The discussion on the themes in the framework presented above, led us to the following conclusions:

- The implementation of a policy needs an integrated approach where all policy and strategy elements are conducted together. Such an approach must include the availability of infrastructure (hardware and software), the human resources development ('humanware'), the involvement of the (local) community and the implementation of the process (procedures).
- This integrated approach should be made operational in a clear plan of activities that includes a clear financial paragraph. This plan of action should take full advantage of all potential resources.
- The involvement of strategic people, bodies and institutions is fundamental for taking responsibility in both the set-up of the process and the implementation.

35

Discussion Group 3 - Guidelines and directions for ICT policy in education

Chair: Anton Knierzinger (Austria)

Rapporteurs: William Newman (Australia)
Stanford M. Gudza (Zimbabwe)

Participants: Florence T. Chinwadzimba (Zimbabwe), Giuliana Dettori (Italy), Bojka Gradinarova (Bulgaria), Tendayi Kakora (Zimbabwe), Joseph Mandibvisa (Zimbabwe), Aaron V.J. Ndlovu (Zambia), Thuto Ntsekhe-Mokhehle (Lesotho)

1 INTRODUCTION

This document does not attempt to prescribe policy. It is provides guidelines and directions that are important in considering the creation of policy. Policy in its final form applies to all schools and as such must be very carefully worded.

2 STRATEGIC OBJECTIVES

The following objectives are designed to encompass a governmental approach to Information Technology (IT). They are designed to improve the range of available services, and encourage economic development and employment growth in industries of the 21st century.

- network - to introduce innovative and competitive telecommunications infrastructure and solutions for the country;
- encourage business and employment growth - to develop an internationally competitive business sector that is confident and proficient in the use of IT; this can be an aim to make students better employable;
- enhance service delivery - to enhance the delivery of services from government and the private sector in the key areas of government, business and home;
- provide new ways to learn - to provide all citizens with the opportunity to learn the skills to use the new technology for their benefit.

3 IMPLEMENTATION

The information in this document relates to primary and secondary levels of education. At both levels there has to be an emphasis on the computer as a tool. It

Capacity Building for IT in Education in Developing Countries
G. Marshall & M. Ruohonen (Eds.)

is important at a primary school level to ensure that IT is not viewed as a specialist subject that only a few people can do. If IT is implemented as a special subject it can have the effect of allowing teachers not involved in the teaching of IT to sit back and do nothing.

At a secondary level IT should also be taught in an integrated way. There is a need to offer IT as a discipline in upper secondary ('O' and 'A' levels) and tertiary levels. It is not necessary to examine IT skills other than in the formal discipline subjects at upper secondary level.

- It is important in formulating policy that the issue of technical support be addressed. Technical support is defined as the fixing of hardware.
- IT sponsorship from industry should be actively sought by individual schools. It is important in doing so that government does not relinquish its responsibility to provide support.
- It is important to focus on the education of IT use rather than on training in IT for its own sake.
- Schools rather than ministries or governments decide on the appropriate hardware and software for the school.
- The emphasis on IT in education should be on function and philosophy, and not on simple skill acquisition.
- It is vitally important to remember that all goals and strategies are inter-related and no one point can be considered in isolation.

4 IMPLEMENTATION STRATEGY

The following areas provide a means whereby the above objectives can be met.

4.1 Sensitisation

Sensitisation is defined as the process of making people aware of the importance and implications of the use of IT in education. It should involve all stakeholders including industry, politicians, parents, principals, teachers and proprietors. It can be achieved by a number of strategies including seminars, information on what is happening elsewhere, demonstrations of what people can do personally, creating a personal interest, demonstrating a need and showing how the resources can be used in the general community.

4.2 Curriculum

- Curriculum needs to be revised on a regular basis.
- Methodologies should be emphasised in the curriculum.

4.3 Support

Support is essential and must have a high priority. In particular, it must concentrate on pre-service and in-service training as well as training the trainers.

- The provision and level of training is important. IT as a discipline should only be taught by teachers qualified to do so.
- All teachers must have the skills to use IT in their teaching of the curriculum. Fundamental to this is the need to provide critical thinking skills in the use of the technology.
- An ongoing professional development program is essential.
- Extensive pre-service training on the use of IT should be compulsory. This training must include methodological guidelines.
- Emphasis must be on teacher training ahead of hardware purchases.
- Teacher training is the cornerstone of any success.
- Continuous support and training of teachers is considered to be essential.

5 CONCLUSION

The above information can be used to create policy. It is not itself policy. Every country will have its own constraints and challenges in formulating and then implementing policy.

36

Discussion Group 4 - IT education delivery and learning

Chair: Bernard Cornu (France)

Rapporteur: Peter Juliff (Australia)

Participants: Raphael Benza (Zimbabwe), Kristina Ekmark (Sweden), Peter Kanengoni (Zimbabwe), Olivia Magaya (Zimbabwe), Rudo Mataranyika (Zimbabwe), Babongile Moyo (Zimbabwe), Rosalie Mitchell (New Zealand), Leonadr Nhembe (Zimbabwe), Nyalugwe Nyalugwe (Zimbabwe), Karen Norwood (USA), Tomás O'Briain (Ireland), Heimir Palsson (Iceland), Shadreck Phiri (Zimbabwe), Faith Samkange (Zimbabwe),Chaweewan Sawetamalya (Thailand), Erling Schmidt (Denmark), Alpheas Shindi (Zimbabwe), Naume Sonhera (Zimbabwe), Lorainne Tafira (Zimbabwe), Alex Tigere (Zimbabwe)

1 INTRODUCTION

The aim of the discussion group was to examine the effects of Information and Communication Technologies (ICT) on the process of learning and the delivery of education. The majority of the group members were involved in education at primary and secondary levels, and the discussion was mainly centered around the issues relating to education at those levels. The focus of the group was the issues relating to the use of computer-related technology in the teaching and learning process, with particular emphasis on the problems encountered in developing countries.

2 KEY ISSUES

In keeping with the theme of the conference, the major questions addressed were :

- the difficulties involved in planning and investing in ICT in education to ensure maximum efficiency and effectiveness;
- the reasons underlying possible under-utilisation of ICT resources;
- lessons to be learned from other countries in the effective adoption of ICT in education;
- remedies available to overcome perceived difficulties;

Capacity Building for IT in Education in Developing Countries
G. Marshall & M. Ruohonen (Eds.)

- the roles to be played by the IFIP community, governments and the private sector in providing a successful outcome to the introduction of ICT into the educational framework.

Three main themes emerged from the group discussion :

- issues relating to the integration of ICT within the broad spectrum of the educational curriculum;
- issues relating specifically to teachers;
- issues relating to the general learning process.

This record of the discussion will attempt to draw together the concerns expressed by members of the group, their experiences in teaching within their own environments, and their suggestions and recommendations on the solution to the problems which were encountered.

3 THE EDUCATIONAL FRAMEWORK

Despite their varied backgrounds, the members of the group portrayed a common environment in which they worked. The factors influencing their educational processes were:

- varying degrees of success in attempting to integrate ICT with other areas of the curriculum;
- mixed levels of computer literacy among teaching staff;
- difficulty in obtaining suitable levels of ICT teaching resources;
- a variety of levels of officially centralised control of syllabuses among the countries represented but at least an unofficial commonality due to the use of common software and common textbooks.

Concern was expressed by representatives of countries where English was not their native language that the adoption of English as the *lingua franca* of Information Technology was seen as having an undesirable effect on the use of the students' native language.

4 INTEGRATING IT WITHIN THE GENERAL CURRICULUM

There is a need both to integrate ICT within the broad spectrum of the educational curriculum and to enable students who wish to do so to pursue specialist studies in that area. Specialisation, however, should be restricted to the last one or two years of the secondary curriculum. The majority of problems associated with the introduction of ICT into primary and secondary education will therefore be associated with its integration across other subject areas.

Integration in this sense refers to computer-based activities which both fulfill the aims of the subject being taught and assist in the acquisition of ICT skills.

Difficulties arise primarily as a result of the lack of appropriate skills on the part of teachers. It is also true that teachers tend to be conservative and to use the same teaching methods as those by which they themselves were taught. If teachers are to pursue the integration of subject matter and ICT, they must be provided with adequate access to appropriate resources. In most cases, this will involve a ranking of a school's priorities to allow sufficient importance to be given to computing resources. This in turn will extend to the political and economic policies set by governments - upon which most education depends.

The utilisation of computing resources must ultimately depend on the judgement of the teaching staff. There must not be engendered an attitude that these resources are under-utilised if they are not fully occupied each hour of the day.

To achieve effective integration of ICT within the curriculum, attention must be given to :

- the design of an imaginative curriculum which encourages teaching by 'entrepreneurial' techniques;
- adequate time allocation to teachers to devise new approaches to their activities;
- appropriate training for teachers to equip them with ICT skills sufficient for the task;
- adequate access to physical resources to be able to develop the necessary courseware.

Teachers need to actively communicate with one another to share skills and experience. This may be done partly by changing teacher training programs but may also be fostered by programmes involving team work and by skilled teachers acting in a mentor capacity for those less skilled.

In addition to the question of curriculum integration, there is also the question of integration with the community-at-large. Students will eventually wish to enter the workforce and the ICT skills acquired at school will play a large part in equipping them with life skills for later use.

5 TEACHERS

Teachers need to regard themselves as agents of the transfer of ICT skills and knowledge. This may mean that they need to be prepared to abandon some time-honoured teaching practices. In turn, this means that they must be given adequate time to retrain and acquire new skills.

Once having acquired the skills needed for these activities, teachers must be given sufficient incentives to remain in the education system. The high turnover associated with the exodus of ICT-skilled teachers into the general workforce leads to discontinuity in the education process. Incentives may be in the form of increased remuneration or time release to pursue further relevant study.

Teachers must adopt the attitude that ICT resources are not solely for the use of computing studies students. This must be aided by the provision of a level of physical resources which ensures that adequate access is available for all students studying all subjects. The computer laboratory must be placed in the same category as the library, *i.e.*, a general resource for all students and staff.

Teacher education needs to expand to ensure that disciplinary teaching methods embrace the means of using computer-based technology in the delivery of the subject matter. This policy must extend beyond the initial teacher training regimen to the re-education of existing teachers. There is an argument for making ICT education a mandatory component for graduation in any teacher education program.

6 LEARNING

The major inhibiting factors in the ICT learning process are closely related to issues already discussed above. Resources are in short supply, leading to frustration among students wishing to improve their skills. Teaching practices often do not encourage students to be innovative in their use of ICT. Existing computing resources are often seen as either the province of computing studies students or as prestigious acquisitions not to be placed at risk by the depredations of unskilled students. One possible means of alleviating the shortage of resources may be to accept equipment which has become surplus to the requirements of business organisations.

The greatest return from the use of ICT in the teaching and learning process occurs when the learning program is interactive rather than one-way and passive. Such interactive programs, however, take time, skill and imagination to develop. These are the very resources likely to be, at least initially, in the shortest supply among existing teaching staff.

Despite the associated difficulties, the scene is changing for the better. The use of pilot projects as exemplars is showing teachers what is possible. More educational software is being developed and is becoming widely available at what is claimed to be affordable prices. Unfortunately, 'affordable' is a subjective quality. Most developing countries are struggling to provide equipment resources and many lack even the commonly-accepted infrastructure of reliable power and telephone communications.

The growth of innovative learning programmes depends on the education or re-education of all sectors of the educational hierarchy. Many teachers complain of inadequate allocation of time, money and equipment resources from principals who themselves have little empathy with the teachers' aims and visions.

7 THE ROLE OF IFIP

The role of IFIP in the IT educational process is seen as largely one of a facilitator. The international nature of IFIP equips it to facilitate such activities as :

- sharing expertise and experience across national, cultural and economic boundaries;
- enabling dialogue between the worlds of education and commerce to better equip educators to prepare students for the vocational component of their life;
- promoting standards and common practices, and enabling dialogue among educators worldwide;
- encouraging government agencies to formulate education policies which promote innovation in curricula.

The conference from which this paper emanates is an example of such an enabling policy and the discussion of which this is a record is the result of much deliberation and sharing of ideas and experience from representatives of ten countries.

8 CONCLUSION

There is a need for educators to strike a balance between the pursuit of technology for its own sake and ignoring it as irrelevant to the essential pedagogical process of equipping students for a useful and rewarding life. There is also a need for balance between a feeling of guilt if technology does not pervade all aspects of a teacher's activities and adopting an attitude that change is not necessary.

Teachers and students, like the population at large, will adopt change and innovation if it is shown to be useful, enjoyable and nonthreatening. All of this takes time and resources. Schools must be given resources appropriate to the expectations of the staff and students. Teachers must be given time to take advantage of those resources. Given these prerequisites, the natural curiosity and enthusiasm of students will ensure that computer-based technology will be embraced as enhancing their education process and preparing them for a world in which these skills are becoming increasingly essential.

37

Discussion Group 5 - Information Technology in institutional administration and management

Chair: Tom Van Weert (The Netherlands)

Rapporteurs: Adrie Visscher (The Netherlands)
Abdulla Suleman (Zimbabwe)

Participants: Alex Fung (Hong Kong), Clement Jumbe, John Kasiyamhuru, Tobias Kuwengwa, Irene Mahamba, Philemon Maramba, Michael Mubatapasango, Joel Munzara, Charles Mutungwazi, Leonard Nhembe, Stephen Raza, Moses Shamu (all of Zimbabwe)

1 INTRODUCTION

The discussion group consisted of representatives from several educational institutions. The group looked at Information Technology in Educational Management (ITEM) in the three countries represented. Moreover, the group discussed which measures could be taken to promote the use of ITEM in Zimbabwe.

2 The CASE OF ZIMBABWE

In Zimbabwe, at the Polytechnic, the need was expressed for a better control on some aspects of its operation. Accounts, hostel room allocation, the amenities fund and examinations have been computerised. Some departments use computers for administrative purposes. The systems have been developed in-house. There is a need to expand and integrate the ITEM. Areas that could be incorporated are: asset control, vocational training loans, examination registration, payments and results, library, expenditure, staffing, timetables and student reports.

The local university is using a system developed internally for administrative purposes.

In the state secondary schools there is very little, if any, ITEM being used. Some of the private schools are using ITEM for accounts. For instance, Speciss College has been using a system called Integrated Tertiary Software (ITS) for two years for the purpose of registrations, fees, statements and class registers. Use in other areas is still to be implemented.

Capacity Building for IT in Education in Developing Countries
G. Marshall & M. Ruohonen (Eds.)

The Discussion Group was informed that the national Zimbabwean EMIS - Educational Management Information System - was out to tender for a countrywide, comprehensive integrated system. The system is for the computerised support of administration of the two ministries involved - Education and Culture, and Higher Education.

3 THE CASE OF HONG KONG

In Hong Kong there are seven autonomous universities, each developing and using its own system, which tends to be task- orientated. There are moves by individual universities to develop an integrated MIS campus-wide. Initially, schools developed their own systems. Since 1993 the SAMS project has been introduced and 1200 schools will be integrated in one system territory-wide for management purposes. The project is due for completion in 1998. Of these schools 800 are primary schools where the computing experience is very low. This centralised system is trying to balance core needs against flexibility for specific or special requirements.

4 THE CASE OF THE NETHERLANDS

Most primary and secondary schools in The Netherlands use some form of computerised system. There are about three systems being used in secondary education. Two of them have been developed by private companies, one resulting from a governmental initiative. Schools can decide for themselves which of these systems they will use since the government cannot prescribe any one system. The available systems support various kinds of administrative activities (*e.g.*, student, personnel, finance) and also assist school managers in planning and evaluating work.

5 ISSUES FOR ZIMBABWE

With regard to Zimbabwe the following issues were highlighted:

1. there is a need for a national policy to lead Zimbabwe into the 21st century; an integrated approach is vital to use the lessons learnt elsewhere and, if deemed necessary, to use outside expertise;
2. the framework should be communicated to the stakeholders - school people, the policy makers (government) and the business sector (suppliers of hardware and software);
3. any amount of funding will not solve the problem, a well thought-out plan is required;
4. the systems should be easy to use for staff at all levels;

Crucial elements of a national strategy for the implementation of ITEM in developing countries using the above scheme are:

- the carefully analyse of the educational institutions concerning their information demands and information flows;

- the definition of the SIS framework, including all the required capabilities that can be obtained from the SIS;
- the step-by-step participative design and development of prototypes for the modules in the SIS framework in iterative design-test-redesign cycles until the modules support users widely in valuable and user-friendly ways, and system designers and users are happy with them;
- the attention paid to the planning and managing of the innovation process (*e.g.*, clear goals and feasible planning);
- the allocation of sufficient resources to the innovation and dispersal of expertise amongst staff;
- the stimulation of users by letting them experience the potential of SISs;
- the preparation and training of users for system use at clerical and managerial level;
- the assurance of the probability of user success during the first innovative activities as high as possible;
- the support of users during the introduction of the SIS (*e.g.*, answer questions, solve problems) and the development of support material users can refer to if problems occur.

6 INSTITUTIONAL PRACTICES

As there is no definitive national policy, institutions could implement their own systems commencing with some administrative work. The options are:

- a do-it-yourself approach of writing programs but this is not cost-effective in the long term; it may be very good staff development and fun learning but not worth pursuing;
- an institution with one PC, using a spreadsheet (*e.g. Excel*) may be able to give some of the statistical information required and this could be easily implemented on a personal level;
- an institution with one PC could use a spreadsheet and a database, (*e.g.*, *Excel* and *Access*) although some assistance will be required to set up the database as the information requirement will determine the structure;
- off-the-shelf packages from a similar school system (*e.g.*, the British SIMS/Dolphin) could be evaluated and implemented.

As in the case of implementing ITEM at a national level, schools working on ITEM should motivate staff, disperse expertise among staff members, pay attention to the innovation process and start with small projects with a high probability of success.

7 ACTION PLAN

As an Action Plan for Zimbabwe and other developing countries, the following are recommended:

1. professional bodies (*e.g.*, the heads of High School Associations) should become interested in ITEM;
2. seminars should be organized by and for the principals on how to use ITEM in the management of their institutions;
3. institution principals could manage upwards and influence the direction of ITEM by getting themselves involved in ITEM issues;
4. principals could start implementing some common systems;
5. principals could also obtain advice/support from IFIP, the Zimbabwe Computer Society and the ministries.

38

Discussion Group 6 - Building resource accessibility in developing countries

Chair: Ian Mitchell (New Zealand)

Particpants: Kersti Hjertqvist (Sweden), J. R. Isaac (India), John Manganye (Zimbabwe), Nathan Matemera (Zimbabwe), Tendeka Matatu (Zimbabwe), Edmore Muchinapo (Zimbabwe), Paul Nleya (Botswana), John Nyamhotsi (Zimbabwe), Alex Tigere (Zimbabwe)

1 PROBLEM DEFINITION

The first step is to clarify the problem.

1.1 Hardware resources

The hardware resources required are:

- PCs, network server, router for connection to the Internet and, possibly later, network computers.

1.2 Software resources

The software resources required are:

- Courseware - *Office* suite, database package, statistics package, Internet browser.

Some software will need to be localised, especially for appropriate teaching examples and, for some countries, languages.

Note: Courseware should not be 'the book' on multimedia. It should be purpose-designed with a sound pedagogical structure.

1.3 Human resources

Trained principals, teachers and technicians will be required. Vocational trainers with work experience will be needed for training practitioners. Courseware developers (subject experts, instructional designers, developers and multimedia designers) will be needed for local courseware development.

Capacity Building for IT in Education in Developing Countries
G. Marshall & M. Ruohonen (Eds.)

1.4 Infrastructural resources

Fundamental requirements are:

- A stable electrical supply, telephone lines with adequate bandwidth and transport to teacher training venues.

2 ACCESSIBILITY

For accessibility the resources must be available, operative with persons knowing how to use them and with confidence to do so. For software to be shared it must be portable and issues of intellectual property rights, language, culture and political will must be addressed. A major inhibitor may be cost. More important than software is the sharing of knowledge, expertise and competency.

3 GOAL RE-STATED

Every child in all developing countries has fun learning 'hands-on' with operative computers running relevant software.

3.1 Short-term goals

Such a goal is ambitious, demanding high levels of resources, efforts and time. Therefore, we focused on shorter-term objectives which might be satisfied within one year and at less than $US 250 000.

4 NATIONAL POLICY

A comprehensive national policy must be developed. It must reflect national goals and aspirations but clearly indicate what principals, teachers and parents may do in the school system with the encouragement of governments.

5 COMMUNITY INVOLVEMENT

An enthusiastic community will make things happen for their children. The community may be engaged by being shown computers being effectively used. The community may then choose which initiatives to support and then commit to contribute resources to the school by fund-raising but also by providing support. An example is the Net Day projects in the USA, where the community helps 'wire' the school.

Some examples are discussed below.

5.1 Teacher training

A donor may provide a computer laboratory for teacher training. As well as hardware and software the donor may provide an expert trainer. The recipient may provide several persons to become trainers and a technician.

Teachers who are about to get computers in their schools should attend a course of 3-5 days. Subsequently the trainers should visit the teachers about two weeks later and again two months later. Therefore the trainers not only give the teachers further support but also learn what are the practical problems that teachers face in the schools.

In subsequent years the aid recipient nationals can take over.

5.2 Mobile laboratory

A mobile laboratory can be installed in a suitable truck. An expert trainer and a technician/driver should travel with the truck. The truck should contain a supplementary generator allowing the laboratory to operate where there is no electrical supply.

The truck might spend a week with the community. The local primary and secondary schools would schedule time for their pupils to use the facilities. Special courses might be run for those needing vocational training. Small business people in the community might be introduced to computers. The laboratory could be used 12 hours per day.

The community awareness of computing in education would be raised. The community could then decide where computers might first be introduced and what they will do to help or encourage the teachers and the school.

5.3 Internet gateway

An Internet service provider might be contracted to run a school's gateway server on behalf of the school system. The server might have substantial cache memory (say 100 GB) so that information fetched from international sources can be held locally and reduce the communications costs for subsequent accesses. Such a computer would cost less than $US 20 000.

The server could have positive or negative stop lists so that pornography and other unsuitable materials can be suppressed. Further caching servers could be placed in each school district to reduce toll loads. Finally, a school should have a network server and this, too, could cache local accesses. Such software could be 'off the shelf'.

A note on the pedagogical uses of the Internet

The pupils should seek whatever information they are interested in on the World Wide Web and increase their knowledge on issues they have chosen themselves. Pupils can collaborate with pupils in their own country or in other countries. Teachers can collaborate with other teachers in their own country or in other countries. Teachers can collect teaching materials that other teachers or institutions have put on the Internet, thus always having up-to-date information. IT teacher training can be followed on the Internet in one's own school instead of traveling to the nearest town.

Pupils can create their own learning materials, which can be used by other pupils when they study. Pupils can produce the learning materials in multimedia presentations. They can quickly learn how to handle a scanner, video capture facilities, digital cameras or a color printer in order to produce multimedia materials.

5.4 Funding teachers' computers

Teachers may be provided with loans, or with finance or leasing arrangements so that they can obtain a computer and gain experience and confidence in using the computer. Alternatively, computers may be funded and placed in public libraries, including traveling libraries, so that more people can become familiar with them. Old computers from business may be given to schools provided they are suitable.

5.5 Seeking donors

To gain donors for a project, a well-prepared proposal must be put forward. Donors must be identified who are interested in the education and capacity-building areas. Most donors operate with governments and therefore you must seek the assistance of your government policy advisers who have this responsibility.

5.6 Government commitment

The government must give a clear commitment to support the use of computers in schools and in vocational training arenas in the use of computers at both user and professional levels. The government should identify the initiatives they will support and clearly commit to donors that successful and proven projects will be replicated and multiplied. A similar commitment will be needed to support community projects.

Alphabetical List of Conference Participants

A

Olayele Adelakun
Turku Centre for Computer Science
and Turku School of Economics
Lemminkaisenkatu 14A, 20520
Turku, Finland
olayele.adelakun@tukkk.fi

Eileen Allen
Speciss College
PO Box 2713
Harare, Zimbabwe
eileenal@speciss.gaia.co.zw

Deane Arganbright
University of Papua New Guinea
Math Department
PO Box 320
University, NCD 134
Papua, New Guinea
100353.163@Compuserve.com

Ben Awuah
University of Botswana
P. Bag 0022
Gaborone, Botswana
awuah@noka.ub.bw

B

Ann Baillie
MJB Software
3 Bowood Road
Mt. Pleasant
Harare, Zimbabwe

Mike Begbie
Prince Edward School
PO Box CY4188, Causeway
Harare, Zimbabwe

Raphael Benza
Ministry of Education
PO Box CY1343, Causeway
Harare, Zimbabwe

David Berg
UNESCO, Learning Without
Frontiers
7, Place de Fontenoy
75352 Paris 07 SP
France
d.berg@unesco.org

Peter Bollerslev
Centre for Applied Informatics
Peder Hvitfeldts Str. 4,3
DK-1173 Copenhagen, Denmark
peter.bollerslev@sembsc.dk

Doug Brown
Birmingham City Council
276 Green Meadow Rd.
Birmingham, B29 4EE
UK
dbrown@lea.birmingham.gov.uk

C

Cornelius Chakabbua
Prince Edward School
Box CY418 Causeway
Harare, Zimbabwe

Walter Chakuzira
Ministry of Education
PO Box CY 1341 Causeway
Harare, Zimbabwe

Felix Chifamba
TEL
PO Box CY2911 Causeway
Harare, Zimbabwe

Florence Chinwadzimba
Belvedere Technical Teachers
College
PO Box BE 100
Belvedere, Zimbabwe
cradu@harare.iafrica.com

Rachel Cohen
72 Rue de l'Est
92100 Boulogne
France
euroboulogne@citi2.fr

Bernard Cornu
IUFM of Grenoble
30 Av. Marcelin Bertholot
38100 Grenoble, France
cornu@grenet.fr

D

Giuliana Dettori
Instituto Matemetica Applicata
C.N.R.
Via De Marini 6,
16149 Genova, Italy
dettori@ima.ge.cnr.it

Pedzisai Dhliwayo
Howard High School
PO Howard
Glendale, Zimbabwe

Dudley Dolan
ECDL Foundation
2 Blackglen Ct.
Sandyford, Dublin 18
Ireland
ecdlf@cs.tcd.ie

E

Kristina Ekmark
Stockholm Municipality School
Kvickensvagen 9
S-123 34
Farsta, Sweden
stina.ekmark@nacka.mail.telia.com

F

Geoff Fairall
CSZ
PO Box Cy164 Causeway
Harare, Zimbabwe

Alex Fung
Hong Kong Baptist University
Department of Education Studies
Kowloon Tong
Hong Kong, China
alexfung@hkbu.edu.hk

G

Boyka Gradinarova
Informatics Department
University of Varna
St. Sveta Ekaterina, 10
9022 Varna-Viniza
Bulgaria
boyka@tu-varna.acad.bg

Klaus-D Graf
Freie University Berlin
Kurstr 5, D-14129
Berlin, Germany
graf@inf.fu-berlin.de

Jacqueline Grierson
Prince Edward School
PO Box CY418 Causeway
Harare, Zimbabwe
peschool@samara.co.zw

Stanford Mbiru Gudza
Ministry of Higher Education
PBag 7711 Causeway
Harare, Zimbabwe

Sam Gumbo
Computer Education Services
PO Box MP 139
Mount Pleasant
Harare, Zimbabwe

H

Hildigunnur Halldorsdottir
Namsgagnastofnun
Laugavegur 166
125 Reykjavik
Iceland
hildig@rvik.ismennt.is

Gilford Hapanwengwi
University of Zimbabwe
PO Box MP 167
Mount Pleasant
Harare, Zimbabwe
gilford@zimbix.uz.zw

Kersti Hjertqvist
Stockholm School Authority
Box 22049
104 22 Stockholm
Sweden
kersti hjertqvist@ett.se

Pieter Hogenbirk
PRINT/CPS
Sector Voortgezet Onderwijs
PO Box 1592
3800 BN Amersfoort
The Netherlands
print@xs4all.nl

Peter Hubwieser
Technical University of Munich
Faculty of Informatics
D-80290 Muenchen
Germany
hubwiese@informatik.tu-muenchen.de

I

James R. Isaac
NIIT Ltd.
8 Balaji Estate
Kalkaji, New Delhi 110019
India
isaac@internet.niit.co.in

J

Zhang Ji-Ping
3663 Zhongshan Bei Rd.
2000062 Shanghai
China
deit@ecnu.edu.cn

Peter Juliff
Deakin University
Burwood 3125
Australia
pjuliff@deakin.edu.au

K

Tsurayuki Kado
Hitachi
27-18 Minami Oi 6-chome
Shinagwaw-ku, Tokyo
140-Japan
t-kado@comp.hitachi.co.ip

Tendayi Kakora
Ministry of Higher Education
PO Box UA275, Union Avenue
Harare, Zimbabwe

Peter Kanengoni
Ministry of Education, Sport and Culture
PO Box CY 1343 Causeway
Harare, Zimbabwe

John Kasiyamhuru
St. Mary's Secondary School
PO Box ZG60, Zengeza
Chitungwiza, Zimbabwe

William Kawdemiiri
Mazoe High School
Private Bag 211A
Harare, Zimbabwe

Immo Kerner
TU Dresden
D-01063
Dresden, Germany

Geoffrey Kiangi
University of Namibia
Private Bag 13301
Windhoek
Namibia
gkiangi@unam.na

Anton Knierzinger
Paedagogische Akademie
Salesianumweg 3
A-4020 Linz
Austria
Kna@mail.padl.ac.at

Juliet Kurebwa
University of Zimbabwe
PO Box MP 167
Mount Plesant
Harare, Zimbabwe

Tobias Kuwengwa
Mutare Technical College
PO Box 640
Mutare, Zimbabwe

M

Anne McDougall
Monash University
Faculty of Education
Clayton 3168
Victoria, Australia
Anne.mcdougall@education.monash.edu.au

Mennas Machawira
Ministry of Higher Education
PO Box BW303
Borrowdale, Zimbabwe
lzimnato@harare.iafrica.com.zw

Olivia Magaya
Vainona High School
PO Box BW490
Borrowdale, Zimbabwe

W.N. Makanga
Ministry of Higher Eudcation
PO Box UA275 Union Avenue
Harare, Zimbabwe

Casper Musindo Mandava
Ministry of Higher Education
PBag 7711 Causeway
Harare, Zimbabwe

John Manganye
Ministry of Higher Education
PO Box UA275, Union Avenue
Harare, Zimbabwe

Philemon Maramba
Harare Polytechnical College
Box 407 Causeway
Harare, Zmbabwe

Joanna Marivara
Groombridge Primary School
Wycombe Avenue
Mount Pleasant
Harare, Zimbabwe

Gail Marshall
2393 Broadmont Ct.
Chesterfield, MO 63017
USA
74055.652@Compuserve.com

Angeline N. Masawi
Harare Polytechical College
Box 407 Causeway
Harare, Zimbabwe

Rudo Mataranyika
Marlborough High School
PO Box MR 199
Marlborough, Zimbabwe

Tendeka Matatu
Falcon College
PO Esigodini
Esigodini, Zimbabwe

Caroline Matemachani
Mutare Technical College
PO Box 640
Mutare, Zimbabwe

Nathan Matemera
Matsine Secondary School
PBag 2107
Wedza, Zimbabwe

Rose Mazhindu-Shumba
University of Zimbabwe
PO Box MP 167
Mount Pleasant
Harare, Zimbabwe
mshumba@zimbix.uz.zw

Ian Mitchell
New Zealand Computer Society
78 Godden Crescent
Mission Bay, Auckland-5
New Zealand
ianm@ie3.co.nz

Marshall Mlambo
Belvedere Technical Teachers College
PO Box BE 100
Belvedere
Harare, Zimbabwe

Uche Modum
University of Nigeria
Box 15735
Enugu Campus
Nigeria

Babongile Moyo
TEL
PO Box CY2911 Causeway
Harare, Zimbabwe

Simon Mphisa
Ministry of Higher Education
PO Box UA275 Union Avenue
Harare, Zimbabwe

Michael Mubatapasango
St. Philips Magwenya High School
PO Box 139
Guruve, Zimbabwe

Edmore Muchunapo
Ministry of Information, Posts and Telecommunications
PO Box CY825 Causeway
Harare, Zimbabwe

Charles Mutungwazi
St. Mark's Diocesan Secondary School
PBag 812
Chegutu, Zimbabwe

Irene Mutungwazi
Ministry of Higher Education
16 Guilford Crescent
Southerton
Harare, Zimbabwe

N

Shailesh Naik
Coopers and Lybrand
PO Box 702
Harare, Zimbabwe
shailesh naik@za.coopers.com

Aaron Ndlovu
Ministry of Science and Technology
and Vocational Training
PO Box 50464
Lusaka, Zambia
dstmstvt@zamnet.zm

Lovemore Ndlodvu
Harare Polytechnical College
Box 407 Causeway
Harare, Zimbabwe

William Newman
30 Raggatt Street
Alice Springs
Northern Territory 0870
Australia
wnewman@pobox.com

Leonard Nhembe
Vainona High School
PO Box BW490
Borrowdale, Zimbabwe

Charles Nherera
University of Zimbabwe
PO Box MP 167 Mount Pleasant
Harare, Zimbabwe
nherera@zimbix.uz.zw

Paul Nicholson
Deakin University
221 Burwood Highway
Burwood
VIC Australia 3125
pauln@deakin.edu.au

Margaret Niess
253 Weniger Hall
Oregon State University
Corvallis, OR 97331
USA
niess@ucs.orst.edu

Paul Nleya
University of Botswana
PBag 0022
Gaborone, Botswana
nleyapt@noka.ub.bw

Karen Norwood
North Carolina State University
326 Poe Hall
Box 7801
Raleigh, NC 27695
USA
karen@poe.coe.ncsu.edu

Thuto Ntsekhe-Mokhehle
Secondary School Inspectorate
PO Box 47
Maseru 100
Lesotho

Nyalugwe Nyalugwe
Mazoe High School
Private Bag 211A
Harare, Zimbabwe

John Nyamhotsi
Ministry of Higher Education
PBag UA 275, Union Avenue
Harare, Zimbabwe

O

Tom O'Briain
St. Mark's SNS and Blackrock
Education Centre
37 Pineview Ave., Tallaght
Dublin 24, Ireland
tobriain@iol.ie

Hajime Ohiwa
Keio University
5322 Endo, Fujisawa
252-Japan
ohiwa@sfc.keio.ac.ip

P

Ravi Palepu
Gweru Technical College
PO Box 137
Gweru, Zimbabwe
palepu@icafe.co.zw

Heimir Palsson
Namsgagnastofnun
Laugavegur 166
125 Reykjavik
Iceland
Heimer@nams.is

Shadreck Phiri
Watershed College
P Bag 3718
Marondera, Zimbabwe

R

Stephen T. Raza
Harare Polytechnic
PO Box CY 407 Causeway
Harare, Zimbabwe

Sindre Røsvik
Giske Kommune
Ovre Nordstrand
N-6050 Valderoy
Norway
sindre@mimer.no

Mikko Ruohonen
Turku School of Economics and Business Administration
P.O. Box 110
FIN-20521 Turku
Finland
mikko.ruohonen@abo.fi

S

Faith Samkange
Gweru Teachers College
PBag 55
Gweru, Zimbabwe

Brian Samways
Birmingham City Council
64 Jervis Cr.
Sutton Coldfield
UK
bsamways@lea.birmingham.gov.uk

Simon Satumba
Harare Polytechnic
PO Box CY407 Causweay
Harare, Zimbabwe

Chaweewan Sawetamalya
Faculty of Education
Srinakharinwirot University
Sukhumvit 23 Klongtoey
Bangkok 10110, Thailand
chawee@psm.swu.ae.th

Erling Schmidt
Educational Computing Centre
Lovebakken 6
DK-9400, Noerresundby
Denmark
eschm@daks.dk

Moses Shamu
Harare Polytechnic College
PO Box 407 Causeway
Harare, Zimbabwe

Alpheas Shindi
Harare Polytechnic
PO Box CY407 Causeway
Harare, Zimbabwe

Hari Gopal Shrestha
Singh Durbas
Kathmandu
PO Box 1573
Nepal
glocom@mos.co.np

Obert Sifile
Chemachinda High School
PO Box 260
Guruve, Zimbabwe

Richard Simango
Oriel Boys School
PO Box CH 346 Chisipite
Harare, Zimbabwe

Matti Sinko
University of Helsinki
Unikkotie 2c
01300 Vantaa
Finland
matti.sinko@helsink.fi

Arthur Sithole
Courseware Development Centre
PO Box CY 1912 Causeway
Harare, Zimbabwe
asithole@zwe.toolnet.org

N. Sonhera
Churchill Boys High School
PO Box CY 616 Causeway
Harare, Zimbabwe

David Squires
School of Education
King's College
Waterloo Road
London SE18WA
UK
david.squires@kcl.ac.uk

Robert Terence Stewart
Thomson Publications
PO Box 1683
Harare, Zimbabwe

Abdulla Suleman
Speciss College
PO Box 2713
Harare, Zimbabwe

T

Lorraine Tafira
Mabelreign Girls High School
Box M96
Mabelreign, Zimbabwe

Alex Tigere
Bernard Mizeki College
PBag 3790
Maronda, Zimbabwe

Enoch Tinofirei
Admiral Tait School
PO Box CY 386 Causeway
Harare, Zimbabwe

Marta Turcsanyi-Szabo
Eotvos Lorand University
Department of Informatic and Methodology
1088 Budapest, Museum krt 6-8
Hungary
turcsanyine@ludens.elte.hu

V

Tom van Weert
University of Nijmegen
PO Box 9010
6500 GL Nijmegen
The Netherlands
tomvw@cs.kun.nl

Adrie Visscher
University of Twente
Department of Educational Administration
PO Box 217
7500 AE Enschede
The Netherlands
visscher@edte.utwente.nl

W

Deryn Watson
School of Education
King's College
Waterloo Road
London SE18WA
UK
deryn.watson@kcl.ac.uk

Marsha Williams
Tennessee State University
PO Box 136 - TSU Downtown
Campus
330 10th Avenue North
Nashville, TN 37203-3401
USA
WILL002@ACAD.TNSTATE.
EDU

INDEX OF CONTRIBUTORS

KEYWORD INDEX

www.ingramcontent.com/pod-product-compliance
Ingram Content Group UK Ltd.
Pitfield, Milton Keynes, MK11 3LW, UK
UKHW020059200726
13856UKWH00002B/280